ASPEN PUBLISHERS

Legal Research Explained

Second Edition

Deborah E. Bouchoux, Esq.
Georgetown University
Washington, D.C.

AUSTIN BOSTON CHICAGO NEW YORK THE NETHERLANDS

To contact Customer Care, e-mail customer.care@aspenpublishers.com, call 1-800-234-1660, fax 1-800-901-9075, or mail correspondence to:

Aspen Publishers
Attn: Order Department
PO Box 990
Frederick, MD 21705

Printed in the United States of America.

2 3 4 5 6 7 8 9 0

ISBN 978-0-7355-8767-0

Library of Congress Cataloging-in-Publication Data

Bouchoux, Deborah E., 1950-
Legal research explained / Deborah E. Bouchoux.—2nd ed.
p. cm.
Includes bibliographical references and index.
ISBN 978-0-7355-8767-0 (alk. paper)
1. Legal research—United States. I. Title.

KF240.B683 2010
340.072'073—dc22

2010008477

About Wolters Kluwer Law & Business

Wolters Kluwer Law & Business is a leading provider of research information and workflow solutions in key specialty areas. The strengths of the individual brands of Aspen Publishers, CCH, Kluwer Law International, and Loislaw are aligned within Wolters Kluwer Law & Business to provide comprehensive, in-depth solutions and expert-authored content for the legal, professional, and education markets.

CCH was founded in 1913 and has served more than four generations of business professionals and their clients. The CCH products in the Wolters Kluwer Law & Business group are highly regarded electronic and print resources for legal, securities, antitrust and trade regulation, government contracting, banking, pension, payroll, employment and labor, and healthcare reimbursement and compliance professionals.

Aspen Publishers is a leading information provider for attorneys, business professionals, and law students. Written by preeminent authorities, Aspen products offer analytical and practical information in a range of specialty practice areas from securities law and intellectual property to mergers and acquisitions and pension/benefits. Aspen's trusted legal education resources provide professors and students with high-quality, up-to-date, and effective resources for successful instruction and study in all areas of the law.

Kluwer Law International supplies the global business community with comprehensive English-language international legal information. Legal practitioners, corporate counsel, and business executives around the world rely on the Kluwer Law International journals, loose-leafs, books, and electronic products for authoritative information in many areas of international legal practice.

Loislaw is a premier provider of digitized legal content to small law firm practitioners of various specializations. Loislaw provides attorneys with the ability to quickly and efficiently find the necessary legal information they need, when and where they need it, by facilitating access to primary law as well as state-specific law, records, forms, and treatises.

Wolters Kluwer Law & Business, a unit of Wolters Kluwer, is headquartered in New York and Riverwoods, Illinois. Wolters Kluwer is a leading multinational publisher and information services company.

Summary of Contents

Contents

Chapter 5: Locating Cases Through Digests and Annotated Law Reports 107

Section III Legal Research: Using Electronic and Computer Resources 215

Chapter 8: The Digital Library: LexisNexis, Westlaw, and Non-Print Research Tools 217

Chapter 9: E-Research: Legal Research Using the Internet 255

Section IV Legal Research: Citing and Validating the Authorities 275

Chapter 10: Legal Citation Form 277

Chapter 11: Updating and Validating Your Research 311

Section V Putting It Together: An Overview of the Research Process 337

Chapter 12: Overview of the Research Process 339

Preface

Introduction

Legal research is likely the most "hands on" subject you will take in the course of your legal education. Although numerous books discuss research methods and techniques, there is no substitute for actually performing the task of legal research. Thus, you will learn the most about legal research, which shortcuts are invaluable, and which techniques are nonproductive, only by *doing* legal research.

Today's legal research projects are simultaneously easier and more difficult than they were years ago. They are easier because there are numerous sources for researchers to consult (including conventional print sources, the computerized legal research systems such as LexisNexis and Westlaw, and the Internet), and they are more difficult for the same reason. There are so many sources to consult that deciding where to begin and what resources to consult calls for careful analysis of the quality of sources and the economics of a research project so you can obtain the best answer to a legal question in the most efficient manner and at the lowest cost to the client.

To that end, library research assignments are placed at the conclusion of each chapter so you can see and use the books discussed in each chapter. Similarly, each chapter includes an Internet Assignment, requiring you to locate information pertinent to the chapter by accessing well-known Internet sites.

Performing legal research can be both frustrating and gratifying. It can be frustrating because there is often no one perfect answer and because there are no established guidelines on how much research to do and when to stop. On the other hand, legal research is gratifying because you will be engaged in a task that requires you to *do* something and one in which you will be rewarded by finding the right case, statute, or other authority.

View legal research as an exciting treasure hunt—a search for the best authorities to answer a question or legal issue. In this sense, the task of using and exploring the law library, LexisNexis or Westlaw, or the

Internet for answers to legal issues or questions should be a welcome relief from the assignments of other classes, which may be passive in nature and involve copious amounts of reading. Take the time to explore the books by reviewing the foreword, table of contents, and index found in each volume. Familiarize yourself with all of the features of the books or electronic resources you use, and you will simplify your legal research.

Consider researching with other students if you are comfortable doing so. Often you will learn a great deal by comparing notes with others who may be able to share successful strategies for effectively using various resources or finding the answers to research problems. Naturally, sharing ideas and tips for research techniques should not be viewed as an excuse not to do the work yourself or a license to use answers discussed by others. In other words, you should research with other students (if you find it useful to do so), but you should never share or copy answers from others. Not only is this practice dishonest, but it will prevent you from effectively learning the skill of legal research. Ultimately, an employer is not interested in how many "points" you obtained on a class exercise or what grade you obtained in a class, but in whether you can be depended upon to research an issue competently.

Structure of the Text

You will be expected "to hit the ground running" when you get a job, yet there is often a significant gap between what is learned in the classroom and the way to apply this knowledge in the real world of a law office environment. *Legal Research Explained* (Second Edition) is meant to bridge this gap by combining a thorough grounding in legal research with a pragmatic approach to the types of legal research assignments you will find in the "real world."

The text is divided into five main sections: The first section begins with a review of the American legal system and discusses the primary authorities used in legal research (namely, cases, constitutions, and statutes that are binding on courts); the second section covers the secondary sources used in legal research that are used to comment upon, explain, and help you locate the primary sources; the third section focuses on computer-assisted legal research using LexisNexis, Westlaw, and the Internet; the fourth section covers citation form for the authorities previously introduced and how to ensure that these sources are still "good law"; and the final section provides an overview of the legal research process, discussing how to begin and end research projects.

Each chapter and section builds on the previous one. For example, once you read Chapter Two's discussion of the federal and state court structure, you will be ready to understand Chapter Three's discussion on reading cases that interpret statutes, paying special attention to cases from higher courts. Similarly, once you read Chapter Four and understand the elements of cases and how they are published, you will be ready for the discussion in Chapter Five about how to locate cases using digests. The text concludes with a pragmatic overview of how to tackle a research problem.

Features of the Text

The text includes a number of features to enhance learning. Each chapter includes the following features:

- **Chapter Overview**. Each chapter begins with a preview of the material that will be presented in the chapter.
- **Key Terms.** The key terms and concepts used in the chapter are presented in italics and are defined in the Glossary at the end of the text.
- **Practice Tips.** Each chapter includes one or more pragmatic practice tips, linking the material in the chapter to "real world" experience.
- **Ethics Alerts.** Each chapter includes an ethics note or comment relating to the material discussed in the chapter.
- **Help Lines.** Each chapter includes at least one "go to" reference source, giving a telephone number or website to call or refer to for additional information on the material discussed in the chapter.
- **CyberSites:** At the conclusion of each chapter, websites are given where you can locate additional information on the topics covered in the chapter. Although every effort has been made to refer to useful websites, those sites can change both their content and addresses without notice. References to websites are not endorsements of those sites.
- **Research and Other Assignments.** Each chapter includes questions requiring you to use the sets of books or other resources discussed in that chapter. You should never have to use a book or set of books that have not been discussed in the chapter you have read or a preceding chapter.
- **Internet Assignments.** Each chapter includes a series of practical questions that require readers to locate information pertinent to the chapter by accessing well-known legal or general-usage Internet sites.
- **Citation Form.** Each chapter demonstrates citation form for the resources discussed in that chapter, in both *Bluebook* and *ALWD* form, in a simple chart format, showing that in many instances the citation form in *The Bluebook* and in *ALWD* are the same. All citations in *Bluebook* form are displayed in the format used by practitioners, not in the "large and small cap" format used for law review articles and journals. When only one citation is given in the text, it is given in *Bluebook* form.

Each chapter also includes charts, graphs, sample forms, and other instructional aids, as needed. For example, Chapter Four includes a chart showing commonly used abbreviations for legal resources, Chapter Eight includes a chart comparing the terms and connectors used by LexisNexis and Westlaw, and Chapter Eleven includes a Frequently Asked Questions section on Shepardizing.

This second edition of the text provides several new features, including the following:

- New practice tips and help tips are included in several chapters.
- Chapter 4 (Case Law) includes new information relating to the use and citation of "unpublished" opinions and information about the 2009 launch of Google Scholar, which allows free and easy access to federal and state court cases.
- Chapter 6 (Secondary Authorities) provides information on the dangers of metadata embedded in forms.
- Chapter 8 (the Digital Library) includes updated information on LexisNexis and its new "Easy Search" feature.
- Chapter 9 (E-Research) includes new material on legal databases available for "apps" on iPhones and other similar devices.
- Chapter 10 (Citation Form) provides new information on the online *Bluebook*.
- Chapter 11 (Updating) requires readers to complete an assignment so they can compare and contrast validating cases using Shepard's on LexisNexis and using Westlaw's KeyCite.
- All new research assignments and Internet legal research assignments have been included.

Textbook Resources

The companion website for *Legal Research Explained*, available at http://www.aspenparalegal.com/bouchoux_explained, includes additional resources for students and instructors, including the following:

- Study aids to help students master the key concepts for this course. Visit the site to access interactive StudyMate exercises such as flash cards, matching, fill-in-the-blank, and crosswords. These activities are also available for download to an iPod or other hand-held device.
- Instructor resources to accompany the text.
- Links to helpful websites and updates.

The text comes packaged with four months of prepaid access to Loislaw's online legal research database, at http://www.loislawschool.com.

Blackboard and eCollege course materials are available to supplement this text. This online courseware is designed to streamline the teaching of the course, providing valuable resources from the book in an accessible electronic format.

Instructor resources to accompany this text include a comprehensive Instructor's Manual, Test Bank, and PowerPoint slides. All of these materials are available on a CD-ROM or for download from our companion website.

Final Thoughts

When you begin reading this book, most of you will be unfamiliar with cases, statutes, constitutions, or the numerous other legal authorities. As you advance in your research class and complete the assignments in the text, you will readily be able to measure your progress. When you complete this text and your legal research class, you will have gained thorough mastery of legal research techniques as well as familiarity with the numerous sets of law books and electronic sources that you will be required to use in your profession.

The vast number of legal authorities available in both a conventional law library and through digital law libraries means that effective legal researchers are flexible. Sometimes the materials you need are not on the shelves, and you will need to switch directions. Sometimes new methods of locating materials emerge. In any event, you will find legal research an interesting hunt for the authorities you need, whether in conventional print sources, on LexisNexis or Westlaw, or on the Internet.

Deborah E. Bouchoux, Esq.

Spring 2010

Acknowledgments

I would like to express my sincere appreciation to the many individuals who contributed to the development of this text. First, as always, I would like to thank Susan M. Sullivan, Program Director at the University of San Diego Paralegal Program. Sue gave me my first teaching position many years ago, and I value and respect her many contributions to the legal profession. My current Program Director, Kelly Holdcraft of Georgetown University, has been unfailingly enthusiastic in support of both my career and that of all of our paralegal students.

Many thanks also to the various reviewers who reviewed the manuscript on behalf of the publisher. Their comments and advice were instructive and insightful. Throughout the more than 20 years I have taught legal research, I have received valuable comments and feedback from my students, who have offered their comments and insight regarding methods of teaching and productive legal research assignments.

Finally, a special thank you to the individuals at Aspen Publishers who generously provided guidance and support throughout the development of the second edition of this text, including Carol McGeehan, Publisher; Melody Davies, Executive Editorial Director; Betsy Kenny, Developmental Editor; David Herzig, Executive Legal Editor; Kaesmene Harrison Banks, Senior Editor; and Susan M. Junkin, Copyeditor.

I would also like to acknowledge the following who permitted me to reproduce copyrighted material for this text.

Chapter 2: The Federal and State Court System

Figure 2-3: Reprinted with permission from West, a Thomson Reuters business.

Chapter 3: Statutory Law

Figure 3-2: Reprinted with permission from Title 35 of U.S.C.A., copyright by West, a Thomson Reuters business.

Figure 3-4: Reprinted with permission from General Index to U.S.C.A., copyright by West, a Thomson Reuters business.

Figure 3-5: Reprinted with permission from U.S.C.A. Popular Name Table, copyright by West, a Thomson Reuters business.

Figure 3-6: Va. Code Ann. § 18-2-256. Copyright by West, a Thomson Reuters business.

Chapter 4: Case Law and Judicial Opinions

Figure 4-1: Reprinted with permission from 595 S.E.2d 697, copyright © 2004 by West, a Thomson Reuters business.

Figure 4-4: Reprinted with permission from 108 S. Ct. at 2611, copyright © 1998 by West, a Thomson Reuters business.

Chapter 5: Locating Cases Through Digests and Annotated Law Reports

Figure 5-2: Reprinted with permission from *Descriptive Word Index to Ninth Decennial Digest, Part 2*, copyright © 1988 by West, a Thomson Reuters business.

Figure 5-3: Reprinted with permission from 29 *Ninth Decennial Digest, Part 2*, page 783, copyright © 1988 by West, a Thomson Reuters business.

Figure 5-4: Reprinted with permission from 29 *Ninth Decennial Digest, Part 2*, page 956, copyright © 1988 by West, a Thomson Reuters business.

Figure 5-5: Reprinted with permission from *American Law Reports* by West, a Thomson Reuters business.

Figure 5-6: Reprinted with permission from *Index to American Law Reports* by West, a Thomson Reuters business.

Chapter 6: Secondary Authorities

Figure 6-1: Reprinted with permission from 87 C.J.S., copyright by West, a Thomson Reuters business.

Figure 6-2: Reprinted with permission from 25 Am. Jur. 2d, copyright by West, a Thomson Reuters business.

Figure 6-3: Reprinted with permission from General Index Update to Am. Jur. 2d, copyright by West, a Thomson Reuters business.

Figure 6-5: Reprinted with permission of the publisher, California Western Law Review, Vol. 41, Number 1, Fall 2004, copyright © 2004.

Figure 6-6: Reprinted with permission of *California Lawyer*, copyright © 2006.

Figure 6-7: Reprinted with permission of The H.W. Wilson Company. Excerpted from the *Index to Legal Periodicals and Books.®*

Figure 6-8: Reprinted with permission from *McCarthy on Trademarks and Unfair Competition*, § 11:32, copyright by West, a Thomson Reuters business.

Figure 6-10: Restatement, Second, Contracts, copyright © 1981 by the American Law Institute. Reprinted with permission. All rights reserved.

Figure 6-11: Reprinted with the permission of LexisNexis.

Figure 6-12: Reprinted with the permission of LexisNexis.

Chapter 8: The Digital Library: LexisNexis, Westlaw, and Non-Print Research Tools

Figure 8-1: Copyright © 2009 LexisNexis, a division of Reed Elsevier Inc. All rights reserved. LexisNexis and the Knowledge Burst logo are registered trademarks of Reed Elsevier Properties Inc. and are used with the permission of LexisNexis.

Figure 8-2: Copyright © 2009 LexisNexis, a division of Reed Elsevier Inc. All rights reserved. LexisNexis and the Knowledge Burst logo are registered trademarks of Reed Elsevier Properties Inc. and are used with the permission of LexisNexis.

Figure 8-3: Copyright © 2009 LexisNexis, a division of Reed Elsevier Inc. All rights reserved. LexisNexis and the Knowledge Burst logo are registered trademarks of Reed Elsevier Properties Inc. and are used with the permission of LexisNexis.

Figure 8-4: Copyright © 2009 LexisNexis, a division of Reed Elsevier Inc. All rights reserved. LexisNexis and the Knowledge Burst logo are registered trademarks of Reed Elsevier Properties Inc. and are used with the permission of LexisNexis.

Figure 8-5: Reprinted with permission from Westlaw, copyright by West, a Thomson Reuters business.

Figure 8-6: Reprinted with permission from Westlaw, copyright by West, a Thomson Reuters business.

Figure 8-7: Reprinted with permission from Westlaw, copyright by West, a Thomson Reuters business.

Figure 8-8: Reprinted with permission from Westlaw, copyright by West, a Thomson Reuters business.

Chapter 9: E-Research: Legal Research Using the Internet

Figure 9-1: Reprinted with permission from FindLaw, a Thomson Reuters business. Copyright © 2006 by West, a Thomson Reuters business.

Figure 9-2: Reprinted with permission from MegaLaw. Copyright ©2006 by MegaLaw.

Chapter 11: Updating and Validating Your Authorities

Figure 11-1: Reprinted with the permission of LexisNexis.

Figure 11-3: Copyright © 2009 LexisNexis, a division of Reed Elsevier Inc. All rights reserved. LexisNexis and the Knowledge Burst logo are registered trademarks of Reed Elsevier Properties Inc. and are used with the permission of LexisNexis.

Figure 11-4: Reprinted with permission from Westlaw, copyright by West, a Thomson Reuters business.

Figure 11-5: Reprinted with permission from West, a Thomson Reuters business.

No copyright is claimed in any material owned by the United States Government, including material shown in Figures 6-14, 7-1, 7-2, 7-3, 7-4, 7-5, or 9-3.

Legal Research

Primary Authorities

Chapter

1

Finding the Law and Introduction to Legal Research

Chapter Overview

This chapter discusses the role of legal professionals in legal research, the ethical duty to perform research competently, types of law libraries and their uses, and the sources of law in the United States. The chapter also examines the classification of law books as either primary or secondary sources. Finally, there is a brief introduction to the major law book publishers, which will be discussed in greater detail in later chapters.

A. The Importance of Legal Research

Legal professionals are expected to perform the task of legal research competently and cost effectively. Performing legal research today is both easier and more difficult than it was just a generation ago. It is easier because many materials are available through electronic sources and the Internet, making it quick and easy to find statutes, cases, and other legal authorities. At the same time, it is more difficult because these new media make so many sources accessible that tracking down the right authority can seem like finding a needle in a haystack.

Today's legal researchers are expected to know how and when to use conventional print sources, the computer-assisted research services LexisNexis and Westlaw, and the Internet to find the best answer to a research question as quickly and effectively as possible.

B. The Ethical Duty to Research Accurately

Perhaps the most fundamental aspect of the attorney-client relationship is the client's absolute trust and confidence in the attorney's competence. In fact, Rule 1.1 of the American Bar Association's Model Rules of Professional Conduct requires that attorneys provide competent representation, meaning the legal knowledge, skill, thoroughness, and preparation necessary for the representation.

Although it is important to *know* the law, particularly in a field in which you may intend to specialize, it is even more important to be able to *find* the law. In this sense, proficiency in legal research is the foundation for a successful legal career. Your employer will not be as interested in your final grade in any specific class as much as your ability to find accurate answers to questions relating to topics, even though you may not have been exposed to those topics in school.

In fact, the duty to perform accurate legal research has been addressed in a number of cases, including *People v. Ledesma*, 729 P.2d 839, 871 (Cal. 1987), in which the court noted that an attorney's first duty is to investigate the facts of a client's case and to research the law applicable to those facts.

Moreover, the failure to research adequately may lead to liability for legal malpractice. In one of the earliest cases on this topic, *Smith v. Lewis*, 530 P.2d 589 (Cal. 1975), *overruled on other grounds*, 544 P.2d 561 (Cal. 1976), the California Supreme Court affirmed a lower court decision awarding $100,000 to be paid to a former client by an attorney who had failed to conduct adequate legal research. The court held that the attorney was obligated to undertake reasonable research and stated, "even as to doubtful matters, an attorney is expected to perform sufficient research to enable him to make an informed and intelligent judgment on behalf of his client." 530 P.2d at 596. In sum, you will be expected to perform competent legal research not only because your employer will insist on it but also because ethical standards demand it. Finally, as further evidence of the importance of legal research, in spring 2006, the National Conference of Bar Examiners announced plans to consider adding a component to the bar exam that will focus on legal research methods and skills.

C. Law Libraries

1. *Types of Law Libraries*

As noted in the preface to this text, legal research is a "hands-on" skill, requiring you to know how to use a law library. Your first task, therefore, is to locate a law library that you may use. There are approximately 3,600 law libraries in the United States. Following is a list of the most common types of law libraries:

- **Law School Libraries.** All accredited law schools have their own law libraries, most of which will have tens of thousands of volumes in print and nonprint forms. Many law school libraries are open only to their students. In a newer trend, many law libraries offer research tutorials and guides on their websites.
- **Federal Depository Libraries.** More than 1,200 libraries throughout the nation have been designated as *Federal Depository Libraries*, meaning that certain U.S. government publications, such as statutes and cases, will be sent to the library for review and access by the general public. In many instances, local public libraries, law school libraries, or university libraries are designated as federal depositories. Identification and location of the depository libraries can be found at the following website: http://www.gpoaccess.gov/libraries.html.
- **Local Law Libraries.** Often a county or city will maintain a law library, and these are usually open to members of the public. These law libraries vary in size, with the largest ones being found in the largest counties. Often they are near a courthouse. The American Association of Law Libraries provides a list of state, county, and court law libraries at the following website: http://www.aallnet.org/sis/sccll/membership/libraries.htm.
- **Courthouse Law Libraries.** Many courts, both federal and state, maintain their own law libraries. Court law libraries are often found in the courthouse for the county seat. Some law libraries are open to the public while others restrict access to courthouse personnel, attorneys, and their paralegals.
- **Bar Association and Private Group Law Libraries.** Often bar associations or private groups, such as insurance companies or real estate boards, will maintain law libraries. These are usually open only to members of the group.
- **Law Firm Libraries.** Almost every law firm will maintain a law library. Large law firms maintain extensive collections. These law libraries are available for use only by employees of the firm.

To find a law library, consult a telephone book or use a general Internet search engine such as Google and call law schools, courthouses, and county offices in your area to determine library policy on use. Additionally, many public and college or university libraries are increasing their collections of law books. Although these libraries typically offer only the major sets of books, you may be able to obtain a quick answer to some legal research questions.

Additionally, law libraries exist in computer databases such as those offered by LexisNexis or Westlaw. In fact, these computer-assisted legal research services offer far more resources than most legal professionals could afford to maintain on their own. Finally, law libraries now exist in cyberspace with vast collections of legal materials available for free "24/7." These virtual law libraries afford quick and easy access to

Help Line: *Library Websites*

Most law libraries now maintain websites, listing their hours, policies, and other pertinent information. Law school libraries often change their hours to comply with law school calendars and exam schedules, so be sure to check their hours of operation. Many law libraries offer online access to their card catalogs, allowing you to plan your research strategy before leaving your house.

asignificant number of legal resources, as discussed in detail in Chapter Nine. See "CyberSites" at the end of this chapter for a list of some websites that provide research guides and tutorials.

2. *Arrangement of Law Libraries*

There is no one standard arrangement for law libraries. Each law library is arranged according to the needs of its patrons. If you cannot obtain a tour of your law library, obtain a copy of the library handbook or guide that will describe the services offered, set forth the library's rules and regulations, and provide a floor plan of the law library. Spend an hour browsing the shelves and familiarizing yourself with the law library's arrangement, organization, and collections. The law library's website may also offer a "virtual" tour.

Few law libraries offer a conventional print card catalog (identical in its alphabetical arrangement to the card catalogs you may have been introduced to in grade school) to help you locate the books you need. The more modern approach is the online catalog or OPAC (online public access catalog). Simply type in or "enter" the title, author, or subject matter you desire in the search box displayed on the screen, and you will then be given the "call number." The shelves or *stacks* in the law library are clearly marked, and locating a book is merely a matter of matching up the call number provided by the card or online catalog with the appropriate stack label.

Most law school and other law libraries use the Library of Congress classification system to arrange their books. This system arranges books on the shelves in subject order. Each book is marked with a three-part

Ethics Alert: *Library Courtesy*

Assume that everyone who uses the law library is as busy as you are. Observe standard library etiquette by reshelving properly every book you use (unless the law library has a preshelving stack for books that are to be reshelved). Do not deface books by turning pages down or marking in them. Do not resort to unfair conduct by hiding or intentionally misplacing books. There is no excuse for such overzealous tactics that not only impede learning but also reflect poorly on one who is joining the legal profession.

> ***Practice Tip:** Legal Abbreviations*
>
> In the beginning of your legal career, you may become confused by the numerous abbreviations used for legal books, case reports, and journals. To determine the meaning of abbreviations such as "Ala." for *Alabama Reports* or "C.J.S." for *Corpus Juris Secundum*, check Appendix A in *Black's Law Dictionary* (9th ed. 2009), which provides an extensive list of abbreviations commonly used in law. Additionally, be patient. Within just a few weeks you will probably know about 90 percent of all of the abbreviations you are likely to encounter. See Chapter Four for a list of some other common legal abbreviations.

classification number, consisting of an alphanumeric combination, which includes letters, a whole number, and a decimal. For example, assume a book is marked "KF503.181." The designation "KF" is the Library of Congress identifier for American legal publications, and "503.181" refers to the book's location in the library stacks.

Law libraries are non-circulating libraries, meaning that few materials may be checked out by patrons.

3. *Other Library Services*

Most law libraries offer a variety of services to help students conduct productive research. You may be able to reserve a carrel so you can store books and materials there while you work on a long-term project. Similarly, you may be able to reserve a group study room so you can meet with other students. Law librarians typically possess degrees in law and library science and may assist you in borrowing materials from other libraries. Many law libraries also offer classes and tutorials to help students conduct research more efficiently.

D. Sources of Law in the United States

1. *Cases and Our Common Law Tradition*

The American legal system is part of what is referred to as the "common law" tradition. *Common law* is defined in part by *Black's Law Dictionary* 313 (9th ed. 2009) as that body of law that derived from judicial decisions rather than from statutes or constitutions. Common law is thus often referred to as "judge-made law."

In early English cases, people training to be lawyers began "taking notes" on what occurred during trials. When judges were called upon to decide cases, they then began referring to these written reports of earlier cases and following the prior cases in similar situations. The English referred to this system as the "common law" because it was applied equally all throughout England and replaced a less-uniform system of law.

This concept of following previous cases, or precedents, is called *stare decisis*, which is a Latin phrase meaning "to stand by things decided." Broadly, the doctrine of stare decisis means that once courts have announced a principle of law, they will follow it in future cases that are substantially similar. It is this doctrine of stare decisis that serves to protect litigants from inexperienced or biased judges. In this way stare decisis advances fairness and consistency in our legal system. Moreover, stare decisis promotes stability in our judicial system because it promotes uniform and predictable rulings.

Under this system or doctrine of precedent following, "the law" was thus found in the written decisions of the judges, and these decisions served as precedents that were followed in later cases involving substantially similar issues. Thus, the first source of law in the United States is judge-made case law.

2. *Constitutions*

A second source of law in the United States is constitutions. A *constitution* sets forth the fundamental law for a nation or a state. It is the document that provides the principles relating to organization and regulation of a federal or state government. We have a United States Constitution, our supreme law of the land, and each state has its own individual constitution.

3. *Statutes*

A *statute*, or law, is defined by *Black's Law Dictionary* 1542 (9th ed. 2009) as "a law passed by a legislative body." In the United States, legislatures did not become particularly active in enacting statutes until the early to mid-1800s, when our economy began changing from a very rural one to a more urban one. This major change in American society was coupled with a tremendous population growth, due largely to immigration. It became clear that rather than having a system that decided disputes on a case-by-case basis, which was slow and cumbersome at best, enacting broader laws that would provide rules to govern public behavior would best serve the needs of a growing society.

4. *Administrative Regulations*

A fourth source of law in the United States is found in the vast number of *administrative rules* or *regulations* promulgated by federal agencies such as the Food and Drug Administration, the Department of Labor, and numerous other agencies. Agencies exist in the individual states as well, and those also promulgate rules and regulations.

The agencies play a unique role in our legal system because they function quasi-legislatively and quasi-judicially. You may recall from basic history classes that our government is divided into three branches: the legislative branch, which makes laws; the judicial branch, which interprets laws; and the executive branch, which enforces laws. Each exercises its own powers, and, by a system usually called "checks and balances," each functions separately from the others.

The agencies, on the other hand, perform two functions: They act like a legislature by promulgating rules and regulations that bind us; and they act like a judiciary by hearing disputes and rendering decisions.

5. *Executive Branch*

Although the primary function of the federal executive branch is to enforce the law, it serves as a source of law itself in three ways. First, treaties are entered into by the executive branch with the advice and consent of the U.S. Senate. These agreements between the United States and other nations serve as a source of law because they may relate to trade and import matters, economic cooperation, or even international boundaries and fishing rights. Second, the President, our chief executive, can issue executive orders to regulate and direct federal agencies and officials. Third, the executive branch exerts influence on the law through policies on enforcing laws. For example, if federal laws relating to possession of small amounts of drugs are rarely enforced, the effect is as if the law does not exist, despite the fact that a statute clearly prohibits such acts. Nevertheless, although such an approach by the executive branch influences the law as well as societal behavior, such influence on the law is indirect and remote. In the event the government prosecutes an individual for violation of a previously unenforced law, the individual usually may not raise the previous laxity as a defense.

The executive branches of the federal and state governments also serve as sources of law in that the chief executive (the President or a state governor) is required to sign a bill to make it legally effective and can veto a bill (although legislatures usually can override such vetoes, generally with a two-thirds vote).

E. Legal Systems of Other Countries

Although every country has its own system of law, most systems are classified as either being part of the common law tradition, described previously, or part of the civil law tradition. *Civil law* systems developed from Roman law, which followed a comprehensive set of codes. In general, civil law countries place much heavier reliance on their collections of statutes than on their much smaller collections of cases. Austria, China, France, Germany, Italy, Japan, Mexico, the Russian Federation, South Korea, Spain, and many of the countries of Africa are civil law countries. Typically, English-speaking countries or those that are prior British Commonwealth colonies are part of the common law system (and are greatly dependent on cases used as precedents), whereas non-English-speaking countries are usually part of the civil law system (which is greatly dependent on codes or statutes). Note that every state in the United States except Louisiana, and every Canadian province except Quebec, is part of the common law tradition. Because Louisiana and Quebec were settled by the French, their legal systems are largely patterned after the law of France, a civil law country. In practice, however, even in many countries with systems based on civil law, case law still plays a significant role. Table T.2 of *The Bluebook* identifies more than 30 foreign countries as either common law or civil law countries.

F. Legal System of the United States

Although the United States adheres to a uniform common law tradition, there is no single legal system in this country. Federal laws are enacted by the U.S. Congress, and cases are decided by the federal courts. Moreover, unless an area of the law has been preempted by the U.S. Constitution or the federal government, each state is free to enact laws as well as to decide cases dealing with state or local concerns.

Thus, there is a tremendous body of legal literature on the shelves of law libraries: federal cases and statutes; state cases and statutes; federal and state administrative regulations; and numerous other texts and journals that explain the law.

All of the great mass of legal authorities can be classified as primary or secondary authority. *Primary authorities* are official pronouncements of the law by the executive branch (namely, treaties and executive orders), legislative branch (namely, constitutions, statutes, and administrative regulations and decisions), and judicial branch (namely, cases).

If a legal authority does not fall within one of the previously mentioned categories, it is a secondary authority. In general, the *secondary authorities* provide comment, discussion, and explanation of the primary authorities, and, equally important, they help researchers locate the primary authorities. Secondary authorities may consist of legal encyclopedias, law review articles written about various legal topics, books or other treatises dealing with legal issues, law dictionaries, and expert opinions and commentary on legal issues.

It is critical to understand thoroughly the differences between primary and secondary authorities because only primary authorities are binding on a court, agency, or tribunal. Thus, if an argument relies on or cites a case, constitution, statute, or administrative regulation that is relevant to the legal issue, it *must* be followed. The secondary authorities, on the other hand, are persuasive only and need not be followed. See Figure 1-1 for a chart showing primary and secondary authorities and other legal research tools.

In addition to the various authorities previously discussed, there are other books in the law library that are in the nature of practical guides or finding tools. These include books such as digests, which help locate cases (see Chapter Five); form books, which provide forms for various legal documents such as wills and contracts (see Chapter Six); and sets of books (and their electronic counterparts) that help you update the authorities you rely upon in any legal writing (see Chapter Eleven).

Figure 1-1
Primary and Secondary Authorities

Primary Authorities (binding)

Authorities	*Source*
Cases (state and federal)	Judiciary
Constitutions (state and federal)	Legislature
Statutes (state and federal)	Legislature
Administrative regulations (state and federal)	Administrative agencies
Executive orders and treaties (federal only)	Executive branch

Secondary Authorities (persuasive)

A.L.R. Annotations
Encyclopedias
Legal periodicals
Texts and treatises
Restatements
Dictionaries

Finding Tools

Digests

Updating Tools

Shepard's Citations (in print and on LexisNexis)
KeyCite (on Westlaw)

G. Law Book Publishing

There is a tremendous amount of publication of legal authorities, both primary and secondary, that occurs each year. Approximately 50,000 cases are published each year. You cannot be expected to know all of the law contained in the published authorities; however, you can be reasonably expected to be able to locate and use these legal authorities. That is the goal of legal research.

The actual publication of these authorities is conducted by only a handful of publishing companies, including the following, which are among the best-known legal publishers:

- **West.** Although West is actually owned by Thomson Reuters, a global information company, in the United States it retains its identification as "West." Founded in 1872, West publishes cases, statutes, secondary authorities, and provides Westlaw, the computer-assisted legal research system. West also owns FindLaw (http://www.findlaw.com), a leader in free online legal information. West is headquartered in Minnesota. In 1996, West acquired a number of other large law book publishers, including the giant Lawyers Cooperative Publishing.
- **LexisNexis Group.** LexisNexis Group is a division of Reed Elsevier PLC and competes head-on with West in the publication of many legal sources, including statutes. LexisNexis also provides its self-named computer-assisted legal research system. Through a series of recent acquisitions, LexisNexis has combined other publishers, including Matthew Bender, The Michie Company, Shepard's, and Martindale-Hubbell. You will likely notice some differences in the presentation of LexisNexis's name on its various publications. For simplicity, this text will generally use "LexisNexis" to refer both to the company's print publications and its electronic research service.
- **Wolters Kluwer.** Headquartered in the Netherlands, Wolters Kluwer includes a number of other "brands," including Aspen Publishers and CCH Incorporated. Wolters Kluwer's computer-assisted legal research system is called Loislaw and is of particular benefit to sole practitioners and smaller law offices.

More information on legal publishers can be found at the following website: *A Legal Publishers List: Corporate Affiliations of Legal Publishers* (2d ed. 2004), http://www.aallnet.org/committee/criv/resources/tools/list.

One of the common features shared by the primary sources (cases, constitutions, statutes, and regulations) as they are initially published is that they are arranged in chronological order. Thus, a set of case reports may include a case related to a will, followed by one related to burglary, followed by one relating to a contract dispute. Similarly, during any given session, a legislature will enact laws relating to motor vehicles, regulation of utilities, and licensing of real estate salespeople. The initial publication of these statutes is in the order in which they were enacted rather than according to subject matter.

This type of organization makes research difficult. If you were asked to locate cases dealing with landlord-tenant law, you would find that they have not been brought together in one specific set of books but rather may be scattered over several hundred volumes of cases. It is clear then that a method of obtaining access to these primary authorities is needed, and in general, the secondary authorities and digests will assist in locating the primary authorities. For example, a secondary source such as a legal encyclopedia will describe and explain landlord-tenant law and will then direct you to cases that are primary or binding authorities relating to this area of the law. These cases, when cited in a legal argument, under the doctrine of stare decisis, must be followed by a court, whereas the encyclopedia discussion is persuasive only and need not be followed by a court.

H. Non-Print Research Media

Until fairly recently, almost all legal research was performed using conventional print volumes in law libraries. With the advent of computer-assisted legal research (see Chapter Eight) and Internet legal research (see Chapter Nine), legal professionals use a variety of media to get the right answers to their research questions and are no longer tied to the law library.

Good researchers must be adept at both methods of performing legal research: using conventional print sources and using newer technology sources such as LexisNexis and Westlaw (the computer-assisted research systems) and the Internet. These newer technologies allow legal professionals to perform research at their desks and on the road.

Some methods are more efficient and cost-effective than others. For example, if you need general background information about an area of the law, consider browsing an encyclopedia or treatise in print form. If you need information about a new or evolving area of law, computer-assisted legal research will likely provide the most current information. Today's researchers need to be flexible in using all methods of legal research in case materials are unavailable: Books can disappear from library shelves and networks can crash.

Successful legal researchers thus combine research media to obtain information for clients. Knowing which media to use requires an analysis of many factors, including the complexity of your task, the costs involved, and time constraints. Many research instructors urge students first to become familiar with the conventional print tools before becoming too wedded to computer-assisted or Internet legal research. Strong skills in conventional legal research provide a good foundation for using Lexis Nexis, Westlaw, and the Internet more effectively. Thus, this text will fully examine the conventional print research tools before discussing newer technologies such as computer-assisted and Internet legal research.

I. Change in Our Legal System

Although stare decisis promotes stability, fairness, and uniformity in our legal system, blind adherence to established precedents in the face of changing societal views and mores may result in injustice. For example, in 1896, the U.S. Supreme Court held that "separate but equal" public facilities for blacks and whites were lawful. *Plessy v. Ferguson*, 163 U.S. 537 (1896). This precedent served to justify segregation for more than 50 years. In 1954, however, in *Brown v. Board of Education*, 347 U.S. 483, 495 (1954), the Supreme Court overruled its earlier decision and held that segregation solely according to race in public schools violated the U.S. Constitution. A strict adherence to stare decisis would have precluded a second look at this issue and would have resulted in continued racial segregation.

Thus, it is clear that as society changes, the law must also change. A balance must be struck between society's need for stability in its legal system and the need for flexibility and change when precedents have outlived their usefulness or result in injustice. Change in established legal precedent comes about by rulings of higher courts, which then bind lower courts in that judicial system or hierarchy. Thus, because *Brown v. Board of Education* was decided by the U.S. Supreme Court, it can only be overruled by the U.S. Supreme Court. Nevertheless, a lower court might try to evade a binding precedent by striving to show that precedent is not applicable or that the facts in the case before it are distinguishable from the facts in the previously decided case. This flexibility in reasoning produces a rich, complex, and often contradictory body of American case law.

Thus, stare decisis means more than following settled cases: It means following settled cases that are factually similar and legally relevant to the case or problem you are researching. Such a factually similar and legally relevant case from a court equivalent to or higher than the court that will hear your particular case is said to be *on point* or "on all fours" with your case. The goal of legal research is to locate cases on point with your particular problem. Such cases are binding upon and must be followed by the court hearing your case.

In the event you cannot locate cases on point in your judicial hierarchy (possibly because your case presents a novel issue not yet considered in your jurisdiction), expand your search for cases on point to other jurisdictions. For example, if Ohio has no precedents on a particular issue, expand your search to another state. The Ohio court, however, is not bound to follow cases from other jurisdictions although it may be persuaded to do so. See Figure 1-2.

Change in our legal system can occur not only as a result of judges expanding or overruling precedents found in cases but also through repeal or amendment of a statute by a legislature or even through judicial interpretation of a statute. Although a court cannot change the plain meaning of a statute, it is free to interpret the statute or to declare it unconstitutional. Thus, even when you locate a statute that appears directly to address your research problem, you cannot stop researching. You must read the cases that have interpreted the statute, because it is the judicial interpretation of a statute rather than its naked language that is binding under the doctrine of stare decisis.

Figure 1-2
Stare Decisis and Our Judicial Hierarchy

- Primary law consists of cases, constitutions, statutes, treaties, executive orders, and administrative regulations. All other legal authorities are secondary.
- Primary law from your state or jurisdiction is binding within your state or jurisdiction.
- Primary law from another state or jurisdiction is persuasive only in your state or jurisdiction.
- If your state or jurisdiction adopts the law or position of another state or jurisdiction, then that position is now binding within your judicial hierarchy.
- Secondary sources (no matter where they originate) are persuasive only.
- Higher courts in any given judicial hierarchy bind lower courts in that hierarchy.
- Higher courts can depart from a previously announced rule of law if there are compelling and important reasons for doing so.

J. Identifying the Holding in a Case

You can readily see that the foundation of the American legal system lies in its rich and varied body of case law. Although analysis of cases will be discussed in great detail in Chapter Four, you should be aware that under the concept of stare decisis, only the actual rule of law announced in a case is binding; that is, only the holding of the case is authoritative. The holding is referred to as *ratio decidendi* or "reason for deciding." Other remarks or judicial comments in the case are often referred to as *dicta*, meaning remarks "in passing." Dictum in a case is persuasive only.

In many instances, distinguishing the holding from the dictum is easily done. Often a court announces its holding by using extremely specific introductory language, such as the following: "Therefore, we hold that . . . ." On other occasions, finding the holding requires more persistence and probing.

You will shortly discover that some cases are difficult to read and use archaic and outmoded language. Do not become discouraged by this. Reading cases takes a great deal of experience and patience. You will find that the more cases you read, the more skillful you will become at locating the holding, distinguishing dicta from the holding, and understanding the relevance of the case for the future.

K. How the Legal Research Process Works: A Research Scenario

Just as it is nearly impossible to put together a puzzle without first seeing a picture of the finished product, it is difficult to understand the process of legal research before actually performing a legal research project. To understand what you will be able to do when you have completed your research class, consider the following scenario, which is typical of the type of task a researcher often encounters.

> Peggie was recently hired by a law firm and asked by her supervising attorney to do some legal research. The attorney met with a client, Grace, whose husband, Phil, died two years ago. Grace is the mother of a ten-year-old boy. The son spends occasional time with Phil's parents. Grace is remarrying and although the grandparents are kind and loving, Grace has decided that it would be better to limit any visits by her son with Phil's parents so that she can begin her new marriage and start her new family. Phil's parents have told Grace that they will go to court to seek visitation. The attorney wants Peggie to find out how the courts in the state handle grandparent visitation. After getting the assignment, Peggie went back to her office to begin the research process. First, she thought about the places she might need to look to find an answer to this question. Because Peggie was unfamiliar with family law, she realized that she would need to learn a bit more about grandparent visitation in general so that she would have the background to understand the materials she would be reading as she worked on this research assignment. Peggie thus reviewed some introductory information in a legal encyclopedia (Chapter Six) to "get her feet wet." Next, she looked to see if her state had any statutes (Chapter Three) that addressed this issue. After reading the statutes, Peggie realized that she needed a better understanding of the meaning of some of the language in the statute, so she looked up some court cases (Chapter Four) that interpreted the statute. One case in particular was relevant to this question, so she used a digest (Chapter Five) to find other cases that dealt with the same issue. She then reviewed a set of books on family law in general and read the chapters relating to grandparent visitation (Chapter Six). Peggie also decided to use LexisNexis or Westlaw to locate the most current information and other specialized articles or texts on grandparent visitation (Chapter Eight). Next, she made sure that the statutes and cases were still in effect and had not been modified or overturned (Chapter Eleven). Finally, Peggie wrote her attorney a memorandum describing what she had found out from her research, being careful to use correct citation form (Chapter Ten).

Peggie's approach to her research problem is only one way that the problem could be solved; another researcher might well approach the problem differently, but both would reach the same conclusion.

It is thus important for researchers to understand thoroughly all of the legal research resources that are available, so that when a project is received, it can be completed efficiently and correctly. Moreover, researchers need to understand the American legal system and court structures (Chapters Two and Four) so that cases can be put into context and researchers can understand which authorities are binding.

Legal research is not so much about following a predicable formula as it is about understanding how the numerous resources fit together so that researchers can make intelligent decisions about performing legal research. Thus, the next chapters will afford you an in-depth understanding of the available resources so that you will know how and where to look for answers, allowing you to fulfill your ethical duties to perform research accurately and efficiently to help clients with their legal problems.

L. Case Citation Form

Although case citation will be discussed in much more depth in Chapter Ten, the sooner you begin examining the books in which our cases are published and reading those cases, the more confident you will become about your ability to research effectively.

All cases follow the same basic citation form: You will be given the case name, the volume number of the set in which the case is published, the name of the set in which the case appears, the page on which it begins, and the year it was decided (and the deciding court, if not apparent from the name of the set). For example, in reading the citation to the United States Supreme Court case *Brown v. Board of Education*, 347 U.S. 483 (1954), you can readily see the following:

- The case name is *Brown v. Board of Education;*
- It is located in volume 347;
- It is found in a set of books entitled *United States Reports*;
- It begins on page 483 of volume 347; and
- It was decided in 1954.

Although this text shows case names, book titles, and other materials in italics, underlining or underscoring is also acceptable according to the two major citation manuals, *The Bluebook: A Uniform System of Citation* (Columbia Law Review Ass'n et al. eds., 18th ed. 2005) ("*The Bluebook*") and ALWD & Darby Dickerson, *ALWD Citation Manual* (3d ed., Aspen Publishers 2006) ("*ALWD*").

As discussed in Chapter Ten, although *The Bluebook* is the standard reference tool for citation form, *ALWD* has gained in popularity due to its commonsense rules and user-friendly format. The citation example given previously complies with both *Bluebook* and *ALWD* rules. There are additional citation systems as well and variation among practitioners, so check with your firm or office to determine if there is a preference.

CyberSites

http://www.lexisnexis.com	Information about LexisNexis products and services.
http://www.west.thomson.com/home	Information about West products and services.
http://www.lectlaw.com	Inter-Law's 'Lectric Library, a variety of legal information together with links to other law-related sites.
http://www.ilrg.com	Internet Legal Research Group, a comprehensive guide to legal resources available online.
http://www.hg.org/publishers.html	HG.org's website, offering a list of legal publishers together with their addresses and telephone numbers.
http://www.loc.gov/law/guide	Guide to Law Online, prepared by the U.S. Law Library of Congress, Public Services Division, providing an annotated guide to sources of information and law available online and links to useful and reliable sites for legal information.
http://www.bc.edu/schools/law/library/research/researchguides.html	Boston College Law Library's legal research guides and videos.
http://www.ll.georgetown.edu/research/index.cfm	Georgetown University Law Library's legal research tutorials and guides.
http://www.law.syr.edu/lawlibrary/electronic/researchguides.asp	Syracuse University College of Law's legal research guides.
http://lib.law.washington.edu/ref/guides.html	University of Washington School of Law's legal research guides.

Research Assignment

1. a. Give the name of the case located at 540 U.S. 93 (2003).
   b. Who represented the plaintiffs in this case?
2. a. Give the name of the case located at 525 U.S. 366 (1999).
   b. Who delivered the opinion of the Court?
3. a. Give the name of the case located at 548 U.S. 521 (2006).
   b. What role did Justice Alito take?
4. a. Give the name of the case at 539 U.S. 90 (2003).
   b. Give the date the case was argued.
   c. Give the date the case was decided.
   d. In brief, what is the subject matter of this case?
   e. Locate a case in this volume in which the defendant's name is *Beaumont*.
   f. Give the citation for the case.
   g. Who dissented in this case?

Internet Assignment

1. Access the website for the National Center for State Courts at http://www.ncsconline.org and locate information about Texas's Supreme Court. Who is the Chief Justice of the Texas Supreme Court?
2. Access the site for GPO Access and identify the name of the library in Ithaca, New York, that is a federal depository library.
3. Access Cornell Law School's Legal Information Institute at http://www.law.cornell.edu. Select "Law About" and then "Lexicon." Provide the first definition for *dicta*.
4. Access the website for the American Association of Law Libraries and review information about the committee called "CRIV" (Committee on Relations with Information Vendors). Review the "CRIV Page — A Legal Publishers List." When did Reed Elsevier PLC acquire Matthew Bender?
5. Access the website for the American Bar Association and review the Model Rules of Professional Conduct. Specifically, review the Comment to Rule 1.1. How can an attorney maintain his or her requisite knowledge and skill?

Chapter 2

The Federal and State Court Systems

Chapter Overview

This chapter provides an overview of the federal and state court systems. To perform research tasks, you should understand these court structures so that when you are confronted with a research assignment or a case citation, you will readily understand the hierarchy of cases within a given court structure, giving greater emphasis to cases from higher courts (such as the United States Supreme Court and the United States Courts of Appeal) than to cases from federal trial courts (called the United States District Courts) or lower state courts.

A. Federalism

At the time of the founding of the nation, there were two conflicting ideas held by the framers of the Constitution. On the one hand, the framers recognized the need for a strong central of "federal" government to act in matters of national concern. On the other hand, the delegates to the Constitutional Convention of 1787 were wary of delegating too much power to a centralized government. The principle of rights for the separate colonies or states was seen as the best protection against encroachment by a federal government.

The result was a compromise: For those delegates devoted to a strong national government, the principle developed that the national government could exercise only those powers specifically enumerated in the Constitution, including borrowing money, collecting taxes, coining money, declaring war, and making any other laws "necessary and proper" for carrying out these delegated powers. As can be readily seen, these specifically enumerated powers are extremely important and gave the emerging federal government wide powers. However, the Constitution was immediately modified by the addition of ten amendments, known collectively as the Bill of Rights, which were designed to protect individual liberties. The Tenth Amendment, in particular, was enacted to reassure those in favor of states' rights. Known as the "reserve clause," the Tenth Amendment provides that any powers not expressly given to the national government are reserved to, or retained, by the individual states.

The result of the historic Constitutional Convention is our "living law"—a unique system referred to as *federalism* in which the states have formed a union by granting the federal government power over national affairs while the states retain their independent existence and power over local matters.

B. Jurisdiction

1. Introduction

The *jurisdiction* (or power to act) of the federal courts does not extend to every kind of case or controversy, but instead only to certain types of matters. You will learn a great deal more about this topic in your litigation or civil procedure classes, but a brief explanation is in order here for you to understand fully why some research projects will be researched through the exclusive use of federal law, and others will be researched through the exclusive review of the law of a particular state.

A party may allege that a court lacks jurisdiction at any time. In fact, lack of jurisdiction is such a fatal defect that any judgment rendered by a court that lacks jurisdiction is void.

There are two types of cases that are resolved by federal courts: those based on federal question jurisdiction (sometimes called *subject matter jurisdiction* cases) and those based on diversity jurisdiction.

2. Federal Question Jurisdiction

Federal courts may decide cases that involve a *federal question*; that is, any case arising under the United States Constitution, a United States (or federal) law, or any treaty to which the United States is a party. Cases arising under the Constitution include cases alleging racial, sexual, or age discrimination; cases involving freedom of speech; cases involving a defendant's right to a fair trial; cases involving federal crimes such as kidnapping or terrorism; and any other actions pertaining to a federal law or the Constitution. Additionally, federal courts may decide controversies between states, between the United States and foreign governments, and any cases involving the U.S. government.

3. *Diversity Jurisdiction*

The other category of cases that is handled by federal courts, those based on *diversity jurisdiction*, is determined not by the issue or subject matter itself (as are federal question cases) but by the status of the parties to the action. Imagine you are a New York resident on vacation in Montana, where you become involved in an automobile accident with a Montana resident. You may have some concern as to whether a court in Montana would treat you, an outsider, the same as it would treat its own citizens, particularly in a locality in which the residents elect their judges.

To ensure that litigants are treated fairly and to eliminate any bias against an out-of-state litigant, the federal courts may resolve cases based on the diversity of the parties; that is, in general, federal courts may hear cases in civil actions between citizens of different states. Note, however, that diversity jurisdiction is conditioned upon satisfying another key element: The amount in controversy must exceed $75,000, exclusive of interest and court costs. For example, if a resident of Oregon sues a resident of Idaho for breach of contract and alleges (in good faith) damages in the amount of $80,000, the matter may be instituted in federal court. There is no monetary jurisdictional limit for cases instituted in federal court based on federal questions.

Diversity must be complete; all plaintiffs must be citizens of different states from all defendants. A federal court in a diversity case will apply the state law of the state in which it is located.

See Figure 2-1 for chart of federal jurisdiction.

Figure 2-1
Federal Jurisdiction

Federal jurisdiction may be based upon the following:

- **Federal question:** Any case arising under the U.S. Constitution or any federal law or treaty (28 U.S.C. § 1331 (2006)); or
- **Diversity:** Generally, cases in which all plaintiffs are from different states from all defendants and in which the matter in controversy exceeds $75,000 (28 U.S.C. § 1332 (2006)).

Additionally, cases originally filed in state court may be removed to a federal court, as follows:

- **Removal:** If a case is originally filed by a plaintiff in state court and federal jurisdiction exists, the case may be *removed* to federal court by the defendant (28 U.S.C. § 1441 (2006)).
- **Remand:** If it appears at any time before final judgment that a case was improperly removed because the district court lacked subject matter jurisdiction, it must be remanded or returned to the state court (28 U.S.C. § 1447 (2006)).

4. *Concurrent Jurisdiction*

If a case may be brought in more than one court, jurisdiction is said to be *concurrent*. For example, racial discrimination is a violation of both California state law and federal law. Thus, a victim of racial discrimination in California may initiate an action either in California state court or in federal court. Matters of trial tactics and strategy often dictate in which court the action will be brought. For example, a plaintiff may wish to proceed in a federal court because it is not as crowded with cases as the local state court, thus providing a more speedy trial and resolution. Moreover, any diversity jurisdiction case (regardless of the amount of money involved) may be brought in a state court rather than a federal court.

5. *Exclusive Jurisdiction*

Some matters are handled exclusively by federal courts and are never the subject of concurrent jurisdiction. For example, all maritime, copyright infringement, and patent infringement cases must be brought in federal court. Generally, statutes govern which cases are subject to *exclusive jurisdiction*.

C. Ground Rules for Cases

Even if a federal question or diversity exists, there still remain some ground rules that must be satisfied before a federal court will hear a case. Although the following discussion relates primarily to federal cases, these ground rules must usually be satisfied for cases brought in state courts as well.

In large part, these ground rules are rooted in Article III of the Constitution, which establishes the jurisdiction of federal courts and restricts federal courts to resolving "cases" and "controversies." There are three ground rules. First, with very few exceptions, federal courts will not consider issues that are "moot" or already resolved. In fact, it is a fraud on a court to continue with a case that is moot. Parties before the court must be involved in an existing, present controversy. Second, a close corollary to this first ground rule is that federal courts will not render advisory opinions, even if asked by the President. The federal courts are constitutionally bound to resolve actual ongoing disputes, not to give advice. Finally, a plaintiff must have personally suffered some actual or threatened legal injury; that is, the plaintiff must be adversely affected by some conduct or threatened conduct of the defendant and cannot base a claim on the rights or interests of some other persons. This requirement is referred to as *standing*, and it ensures that parties before the court have a personal stake in the outcome of the controversy.

D. The Federal Court Structure

1. *Introduction*

Article III, Section 1, of the Constitution created the federal court system. This section provides in part that "the judicial power of the United States shall be vested in one Supreme Court and in such inferior courts as Congress may from time to time ordain and establish." Thus, only the existence of the Supreme Court was assured. It was left up to Congress to determine its composition and to create any other federal courts. In fact, the first Congress created the federal court structure that still exists today. Although the numbers of courts and judges have increased, the basic structure of our federal court system remains as it was in 1789: district courts, intermediate courts of appeal, and one United States Supreme Court. Judges appointed to these courts are often referred to as *Article III judges*.

There are three levels of courts in the federal system. Starting with the lowest courts, they are the district courts, the courts of appeal, and the United States Supreme Court. All judges in the federal court system are nominated by the President and confirmed by the United States Senate.

2. *United States District Courts*

The *district courts* are the trial courts in our federal system. At present, there are 94 district courts scattered throughout the 50 states, the District of Columbia, and the territories and possessions of the United States. There is at least one district court in each state, and the more populous states, namely, California, New York, and Texas, have four district courts within their territorial borders. Other less populous states, such as Alaska and Utah, each have only one district court (although they may have divisions in other parts of the state to allow easy access for litigants). Although Congress has the authority to create new district courts, it has not done so since 1971, when a new district was created by splitting an existing district in Louisiana. See Figure 2-2 for a list of the district courts.

Help Line: *Federal Court Websites and Opinions*

All federal courts maintain websites, all of which can be accessed through a site entitled U.S. Courts at http://www.uscourts.gov. This site provides a map of the federal courts of appeal; direct linking to the websites for all federal courts; and access to opinions and to the federal rules of civil procedure, criminal procedure, and evidence.

Figure 2-2
United States District Courts and Courts of Appeal

Alabama	11th Cir.
M.D. Ala.	
N.D. Ala.	
S.D. Ala.	
Alaska	9th Cir.
D. Alaska	
Arizona	9th Cir.
D. Ariz.	
Arkansas	8th Cir.
E.D. Ark.	
W.D. Ark.	
California	9th Cir.
C.D. Cal.	
E.D. Cal.	
N.D. Cal.	
S.D. Cal.	
Colorado	10th Cir.
Connecticut	2d Cir.
D. Conn.	
Delaware	3d Cir.
D. Del.	
District of Columbia	D.C. Cir.
D.D.C.	
Florida	11th Cir.
M.D. Fla.	
N.D. Fla.	
S.D. Fla.	
Georgia	11th Cir.
M.D. Ga.	
N.D. Ga.	
S.D. Ga.	
Hawaii	9th Cir.
D. Haw.	
Idaho	9th Cir.
D. Idaho	
Illinois	7th Cir.
C.D. Ill.	
N.D. Ill.	
S.D. Ill.	
Indiana	7th Cir.
N.D. Ind.	
S.D. Ind.	
Iowa	8th Cir.
N.D. Iowa	
S.D. Iowa	
Kansas	10th Cir.
D. Kan.	
Kentucky	6th Cir.
E.D. Ky.	
W.D. Ky.	
Louisiana	5th Cir.
E.D. La.	
M.D. La.	
W.D. La.	
Maine	1st Cir.
D. Me.	
Maryland	4th Cir.
D. Md.	
Massachusetts	1st Cir.
D. Mass.	
Michigan	6th Cir.
E. D. Mich.	
W.D. Mich.	
Minnesota	8th Cir.
D. Minn.	

Figure 2-2 *(Continued)*

Mississippi 5th Cir.
N.D. Miss.
S.D. Miss.

Missouri 8th Cir.
E.D. Mo.
W.D. Mo.

Montana 9th Cir.
D. Mont.

Nebraska 8th Cir.
D. Neb.

Nevada 9th Cir.
D. Nev.

New Hampshire 1st Cir.
D.N.H.

New Jersey 3d Cir.
D.N.J.

New Mexico 10th Cir.
D.N.M.

New York 2d Cir.
E.D.N.Y.
N.D.N.Y.
S.D.N.Y.
W.D.N.Y.

North Carolina 4th Cir.
E.D.N.C.
M.D.N.C.
W.D.N.C.

North Dakota 8th Cir.
D.N.D.

Ohio 6th Cir.
N.D. Ohio
S.D. Ohio

Oklahoma 10th Cir.
E.D. Okla.
N.D. Okla.
W.D. Okla.

Oregon 9th Cir.
D. Or.

Pennsylvania 3d Cir.
E.D. Pa.
M.D. Pa.
W.D. Pa.

Rhode Island 1st Cir.
D.R.I.

South Carolina 4th Cir.
D.S.C.

South Dakota 8th Cir.
D.S.D.

Tennessee 6th Cir.
E.D. Tenn.
M.D. Tenn.
W.D. Tenn.

Texas 5th Cir.
E.D. Tex.
N.D. Tex.
S.D. Tex.
W.D. Tex.

Utah 10th Cir.
D. Utah

Vermont 2d Cir.
D. Vt.

Virginia 4th Cir.
E.D. Va.
W.D. Va.

Washington 9th Cir.
E.D. Wash.
W.D. Wash.

West Virginia 4th Cir.
N.D.W. Va.
S.D.W. Va.

Figure 2-2 *(Continued)*

Wisconsin E.D. Wis. W.D. Wis.	7th Cir.	**N. Mariana Islands** D.N. Mar. I.	9th Cir.
Wyoming D. Wyo.	10th Cir.	**Puerto Rico** D.P.R.	1st Cir.
Miscellaneous		**Virgin Islands** D.V.I.	3d Cir.
Canal Zone D.C.Z. **(abolished 1982)**	5th Cir.	**U.S. Court of Appeals for the Federal Circuit**	Fed. Cir.
Guam D. Guam	9th Cir.	**U.S. Court of Federal $$$Claims**	Fed. Cl.

These district courts have jurisdiction over a wide variety of cases. In any given day, a district court judge may hear cases involving a bank robbery, a civil rights question, and a crime committed on an Indian reservation. Bankruptcy courts are also considered units of our district courts with judges appointed by the courts of appeal for 14-year terms. Each district includes a United States Bankruptcy Court.

The number of judges assigned to a particular district court will vary depending upon the number of cases the court is called upon to adjudicate. Thus, there may be as few as one district court judge assigned to a district court, as is the case for the Green Bay Division of the Eastern District of Wisconsin, or there may be nearly 50, as is the case for the increasingly busy Southern District of New York.

The district court judges, who are paid more than $165,000 annually, usually sit individually; that is, they hear cases and render decisions by themselves rather than as a panel or group as the United States Supreme Court justices sit.

The vast majority of all federal cases end at the district court level; only approximately 10 percent of these federal cases are appealed. In recent years, the number of civil filings in the district courts has remained relatively stable (or even dropped slightly), perhaps as a result of litigants seeking various forms of alternative dispute resolution, such as mediation and arbitration, and reforms aimed at reducing the number of frivolous petitions filed by prisoners. In 2008, nearly 250,000 civil cases were commenced in the various district courts.

3. United States Courts of Appeal

The 13 United States Courts of Appeal, sometimes called the *circuit courts*, are the intermediate courts in our federal system. The theory of our judicial system is that a litigant should have a trial in one court before one judge and a right to an appeal in another court before a different judge or judges. In fact, a federal statute directs that no judge may hear an appeal of a case originally tried by him or her.

It is critical to remember the difference between the district courts, which are trial courts that hear evidence, listen to witnesses testify, and render decisions, and the courts of appeal, whose primary function is to review cases from these district courts. The courts of appeal do not retry a case. They merely review the record and the briefs of counsel to determine if a prejudicial error of law was made in the district court below. A second important function of the United States Courts of Appeal is to review and enforce decisions from federal administrative agencies such as the FCC or NLRB.

The United States is divided into 12 geographical regions called "circuits," and there is a court of appeal in each of these circuits (including one for the District of Columbia circuit). Additionally, there is a Court of Appeals for the Federal Circuit, located in Washington, D.C., which has nationwide jurisdiction and handles specialized cases, such as patent and international trade cases. Figure 2-3 shows the grouping of states that make up each circuit. It is not critical to know which states or district courts fall within the boundaries of which circuits. Maps of the circuit courts are readily available in the front of each volume of West's *Federal Reporter*, a set of books that reports decisions from the various courts of appeal. You should, however, know which circuit covers the state in which you will be working and that 11 of the 13 circuits are assigned a number and will have several states (and their district courts) within their boundaries. For example, the Ninth Circuit covers California and most of the western states. Thus, if a trial occurs in the Northern District of California, the appeal is filed in the Ninth Circuit Court of Appeals. Similarly, if a trial occurs in the Southern District of New York, the appeal is filed in the Second Circuit Court of Appeals. In 2008, approximately 58,000 appeals were filed in the U.S. Courts of Appeal.

Each of the intermediate circuit courts of appeal is free to make its own decisions independent of what the other circuits have held; in practice, however, the circuit courts are often guided by decisions from other courts. Decisions from the U.S. Supreme Court often resolve conflicts among the circuits.

Congress has the authority to create additional circuits, but it has not done so since 1981, when it created the Eleventh Circuit by dividing the Fifth Circuit, which had seen an increasingly heavy caseload as population grew in the South.

Figure 2-3
The Thirteen Federal Judicial Circuits (See 28 U.S.C.A § 41 (2006))

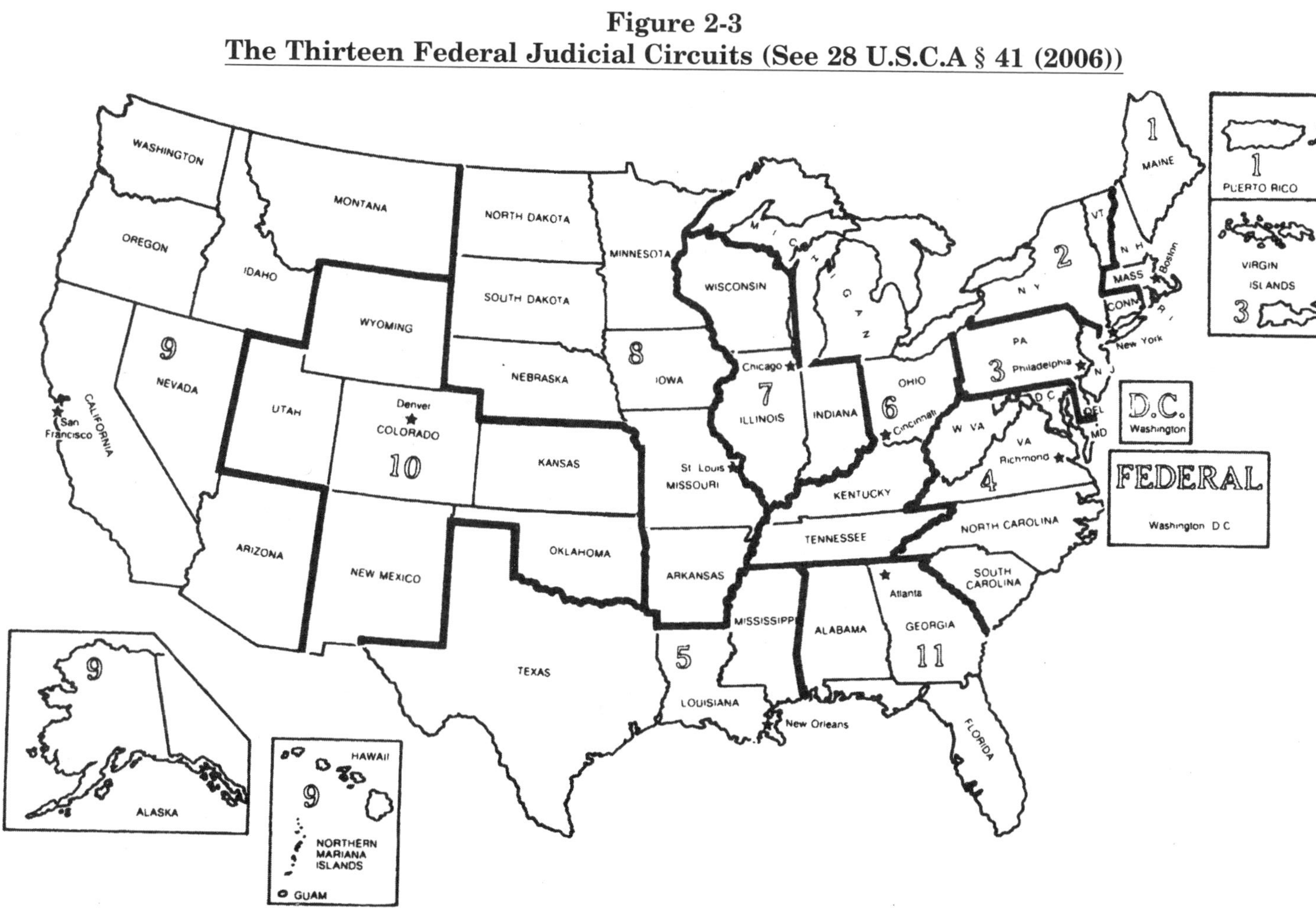

Each of the courts of appeals has at least six judges and as many as 28 judges assigned to it, depending on the caseload for the circuit. The judges usually hear the appeals from the district courts as a panel of three judges, although they may sit *en banc*, with all judges present. These federal judges earn an annual salary of approximately $180,000. The United States Courts of Appeal typically issue more than 15,000 opinions each year (although not all of them are published).

For the vast majority of litigants, these intermediate courts of appeal represent the last opportunity to prevail. As you will see, the popular notion that everyone has access to the Supreme Court is unfounded; for most litigants, the court of appeals is the last chance to win, because one who wishes to appeal a case to the U.S. Supreme Court is largely dependent on the Court's discretion in accepting the case for review.

4. United States Supreme Court

The United States Supreme Court consists of eight associate justices and one chief justice. Although the chief justice draws a higher salary than the associate justices (roughly $217,000 to their annual salaries of $208,000) and has prestige and certain authority by virtue of seniority, the chief justice's vote counts equally with that of any associate justice. Nevertheless, as the presiding officer of the Supreme Court, he or she is responsible for administration of the Court and leadership of the federal judicial system. Upon the death or resignation of a chief justice, the President may either appoint one of the eight existing associate justices to the position of chief justice or may appoint an "outsider" as chief justice.

As are all approximately 870 judges in the federal system, the Supreme Court justices are nominated by the President and hold office "during good behavior." This means they are not subject to mandatory retirement and may sit as federal judges until they voluntarily resign or retire. Many have served for extremely long periods—notably Chief Justice John Marshall, widely regarded as the finest jurist produced by the United States, who served for 34 years, and Associate Justice William O. Douglas, who served for 36 years. Although federal judges may be impeached by Congress, this drastic remedy is seldom used, and only a few have actually been removed through impeachment.

The individuals who sit on the United States Supreme Court (or a state's highest court) are usually referred to as *justices*, whereas the individuals who sit on lower courts are referred to as *judges*. Occasionally, individuals who sit on intermediate appellate courts are also referred to as "justices," although typically the term "justice" is reserved for individuals on the United States Supreme Court or a state's highest court.

In addition to their primary activities of hearing cases and writing opinions, each justice is assigned to one of the federal judicial circuits for the purpose of handling special and emergency matters such as stays of execution and injunctions. Because there are thirteen federal courts of appeal and only nine Supreme Court justices, some justices are assigned to more than one circuit. Assignment to the circuits is made annually by the chief justice.

By federal law, the term of the Court commences on the first Monday in October, and the term typically ends at the end of June nine months later. In recent years, the Court has been reducing its docket. During the 1980s, the Court routinely decided roughly 150 cases each term. In its 2007-2008 term, the Court issued only 67 full written opinions, although the average number of pages and footnotes per opinion has increased steadily over the years.

By the authority of the Constitution, the United States Supreme Court has the jurisdiction to act not only as an appellate or reviewing court but also in very limited instances (usually disputes between two states) can act as a court of original jurisdiction or trial court. The Court usually hears fewer than five original jurisdiction cases per term. See Figure 2-4 for a chart showing the jurisdiction of the Supreme Court.

Figure 2-4
Jurisdiction of United States Supreme Court

I. Original Jurisdiction (28 U.S.C. § 1251 (2006))
   A. Controversies between two or more states (exclusive jurisdiction)
   B. Actions in which ambassadors or other public ministers, consuls, or vice-consuls of foreign states are parties (non-exclusive jurisdiction)
   C. Controversies between the United States and a state (non-exclusive jurisdiction)
   D. Actions by a state against the citizens of another state (non-exclusive jurisdiction)

II. Appellate Jurisdiction (28 U.S.C. §§ 1253, 1254, 1257 (2006))
   A. Cases from federal courts
      1. United States District Courts (special statutes allow direct appeals as well as appeals from three-judge district courts granting or denying injunctive relief to be directly appealed to the United States Supreme Court)
      2. United States Courts of Appeal
         a. Certiorari
         b. Certification (granted only in exceptional cases)
   B. Cases from highest state courts that present a federal question (reviewed by writ of certiorari)

The most important function of the United States Supreme Court is its appellate jurisdiction, namely, its authority to review decisions from lower courts. Nearly all cases come to the Supreme Court from the lower federal courts or from the highest court in any state.

Although a few cases, such as some cases under the Interstate Commerce Act, are directly appealable from the district courts to the

United States Supreme Court, the vast majority of federal cases that the Supreme Court reviews proceed to the Court in the expected "stair step" fashion: trial in the district court, an intermediate appeal to the appropriate circuit court, and a final appeal to the United States Supreme Court.

The most widely used means to gain access to the United States Supreme Court from the lower circuit courts of appeal is the writ of certiorari. *Certiorari* is a Latin word meaning "to be more fully informed." A litigant who has lost an appeal in the intermediate circuit court will file a document or petition with the Supreme Court called a Petition for Writ of Certiorari, setting forth the basis for appeal. The Supreme Court will either grant the petition and direct the lower court to send its records and files to the Supreme Court or will deny the petition, meaning that the lower court decision will stand. Issuance of the writ, or "granting cert," is discretionary with the Supreme Court; a litigant does not have an absolute right to have the Supreme Court review a case.

Approximately 8,000 petitions for certiorari are filed with the United States Supreme Court each year, and the justices typically grant cert in fewer than 100 of these cases. Full signed opinions are issued in approximately 70 cases, and the remaining cases are disposed of without oral argument or formal written opinions.

There are no clearly articulated or published criteria followed by the justices in determining which petitions will be deemed "cert worthy." Court rules provide that certiorari will be granted if there are "compelling" reasons for doing so. Sup. Ct. R. 10. In general, however, a review of the cases accepted by the Supreme Court reveals some common elements: If the lower courts are in conflict on a certain issue and the circuit courts of appeal are issuing contradictory opinions, the Supreme Court often grants certiorari so that it can resolve such a conflict; or if a case is of general importance, the Court may grant certiorari.

Denial of the writ of certiorari is not to be viewed as an endorsement by the Court of a lower court's holding but rather its determination that for reasons of judicial economy not every case can be heard. Once a petition for certiorari has been granted, the attorneys or parties are notified and instructed to submit their written arguments, called briefs, which are then filed with the Court and made public. Oral arguments are then scheduled after which the justices meet in conference to decide the case. A preliminary vote is taken to determine the Court's disposition of the case. The justice who is the most senior in the majority group then assigns the opinion to be drafted by another justice or may decide to author the opinion himself or herself. While one justice is drafting the majority opinion, others may be writing separate dissents or concurring opinions (see Chapter Four). Drafting the majority opinion may take weeks or even months. When the opinion is complete, it is circulated to the justices for comments and then released to the public and authorized for printing in the *United States Reports*, the official publication of the Court's work.

Although most cases arrive at the Court from the various United States courts of appeal by means of the writ of certiorari, there is one other means by which cases from these lower federal courts may be reviewed by the Supreme Court: certification. Certification is the process by which a court of appeals (rather than the parties) refers a question to the Supreme Court and asks for instructions. Certification is a rarely used process.

Cases from the state courts may be appealed to the United States Supreme Court from the highest court in a state if and only if a federal question is involved. Even then the Court may, in its discretion, refuse to grant certiorari, thus rendering the state court decision final. State court litigants seeking access to the United States Supreme Court have no absolute right to an appeal and are entirely dependent on the Court granting certiorari, which it does for roughly one percent of cases. See Figure 2-5 for a diagram of our federal court structure.

Figure 2-5
Structure of Federal Court System

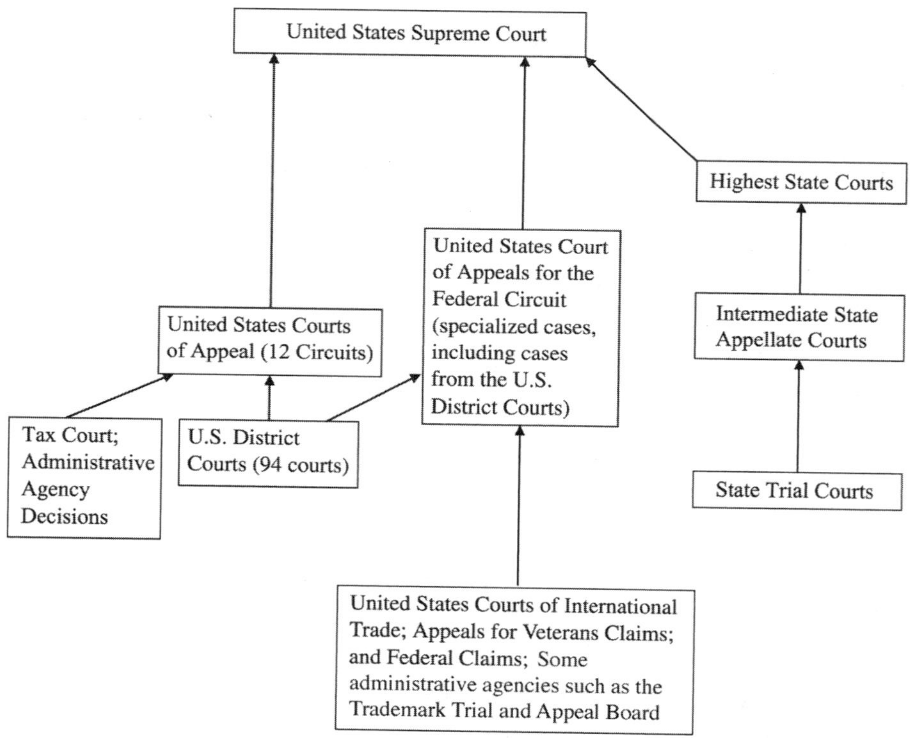

United States Supreme Court Trivia

- No new judgeships have been authorized for the federal appellate courts since 1990, although appeals filings increased 68 percent since that date through 2005.
- The present composition of nine justices on the Supreme Court has existed since 1869. At its beginning, the Court had only six justices. At one time, it had ten justices.
- A 2006 nationwide poll by Zogby International found that while 77 percent of those polled could name two of Snow White's dwarfs, only 24 percent could name two Supreme Court justices.
- Since the late 1800s, as the justices take their seats on the bench and at the beginning of the case conferences at which they meet and review cases, each justice formally shakes hands with each of the other justices. This handshake serves as a visible reminder that although the justices may offer differing views of the law, they are united in their purpose of interpreting the U.S. Constitution.
- On rainy days, the early justices would enliven case conferences with wine. On other days, even if the sun were shining, Chief Justice John Marshall would order wine anyway, saying, "Our jurisdiction is so vast that it must be raining somewhere."

5. *Specialized Courts*

In addition to the district courts, the intermediate circuit courts of appeal, and the United States Supreme Court, certain specialized courts exist in the federal judicial system to determine particular issues, such as the United States Tax Court, which issues decisions in tax matters, and the United States Court of Federal Claims, which considers private claims seeking monetary damages from the United States government. Other specialized courts include the United States Court of Appeals for Veterans Claims (which reviews determinations regarding matters pertaining to veterans of the armed services, such as disability determinations) and the United States Court of International Trade (which handles trade and customs disputes).

These specialized courts are often referred to as *legislative courts*, as distinguished from the district courts, intermediate courts of appeal, and Supreme Court, which are referred to as *constitutional courts* or "Article III courts" because they exist under Article III of the Constitution.

Ethics Alert: *Court Rules*

You must comply with all court rules when submitting any document to a court. Failure to follow local court rules may result in the court's refusal of your document, which could lead to liability for legal malpractice. In addition, you may not circumvent court rules relating to length of documents by using smaller typeface or font. U.S. Supreme Court Rules provide that briefs must be typeset in a "Century" family typeface in 12-point type. Sup. Ct. R. 33(1)(b). Nearly all courts post their rules on their websites. See Table T.1 of *The Bluebook* for identification of each state's judicial website.

E. State Courts

In addition to the federal court structure discussed above, each of the 50 states and the District of Columbia has its own arrangement for its court system. Although the names of these courts vary from state to state, the general organization is the same: A trial is held in one court and the losing party will usually have the right to at least one appeal in an appellate court.

Minnesota's court system is typical of many states and is shown in Figure 2-6. Note that in some states, trials involving lesser amounts of money and misdemeanors are held in courts called municipal courts or district courts, whereas trials involving greater amounts of money and felonies are held in the superior courts or circuit courts. In Minnesota, intermediate appeals are heard by the court of appeals, with the Minnesota Supreme Court serving as the court of last resort.

Although the majority of states have a two-tier appellate system, in 11 jurisdictions (Delaware, District of Columbia, Maine, Montana, Nevada, New Hampshire, Rhode Island, South Dakota, Vermont, West Virginia, and Wyoming) there is no intermediate court of appeal, and dissatisfied litigants proceed directly from the trial court, usually called the *court of first resort*, to the *court of last resort* in the state, usually called the supreme court in most states (see Figure 2-7). The U.S. Supreme Court is also referred to as a court of last resort.

In 48 jurisdictions, the highest state court is called the supreme court, supreme judicial court, or supreme court of appeals. Maryland and the District of Columbia, however, call their highest courts the court of appeals. New York also calls its highest court the court of appeals and calls one of the courts below it, which handles felonies, marriage dissolutions, and miscellaneous civil actions, the supreme court, which can cause some confusion.

Figure 2-6
Minnesota Court Structure
(with intermediate appellate court)

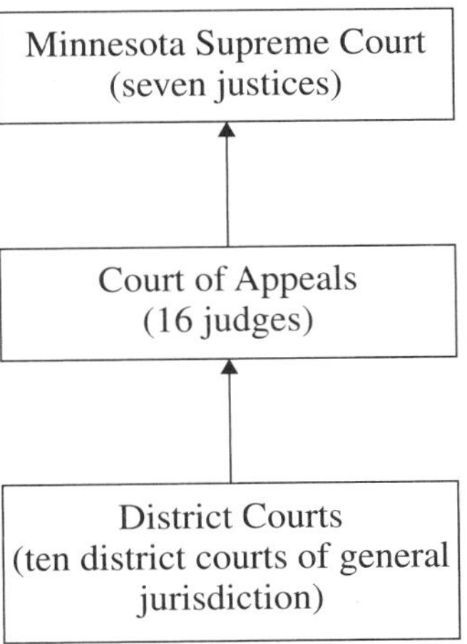

Figure 2-7
Nevada Court Structure
(no intermediate appellate court)

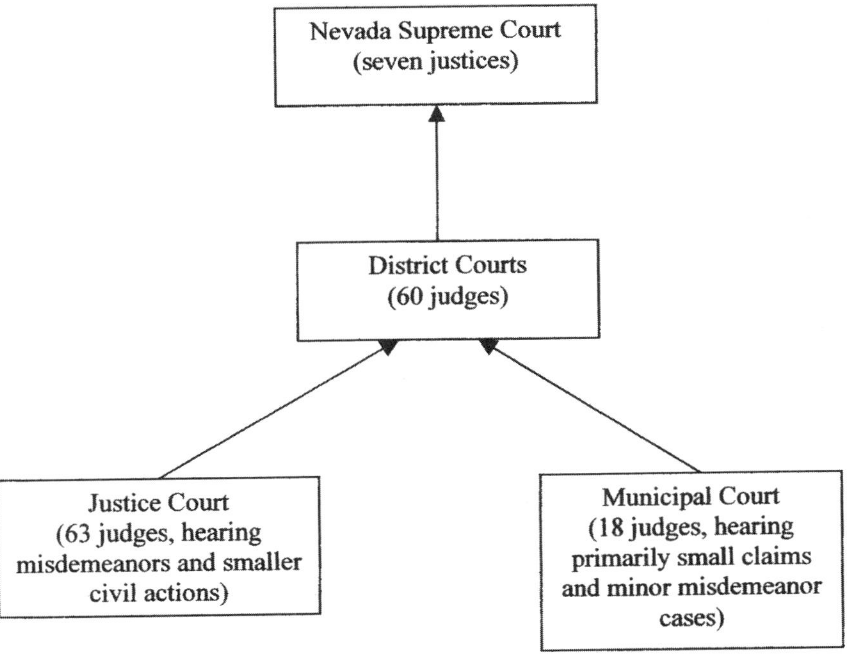

Practice Tip: *Reading Citations*

Gain as much information from citations as you can. When you see the word "App." in a case citation, immediately think to yourself that the case is likely *not* from the state's highest court, but rather from its intermediate court of appeals. Similarly, the absence of the word "App." from a state court case citation is typically a signal that the case is a strong one and is from your state's court of last resort.

Decisions by the highest courts in all states are rendered by odd-numbered panels of justices who function in a collective fashion. Seventeen of the 50 states have a five-member supreme court; 28 of the states have a seven-member supreme court; and five of the states and the District of Columbia have a nine-member supreme court. Diagrams of the structures of all state courts can be found at the website of the National Center for State Courts at http://www.ncsconline.org.

As of 2008, the median annual salary for justices on the highest state courts is approximately $142,000. The median salary for state trial court judges is approximately $130,000. Note that all of these salaries are approximately the same as the starting salaries paid to new attorneys in the nation's largest law firms, where annual salaries range from $125,000 to $160,000.

Although all judges in the federal system are nominated by the President and are confirmed by the United States Senate, there is great variation among the states with regard to the selection of state court judges. The majority of states use a merit selection method (somewhat similar to the federal presidential appointment method), in which the governor appoints a judge from a list of nominees provided to him or her by a judicial nominating commission. Other states elect their judges either by vote of the state legislature or the general population for specific terms.

Practice Tip: *State Court Names*

Review Table T.1 of *The Bluebook* or Appendix 1 of *ALWD* to learn about your state courts. Both *The Bluebook* and *ALWD* identify the formal names of the courts in each state, identifying higher state courts first and then lower state courts.

F. Citation Form

	Bluebook (for practitioners)	*ALWD*
Federal Cases		
• United States Supreme Court	• *Ewing v. California*, 538 U.S. 11 (2003).	• *Ewing v. California*, 538 U.S. 11 (2003).
• United States Courts of Appeal	• *Bailey v. Talbert*, 585 F.2d 968 (8th Cir. 1989).	• *Bailey v. Talbert*, 585 F.2d 968 (8th Cir. 1989).
• United States District Court	• *Peters v. May*, 697 F. Supp. 101 (S.D. Cal. 1988).	• *Peters v. May*, 697 F. Supp. 101 (S.D. Cal. 1988).
State Cases		
• When parallel citations are not required	• *Janson v. Keyser* , 415 N.E.2d 891 (Mass. 1976).	• *Janson v. Keyser* , 415 N.E.2d 891 (Mass. 1976).
• When parallel citations are required by court rules	• *Janson v. Keyser*, 204 Mass. 617, 415 N.E.2d 891 (1976).	• *Janson v. Keyser*, 204 Mass. 617, 415 N.E.2d 891 (1976).

CyberSites

http://www.uscourts.gov	Official listing of all federal courts with direct links to district courts, circuit courts of appeal, and United States Supreme Court.
http://www.fjc.gov	Federal Judicial Center, the education and research agency for the federal courts.
http://www.supremecourtus.gov	Website of U.S. Supreme Court with general information about the Court and access to opinions.
http://www.megalaw.com	Select "state law" and then the desired state for access to each state's courts, statutes, and cases.
http://www.ncsconline.org	National Center for State Courts, offering diagrams for each state's court structure and statistics about state court caseloads.
http://www.usa.gov	USA.gov, the federal government's official web portal with links to all units of the federal judicial branch and a vast array of excellent information about the federal government (formerly called "FirstGov").
http://www.law.cornell.edu	Cornell Law School's site, providing access to decisions of the U.S. Supreme Court and other federal and state courts.
http://www.findlaw.com	FindLaw, allowing access to federal and state cases as well as a wide variety of law-related information.

Research Assignment

1. a. Locate a case in volume 546 of the *United States Reports* in which the defendant's name is *Garcia Espitia* and give the full name and citation for the case.
   b. Give the result reached in the case.
   c. During the period of time covered by this volume, which United States Supreme Court justice was assigned or allotted to the Sixth Circuit?
2. a. Locate a case in volume 531 of the *United States Reports* in which the plaintiff's name is *Whitman* and give the full name and citation for the case.
   b. Who was the United States Attorney General at the time this case was decided?
3. a. Give the name of the case located at 240 F.3d 18.
   b. Which of the United States Courts of Appeal decided this case?
   c. Which judge issued the opinion of the court (give the full name)?
4. a. Give the name of the case located at 101 F. Supp. 2d 866.
   b. Which of the United States District Courts decided this case?
   c. Who represented the petitioner in this case?

Internet Assignment

1. Access the site U.S. Courts (http://www.uscourts.gov) and answer the following questions.
   a. What is the address and phone number for the United States District Court for the Northern District of Texas (in Dallas)?
   b. In which city is the office for the United States District Court for Colorado?
   c. Federal Judge Johnson would like to serve on the board of a public law school. Review the Code of Conduct for U.S. Judges and determine whether this is permissible. What Canon governs your answer?
2. Access the site for the National Center for State Courts at http://www.ncsconline.org and locate the "Court Structure Charts."
   a. How many justices sit on the Arizona Supreme Court?
   b. If you wish to bring an action in Arizona for breach of a contract involving $20,000, in which court would you initiate the action?
3. Within the site for the National Center for State Courts, select "Court Statistics Project" and then locate "State Court Caseload Statistics." Review the Caseload Tables for Appellate Courts

(Table 11). How many total mandatory cases were filed in the California courts of appeal and the California Supreme Court?

4. Access the website for the United States Supreme Court.
   a. Review the section relating to the Court and its traditions.
      (i) How are the justices seated?
      (ii) Do any attorneys wear formal clothes to the Court?
   b. Review the biographies for the justices.
      (i) For which Supreme Court Justice did Chief Justice John Roberts, Jr., serve as a law clerk?
      (ii) Which president nominated Justice Stevens?

Chapter 3

Statutory Law

Chapter Overview

Recall from Chapter One that courts are free to interpret statutes. This chapter focuses on statutory law because the logical progression many researchers follow when given a task is to first determine whether a statute relates to the issue. If so, they begin by reading the statute itself and then reviewing the cases and other sources that interpret it. Thus, this chapter discusses the enactment, publication, and codification of federal and state statutes and the research techniques that enable you to find statutes.

A. Federal Legislation

1. Enactment of Federal Statutes

The chief function of the U.S. Congress is its lawmaking task. Congress is a *bicameral* (two-chamber) legislature and consists of 100 members of the Senate (two from each state, regardless of state population) and 435 members of the House of Representatives (based on population of the state).

The framers of the Constitution anticipated that most legislation would originate in the House, and this is the case (although certain types of legislation can be introduced in the Senate). For example, during the 110th Congress, from January 4, 2007, until January 2, 2009, 7,340 bills and resolutions were introduced in the House while 3,741 were introduced in the Senate. The Constitution provides that only the House of Representatives can originate revenue-raising bills. By tradition, the House also initiates appropriations or spending bills. Legislation can be proposed by anyone, including members of Congress, executive departments of the federal government, and private individuals (who transmit their proposals to their representatives).

Following are the steps in the enactment of legislation. Assume the legislation is originating in the House:

- **Introduction in House.** The *bill* (a proposed law) is introduced by its sponsor, who gives it to the Clerk of the House or places it in a box (called the "hopper"). The Clerk assigns a legislative number to the bill, with "H.R." used for bills originating in the House and "S." used for bills introduced in the Senate. The bill is printed by the Government Printing Office and distributed to each member of the House.
- **Assignment to Committee.** The bill is assigned to a committee by the Speaker of the House so that it can be studied. The House has 20 permanent or standing committees (for example, the House Armed Services Committee). The committee studies the bill, holds hearings, and will take one of three actions: It will release the bill with a recommendation to pass it (called "reporting it out"); revise the bill and release it; or set it aside (called "tabling" the bill).
- **House Rules Committee Action.** The bill is now placed on a calendar of bills awaiting action and scheduled for debate on the floor of the House. The House Rules Committee may call for the bill to be voted on quickly if it is important.
- **Voting.** The bill now proceeds to the floor of the House for voting. If the bill passes by a simple majority (218 votes of 435), it moves to the Senate.
- **Introduction in Senate.** The bill is introduced in the Senate.
- **Assignment to Committee.** Just as in the House, the bill is then assigned to the appropriate committee. The Senate has 16 permanent committees. The committee studies the bill and either releases it (with or without modification) or tables it (just as occurred in the House).
- **Voting.** Once released, the bill proceeds to the Senate floor for debate and consideration. A simple majority (51 of 100) is required to pass the bill.
- **Signature by President.** If the bill passed by the Senate is identical to the one passed by the House, it goes to the President for signature.
- **Conference Committee Action.** If the House and Senate versions of the bill differ in any respect, the bill moves to a *conference committee*, composed of members of the House and Senate. The conference committee works out any differences between the two bill versions. The revised bill is then sent to both the House and the Senate for final approval.
- **Signature by President.** The final bill is sent to the President for signature. The President has ten days to sign or veto the bill. If the President vetoes the bill, it can still become a law if two-thirds of the House and two-thirds of the Senate approve it. When the President signs the bill is it now called a "law" or "statute."

2. *Classification of Federal Statutes*

Federal statutes are classified as public or private and as permanent or temporary.

- **Public laws.** A *public law* is one that affects the public generally, such as a bankruptcy or tax law.
- **Private law.** A *private law* is one that affects only one person or a small group of persons, granting them some special benefit not afforded

to the public at large. Most private laws are those dealing with immigration or naturalization.

• **Permanent law.** A *permanent law* remains in effect until it is expressly repealed.

• **Temporary law.** A *temporary law* has limiting language in the statute itself, such as the following: "This law shall have no force or effect after December 31, 2009."

3. *Publication of Federal Statutes*

a. United States Statutes at Large

As each federal law is passed by Congress, it is published by the United States Government Printing Office as a looseleaf unbound pamphlet or sheet of paper, referred to as a *slip law*. At the end of each congressional session, these slips are taken together and are published in a hardback set of volumes called *United States Statutes at Large*. All of our federal laws since 1789 are contained in this set.

The laws in *United States Statutes at Large* appear in chronological order—namely, in the way in which they were passed by Congress—rather than by topic, making the slip laws extremely difficult to research. Moreover, there is no one master index to this set, and laws relating to the same topic are scattered throughout several volumes. Thus, *United States Statutes at Large* serves more as a historical overview of Congress's work than as a viable research tool.

Practice Tips: *Early Access to Federal Statutes*

To obtain the exact wording of a federal statute without waiting for *United States Statutes at Large* to be published (which can take one year), consult the following:

- **Slip Laws.** The slips themselves are available in the more than 1,200 federal depository libraries (see Chapter One).
- ***United States Code Congressional and Administrative News Service.*** This monthly West publication provides the text of public laws passed during the previous month.
- ***United States Law Week.*** Law firms and law libraries subscribe to this weekly publication for rapid access to public laws.
- **Congressional Representatives.** Contact your congressional representative to ask for the complete text of a recently enacted law.
- **LexisNexis and Westlaw.** The computerized legal research systems provide access to recently enacted federal statutes.
- **THOMAS.** One of the best websites for legislative information is THOMAS, provided by the Library of Congress to make federal legislation available to the public. Access http://thomas.loc.gov (see Figure 9-3). Searching may be done by key word or bill number.

b. United States Code

Because the organization and lack of indexing of *United States Statutes at Large* makes using the set so difficult, it became readily apparent to researchers that a set of books should be developed to eliminate these barriers to efficient research. The process of developing a set of books that compiles currently valid laws on the same subject together with any amendments to those laws is referred to as *codification*, and the result is a *code*.

The current codification of *United States Statutes at Large* that legal professionals use to find federal statutes is called the *United States Code* (U.S.C.). The set U.S.C. arranges all federal laws by topic or subject matter into 50 different alphabetically arranged categories, called *titles* (see Figure 3-1).

Figure 3-1
Titles of United States Code

1. General Provisions
2. The Congress
3. The President
4. Flag and Seal, Seat of Government, and the States
5. Government Organization and Employees
6. Surety Bonds
7. Agriculture
8. Aliens and Nationality
9. Arbitration
10. Armed Forces
11. Bankruptcy
12. Banks and Banking
13. Census
14. Coast Guard
15. Commerce and Trade
16. Conservation
17. Copyrights
18. Crimes and Criminal Procedure
19. Customs Duties
20. Education
21. Food and Drugs
22. Foreign Relations and Intercourse
23. Highways
24. Hospitals and Asylums
25. Indians
26. Internal Revenue Code
27. Intoxicating Liquors
28. Judiciary and Judicial Procedure
29. Labor
30. Mineral Lands and Mining
31. Money and Finance
32. National Guard
33. Navigation and Navigable Waters
34. Navy (see Title 10, Armed Forces)
35. Patents
36. Patriotic Societies and Observances
37. Pay and Allowances of the Uniformed Services
38. Veterans' Benefits
39. Postal Service
40. Public Buildings, Property, and Works
41. Public Contracts
42. The Public Health and Welfare
43. Public Lands
44. Public Printing and Documents
45. Railroads
46. Shipping
47. Telegraphs, Telephones, and Radiotelegraphs
48. Territories and Insular Possessions
49. Transportation
50. War and National Defense

For example, Title 11 includes all federal bankruptcy laws, and Title 35 contains all patent laws. Within the titles, statutes are further divided into sections. Citations to federal statutes in U.S.C. appear as follows:

42	U.S.C.	§	1390	(2006)
Title	*Set*	*Abbr. for section*	*Section no.*	*Year of code*

It is not important to know what subject each of the 50 titles refers to. It is sufficient to understand that there are, in fact, 50 groups or titles of federal statutes, that they are arranged alphabetically, and that these titles are permanently established, meaning, for example, that any federal statute relating to patents will always be found in Title 35.

The *United States Code* is *official*, a term meaning that its publication is approved by the government. A new edition of the *United States Code* is published every six years.

c. Annotated Versions of the United States Code

Although the *United States Code* (U.S.C.) is an efficiently organized set of federal statutes, it has one glaring drawback from the perspective of legal researchers: Although it includes the exact language of our federal statutes, it does not send researchers to cases that might interpret those statutes. Under the concept of stare decisis, discussed in Chapter One, it is not the naked statutory language that controls a given situation but a court's interpretation of that statute. Thus, because U.S.C. simply recites the exact text of a federal statute without providing any comment regarding the law or any reference to any cases that may have interpreted the law, two private publishers, LexisNexis and West, have separately assumed the task of providing this critical information to legal professionals. Because the publication of their sets is not government approved, these publications are referred to as *unofficial*. Note that the terms "official" and "unofficial" relate to whether the publication of a set is government approved or not. The terms do not relate to the accuracy or credibility of a set. The text of a statute will be the same whether it is published in the official set, U.S.C., or in one of the unofficial sets, namely, U.S.C.A. or U.S.C.S. Both U.S.C.A. and U.S.C.S. are referred to as *annotated* codes, meaning that they include "notes" referring readers to cases interpreting statutes.

You will see from the discussion below that the two sets are highly similar. Generally, researchers will use one set rather than another, primarily based on habit and convenience. In most respects the two sets are *competitive*, meaning they are equivalent. For a typical research project you would ordinarily use one set—not both.

(1) United States Code Annotated *and* United States Code Service

West's set is called *United States Code Annotated* (U.S.C.A.); LexisNexis's set is *United States Code Service* (U.S.C.S.). Both are divided into the same 50 titles as U.S.C. and both include a multi-volume general index at the end of the set. The value of these sets is found not in their providing the language of federal statutes—U.S.C. provides that. Rather, these unofficial sets are valuable because of the helpful "extra" features they provide, which are nearly identical. These features are shown in Figure 3-2 and include the following. (Note that the names of these features vary slightly in U.S.C.A. and U.S.C.S.):

- **Historical and statutory notes.** Historical notes provide an overview of the history of a statute, including the Public Law number, the effective date of the statute, its citation in *United States Statutes at Large*, and an indication of the date(s) on which certain parts or subsections were amended, added, or deleted.
- **Cross-References.** Following the historical notes you will be sent to other federal statutes that may help you understand this federal statute.
- **Library References.** Library references (called "Research Guide" in U.S.C.S.) direct you to other sources in the law library (including form books, practice manuals, texts and treatises, encyclopedias, and law review articles) that deal with the topic covered by the statute.
- **Annotations.** The annotations (called "Notes of Decisions" in U.S.C.A. and "Interpretive Notes and Decisions" in U.S.C.S.) are the most valuable part of U.S.C.A. and U.S.C.S. because they will direct you to cases that have interpreted the statute you have just read. You will be given a one-sentence description of the case and then its citation. You can then decide whether to read the case in full. Both U.S.C.A. and U.S.C.S. organize these annotations for you by topic, making it easy for you to select the right cases to read.

(2) Pocket Parts and Updating

Because federal statutes are amended so frequently, U.S.C.A. and U.S.C.S. are kept current by the most typical method of updating legal volumes: annual cumulative pocket parts. A slit or "pocket" has been created in the back cover of each volume of U.S.C.A. and U.S.C.S. During each year, West and LexisNexis mail small, softcover pamphlets called *pocket parts* to law firms and law libraries. These pocket parts slide into the slits in the back of each volume of U.S.C.A. and U.S.C.S. and provide current information about the statutes in that volume, including amendments to the statute and references or annotations to cases decided since the hardback volumes were placed on the library shelves. The numbering of statutes in the pocket parts is identical to that in the hardback volumes. Eventually, if a book becomes worn out, the publisher will replace that single volume. On occasion, a softcover book, called a *supplement*, is placed on the shelf next to a hardbound volume to update it.

There are few invariable or inflexible rules in legal research, but one of them is that you must always consult a pocket part (or supplement) if the volume you are using is updated by one.

Figure 3-2
Sample Pages from U.S.C.A. (Title 35)

35 § 287 PATENTS; PROTECTION OF RIGHTS PT. III
Note 36

Gibson-Stewart Co., D.C.Ohio 1961, 202 F.Supp. 6.

There can be no recovery for period before a defendant is expressly notified by patentee that it is infringing a particular patent. International Nickel Co. v. Ford Motor Co., D.C.N.Y.1958, 166 F.Supp. 551.

In patent infringement action, accounting period was properly commenced on date when written infringement notice was given to infringer rather than on date of patent grant. Mathey v. United Shoe Machinery Corporation, D.C.Mass.1944, 54 F.Supp. 694.

In patent infringement suit, where evidence showed that defendant corporation's employee, whom plaintiff told that defendant would be held liable if it infringed patent, had no authority to receive such notice and communicate it to defendant, and there was no proof of defendant's manufacture or sale of infringing machine after actual notice of infringement in letter to defendant from plaintiff's attorney, plaintiff was not entitled to accounting for profits or damages. Federal Machine & Welder Co. v. Mesta Mach. Co., D.C.Pa. 1939, 27 F.Supp. 747, reversed on other grounds 110 F.2d 479.

The filing of bill of complaint and service thereof on defendant in patent infringement suit did not of itself constitute such a compliance with this section as to entitle plaintiff to an accounting for infringement by defendant occurring pendente lite. Hazeltine Corporation v. Radio Corporation of America, D.C. N.Y.1937, 20 F.Supp. 668.

37. Injunction

This section, limiting damages in patent infringement suit, pertains only to damages and does not preclude grant of injunctive relief. Eversharp, Inc. v. Fisher Pen Co., D.C.Ill.1961, 204 F.Supp. 649.

Where infringement of patent had not interfered with patentee's business, patentee was not entitled to any damages but infringer would be enjoined from making article and selling same. Metal Stamping Co. of Greenville v. General Mfg. Co., D.C.Tex.1957, 149 F.Supp. 508.

Defendant's motion for preliminary injunction restraining plaintiff from sending notices of infringement to defendant's customers and from threatening or starting suit against defendant's customers would be denied, where there was nothing in moving papers to justify conclusion that such letters were sent out in bad faith or otherwise than as notices of infringement as provided for in this section. Glatt v. Notion Accessories, D.C.N.Y.1954, 129 F.Supp. 297.

§ 288. Action for infringement of a patent containing an invalid claim

Whenever, without deceptive intention, a claim of a patent is invalid, an action may be maintained for the infringement of a claim of the patent which may be valid. The patentee shall recover no costs unless a disclaimer of the invalid claim has been entered at the Patent and Trademark Office before the commencement of the suit.

Text of Statute

(July 19, 1952, c. 950, § 1, 66 Stat. 813; Jan. 2, 1975, Pub.L. 93–596, § 1, 88 Stat. 1949.)

Historical and Revision Notes

Reviser's Note. Based on Title 35, U.S.C., 1946 ed., § 71 (R.S. 4922 [derived from Act July 8, 1870, c. 230, § 60, 16 Stat. 207]).

The necessity for a disclaimer to recover on valid claims is eliminated. See section 253.

Language is changed.

1975 Amendment. Pub.L. 93–596 substituted "Patent and Trademark Office" for "Patent Office".

Effective Date of 1975 Amendment. Amendment by Pub.L. 93–596 effective Jan. 2, 1975, see section 4 of Pub.L. 93–596, set out as a note under section 1111 of Title 15, Commerce and Trade.

Legislative History. For legislative history and purpose of Pub.L. 93–596, see 1974 U.S. Code Cong. and Adm.News, p. 7113.

Historical and Statutory Notes

Figure 3-4 *(Continued)*

CH. 29 INFRINGEMENT—INVALID CLAIMS **35 § 288**
Note 2

Cross References

Cross References

Costs as excluded from judgment in infringement action unless disclaimer was filed in Patent and Trademark Office prior to commencement of action, see section 1928 of Title 28, Judiciary and Judicial Procedure.
Filing fee, see section 41 of this title.
Infringement of patent, see section 271 of this title.
Right to disclaim and requisites and effect of disclaimer, see section 253 of this title.

Federal Rules

Effect of rule 54 on former section 71 of this title, see note by Advisory Committee under said rule 54, Federal Rules of Civil Procedure, Title 28, Judiciary and Judicial Procedure.
Judgment and costs, see rule 54, Federal Rules of Civil Procedure, Title 28.
One form of action, see rule 2, Federal Rules of Civil Procedure, Title 28.

Library References

Code of Federal Regulations

Disclaimer, see 37 CFR 1.321, set out in the Appendix.

Library References

Patents ⚷226 et seq. C.J.S. Patents § 282.

Notes of Decisions

Index to Numbered Annotations

Abandonment of claims 5
Appellate costs 18
Burden of proof 14
Combination claims 6
Compliance with section 3
Construction with other laws 1
Costs
Generally 17
Appellate costs 18
Partial success 19
Deception 10
Dismissal 22
Failure to file disclaimer
Generally 7
Unreasonable neglect or delay 8
Fraud or deception 10
Material and substantial parts 4
Partial success, costs 19
Persons entitled to sue 12
Pleadings 13
Prerequisites to action 11
Purpose 2
Questions of fact 16
Res judicata 20
Scope of
Determination 15
Review 21
Substantial parts 4
Unreasonable neglect or delay, failure to file disclaimer 8
Validation 9

---

1. Construction with other laws

This section should be construed in connection with former section 65 [now 253] of this title. Sessions v. Romadka, Wis.1892, 12 S.Ct. 799, 145 U.S. 29, 36 L.Ed. 609.

Annotations

This section, construed in connection with former section 65 [now 253] of this title, gives no authority for amending a patent by means of a disclaimer. Hailes v. Albany Stove Co., N.Y.1887, 8 S.Ct. 262, 123 U.S. 582, 31 L.Ed. 284.

Where certain claims were not put in issue by either party in action for infringement, any determination as to the validity would have been error and would have violated rights reserved to patentee by section 253 of this title and this section, which were enacted to mitigate earlier rule under which patent was held void if any claims thereof were found to be invalid. Chemical Const. Corp. v. Jones & Laughlin Steel Corp., C.A.Pa.1962, 311 F.2d 367.

Section 253 of this title providing for filing of disclaimers of claims in patent and this section providing for actions for infringement of patents which include unpatentable claims, should be read together. Del Riccio v. Photochart, 1954, 268 P.2d 814, 124 C.A.2d 301.

2. Purpose

Object of this section is to legalize and uphold suits brought on such patents as are mentioned in former section 65 [now 253] of this title, to the extent that the patentees are entitled to claim the inventions therein patented. Hailes v. Albany Stove Co., N.Y. 1887, 8 S.Ct. 262, 265, 123 U.S. 582, 31 L.Ed. 284. See, also, General Electric Co. v.

587

You can easily see the advantage of the pocket parts and supplements: rapid supplementation of the statutes and annotations at a cost much lower than replacing the nearly 300 volumes of U.S.C.A. or the approximately 200 volumes of U.S.C.S. each year.

The publishers of U.S.C.A. and U.S.C.S. also publish additional pamphlets to help researchers update statutes before the publication of next year's pocket part. Therefore, after you check the pocket part (published yearly) when using West's U.S.C.A., check West's Statutory Supplements (published bimonthly) to determine if more recent changes have occurred. When using LexisNexis's U.S.C.S., check its pamphlets called *Cumulative Later Case and Statutory Service* and *U.S.C.S. Advance*. The weekly publication *United States Law Week* also provides information about recent legislative activity. Of course, LexisNexis and Westlaw (the computerized legal research systems) provide "one-stop" immediate updating and offer hyperlinks to relevant cases, making statutory research using LexisNexis and Westlaw easy and effective.

Finally, you may be able to do some updating using the following online sources:

- Office of the Law Revision Counsel (http://uscode.house.gov/lawrevisioncounsel.shtml) lists the sections of the United States Code affected by recently enacted laws.
- GPO Access (http://www.gpoaccess.gov/uscode/index.html) attempts to ensure that its online references to the United States Code are always current.

See Figure 3-3 for a chart showing how to update research of federal statutes.

Figure 3-3
Updating Federal Statutory Research

U.S.C.	*U.S.C.A.*	*U.S.C.S.*
Read statute in main hardbound volume.	Read statute in main hardbound volume.	Read statute in main hardbound volume.
Check annual hardbound supplements.	Check annual pocket part or softcover supplements.	Check annual pocket part or softcover supplements.
Check slip laws or *U.S. Law Week*.	Check U.S.C.A.'s Statutory Supplements.	Check U.S.C.S.'s *Cumulative Later Case and Statutory Service* and then the *Advance* pamphlets.

Figure 3-3 *(Continued)*

U.S.C.	*U.S.C.A.*	*U.S.C.S.*
	Check slip laws or *U.S. Law Week*	Check slip laws or *U.S. Law Week*.
Check the GPO website at http://www.access.gpo.gov/uscode or the website http://uscode.house.gov/lawrevisioncounsel.shtml.	Check the GPO website at http://www.access.gpo.gov/uscode or the website http://uscode.house.gov/lawrevisioncounsel.shtml.	Check the GPO website at http://www.access.gpo.gov/uscode or the website http://uscode.house.gov/lawrevision counsel.shtml.

d. Use of U.S.C., U.S.C.A., and U.S.C.S.

Researchers often wonder which set they should use when researching federal statutes. Here are some tips:

- Use U.S.C. only when you need the exact wording of a federal statute and do not need references to cases or other authorities interpreting the statute. For example, if you needed to determine the term of existence for a patent, a simple check of U.S.C. would suffice. Many researchers use U.S.C. only infrequently.
- Use either U.S.C.A. or U.S.C.S. when you are interested in researching the history of a statute, finding other sources in the law library that discuss that statute, and, most important, reviewing judicial decisions that have interpreted the statute. Remember that in most respects, U.S.C.A. and U.S.C.S. are *competitive* sets, meaning they are essentially the same. The choice of which set you ultimately use will likely depend on habit or convenience. Some researchers prefer an integrated approach to all legal research and will consistently use all West publications when possible, whereas others prefer to use LexisNexis's sets. Only in the most detailed research project should you consult both sets. Ordinarily, one set will be sufficient for nearly all of your research needs, and most law firms, corporations, and agencies purchase one set or the other, but not both.

Ethics Alert: *How to Use the Annotations*

Never fully rely on the one-sentence annotations or descriptions of cases provided by U.S.C.A., U.S.C.S., or any other annotated set. It is not possible to convey complex case analysis in one sentence. Similarly, never quote from an annotation. They are not the law but rather very brief summaries of the law that are prepared by commercial publishers, not courts, solely for the convenience of readers.

4. *Research Techniques*

Researchers generally use one of the three following techniques to find statutes:

a. Descriptive Word Approach

Both U.S.C.A. and U.S.C.S. have a multivolume general index, which is arranged alphabetically and is usually located after Title 50, the last title in both sets. These softcover general indices are replaced and updated every year. When you are assigned a legal research problem, think of key words and phrases that describe this problem, and then look up these words or phrases in the general index of either U.S.C.A. or U.S.C.S., which will then direct you to the appropriate title and section you need. This technique, usually called the *descriptive word approach* or *index method*, is the simplest and most reliable way to locate federal statutes.

The indices for U.S.C.A. and U.S.C.S. are both very "forgiving." For example, if you selected "landlord" and the statute is indexed under "tenant," both U.S.C.A. and U.S.C.S. will guide you to the appropriate word, as follows:

Landlord. Tenant, this index

U.S.C.A. and U.S.C.S. will direct you to the appropriate statute by listing the title first and then identifying the specific statute section, as follows:

Citizenship, **8 § 1409**

You are thus directed to Title 8, Section 1409. See Figure 3-4 for a sample page from U.S.C.A. General Index.

This descriptive word approach (sometimes called the "index method" because you use the general index to find statutes) is usually the easiest and most efficient way to locate a statute, particularly for beginning researchers. Use this technique until you are extremely familiar with the organization of U.S.C.A. and U.S.C.S. and feel comfortable using the next method of statutory research: the title/topic approach.

b. Title or Topic Approach

You may become so familiar with the organization of U.S.C.A. or U.S.C.S. that when given a research problem you can bypass the general index and go directly to the appropriate title. This is the *title* or *topic approach*. For example, if you know that a bankruptcy statute is in Title 11, you can retrieve the appropriate volume and look at the table of contents for Title 11 at the beginning of Title 11, or go directly to the index for all of the bankruptcy statutes found at the end of the title. You will then review the statutes and annotations.

This title/topic approach is best employed by researchers who are sufficiently familiar with U.S.C.A. and U.S.C.S. so they can confidently select the one relevant title of the 50 titles available and review the statutes therein.

Figure 3-4
Sample Page from U.S.C.A. General Index

753 **TRADEMARKS**

TRADE SECRETS—Cont'd
Steel and aluminum energy conservation, 15 § **5104**
Technical Study Group on Cigarette and Little Cigar Fire Safety, **15 § 2054 nt**
Trade agreements, **19 § 2155**
United States Court of International Trade, **28 § 2641**
Water Pollution, this index

TRADE SHOWS
Exports and imports, regulation and control of, Peoples Republic of China, goods for, license applications, approval, national security controls, **50 App. § 2404**
Income Tax, this index
Secretary of Commerce, authority, **15 § 4724**
Small businesses, definitions, authority of Secretary of Commerce, **15 § 4724**
United States business, definitions, authority of Secretary of Commerce, **15 § 4724**

Reference to other part of U.S.C.A. Index

TRADE UNIONS
Labor Organizations, generally, this index

TRADE ZONE
Foreign Trade Zones, generally, this index

Reference to 15 U.S.C.A § 1051

TRADEMARK ACT
Generally, **15 § 1051 et seq.**

TRADEMARK AMENDMENTS ACT OF 1999
See Popular Name Table

TRADEMARK CLARIFICATION ACT OF 1984
See Popular Name Table

TRADEMARK COUNTERFEITING ACT OF 1984
See Popular Name Table

TRADEMARK LAW REVISION ACT OF 1988
See Popular Name Table

TRADEMARK REMEDY CLARIFICATION ACT
See Popular Name Table

TRADEMARK TRIAL AND APPEAL BOARD
Appeal to,
- Board from a decision of examiner, **15 § 1070**
- United States Court of Appeals for the Federal Circuit on Board's decision, **15 § 1071**

Composition, **15 § 1067**
Determination of respective rights of registration, **15 § 1067**
Election of remedies on dissatisfaction with Board's decision, **15 § 1071**
Fee on appeal to Board from examiner's decision, **15 § 1070**
Hearing on application for cancellation of registration on supplemental register, **15 § 1092**

TRADEMARK TRIAL AND APPEAL BOARD
—Cont'd
Notice to registrant of application for cancellation of registration on supplemental register, **15 § 1092**
Number of members to hear cases, **15 § 1067**
Reference to board of application for cancellation of registration on supplemental register, **15 § 1092**
United States Court of Appeals for the Federal Circuit, jurisdiction of appeals from decisions, **28 § 1295**

TRADEMARKS AND TRADE NAMES
Generally, **15 § 1051 et seq.**
Abandonment, **15 §§ 1062, 1127**
- Defense, infringement suit, **15 § 1115**
- Definitions, **15 § 1127**
- Foreign countries, **15 § 1141c**
- Time for petitioning to cancel registration, **15 § 1064**

Acknowledgments, **15 § 1061**
- Assignment, **15 § 1060**

Actions and proceedings, **15 § 1114 et seq.**
- Civil action, against persons using deceptive conduct, false or misleading descriptions in attempts to deceive, **15 § 1125**
- Cyberpiracy, **15 §§ 1125, 1129**
- False designations of origin, false descriptions and dilution, **15 § 1125**
- Foreign register mark or name, **15 § 1126**
- Infringement, generally, post
- Pending actions not affected by repeal of laws, **15 § 1051 nt**
- Postal emergency, relief as to filing date of trade-mark application or registration, **35 § 111 nt**
- United States Olympic Committee, **36 § 220506**
- Waiver or election by adverse party, civil actions, dissatisfaction with decision of Commissioner or Trademark Trial and Appeal Board, **15 § 1071**

Adjustment, fees, filing, application, **15 § 1113, 1113 nt**
Advertisements,
- Certification mark, **15 § 1064**
- Destruction of infringing trademark, **15 § 1118**
- Injunction against presenting advertising matter containing trademark, **15 § 1114**

Affidavits,
- Duration, affixing specimen or facsimile, **15 § 1058**
- Foreign countries, **15 § 1141k**
- Obtain incontestable right to use mark, **15 § 1065**
- Use of trademarks, **15 § 1058**
  - Appeals to court by registrant who has filed, dissatisfaction with decisions of Commissioner or Trademark Trial and Appeal Board, **15 § 1071**

Agent for service of process, foreign countries, **15 §§ 1141h, 1141k**
Alien property, divestment, **50 App. § 43**

Practice Tip: Infra *and* Supra

When using indices for almost any set of law books, you may encounter the words *infra* (meaning "below") and *supra* (meaning "above"). These are signal terms that direct you to other pages within the index. For example, if you look up the word "tenant" in an index, you may see the instruction "See landlord, *supra*," meaning that you should look at the entries listed under the word "landlord" given previously in the index.

c. Popular Name Approach

Many of our federal statutes are known by a popular name—either that of the sponsors of the legislation (for example, the Sarbanes-Oxley Act of 2002) or that given the legislation by the public or media (for example, the AMBER Alert Act). If you are asked to locate one of these statutes, you can easily do so in either U.S.C.A. or U.S.C.S. by using the *popular name approach*.

In U.S.C.A., locate the volume entitled *Popular Name Table*, which lists in alphabetical order federal laws known by their popular names. Simply look up the law you are interested in, and you will be directed to the appropriate title and section. When using U.S.C.S., consult the *Popular Name* table found in a separate volume of the set, which also lists the federal statutes known by a popular name in alphabetical order. See Figure 3-5 for a sample page from U.S.C.A.'s Popular Name Table.

Finally, if you have only a public law number (such as Pub. L. No. 109-114) or a reference to the statute from *United States Statutes at Large* (such as 117 Stat. 660), both U.S.C.A. and U.S.C.S. have separate volumes marked "Tables," which convert a public law number or a *United Statutes States at Large* citation into a citation to U.S.C.A. or U.S.C.S.

5. *The United States Constitution*

Although the United States Constitution is not one of the 50 titles of the *United States Code*, nevertheless both U.S.C.A. and U.S.C.S. contain volumes for the Constitution. When conducting constitutional research in U.S.C.A. or U.S.C.S. you will be provided with the text of the pertinent constitutional provision and then, by the use of annotations, you will be referred to cases that interpret it. The three primary research techniques described above should also be used when you research a constitutional law issue. Don't forget to review the pocket parts.

Help Line: *Personal Research Assistance*

If you have any difficulty performing statutory research, you may call either LexisNexis (800-897-7922) or West (800-733-2889) to receive personal assistance from reference attorneys.

Figure 3-5
Sample Page from U.S.C.A. Popular Name Table

973 **POPULAR NAME TABLE**

San Carlos Apache Tribe Water Rights Settlement Act of 1992
Pub.L. 102–575, Title XXXVII, Oct. 30, 1992, 106 Stat. 4740 (25 §§ 390, 390 note; 43 §§ 1524, 1524 note)
Pub.L. 103–263, § 2(a), May 31, 1994, 108 Stat. 708
Pub.L. 103–435, § 13, Nov. 2, 1994, 108 Stat. 4572 (25 §§ 390 note)
Pub.L. 104–91, Title II, § 202(a), Jan. 6, 1996, 110 Stat. 14 (25 § 390 note)
Pub.L. 104–261, § 3, Oct. 9, 1996, 110 Stat. 3176 (25 § 390 note)
Pub.L. 105–18, Title II, § 5003, June 12, 1997, 111 Stat. 181 (25 § 390 note)

San Carlos Indian Irrigation Project Divestiture Act of 1991
Pub.L. 102–231, Dec. 12, 1991, 105 Stat. 1722
Pub.L. 102–497, § 6, Oct. 24, 1992, 106 Stat. 3256

San Carlos Mineral Strip Act of 1990
Pub.L. 101–447, Oct. 22, 1990, 104 Stat. 1047

San Domingo Resolution
Jan. 12, 1871, No. 7, 16 Stat. 591

San Francisco Maritime National Historical Park Act of 1988
Short title, see 16 USCA § 410nn note
Pub.L. 100–348, June 27, 1988, 102 Stat. 654 (16 §§ 410nn, 410nn note, 410nn–1 to 410nn–4, 460bb–3)
Pub.L. 103–437, § 6(d)(11), Nov. 2, 1994, 108 Stat. 4584 (16 §§ 410nn, 410nn–2)

San Gabriel River Watershed Study Act
Pub.L. 108–42, July 1, 2003, 117 Stat. 840

San Juan Basin Wilderness Protection Act of 1984
Pub.L. 98–603, Oct. 30, 1984, 98 Stat. 3155 (16 § 1132 note; 25 § 640d–10)
Pub.L. 101–556, § 6, Nov. 15, 1990, 104 Stat. 2764
Pub.L. 104–333, Div. I, Title X, Subtitle C, § 1022(b) to (e), Nov. 12, 1996, 110 Stat. 4211 to 4213 (16 § 1132 note; 43 § 1785)
Pub.L. 106–176, Title I, § 124, Mar. 10, 2000, 114 Stat. 30 (43 § 1785)

Referecnce to 43 U.S.C.A. § 1785

San Juan Island National Historical Park Act
Pub.L. 89–565, Sept. 9, 1966, 80 Stat. 737 (16 §§ 282–282c)

San Luis Rey Indian Water Rights Settlement Act
Pub.L. 100–675, Title I, Nov. 17, 1988, 102 Stat. 4000
Pub.L. 102–154, Title I, § 117, Nov. 13, 1991, 105 Stat. 1012
Pub.L. 106–377, § 1(b) [Title II, § 211], Oct. 27, 2000, 114 Stat. 1441, 1441A–70

Sand Creek Massacre National Historic Site Establishment Act of 2000
Pub.L. 106–465, Nov. 7, 2000, 114 Stat. 2019 (16 § 461 note)

Sand Creek Massacre National Historic Site Study Act of 1998
Pub.L. 105–243, Oct. 6, 1998, 112 Stat. 1579

Sanitary Food Transportation Act of 1990
Pub.L. 101–500, Nov. 3, 1990, 104 Stat. 1213 (49 § 521; 49 App. §§ 1814, 2501 note, 2801, 2801 notes, 2802 to 2812)
Pub.L. 103–272, § 7(b), July 5, 1994, 108 Stat. 1398 (49 App. §§ 1814, 2501 note, 2801 to 2812)
Pub.L. 103–429, § 8(15), Oct. 31, 1994, 108 Stat. 4391 (49 App. §§ 2501 note, 2801 note)

Santa Fe Indian School Act
See, also, Omnibus Indian Advancement Act
Pub.L. 106–568, Title VIII, Subtitle B (§§ 821 to 824), Dec. 27, 2000, 114 Stat. 2921

Santa Monica Mountains National Recreation Area Boundary Adjustment Act
Short title, see 16 USCA § 1 note
Pub.L. 107–236, Oct. 9, 2002, 116 Stat. 1483 (16 §§ 1 note, 460kk)

Santa Rosa and San Jacinto Mountains National Monument Act of 2000
Pub.L. 106–351, Oct. 24, 2000, 114 Stat. 1362 (16 § 431 note)
Pub.L. 106–434, § 2, Nov. 6, 2000, 114 Stat. 1912 (16 § 431 note)

Santini-Burton Act
Pub.L. 96–586, Dec. 23, 1980, 94 Stat. 3381 (16 §§ 461 note, 467, 467a, 467a–1)

B. State Legislation

1. *Introduction*

The process of enacting and publishing legislation at the state level is substantially similar to the process described previously for the federal level. Just as the U.S. Congress is divided into two chambers—the House of Representatives and the Senate—each state except for Nebraska has a legislature divided into two chambers. Nebraska has a one-house or unicameral legislature. The names given to the two chambers, however, will vary from state to state.

Similar to the process of enacting federal law, much of the work in enacting state law is done by committees. When a final version of a bill is agreed upon, it will be sent to the governor of the state for signature, at which time it is now a "law" or "statute" rather than a bill. The website of the National Conference of State Legislatures (http://www.ncsl.org) provides direct links to each state's legislative home page.

2. *Publication and Codification of State Statutes*

State statutes initially appear in slip form and are then compiled in sets of books generally called *session laws*. The session laws are analogous to *United States Statutes at Large* in that they contain laws, but due to their chronological arrangement, they are not particularly helpful to researchers. Thus, the states have codified their session laws to bring together all the current laws on the same subject and eliminate repealed laws. These state codifications may be called "codes," "compilations," "revisions," or "consolidations," depending on the state.

Most states arrange their statutes by titles and chapter, for example, Va. Code Ann. § 18.2-256 (1996). A few states, usually the more populous ones, arrange their statutes in named titles, for example, Cal. Evid. Code § 115 (West 1998). The numbering and format vary from state to state.

Most states have annotated codes, meaning that after you are given the wording of the pertinent statute, you will be directed to cases that interpret the statute. West publishes annotated codes for approximately 30 of the states and The Michie Company (now part of LexisNexis) publishes statutes for most of the remaining states. An identification of the publisher for each state's statutes can be found in Table T.1 of *The Bluebook* and Appendix 1 of *ALWD*.

Although the publication of each state's statutes will vary somewhat, and the publication may be unofficial or official, most state codes share the following features:

- The state's constitution is usually included in the state's code;
- The statutes will be organized by subject matter so that all of the corporate statutes are grouped together, all of the probate statutes are grouped together, and so forth;

- There will be a general index to the entire set and often each title (such as "Probate") begins or ends with its own index;
- The statutes are kept current by annual cumulative pocket parts or supplements;
- Annotations will be provided to direct you to cases interpreting the statutes, typically through the use of a one-sentence summary of the case and the case citation, similar to the organization of U.S.C.A. and U.S.C.S. annotations;
- "Extra" features, such as historical notes and library references will be provided to assist you in interpreting the statute; and
- Conversion tables are provided in each volume so that if a state statute has been repealed or renumbered, you will be informed of the repealing or provided with the new section number. See Figure 3-6 for a sample page showing a state statute.

3. Research Techniques

The same techniques used to locate federal statutes are used to locate state statutes. They are as follows:

- **Descriptive Word Approach.** This method requires you to determine which words or phrases relate to the issue you are researching and then locate those words or phrases in the general index, which will then direct you to the pertinent statute.
- **Title/Topic Approach.** This technique may be used when you have become so familiar with your state code that you bypass the general index and immediately locate the particular title or section that deals with the research problem.

Figure 3-6
Sample Page from Code of Virginia

§ 18.2-256. Conspiracy. — Any person who conspires to commit any offense defined in this article or in the Drug Control Act (§ 54.1-3400 et seq.) is punishable by imprisonment or fine or both which may not be less than the minimum punishment nor exceed the maximum punishment prescribed for the offense, the commission of which was the object of the conspiracy. (Code 1950, § 54-524.104; 1970, c. 650; 1972, c. 798; 1975, cc. 14, 15; 1978, c. 130.)

Cross references. — As to exception of offenses defined in this chapter from the provisions of the general statute governing conspiracy to commit felony, see § 18.2-22 (d).

Law Review. — For survey of Virginia criminal law for the year 1972-1973, see 59 Va. L. Rev. 1458 (1973).

A single agreement can form the basis for multiple violations of this section. Otherwise, criminals would be encouraged to plot a number of drug-related crimes simultaneously, because only one conspiracy would exist. This could not have been the intention of the General Assembly. Wooten v. Commonwealth, 235 Va. 89, 368 S.E.2d 693 (1988).

Conspiring with police officer and officer's informant. — An accused may not be convicted under this section for conspiring to distribute cocaine with a police officer and the officer's confidential informant. Fortune v. Commonwealth, 12 Va. App. 643, 406 S.E.2d 47 (1991).

Evidence of acts of co-conspirators. — Where the Commonwealth's evidence established a prima facie case of conspiracy, the trial court did not err in admitting evidence of acts of co-conspirators in furtherance of that conspiracy. Barber v. Commonwealth, 5 Va. App. 172, 360 S.E.2d 888 (1987).

Evidence of another conspiracy was properly admitted to prove defendant's intent and to show that both conspiracies were part of a common scheme or plan. Barber v. Commonwealth, 5 Va. App. 172, 360 S.E.2d 888 (1987).

Evidence that defendants constructively possessed cocaine was probative of the object of the conspiracy. Hodge v. Commonwealth, 7 Va. App. 351, 374 S.E.2d 76 (1988).

• **Popular Name Approach.** This method of locating statutes is used in those instances in which a state statute is known by a popular name, such as the "Megan's Law" in your state. Look up the name of the statute in the alphabetically arranged general index.

Finally, there is no single set of books that will provide you with all of the laws for all 50 states. Such a set would be unwieldy, expensive, and generally not very useful, because researchers in one state are usually not interested in the statutes of another state.

4. *Final Research Steps for Federal and State Statutory Research*

After you locate any statute or constitutional provision you are interested in, whether federal or state, read it carefully. Examine the historical notes, and review the library references to determine whether other sources in the library provide further information on this statute or its subject matter. Then read the annotations carefully, and decide which cases you will read in full based on your initial reading of the brief descriptions of these cases. Finally, check the pocket part and any of the interim pamphlets or supplements to determine if the statute has been amended or repealed and to look for annotations or references to cases that have interpreted the statute or provision after the hardback volume was published.

Practice Tip: *Tracking Pending Legislation Online*

On many occasions, you may need to monitor pending legislation. A client may be interested in the progress of a bill. There are several online resources that will help you track pending legislation, including the following:

- LexisNexis's service called *Congressional* provides bill tracking. Similarly, its service called "Alerts" will provide you with monthly, weekly, daily, or more frequent updates on legislation you are following.
- Westlaw also provides bill tracking through its "Bill Tracking" database. Its clipping service, WestClip, delivers periodic updates to your email account about legislation you are monitoring.
- THOMAS does not provide automatic alerts to you regarding changes in legislative status, but by routinely checking the status and summary of a bill, you can track its progress.
- Many states now automatically provide email updates on pending legislation. For example, California provides a bill status updating service that sends you an email to alert you to actions affecting the legislation you are monitoring. The free tracking service is located at http://www.leginfo.ca.gov.

Additional information about bill tracking is found in Chapter Seven.

C. Rules of Procedure and Court Rules

1. *Introduction*

To promote efficient operation, courts are empowered to enact certain rules relating to various court procedures and administrative matters, such as the correct size of paper to be used, when papers must be filed, and the format of papers presented to the court. In addition to rules relating to such administrative matters, there are rules relating to more substantive matters, such as rules of evidence and rules of civil and criminal procedure. Although these rules are not statutes or laws, they are binding on those practicing before the court, and thus they are discussed here.

In civil actions, all federal district courts follow the Federal Rules of Civil Procedure (FRCP), which provide rules on pleadings, motions, discovery, and civil trials. In addition, the district courts may make their own rules governing practice in their courts. For example, the United States District Court for New Hampshire follows the FRCP and also has its own rules relating to the maximum length of memoranda that may be submitted to the court.

Similarly, nearly all states have modeled their own civil procedural rules after the FRCP, and in addition have local or court rules governing practice before the courts. For simplicity, this discussion will refer to the more significant rules (such as the FRCP) as *rules of procedure* and the more local rules, which generally govern less substantive matters (for example, the format of documents) as *court rules*.

2. *Federal Rules of Procedure*

The FRCP, which became effective in 1938, govern the conduct of all civil litigation in the United States District Courts. The FRCP govern all trial-related matters from the commencement of an action, through the pleadings allowed, to motions and discovery practice, to the trial itself. The FRCP can be found in both U.S.C.A. and U.S.C.S. and can be located by any of the standard research techniques used for locating statutes: the descriptive word approach, the topic approach, or the popular name approach. Once you review the rule, scan the annotations, and then select cases to read that have interpreted the rule.

Appellate practice in the federal courts of appeal is governed by the Federal Rules of Appellate Procedure. Matters of evidence are governed by the Federal Rules of Evidence, and matters relating to criminal procedure are governed by the Federal Rules of Criminal Procedure. All of the major federal rules (the Federal Rules of Civil Procedure, Federal Rules of Criminal Procedure, Federal Rules of Appellate Procedure, and Federal Rules of Evidence) are available through the U.S. Courts website at http://www.uscourts.gov/rules/newrules4.html. Additionally, the text of proposed amendments and forms is provided. Finally, the U.S. Supreme Court has its own set of rules, posted on its website at http://www.supremecourtus.gov.

Several sets of books are useful in interpreting the federal rules, such as *Federal Rules Service, 3d*, which includes the text of the federal rules and directs you to cases interpreting the rules. Moreover, the following two sources are invaluable in interpreting federal rules:

- *Moore's Federal Practice*, a 33-volume set including the full text of the federal rules together with extensive commentary and analysis; and
- *Federal Practice and Procedure* by Charles Alan Wright and Arthur R. Miller, a more than 60-volume set of books with full coverage and analysis of all aspects of federal civil, criminal, and appellate procedure, offering relevant forms for federal practice.

3. *Federal Court Rules*

In addition to the significant and substantive federal procedural rules that govern practice in our nation's federal courts, the lower federal courts themselves are free to enact their own more local rules of court. Often these rules are administrative and relate to matters such as the maximum length of a brief or citation form. Other rules are more substantive and might impose a duty upon counsel to meet and confer regarding disputed issues.

With 94 district courts and 13 circuits, determining the specific rules for each court can be a daunting task. All of these rules are now available on the Internet at http://www.uscourts.gov/rules/newrules8.html.

4. *State Rules of Procedure and Court Rules*

To promote efficiency in litigation, states have also adopted rules of procedure and rules of court. Most states now publish their rules on their websites. Failure to follow the local rules regarding even such seemingly minor matters as the type size to be used may result in rejection of documents and pleadings. If your pleading is rejected for nonconformance with local rules and the time limit for filing the pleading expires before you can submit an acceptable pleading, the client's rights may be jeopardized, and your firm may be subject to a claim of legal malpractice.

To obtain a copy of the local rules, contact the clerk of the court and arrange to purchase a set of the rules. Alternatively, access MegaLaw at http://www.megalaw.com/rules.php, which will link you to many local court rules for each state. Review *Bluebook* Bluepages Table BT.2 for references to local rules on citation form and Table T.1 of *The Bluebook* for a reference to each state's judicial website (which usually provides the court's rules). Additionally, Appendices 1 and 2 of *ALWD* provide information on citation rules of the state courts.

D. Uniform and Model Laws

Uniform laws are those drafted for topics of the law in which uniformity is desirable and practical. For example, a set of laws relating to the formation, operation, and dissolution of partnerships, called the Uniform Partnership Act, has been adopted by nearly all U.S. jurisdictions. Once adopted in a state, a uniform law is then a state statute like any other and can be located using any of the research techniques discussed previously. Many states, however, often make changes and modifications to the uniform laws, resulting in laws that are highly similar from state to state but that are not perfectly uniform across the nation. Uniform laws and model acts are discussed further in Chapter Six.

E. Statutory Research Overview

When you are undecided whether to begin a project by examining federal or state statutes, keep in mind that some matters are exclusively presumed to be federal in nature. For example, patent law is the exclusive province of the federal government, which eliminates the confusion that would result if each state issued its own patents. On the other hand, states have the power to enact laws relating to local concerns, such as residency laws for obtaining a divorce and statutes of limitation for breach of contract matters. If you are uncertain whether an area of law is governed by federal or state law, examine the federal statutes first, and then proceed to examine your state statutes if the topic is not covered by federal statute.

Following are some tips to help you research statutes more efficiently:

- Quickly review the entire scope of the statutes governing your topic. Generally, terms used in the act are first defined. Definitions are usually followed by the rules announced in the statute and then by penalties for violations of the statute.
- Assume that each word in the statute is there for a purpose, and the words are to be given their plain meaning.
- If the statute is vague or ambiguous, examine the cases that discuss the statute to determine how courts have interpreted the statute.

Remember that it is the province of our courts to apply and interpret statutes and even strike down statutes as unconstitutional.

Finally, although the rules and regulations of administrative agencies such as the Food and Drug Administration or Securities and Exchange Commission are as binding as statutes (in that violations can be punished, usually by fines), administrative law is discussed in Chapter Seven because it is somewhat of a "specialized" field of research and not commonly performed by most legal professionals.

F. Citation Form

	Bluebook *(for practitioners)*	*ALWD*
Federal Statutes	• 11 U.S.C. § 1327 (2006). • 11 U.S.C.A. § 1327 (West 2004). • 11 U.S.C.S. § 1327 (LexisNexis 2001).	• 11 U.S.C. § 1327 (2006). • 11 U.S.C.A. § 1327 (West 2004). • 11 U.S.C.S. § 1327 (Lexis 2001).
State Statutes (Citation form may vary between *Bluebook* and *ALWD*.)	• Ind. Code Ann. § 14-11-2-2 (West 1998). • Wash. Rev. Code § 8.04 (1997).	• Ind. Code Ann. § 14-11-2-2 (West 1998). • Wash. Rev. Code § 8.04 (1997).
Court Rules	• Fed. R. Civ. P. 12(b). • Cal. R. Ct. 3.60. • Sup. Ct. R. 21.	• Fed. R. Civ. P. 12(b). • Cal. R. Ct. 3.60. • Sup. Ct. R. 21.

CyberSites

http://thomas.loc.gov	THOMAS contains the full text of pending bills, key legislation, committee and congressional information, and additional information.
http://www.gpoaccess.gov/index.html	GPO Access, the U.S. Government Printing Office site, offers access to bills, public and private laws, and the United States Code.
http://uscode.house/gov/lawrevisioncounsel.shtml	The Law Revision Counsel provides information about and searching of the United States Code.
http://www.uscourts.gov	U.S. Courts provides direct links to all federal courts and federal rules.
http://www.law.cornell.edu	Cornell University Law School's site offers easy access to federal and state statutes and federal and state court rules.
http://www.megalaw.com	MegaLaw is a general legal site, allowing researchers to find statutes, court rules, and a wide variety of other legal materials.

Research Assignment

1. What title of the *United States Code* relates to Shipping?

2. Use U.S.C.A. and cite the title and section that govern the following:
   a. Awards of National Medals of Art by the President.
   b. Support of children by deadbeat parents.

3. Use either U.S.C.A. or U.S.C.S. and cite the title and section that govern the following:
   a. Aggravated identity theft.
   b. Misbranding of textiles.

4. Use the Popular Name tables as directed and cite the title and section for the following:
   a. Use U.S.C.A. and give the citation for the short title of the Child Pilot Safety Act.
   b. Use U.S.C.A. and give the citation for the short title of the Freedom to E-File Act.
   c. Use either U.S.C.A. or U.S.C.S. and give the citation for the Beef Promotion and Research Act of 1985.
   d. Use either U.S.C.A. or U.S.C.S. and give the citation for the Eagle Protection Act (1962).

5. Use either U.S.C.A. or U.S.C.S. and indicate whether the following types of eggs fall within the definition of "egg" under federal law. What statute governs your answer?
   a. Turkey egg
   b. Goose egg
   c. Quail egg
   d. Ostrich egg

6. Use the U.S.C.A. volumes for the Constitution. Answer the following questions and cite the best case to support your answer. Give case names only.
   a. Under the First Amendment (Freedom of Religion—Public Schools), may a school board store on the grounds of public high schools monuments inscribed with the Ten Commandments?
   b. Under the Eighth Amendment (Sentence or Punishment), is shooting as a means of enforcing a death penalty sentence for murder in the first degree cruel and unusual punishment?

7. Use U.S.C.A.
   a. Under 18 U.S.C.A. § 2199, may aiding and abetting a stowaway on an aircraft be a violation of § 2199? Answer the question and cite the best case to support your answer. Give the case name only.
   b. What is the most recent A.L.R. annotation you are directed to in order to better understand this statute? Give the citation only.
   c. Give the original *U.S. Statutes at Large* citation for this statute.

8. Use U.S.C.S.
   a. Under 10 U.S.C.S. § 849, may a videotape of a deposition be viewed by a military judge?
   b. Are paper containers and cardboard tubes sold and intended to be used to produce banned fireworks "banned hazardous substances" under 15 U.S.C.S. § 1263?
9. Use *U.S. Statutes at Large.*
   a. What is the short title of Public Law 109-415?
   b. Give the citation for this law in *U.S. Statutes at Large.*
   c. What was its designation in the House of Representatives?
10. Use *U.S. Statutes at Large.*
    a. For whose relief was Private Law 108-3 enacted?
    b. Briefly, what was the purpose of this private law?

Internet Assignment

1. Access THOMAS.
   a. What is the title of bill number H.R. 220 introduced in the 100th Congress?
   b. Who were the sponsors of the legislation?
   c. Review the "Bill Summary and Status" for the legislation. What was the latest major action taken?
2. Access THOMAS and review the information for the United States Senate. Give the address and telephone number for Senator Kay Hagan.
3. Access THOMAS and review the information about "The Legislative Process." Review the materials on how our laws are made. What is "markup"?
4. Access THOMAS and locate the information about the U.S. Constitution. How many months of debate occurred before the Constitution was submitted to the states for approval?
5. Access the website for GPO Access. Browse the public and private laws for the 108th Congress. For whose relief was Private Law 108-006 enacted?
6. Access the website for the United States Supreme Court. Review the Rules for the Supreme Court.
   a. Under Rule 24, when must a brief on the merits include a table of contents and a table of authorities?
   b. Under Rule 25, must briefs be submitted electronically?
7. Using Cornell University's Law School's website, locate the Federal Rules of Civil Procedure. When may a district court adopt rules relating to its practices? What rule governs your answer?

8. Access the website for MegaLaw and select "California." Review the local rules for the Los Angeles Superior Court, specifically Chapter 8.
   a. Where does the plaintiff's attorney sit?
   b. Is it permissible to address a judge as "Sir" or "Judge"?

9. Review either Table T.1 of *The Bluebook* or Appendix 1 of *ALWD*.
   a. Who is the publisher of the Oregon Revised Statutes?
   b. Who is the publisher of Hawaii Revised Statutes Annotated?

Chapter 4

Case Law and Judicial Opinions

Chapter Overview

This chapter discusses judicial opinions and provides you with an understanding of the publication of cases, the elements of a typical court case, and the types of opinions written by judges. The chapter also discusses West's *National Reporter System,* a thorough and comprehensive series of case reporters, which publishes both federal and state court cases. Finally, the process of analyzing and briefing cases is addressed.

A. Selective Publication of Cases

1. Standards for Publishing Cases

Not all cases are published or "reported." In general, and with the exception of some trial cases from our federal courts, trial court decisions are not published. If you consider the overwhelming number of routine assault and battery cases or cases relating to the possession of narcotics, you can readily see why trial court decisions are not usually published. Many of these cases add little to our body of precedents. Generally, only the decisions of the courts of last resort in a jurisdiction are published in full. For example, all of the decisions of the U.S. Supreme Court and the California Supreme Court are published in full, but not all decisions of the lower federal courts and lower California courts are. In fact, in 2007, more than 80 percent of cases from the U.S. Courts of Appeal were not published.

In many instances, the courts themselves decide whether a case merits publication. For example, California Rule of Court 8.1105 provides that cases that meet the following criteria, among others, should be considered by appellate courts in determining which cases should be officially published:

- those that establish a new rule of law or alter or criticize an existing rule;
- those that address an apparent conflict of authority in the law;
- those that involve a legal issue of continuing public interest; or
- those that make a significant contribution to legal literature.

In sum, only appellate court cases that advance legal theory are published. Publishing every case decided in the United States this year would not be of any great value to researchers and would simply result in needless publication. Thus, a certain amount of "weeding out" or selectivity occurs in the publication of cases.

2. *The Controversy Surrounding Unpublished Opinions*

As discussed previously, generally a court decides which cases to publish by certifying them for publication after determining that the cases meet the court's standards for publication. In recent years, however, the issue whether legal professionals may cite cases that have *not* been designated for publication has sparked a great deal of controversy. In *Anastasoff v. United States,* 223 F.3d 898 (8th Cir. 2000), the court ruled that allowing judges to ignore unpublished cases was unconstitutional and gave them arbitrary power. Although *Anastasoff* was later vacated as moot on other grounds, *see Anastasoff v. United States,* 235 F.3d 1054 (8th Cir. 2000), the issue regarding the precedential value of unpublished decisions continued to engender heated debate.

Remember that "unpublished" does not mean "unavailable"; it simply means that the case will not be printed in a conventional hardbound book. As courts have published their opinions on their own websites and released them to LexisNexis and Westlaw, the online legal research systems, the public has been able to access these otherwise *unpublished* or *unreported decisions,* and attorneys and litigants have wanted to refer to, cite to, and rely upon these unpublished decisions to support their arguments and their clients' positions. Moreover, in 2001 West created the *Federal Appendix,* a set that prints the unpublished federal courts of appeals decisions, together with headnotes, key numbers, and topic names, making these unpublished cases even more readily available to researchers. Finally, pursuant to the E-Government Act of 2002, all federal appellate courts must provide access over the Internet to all of their written opinions, regardless of whether such opinions are to be published. Thus, researchers were able to locate and access these "unpublished" cases through numerous means and demanded the right to cite to them in their briefs.

Yet many courts retained "no citation" rules, meaning that unless the case had been designated by the court for publication, it could not be cited in court briefs and other documents. The issue was settled on December 1, 2006, when the Federal Rules of Appellate Procedure were amended to permit citation in briefs of cases that have been designated as "not for publication." Fed. R. App. P. 32.1. However, it was left up to the individual circuits to decide what effect or precedential value these unpublished opinions would have.

State courts also differ in their treatment of unpublished decisions, with about one-half of the states allowing citation of unpublished decisions, although most of these agree that these unpublished decisions are not binding precedent under the doctrine of stare decisis. Others, such as California (which publishes only about 10 percent of its appellate cases each year), strictly prohibit courts and parties from citing or relying upon opinions not certified for publication except in extraordinary circumstances. Cal. R. Ct. 8.1115. Similarly, the federal courts have varying rules relating to the effect of unpublished cases. For example, Rule 36-3 for the Ninth Circuit Court of Appeals provides that except in limited situations, unpublished decisions are not binding precedent.

You may wonder whether you have an obligation to locate and cite to one of these numerous unpublished authorities if it supports a client's position. At present there is no legal obligation to locate authorities that may be persuasive only; thus, failure to cite to such unpublished opinions would likely not constitute malpractice.

B. Elements of a Case

When an appellate court has reviewed the transcript of the trial court, read the written arguments (called "briefs") that were submitted by the parties, and perhaps heard oral argument, the court will render its decision in a written opinion. Cases that are published or reported typically contain the following elements (see Figure 4-1):

1. Case Name

The name or title of a case identifies the parties involved in the action and also provides additional information about the nature of the proceeding. There are several types of case names, including the following:

• *Smith v. Jones.* A case name with a "v." in its title indicates an adversarial proceeding.

• *In re Smith.* The phrase "in re" means "regarding" or "in the matter of." This case name usually designates a case that is not adversarial in nature, such as a bankruptcy proceeding or probate matter involving only one party. Additionally, "in re" is used to designate civil cases involving multiple claims that are transferred to one federal court for coordinated and consistent handling, such as the case *In re Vitamin Antitrust Litigation.*

• *State v. Smith* (or *United States v. Smith).* This case name generally indicates a criminal proceeding, initiated by the state or federal government on behalf of its citizens, all of who are injured by a crime.

• *In re Alison A.* Case names that provide only a party's first name or initials (such as *In re A.S.)* are typically used to designate matters involving minors.

• *Ex rel. Smith.* The phrase "ex rel." is short for "ex relatione," meaning "upon relation or information." Such a case name indicates a legal proceeding initiated by an attorney general or some other state or governmental official on behalf of a state but at the instigation of a private party who has an interest in the matter. The case caption may read *United States ex rel. Smith v. Dowd.*

2. Docket Number and Deciding Court

Immediately beneath the case name you will be given the docket number of the case, which is a number used by the court to identify the case as it progresses through the court system. Following the docket number, the deciding court is usually identified.

3. Date of Decision

The date the case was decided by the court will be given. If two dates are given, one will be identified as the date the case was argued, and the other will be the date the case was decided. For citation purposes, the critical date is the date of decision.

Figure 4-1
Sample of a Published Case

STATE v. BOYD N.C. 697

Cite as 595 S.E.2d 697 (N.C.App. 2004)

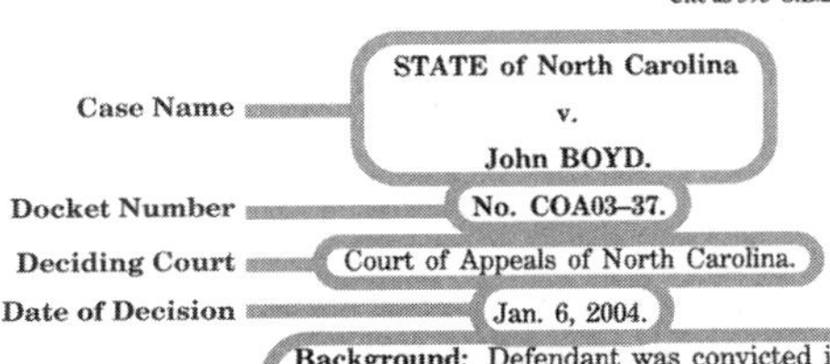

STATE of North Carolina
v.
John BOYD.

No. COA03–37.

Court of Appeals of North Carolina.

Jan. 6, 2004.

Case Summary or Synopsis

Background: Defendant was convicted in the Superior Court, Mecklenburg County, J. Gentry Caudill, J., of conspiracy to sell a controlled substance and was acquitted of sale of a controlled substance, contributing to the delinquency of a minor, and employing and using a minor to commit a controlled substance offense. He appealed conviction and sentence.

Holdings: The Court of Appeals, Wynn, J., held that:

(1) even if issue had been properly preserved for appeal, evidence was sufficient to sustain denial of defendant's motion to dismiss charge of conspiracy to sell a controlled substance, and

(2) defendant's acquittals did not preclude trial court from considering sentencing aggravating factor that defendant involved a person under 16 in commission of conspiracy.

Affirmed.

Headnote

1. Criminal Law ⟹1044.2(2)

Defense counsel, who did not avail himself of his opportunity to move to dismiss conspiracy charge at the close of State's evidence, could not renew nonexistent motion at close of all evidence, as was required to attack on appeal sufficiency of evidence supporting conviction for conspiracy to sell a controlled substance. Rules App.Proc., Rule 10(b)(3).

2. Conspiracy ⟹47(12)

Even if issue had been properly preserved for appeal, evidence was sufficient to sustain denial of defendant's motion to dismiss charge of conspiracy to sell a controlled substance; evidence showed defendant approached undercover police officers in response to juvenile's call, that officer told defendant he wanted to find some cocaine, that defendant told officer to pull his car over and wait while he went down the street to get "it," that defendant and juvenile crossed street, and that juvenile returned and handed officer clear plastic bag containing a rock of crack cocaine, which officer paid for with a marked twenty dollar bill.

3. Sentencing and Punishment ⟹98

Fact that defendant was acquitted of contributing to the delinquency of a minor and employing and using a minor to commit a controlled substance offense did not preclude trial court from considering the sentencing aggravating factor that defendant involved a person under 16 in the commission of conspiracy to sell a controlled substance. West's N.C.G.S.A. § 15A–1340.16(d)(13); § 15A–1340.4(a) (Repealed).

Appeal by Defendant from judgment entered 13 August 2002 by Judge J. Gentry Caudill in Superior Court, Mecklenburg County. Heard in the Court of Appeals 28 October 2003.

Names of Counsel

Assistant Attorney General Martin T. McCracken, for the State.

Robert W. Ewing, Winston-Salem, for the Defendant.

Author of Opinion

WYNN, Judge.

From his conviction for Conspiracy to Sell a Controlled Substance, Defendant, John Boyd, argues on appeal that the trial court erred by failing to grant his motion to dismiss, and considering as an aggravating sentencing factor that he involved a person under 16 years of age in the commission of a crime. We find no error in Defendant's trial.

At trial, the State's evidence tended to show that on 25 October 2001, while conducting undercover drug buys, Charlotte Police Officers Eric Duft and Susan O'Donohue stopped two juveniles in the Colony Acres Drive neighborhood and asked for some "hard" or "rock"—slang terms for the drug crack cocaine. In response, Quintine Hamp-

Figure 4-1 *(Continued)*

ton, one of the youths, pointed across the street and yelled for "J.B." to come over to the car. Responding to Hampton, Defendant approached the officers' car. Officer Duft reiterated his desire to find some "hard," but before discussing the drug request, Defendant asked the officers whether they were police. Officer Duft denied being a police officer and assured Defendant he "just wanted to get hooked up." Apparently satisfied, Defendant told Officer Duft to pull his car over and wait while he went down the street to get "it."

The officers then observed Hampton and Defendant cross Colony Acres Drive before losing sight of them. After two or three minutes, Hampton returned alone and handed Officer Duft a clear plastic bag containing a rock of crack cocaine. Officer Duft paid Hampton with a marked twenty dollar bill. Thereafter, Defendant and Hampton were arrested separately.

After estimating that he had conducted approximately 200–300 similar undercover drug buy stings, Officer Duft testified that "it is common for more than one person to be involved in the [drug] transaction" and sometimes, "they will use a younger person to sell them [because] [t]here is less consequences for a juvenile than there is for an adult." The arresting officer testified that, when Defendant was apprehended, "He stated to me; and I, quote, 'I did not sell shit. All I did was get a piece of the rock.' " At the close of the State's evidence, defense counsel did not "care to be heard" on the conspiracy charge, but did move to dismiss all remaining charges; the motions were denied.

In his defense, Defendant denied the statement attributed to him by the arresting officer. Rather, Defendant testified that he was walking towards Hampton to warn him that Officers Duft and O'Donohue were police officers. When Defendant "couldn't catch [Hampton's] bicycle" he turned around to go home. Defendant maintained "I don't have nothing to do with it."

Ultimately, the jury convicted Defendant of Conspiracy to Sell a Controlled Substance but acquitted him of the remaining charges of Sale of a Controlled Substance, Contributing to the Delinquency of a Minor [1], and Employing and Using a Minor to Commit a Controlled Substance Offense.[2] The trial judge found one aggravating factor (that Defendant involved a person under the age of 16 in the commission of the offense) outweighed mitigating factors (that Defendant had a support system in the community and was gainfully employed) and sentenced Defendant in the aggravated range of 18 to 22 months imprisonment. Defendant appealed.

[1] Defendant first argues the trial court erred by denying his motion to dismiss the charge of Conspiracy to Sell a Controlled Substance. For procedural reasons, we disagree.

N.C.R.App. P. 10(b)(3) provides that "a defendant in a criminal case may not assign as error the insufficiency of the evidence to prove the crime charged unless he moves to dismiss the action. . . ." The rules further provide that by presenting evidence after the close of the State's case, a defendant waives any previous motion to dismiss, and in order to preserve an insufficiency of the evidence argument for appeal, defendant must renew his motion to dismiss at the close of all evidence.

[2] At the close of the State's case, the trial judge in the instant case asked defense counsel whether he cared to make "any motions for the defendant?" Defense counsel responded:

> Yes, Your Honor. I think, taking the evidence in the light most favorable to the state, their strongest case seems to be for conspiracy. And so, I don't care to be heard on that ... I'll ask you to dismiss the sale, at the close of evidence.

1. N.C.G.S. § 14.316.1: "to knowingly or willfully cause, encourage or aid any juvenile within the jurisdiction of the court to be in a place or condition, or to commit an act whereby the juvenile could be adjudicated delinquent, undisciplined, abused or neglected."

2. N.C.G.S. § 90–95.4: "to hire or intentionally use a minor to violate G.S. § 90–95(a)(1)."

Figure 4-1 *(Continued)*

At the close of all evidence, Defense counsel renewed prior motions to dismiss: "We would rest and renew our motions to dismiss; and, re-adopt our arguments, special as they relate to the sale, conspiracy, contributing to the delinquency of a minor; and, the engaging a minor in drug trafficking." By that statement, defense counsel renewed his argument that he "didn't care to be heard" on the conspiracy charge because "their strongest evidence seems to be for conspiracy." Defense counsel did not avail himself of his opportunity to move to dismiss the conspiracy charge at the close of the State's evidence, and thus, he could not renew a nonexistent motion at the close of all evidence. Accordingly, we are precluded from reviewing the merits of Defendant's argument. *See State v. Stocks,* 319 N.C. 437, 439, 355 S.E.2d 492, 492 (1987) (holding that "a defendant who fails to make a motion to dismiss at the close of all the evidence may not attack on appeal the sufficiency of the evidence at trial."). We note, however, that even if this issue had been properly preserved for appeal, the evidence in the record sustains the trial court's denial of Defendant's motion to dismiss this charge.

[3] Defendant next argues that because Hampton's age was an element of the crimes for which he was acquitted, Contributing to the Delinquency of a Minor and Employing and Using a Minor to Commit a Controlled Substance Offense, the trial court erred by considering the sentencing aggravating factor that he "involved a person under 16 in the commission of a crime." We disagree.

In North Carolina, a trial court may consider any aggravating factors it finds proved by the preponderance of the evidence that are reasonably related to the purposes of sentencing. N.C.G.S. § 15A-1340l.4(a). N.C.G.S § 15A-1340.16(d)(13) allows a court to aggravate a defendant's sentence from the presumptive range when "defendant involve[s] a person under the age of 16 in the commission of the crime."

In *State v. Marley,* 321 N.C. 415, 424, 364 S.E.2d 133, 138 (1988), our Supreme Court stated that "once a defendant has been acquitted of a crime he has been set free or judicially discharged from an accusation; released from ... a charge or suspicion of guilt." Therefore, our Supreme Court held "to allow the trial court to use at sentencing an essential element of a greater offense as an aggravating factor, when the presumption of innocence was not, at trial, overcome as to this element, is fundamentally inconsistent with the presumption of innocence itself." In *Marley,* the defendant had been tried for first degree murder upon the theory of premeditation and deliberation. The jury found the defendant guilty of second degree murder. Thus, one can infer from the jury's verdict in *Marley* that the jury determined there was insufficient evidence of premeditation and deliberation.

In this case, it cannot be inferred from the jury's acquittal of Defendant on the contributing to the delinquency of a juvenile and employing and intentionally using a minor to commit a controlled substance offense charges that it found there was insufficient evidence to conclude beyond a reasonable doubt that Hampton was a minor. Indeed, the parties in this case stipulated Hampton was thirteen years old. Unlike Marley, where the difference between first degree murder and second degree murder was the jury "decided that there [was] not sufficient evidence to conclude beyond a reasonable doubt that defendant premeditated and deliberated the killing," *Marley,* 321 N.C. at 424, 364 S.E.2d at 138, in this case, we are unable to explain rationale behind the jury's verdict. Thus, by convicting Defendant of conspiracy to sell a controlled substance, the jury concluded that Johnny Boyd and Quintinie Hampton were conspirators. Therefore, we uphold the trial court's consideration as an aggravating sentencing factor that Defendant involved a person under the age of 16 in the commission of a crime.

No error. — **Decision**

Judges TIMMONS-GOODSON and ELMORE concur.

4. *Case Summary or Synopsis*

Before you are given the actual opinion of the court, you will be provided with a brief paragraph summarizing the nature and background of the case, a description of the parties, a summary of what occurred in the court below, and an overview of this court's decision. This summary is typically prepared by the legal publishing companies (usually West), not by the court. This case summary serves as a quick introduction to the case, and helps you weed out irrelevant cases, but it can never be quoted from or relied on as authority because it was not prepared by the court.

5. *Headnotes*

Before the actual opinion of the court, you will be provided with short paragraphs, each of which is assigned a number and a title, such as **"4. Damages."** These are called *headnotes*. Each point of law discussed in the case is assigned a headnote. Thus, if the case discusses six points of law, there will be six headnotes. The headnotes provide a condensed overview or snapshot of the case and reduce the time you might spend reading a case that ultimately proves to be of no value to you. Headnotes may be thought of as the table of contents to your case. Because the headnotes are typically prepared by publishers and not judges, you cannot rely on them or quote from them, although they serve as excellent overviews of the issues in the case to follow. West reporters also include a pictorial diagram of a key, a topic name, and a number. This Key Number System is a method of finding other cases on the same topic and is discussed in detail in Chapter Five.

6. *Names of Counsel*

The names of the attorneys who represented the parties in the case are provided so that you can make contact with them. Although you can readily obtain copies of the briefs and papers filed in a court case from the court itself, discussing the case with the attorney involved may be of particular help to you.

7. *Opinion*

The beginning of the opinion of the court is almost always marked by an identification of the author of the opinion. This is a signal that everything that follows is the court's opinion. Some sets of case reports include introductory summaries before the case begins. For example, the set *United States Reports,* which publishes decisions of the U.S. Supreme Court, includes a *Syllabus* before most opinions, which is a summary of the decision to follow. The *Syllabus* is prepared by the Court's Reporter of Decisions, who is responsible for editing and publishing cases, and most cases include the following disclaimer by the Court: "The *Syllabus* constitutes no part of the opinion of the Court but has been prepared . . . for the convenience of the reader." Similarly, some older sets of case reports and some of the unofficial sets include summaries of the arguments advanced by each party or summaries of the opinion to follow. Make sure you understand the difference between these useful editorial enhancements and the actual opinion. Only the court's opinion is binding; summaries or syllabi are helpful overviews of the case to follow, but they are usually prepared by a court official or a private publisher, and you may not quote from them or rely on them.

Most opinions begin with a recital of the facts of the case. There are various types of opinions:

- *Majority opinions* are those written by a member of the majority after the court has reached its decision. The holding of the majority is the law and serves as binding authority.
- *Plurality opinions* are those lacking sufficient votes by appellate judges to constitute a majority; separate opinions are written by members of the majority and no single opinion receives the support of a majority of the judges hearing the case. Plurality opinions are usually said to establish no precedent for future cases. The result carries precedential weight but the reasoning in a plurality opinion does not.
- *Concurring opinions* are opinions written by justices or judges who agree with the actual result reached in a case (for example, that the case should be affirmed) but disagree with the reasoning of the majority opinion. Concurring opinions are persuasive and not binding.
- *Dissenting opinions* are those written by members of the minority. They are persuasive only.
- *Per curiam opinions* are opinions of the whole court in which no specific author is identified.
- *Memorandum opinions* report routine decisions. They provide a holding or result but little, if any, reasoning therefor. A memorandum decision may state only, "For the reasons given by the court below, we also affirm."

Ethics Alert: *Reliance on Non-Majority Opinions*

Whenever you cite a case in a document, the reader will assume that you are relying on the majority opinion. If you are relying on anything other than the majority opinion, such as a dissent or a concurring opinion, you must inform the reader by indicating such, as follows: *Circuit City Stores v. Adams,* 532 U.S. 105, 125 (2001) (Stevens, J., dissenting).

8. *Decision*

The final element in a case is the actual decision reached by the court. The final decision may be to affirm or uphold the determination of the lower court, to reverse or overturn the determination reached below, or to remand or return the case to the lower court for further action consistent with the court's findings. Although strictly speaking, the word *decision* refers only to the final disposition of a case, in many instances and in common usage, the words "opinion," "judgment," "decision," "case," and "holding" are often used interchangeably to refer to an entire case from the name of the case to the final decision.

C. Publication of Cases

1. *Official and Unofficial Publication*

The books in which cases are published are referred to as *reports* or *reporters* and each one has a specific abbreviation. If cases are published pursuant to some statutory directive or court rule, the set of books in which they are collected are referred to as *official reports.* Cases published without this type of governmental approval are collected in sets of books called *unofficial reporters.* The terms "official" and "unofficial" have nothing to do with accuracy or quality—the terms relate solely to the method of publication. The fact that many cases are published both officially and unofficially means that researchers have a choice as to what set of books to use to locate a case. As discussed previously, statutes are also published officially and unofficially. It is also important to understand the difference between official and unofficial sets because in many instances citation rules require one form of citation over another or may require that a writer provide both citations, giving the official citation first.

For example, consider the following citation: *Jones v. Smith,* 236 Va. 109, 402 S.E.2d 16 (1995). Citations to cases always include the same elements: the name of the case; a reference to the volume number, name of the set, and page number on which the case begins; the date of decision; and the deciding court, if not apparent from the name of the set. Thus, the citation given above informs the reader that the case named *Jones versus Smith* can be located in volume 236 of a set of books called *Virginia Reports* at page 109 and the same case can also be located in volume 402 of a set of books called *South Eastern Reporter, Second Series,* at page 16. The case was decided in 1995. The two citations are called *parallel citations,* and the first one given above is the official citation, and the second one is the unofficial citation. The case opinion itself will be exactly the same in both sets because what the judge has said in issuing the opinion is "etched in stone." What will vary will be type size, quality of paper, and some "extra" features provided by the respective publishers, such as the headnotes and case summary or synopsis. Note that when citing cases, writers should also provide not only the page on which the case begins but also the page in the case where the specific material can be found. These "pinpoint" citations are discussed in Chapter Ten.

2. *Series of Case Reports*

You may have noticed that some of the case reports on the shelves are marked, for example, *Pacific Reporter,* while others indicate *Pacific Reporter 2d Series* on their spines. The switch to a new series by a publisher merely indicates newer cases. You do not need to know which years are covered by which series. It is sufficient to know, for example, that any case in *Federal Reporter 3d Series* is newer than any case published in *Federal Reporter 2d Series,* and so forth.

3. *Advance Sheets*

Cases are first published in slip form and are then published in *advance sheets,* which are temporary softcover publications that appear a few weeks after release of the court's opinion and are published to provide rapid access to cases. Eventually, after several months, the cases will be published in hardback volumes, and the softcover advance sheets will be discarded. The permanent volumes will share the identical volume number and pagination as the earlier advance sheets. Therefore, you may readily rely upon and quote from cases appearing in the advance sheets because a citation to the page a quote appears on in the advance sheet will be identical to the page a quote appears on in the later published hardbound volume.

D. Publication of State Cases

1. West's National Reporter System

In 1879, West created and published the *North Western Reporter* to publish decisions from the northwestern region of the United States. In many instances, these cases were already being published officially. Thus, for example, a Minnesota case would appear both officially in the *Minnesota Reports* and unofficially in the *North Western Reporter.* Practitioners became so enthusiastic about the various features offered by West's *North Western Reporter* and its groupings of cases from neighboring states that West followed it by creating reporters for other geographical regions of the United States. West's sets of books that collect state and federal cases are collectively referred to as the *National Reporter System.* In these sets of books West publishes all of the cases released by courts for publication, as well as adding thousands of cases not released for official publication and those that were reported as memorandum decisions. Within the *National Reporter System* there are various units or sets of case books. The states that compose each unit of the *National Reporter System* can be seen in Figure 4-2.

Figure 4-2
Major Units of West's National Reporter System

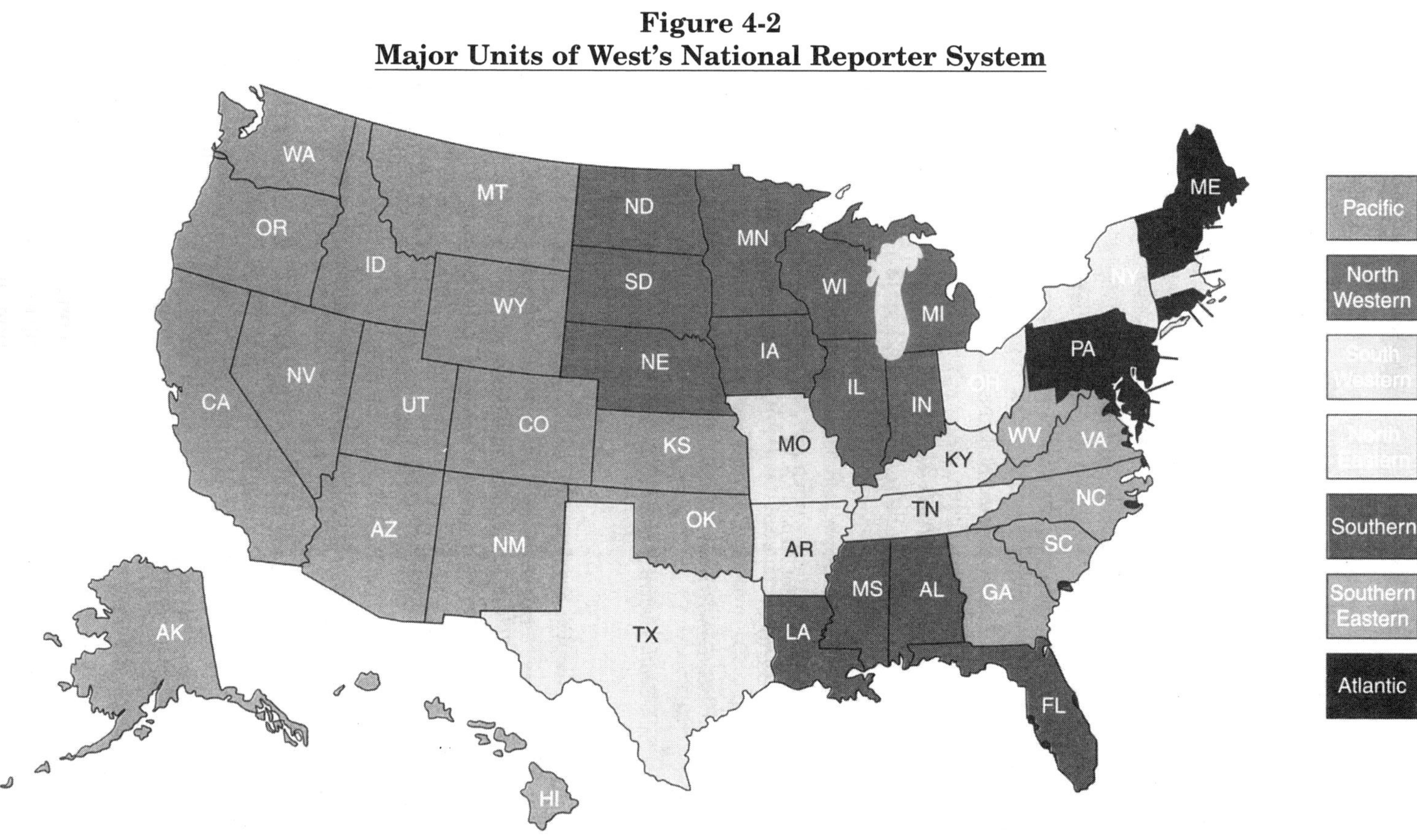

Figure 4-2 *(Continued)*

Name of Case Reporter and Abbreviation	Courts Covered
North Western Reporter N.W., N.W.2d	State courts in Iowa*, Michigan, Minnesota*, Nebraska, North Dakota*, South Dakota*, Wisconsin
Pacific Reporter P., P.2d, P.3d	State courts in Alaska*, Arizona, California, Colorado*, Hawaii, Idaho, Kansas, Montana, Nevada, New Mexico, Oklahoma*, Oregon, Utah*, Washington, Wyoming*
North Eastern Reporter N.E., N.E.2d	State court cases in Illinois, Indiana*, Massachusetts, New York, Ohio
Atlantic Reporter A., A.2d	State court cases in Connecticut, Delaware*, Maine*, Maryland, New Hampshire, New Jersey, Pennsylvania, Rhode Island*, Vermont, Washington, D.C.*
South Western Reporter S.W., S.W.2d, S.W.3d	State court cases in Arkansas, Kentucky*, Missouri*, Tennessee*, Texas*
Southern Reporter So., So. 2d	State court cases in Alabama*, Florida*, Louisiana*, Mississippi*
South Eastern Reporter S.E., S.E.2d	State court cases in Georgia, North Carolina, South Carolina, Virginia, West Virginia
New York Supplement N.Y.S., N.Y.S.2d	Cases from various New York state courts
California Reporter Cal. Rptr., Cal. Rptr. 2d, Cal. Rptr. 3d	Cases from the California Supreme Court, California Court of Appeal, and Appellate Departments of the California Superior Courts
Illinois Decisions Ill. Dec.	Cases from the Illinois Supreme Court and Illinois Appellate Court
Supreme Court Reporter S. Ct.	Cases from U.S. Supreme Court
Federal Reporter F., F.2d, F.3d	Cases from U.S. Courts of Appeal
Federal Supplement F. Supp., F. Supp. 2d	Cases from U.S. District Courts
Federal Rules Decisions F.R.D.	Cases interpreting federal rules of civil procedure, criminal procedure, and evidence (and some legal articles)

* State no longer publishes official versions of its cases.

It is not important to memorize or know which state is published or covered in which unit. It is sufficient if you understand the general structure of West's *National Reporter System:* It is a set of books, published unofficially, which reports many cases already published officially by many states themselves. You should know, however, which unit covers the state in which you will be working.

After West created the regional units to report decisions from groups of neighboring states, it created specialized sets for three states because of the volume of litigation in those states: *California Reporter, Illinois Decisions,* and the *New York Supplement.* Thus, there may be three parallel citations to a California case, as follows:

> *Powers v. City of Richmond,* 10 Cal. 4th 85, 893 P.2d 1160, 40 Cal. Rptr. 2d 839 (1995).

This citation shows that the *Powers* case can be located in three separate sets of books. The opinion issued by the court in *Powers* will be the same no matter which of the three sets you select to locate the case. What will differ, however, may be the color of the covers, the quality of the paper used, the typeface, and the editorial enhancements such as headnotes and the case summary or synopsis.

One of the advantages of the *National Reporter System* units lies in its groupings of states. A law firm in Ohio that purchases the official *Ohio State Reports* will acquire a set of books that contains cases only from Ohio. If that firm purchases the *North Eastern Reporter,* however, it acquires a set of books that contains decisions not only from Ohio but also from Illinois, Indiana, Massachusetts, and New York. This allows legal professionals to review decisions from other neighboring states, which decisions might be helpful if a case of first impression arises in Ohio.

The sets of books in the *National Reporter System* offer a variety of useful features, including the following: an alphabetical table of the cases in that volume; a table of statutes directing you to cases in the volume that interpret statutes; and a table of words and phrases directing you to cases in the volume that interpret a word or phrase (for example, "assault"), although this feature is not found in all volumes. Moreover, all books in the *National Reporter System* participate in West's Key Number System, a method of allowing researchers to locate other similar cases, and which is discussed in Chapter Five.

Interestingly enough, and perhaps because of its publishing expertise, West has been recognized as the official or primary source of decisions in a majority of the states. Thus, although *Arizona Reports* and *Ohio Sate Reports* are the official sets of the respective states, the actual publication of the books is accomplished by West. Similarly, some states have adopted West's regional reporters as their official state reporters.

Practice Tip: *Citations in Case Reports*

The citations that appear in published cases are generally not in correct *Bluebook or ALWD* form. For space reasons, publishers often take shortcuts in citing cases and other authorities. Rely on *The Bluebook* or *ALWD* when citing legal authorities and not the way the citations look in the books themselves or on LexisNexis or Westlaw.

2. *Citation Form*

Although citation form will be covered in depth in Chapter Ten, at this point you should know one importance of distinguishing an official citation from an unofficial one. Many courts require that citations to state court cases include a citation to the official state report followed by a parallel citation to West's regional reporter. Thus, you will need to know the major units in West's *National Reporter System* so that when you are confronted with a case citation such as *Deyo v. Deyo,* 474 Mich. 952, 707 N.W.2d 339 (2005), you will know that because the *North Western Reporter* is one of West's *National Reporter System* unofficial units, the citation to it should follow the official *Michigan Reports* citation. Under *The Bluebook* and *ALWD* (unless local rules require otherwise), the citation would include only the West regional reporter and not the official citation, as follows: *Deyo v. Deyo,* 707 N.W.2d 339 (Mich. 2005).

3. *Discontinuation of Some Official Reports*

Because of the popularity of West's *National Reporter System,* about 20 states stopped publishing their cases officially. Generally, the states that have stopped official publication are smaller states (for example, North Dakota and Iowa). In those states, you will be able to locate cases only in West's respective regional reporter, and there will be only one citation for any case decided after the state stopped publishing officially. Figure 4-2, Table T.1 of *The Bluebook,* and Appendix 1 of *ALWD* identify which states have ceased official publication.

E. Publication of Federal Cases

1. *United States Supreme Court Cases*

United States Supreme Court cases are published in the following three sets of books: *United States Reports* (the official set), *Supreme Court*

Reporter (West's unofficial set), and *United States Supreme Court Reports, Lawyers' Edition* (LexisNexis's unofficial set, commonly called *Lawyers' Edition).*

Thus, there are at least three parallel citations for all United States Supreme Court cases, and you can locate the 1986 case *Batson v. Kentucky,* in three locations: 476 U.S. 79, 106 S. Ct. 1712, and 90 L. Ed. 2d 69. In the event of any conflict in versions of the cases reported in these volumes, the version of a case found in the official *U.S. Reports* governs.

For rapid access to United States Supreme Court cases, you may use *United States Law Week,* a journal that publishes the full text of United States Supreme Court cases published during the previous week; you may access the Court's website at www.supremecourtus.gov (which posts opinions within hours after they are released); or you may use the computer-assisted research services LexisNexis or Westlaw, which usually have the full text of a United States Supreme Court case within one hour after the decision is released.

2. United States Courts of Appeal Cases

The set of books that publishes cases from the intermediate courts of appeal (for example, First Circuit, Second Circuit, and so forth) is the *Federal Reporter* (abbreviated "F.") and the *Federal Reporter, Second Series* and *Third Series* (abbreviated as "F.2d" and "F.3d"). Although the primary function of the *Federal Reporter* is to publish decisions from the United States Courts of Appeal, it has published cases from various other courts as well (see Figure 4-3).

This set of reporters is unofficial and is yet another of the units in West's *National Reporter System.* In fact, the *Federal Reporter* is the *only* set that reports decisions from these intermediate courts of appeal. Thus, there are no parallel citations for cases from these courts of appeal. The cases are initially published in softcover advance sheets that are later replaced by hardbound permanent volumes.

3. United States District Court Cases

The beginning of this chapter noted that trial court decisions are not usually published. An exception to this general rules lies in the *Federal Supplement* and *Federal Supplement, Second Series* (abbreviated as "F. Supp." and "F. Supp. 2d"), created in 1932 by West and which publishes decisions from the United States District Courts, our federal trial courts. Although the *Federal Supplement* and *Federal Supplement, Second Series* publish decisions from some other courts as well (for example, the sets publish decisions from the U.S. Court of International Trade), their key function is to report decisions from these United States District Courts (see Figure 4-3). The *Federal Supplement* and *Federal Supplement, Second Series* are the primary sets of books that publish

United States District Court cases. Thus, there are no parallel citations for cases from these courts. Just as with other case reports, cases appear first in advance sheets and later in hardbound volumes.

Figure 4-3
Coverage of the *Federal Reporter* and *Federal Supplement*

Date	*Federal Reporter* (F., F.2d, and F.3d)
1880-1912	U.S. Courts of Appeals
1911-1913	Commerce Court of the United States (abolished in 1932)
1880-1932	U.S. District Courts (after 1932, cases reported in *Federal Supplement* and *Federal Supplement, Second Series*)
1929-1932, 1960-1982	U.S. Court of Claims
1891-Date	U.S. Courts of Appeal
1929-1982	U.S. Court of Customs and Patent Appeals
1943-1961	U.S. Emergency Court of Appeals
1972-1993	Temporary Emergency Court of Appeals

Date	*Federal Supplement* and *Federal Supplement, Second Series* (F. Supp. and F. Supp. 2d)
1932-1960	U.S. Court of Claims
1932-Date	U.S. District Courts
1956-Date	U.S. Court of International Trade (previously called U.S. Customs Court)
1968-Date	Judicial Panel on Multidistrict Litigation
1973-1996	Special Court, Regional Rail Reorganization Act (abolished in 1996)

4. *Cases Interpreting Federal Rules*

Yet another unit in West's *National Reporter System,* the *Federal Rules Decisions* set, publishes cases that have not been published in F. Supp. or F. Supp. 2d that interpret and construe the Federal Rules of Civil Procedure, Federal Rules of Criminal Procedure, Federal Rules of Evidence, Federal Rules of Appellate Procedure, Federal Sentencing Guidelines, and other rules. Thus, the name of this set, *Federal Rules Decisions* (abbreviated as "F.R.D."), is perfectly descriptive of its function: It publishes cases that construe federal rules, whether those rules relate to rules of procedure for civil cases, rules of evidence, and so forth. Articles that provide comment on the federal rules are also included.

Practice Tip: *Google Scholar*

A new feature introduced by Google is "Google Scholar," which allows free and easy searching of court opinions from federal and state courts. Access http://scholar.google.com and select the "Legal opinions and journals" button. Type in your case name or your search terms in plain English and you will be directed to cases relating to your topic. You may also explore related cases and cases that have cited your case.

F. Star Paging

Citation form will be thoroughly discussed in Chapter Ten, but for now it is sufficient if you are aware that many state rules require that citation to state cases include all parallel citations. The rule for U.S. Supreme Court cases is far different. *The Bluebook* requires that for these cases, you are to cite only to the official *United States Reports.* The *ALWD* rule is substantially similar, although *ALWD* notes that giving all parallel citations for U.S. Supreme Court cases is permitted but not preferred.

Obviously, therefore, the publishers at West and LexisNexis were in a dilemma. It would be extremely difficult for these publishers to attempt to market their sets of books *(Supreme Court Reporter* and *United States Supreme Court Reports, Lawyers' Edition,* respectively) because no matter how wonderful the sets might be, law firms and other users would be highly unlikely to purchase a set of case books that could not be cited or quoted.

The publishers at West and LexisNexis thus developed a technique of continually indicating throughout their sets which volume and page a reader would be on if that reader were using the official *United States Reports.* This technique of indicating page breaks in the official set is called *star paging* because the early method of indicating when a new page began was through the use of a star or asterisk (*). West now uses an inverted "T" as shown in Figure 4-4, and LexisNexis now uses boldface print as in **[516 US 14]** to indicate the page breaks.

Practice Tip: *Common Legal Abbreviations*

Newcomers to the legal profession are often bewildered by the numerous odd abbreviations found in law books. With just a little time and effort, you will be able to understand and translate the quirky abbreviations you see. *Black's Law Dictionary* (9th ed. 2009) includes a table of abbreviations, and both *The Bluebook* and *ALWD* are helpful in interpreting legal abbreviations. Following are some of the more common abbreviations you will encounter:

A.	Atlantic	Super.	Superior
P.	Pacific (or Procedure)	D. or Dist.	District
S.E.	South Eastern		
S.W.	South Western	C.D.	Central District
N.E.	North Eastern	E.D.	Eastern District
N.W.	North Western	M.D.	Middle District
So.	Southern	N.D.	Northern District
F.	Federal	S.D.	Southern District
R.	Rule, Rules	W.D.	Western District
Supp.	Supplement	J.	Judge, Justice (or Journal)
App.	Appellate		
		JJ.	Judges, Justices
Div.	Division	A.J.	Associate Judge, Associate Justice
Ch.	Chapter or Chancery		
Cl.	Claims	C.J.	Chief Judge, Chief Justice
Cir.	Circuit		
Civ.	Civil	P.J.	Presiding Judge
Crim.	Criminal	L.	Law
Ct.	Court		

Star paging thus allows you to read a U.S. Supreme Court case in one of the unofficial sets and yet know what page you would be on if you were holding the official *United States Reports*. Figure 4-4 shows a sample page illustrating star paging. Star paging is also found in some other West sets, including the *California Reporter* and the *New York Supplement*, directing you to pagination for the official California and New York reports. Star paging is also used by LexisNexis and Westlaw so that as you review a case on your computer screen, you can determine the page you would be reviewing if you were holding a hardbound volume of case reports.

Figure 4-4
Sample Page from West's Supreme Court *Reporter Showing* "Star Paging"

Reference to volume and page in official *United States Reports*

Star Paging (the word "to" appears on page 675 of volume 487 of the *United States Reports,* while the word "impair" appears on page 676 of the volume)

487 U.S. 677

MORRISON v. OLSON

Cite as 108 S.Ct. 2597 (1988)

2611

ter the addition of "Consuls" to the list, the Committee's proposal was adopted, *id.*, at 539, and was subsequently reported to the Convention by the Committee of Style. See *id.*, at 599. It was at this point, on September 15, that Gouverneur Morris moved to add the Excepting Clause to Art. II, § 2. *Id.*, at 627. The one comment made on this motion was by Madison, who felt that the Clause did not go far enough in that it did not allow Congress to vest appointment powers in "Superior Officers below Heads of Departments." The first vote on Morris' motion ended in a tie. It was then put forward a second time, with the urging that "some such provision [was] too necessary, to be omitted." This time the proposal was adopted. *Id.*, at 627–628. As this discussion shows, there was little or no debate on the question whether the Clause empowers Congress to provide for interbranch appointments, and there is nothing to suggest that the Framers intended to prevent Congress from having that power.

We do not mean to say that Congress' power to provide for interbranch appointments of "inferior officers" is unlimited. In addition to separation-of-powers concerns, which would arise if such provisions for appointment had the potential to ⌊676impair the constitutional functions assigned to one of the branches, *Siebold* itself suggested that Congress' decision to vest the appointment power in the courts would be improper if there was some "incongruity" between the functions normally performed by the courts and the performance of their duty to appoint. 100 U.S. (10 Otto), at 398 ("[T]he duty to appoint inferior officers, when required thereto by law, is a constitutional duty of the courts; and in the present case there is no such incongruity in the duty required as to excuse the courts from its performance, or to render their acts void"). In this case, however, we do not think it impermissible for Congress to vest the power to appoint independent counsel in a specially created federal court. We thus disagree with the Court of Appeals' conclusion that there is an inherent incongruity about a court having the power to appoint prosecutorial officers.[13] We have recognized that courts may appoint private attorneys to act as prosecutor for judicial contempt judgments. See *Young v. United States ex rel. Vuitton et Fils S.A.*, 481 U.S. 787, 107 S.Ct. 2124, 95 L.Ed.2d 740 (1987). In *Go–Bart Importing Co. v. United States,* 282 U.S. 344, 51 S.Ct. 153, 75 L.Ed. 374 (1931), we approved court appointment of United States commissioners, who exercised certain limited prosecutorial powers. *Id.*, at 353, n. 2, 51 S.Ct., at 156, n. 2. In *Siebold,* as well, we indicated that judicial appointment of federal marshals, who are "executive officer[s]," would not be inappropriate. Lower courts have also upheld interim judicial appointments of United States Attorneys, see *United States v. Solomon,* 216 F.Supp. 835 (SDNY 1963), and Congress itself has vested the power to make these interim appointments in the district courts, see 28 ⌊677U.S.C. § 546(d) (1982 ed., Supp. V).[14] Congress, of course, was concerned when it created the office of independent counsel with the conflicts of interest that could arise in situations when the Executive Branch is called upon to investigate its own high-ranking officers. If it were to remove the appointing authority from the Executive Branch, the most logical place to put it was in the Judicial Branch. In the light of

13. Indeed, in light of judicial experience with prosecutors in criminal cases, it could be said that courts are especially well qualified to appoint prosecutors. This is not a case in which judges are given power to appoint an officer in an area in which they have no special knowledge or expertise, as in, for example, a statute authorizing the courts to appoint officials in the Department of Agriculture or the Federal Energy Regulatory Commission.

14. We note also the longstanding judicial practice of appointing defense attorneys for individuals who are unable to afford representation, see 18 U.S.C. § 3006A(b) (1982 ed., Supp. V), notwithstanding the possibility that the appointed attorney may appear in court before the judge who appointed him.

G. Specialized *National Reporter System* Sets

There are additional sets of books that are also a part of West's *National Reporter System* series. These reporters publish very specialized cases and include the following:

- **West's *Military Justice Reporter*.** This set publishes decisions from the United States Court of Appeals for the Armed Forces and the Military Service Courts of Criminal Appeals.
- **West's *Veterans Appeals Reporter*.** This set publishes cases decided by the United States Court of Appeals for Veterans Claims, created in 1988, and previously named the United States Court of Veterans Appeals.
- **West's *Bankruptcy Reporter*.** The *Bankruptcy Reporter* publishes cases decided by U.S. Bankruptcy Courts and U.S. District Courts dealing with bankruptcy matters. Also included are bankruptcy decisions by the U.S. Supreme Court and U.S. Courts of Appeals.
- **West's *Federal Claims Reporter*.** This set publishes decisions from the United States Court of Federal Claims. Cases include tax refund suits, government contract disputes, environment and natural resource disputes, and civilian and military pay questions.
- ***Federal Cases*.** Until 1880, when West began publishing cases from the lower federal courts, there was no one comprehensive set of books that reported decisions from these courts. Although several sets existed, none were adequate. Therefore, in 1880, West collected all of these lower federal court cases together and republished them in a set of books titled *Federal Cases*. Rather than arranging cases in chronological order, as is the usual format used for case reports, this set arranges the cases in alphabetical order. Because *Federal Cases* covers much older cases, it is often available only at larger law libraries.
- **State-Specific Sets.** For the convenience of practitioners, West also publishes case reporters for individual states. For example, the *Minnesota Reporter* includes decisions from Minnesota state courts that are published in the *North Western Reporter* (but omits cases from other states covered by the *North Western Reporter*, such as Michigan cases). Practitioners use these sets, but they are not cited; because these separate sets retain the pagination of the regional reporter, practitioners cite to the relevant regional reporter. These separate sets, however, offer ease of use to practitioners and include helpful features such as Key Number references, headnotes, and other editorial enhancements. These specialized sets have various names, such as *Alaska Reporter*, *Arkansas Cases*, and *Kentucky Decisions*.

H. Features of West's *National Reporter System*

The case reporters in West's *National Reporter System* possess a number of useful editorial features that aid in and simplify legal research. These features are found in both the advance sheets and the permanent hardbound volumes (except as noted) and are as follows:

1. Table of Cases Reported

There will be at least one alphabetical table of cases in each reporter volume. For example, each volume of the *Supreme Court Reporter* includes a complete alphabetical list of all of the cases in that volume. This feature is useful if you know the approximate date of a Supreme Court case and need to examine a few volumes of the set to locate a case or if you mistakenly transpose numbers in a citation. Cases can be found by using either the plaintiff's or defendant's name.

Some sets of books have two tables of cases. For instance, any volume in the *Pacific Reporter* will contain one complete alphabetical list of the cases in that volume as well as an alphabetized list of the cases arranged by state, so that the Alaska cases are separately alphabetized, the Arizona cases are separately alphabetized, and so on.

2. Tables of Statutes and Rules

The Table of Statutes will direct you to cases in a volume that have interpreted any statutes or constitutional provisions. Thus, if you are interested in whether any recent cases have interpreted Cal. Evid. Code § 2211 (West 2000), you can consult the table of statutes in a volume of the *California Reporter,* and you will be directed to any page in the volume that interprets that statute. Similarly, there are tables listing federal rules of civil and criminal procedure and so forth that are construed by any cases in a particular volume. Some sets include separate tables for statutes and rules, some sets combine the two into one table, and some sets no longer include this feature.

3. Table of Words and Phrases

This table alphabetically lists words and phrases that have been interpreted or defined by any cases in a volume. For example, you can consult the Table of Words and Phrases and determine if the word "negligence" has been construed by any cases in a volume, and you will be directed to the specific page in a volume on which the word is interpreted. This feature is not found in all volumes or sets.

4. *List of Judges*

This feature (found only in the hardbound volumes of the *National Reporter System*) allows you to identify judges sitting on the courts covered by that particular volume.

5. *Key Number System*

West's Key Number System will be described in the next chapter; for the present, it is sufficient to know that all of the books in the *National Reporter System* are participants in the Key Number System, West's integrated research system that helps you find cases discussing similar points of law.

I. Finding Parallel Citations

On occasion, you may have one parallel citation and need the other(s). This could be because citation rules require all parallel citations or because the volume you need is missing from the law library shelf, and you must obtain the parallel citation to locate the case you need. There are several techniques you can use to find a parallel citation:

- **Cross-References.** Many cases provide all parallel citations. For example, if you open a volume of *California Reports* to the case you need, at the top of each page, in the *running head,* you are given all parallel citations for this case. West's reporters provide the official citation for cases they report unofficially. LexisNexis and Westlaw screens also provide parallel citations.
- ***National Reporter Blue Book* and State *Blue and White Books.*** A book published by West and titled the *National Reporter Blue Book* gives you tables converting official citations to unofficial regional citations. Similarly, about one-half of the states have state *Blue and White Books,* which provide conversion tables with parallel citations. For example, the *Nebraska Blue and White Book* includes blue pages giving citations from the official reports to the unofficial reporter and white pages that provide the reverse function (giving citations from the unofficial regional reporter back to the official reports).
- ***Shepard's Citations* and KeyCite.** As you will learn in Chapter Eleven, when you Shepardize or KeyCite either an official or an unofficial citation, you are given the parallel citation.
- **State Digests.** West has published sets of books called "digests" for each state except Delaware, Nevada, and Utah. These digests contain tables of cases that provide parallel citations. Thus, if you look up a case by name in the Table of Cases for the *Wisconsin Digest,* you will be given the case's citation in the official *Wisconsin Reports* and in the unofficial *North Western Reporter.*

J. Summary of West's *National Reporter System*

West's *National Reporter System* is a series of sets of case reporters that publishes cases from state appellate courts and from federal trial and appellate courts. All of the sets of books in the *National Reporter System* are unofficial because the books are published privately by West rather than pursuant to some government mandate. Although West's *National Reporter System* is the largest collection of case reporters, West is not the only publisher of cases. For example, LexisNexis publishes U.S. Supreme Court cases in its unofficial set *United States Supreme Court Reports, Lawyers' Edition.*

- **State Court Cases.** West publishes state court cases in seven regional units, each of which contains cases from a particular geographical area. The regional units are as follows:
  - *North Western Reporter*
  - *Pacific Reporter*
  - *North Eastern Reporter*
  - *Atlantic Reporter*
  - *South Western Reporter*
  - *Southern Reporter*
  - *South Eastern Reporter*
  - West also created the following separate sets for three states:
  - *California Reporter*
  - *Illinois Decisions*
  - *New York Supplement*
- **Federal Cases.** Federal cases are published in these sets of books:
  - *Supreme Court Reporter* (cases from the U.S. Supreme Court)
  - *Federal Reporter* (cases from the U.S. Courts of Appeal)
  - *Federal Supplement* (cases from the U.S. District Courts)
  - *Federal Rules Decisions* (cases interpreting federal rules)

Finally, West publishes other sets, each of which is descriptively titled: the *Military Justice Reporter,* the *Veterans Appeals Reporter,* the *Bankruptcy Reporter,* the *Federal Claims Reporter,* and specialized sets for some states, such as *Oregon Decisions* and *Texas Cases.*

All of the books in West's *National Reporter System* possess a variety of useful features and all are participants in West's Key Number System, which is described in Chapter Five. See Figure 4-5 for a summary of case law publication.

Figure 4-5
Summary of Case Law Publication

	Highest Court	*Intermediate Appellate Courts*	*Trial Courts*
Federal Cases	United States Supreme Court • *United States Reports** • *Supreme Court Reporter* • *United States Supreme Court Reports, Lawyers' Edition* • *United States Law Week*	United States Courts of Appeal cases are published in West's *Federal Reporter* (F., F.2d, and F.3d)	United States District Court cases are published primarily in West's *Federal Supplement* (F. Supp. and F. Supp. 2d)
State Cases	State Supreme Courts (example of official sets are *California Reports** and *Georgia Reports**; example of unofficial set is *Pacific Reporter*)	State Appellate Courts (example of official sets are *California Appellate Reports** and *Georgia Appeals Reports**; example of unofficial set is *South Eastern Reporter*)	Generally, state trial court cases are not published

*Designates official set.

K. Briefing Cases

1. *Introduction and Purpose of Case Briefs*

The importance of cases in our common law system has already been discussed. You will also recall that in our legal system it is not sufficient to merely read a statute assuming that it will provide the answer to a question or problem because it is the task of our courts to interpret and construe statutory language. Thus, reading, interpreting, and analyzing cases are of critical importance to all legal professionals.

Few people find it natural to read cases. The language used by courts is often archaic, and the style of writing can make it difficult to comprehend the court's writing. Moreover, the topics discussed in cases are often complex. The most common technique used to impose some order or structure on the confusing world of case law is case briefing. A *case brief* or *brief* is a short, written summary and analysis of a case.

It is extremely common for law students to brief cases so that in the event they are called on in class to discuss a case, they will have a convenient summary to use. Moreover, practicing attorneys often desire to have cases briefed so they may save time by reading the briefs first and then, based upon their initial reading, analyze only selected cases in full. In some instances, months can go by between hearings in court or new professionals may join the legal team. The case briefs for a matter handled by the team should be sufficiently readable and useful that new team members can be immediately brought "up to speed" by reviewing the briefs. Do not confuse the word "brief" in this context (meaning a summary of the key elements of case) with the written argument an attorney submits to a court, which is also called a "brief."

One of the best reasons for briefing cases is to learn how to focus on the important parts of the case in order to obtain a thorough understanding of the case and its reasoning. Although you may be tempted to view case briefing as busywork and may believe you can understand a case by simply reading it through, research has shown that people tend to read quickly and see words in groupings. Briefing a case will force you to slow down and concentrate on the critical aspects of the case.

Preparing a case brief requires you to tear the case apart and rebuild it in a structure that helps you and others understand it. Case briefing helps develop your analytical skills and forces you to focus on the critical parts of the court's opinion. In a sense, you are taking notes on the cases you read, and just as explaining a difficult concept to another helps you understand it better, preparing a case brief will help clarify your comprehension of the case. Thus, case briefing is a first step in learning how to write legal memoranda and court documents. After you have mastered case briefing and thus trained yourself to analyze cases properly, you may be able to dispense with separately prepared written briefs and be able to brief cases by merely highlighting the key portions of printed cases. Consider using the abbreviations shown in Figure 4-6.

The first briefs you prepare may be nearly as long as the case itself. This is because it takes practice to learn to recognize the essential elements of a case. Initially, every part of the case will seem critical to you. With time, however, you will develop skill at briefing and will be able to produce a concise summary of cases. Ideally, a case brief should be one typed page, although longer and more complex cases may require a longer brief.

Figure 4-6
Note-Taking Abbreviations

To be efficient, you need to develop a system of abbreviations for taking notes on the job or when briefing cases. Although there are some common legal and general symbols, any symbol or abbreviation will be satisfactory so long as you understand it.

Figure 4-6 *(Continued)*

Legal Abbreviations and Symbols	
Π	plaintiff
Δ	defendant
§	section
K	contract
Atty	attorney
Cert	certiorari
Dep	deposition, deponent
J, J'ment	judgment
JNOV	judgment notwithstanding the verdict
Re:	regarding
SJ	summary judgment
S/F	statute of frauds
S/L	statute of limitations
v., vs.	versus, as opposed to, against

There is no one perfect form for a case brief. Some large law firms provide suggested formats. If no form is given to you, use a style that best suits your purpose and helps you understand the case and its significance as a precedent for the research problem on which you are working. Read through a case at least once before you begin to brief it so you will have a general idea as to the nature of the issues involved and how the court resolved these issues. Resist the temptation to read only the headnotes or to skim the case. A close scrutiny of the case may reveal critical analysis likely to be overlooked in a cursory reading. See Figure 4-7 for some reading strategies.

It may take you several readings of a case to understand it thoroughly. You may need to take notes and prepare a diagram or flowchart showing the path the case followed in reaching this court and the relationship of the parties to each other.

2. *Elements of Case Briefs*

The most common elements to be included in a case brief are the following:

- **Case Name.** Give the case name following *Bluebook* or *ALWD* rules or as it appears in the running head on the top of each page of the case.
- **Citations.** All parallel citations should be included, as well as the year of decision. These citations will enable you to retrieve the case later if you need to locate it. Use correct citation form.
- **Procedural History.** A *procedural history* describes how the case got to this court and how this court resolves the case. It will be significant whether the prior decision is a trial court decision or an

> ***Practice Tip:*** *Determining Procedural History*
>
> Westlaw has added a new feature called "Graphical History" to allow you to view the procedural background of cases. When you access a case on Westlaw, click on "Direct History (Graphical View)," which will be displayed on the screen. You will be given a flowchart, showing the path a case has followed through the courts. These easy-to-understand timelines display in graphical manner, with boxes and arrows, a case's route through the court system, allowing you to visually grasp a case's procedural history. Although LexisNexis does not show the procedural history of a case in a flowchart format, it includes a brief description of a case's subsequent and prior history when a case is displayed on the screen.

Figure 4-7
Case Reading Strategies

Consider the following strategies to help you better understand the cases you read and to help prepare case briefs.

- During your first reading, review the headnotes and the case. Focus on who the parties are and what relief they wanted from the court. Ask, "What is the plaintiff's gripe?" and "What is the defendant's defense?"
- Figure out what happened at the court(s) below, and then determine what this reviewing court's decision is. Knowing the court's decision in advance will help you make sense of the case when you read it more thoroughly.
- Look for clues. Watch for language in the court's opinion such as "it is critical to note that," "although we have previously held that," and other signals that what follows such expressions is key to the court's decision.
- Look up all Latin terms or phrases and any words you don't understand.

appellate court decision. Briefly identify the parties, describe the nature of the action, the relief sought, and defenses raised. Then state what the court(s) below held and the final disposition by this reviewing court. In many instances, the procedural history or background can be summed up in one or two sentences.

> ***Example:*** The case was appealed by the defendant employer to the Florida District Court of Appeals after a trial court awarded monetary damages to the plaintiff employee for sexual harassment. The Florida District Court of Appeals affirmed the decision of the trial court.

•**Statement of Facts.** A case brief should include a concise summary of the facts of the case. You need not include all facts but rather only the significant facts relied on by the court in reaching its decision. Facts that affect the outcome of a case are called *relevant* or *material facts*. Identify the parties by name and indicate whether a party is a plaintiff, defendant, and so forth. The facts are more readable if they are presented in a narrative rather than outline or "bullet" format. Discuss facts in the past tense. A chronological presentation of the facts is usually the most helpful to the reader; however, if the facts have no temporal relationship to each other, consider grouping the facts by topic or by the claims or causes of action presented by the plaintiff. Tell the story in plain English. If certain facts are disputed, indicate such. Some individuals prefer to place the statement of facts after the case name and citations (and before the procedural history). Providing the statement of facts first may aid comprehension of a case's procedural history (especially if the procedural history is complex).

•**Issue(s).** You must formulate the question(s) or issue(s) being decided by this court. Focus on what the parties asked to court to determine. In some instances, courts will specifically state the issues being addressed, using language such as, "The issue we are called upon to decide is whether . . . ." In other instances, the issues are not expressly provided, and you will have to formulate the issue being decided. Phrase the issue so that it has some relevance to the case at hand. Thus, rather than stating the issue in a broad fashion, such as, "What is an assault?", state the issue so it incorporates some of the relevant facts of the case, such as, "Does a conditional threat constitute an assault?" Keep your issues or questions to one sentence in length.

If you have trouble determining the issue, locate the rule that the court announces and then convert this into question form.

> ***Example of rule:*** The goodwill of a celebrity is a marital asset that can be evaluated and distributed in a divorce.
>
> ***Example of issue:*** Is a celebrity's goodwill acquired during a marriage a property asset that can be evaluated and distributed in a divorce?

In any event, the issue should be phrased so that it can be answered "yes" or "no." If there are several issues, number each one. Do not number a single issue.

There are three ways issues can be phrased: a direct question, the "whether" format, or the "under" format. A direct question might ask, "Is pointing an unloaded gun at a person an assault?" The "whether" format would phrase the same question as follows: "Whether pointing an unloaded gun at a person is an assault." The "under" format would result in the following phrasing: "Under California law, is pointing an unloaded gun at a person an assault?" Generally, any of these formats is acceptable, although some attorneys dislike the "whether" form of issue because it produces a fragment rather than a complete sentence. Pick one format and use it for all of your issues.

•**Answer(s)** or **Holding(s).** Provide an answer(s) to the question(s) you phrased. Rather than merely stating "yes" or "no," phrase the answer in a complete sentence and incorporate some of the reasons for the answer.

> ***Example:*** *A* conditional threat does not constitute an assault because a condition negates a threat so that the hearer is in no danger of immediate harm.

If you have set forth three issues, you will need three separate answers. Each answer should be no more than two sentences in length. Do not include citations.

•**Reasoning.** The reasoning is the most important part of a brief. This is the section in which you discuss *why* the court reached the conclusions it did. Were prior cases relied upon? Did the court adopt a new rule of law? Did the court discuss any social policy that would be served by its decision? Fully discuss the reasons why the court reached its decision and the thought process by which it arrived at this decision. Make sure you apply the court's reasoning to the facts of your case. Re-read your questions and then ensure that the reasoning section is directly responsive to the questions you framed. Citations may be included in this section, but are often not necessary. Use your own words in summarizing and explaining the court's reasoning rather than over-quoting from the case. This will help ensure that you understand the rationale for the court's decision. Don't be concerned that there will be some repetition in your case brief. As you have seen, the brief answer or holding nearly parrots the language of the issue. The same or similar language will then reappear as part of your reasoning section. A case brief is not meant to be a thrilling work of literature. It is meant to help you develop your analytical skills and provide a convenient summary of a case.

•**Holding.** Include the actual disposition of this case, such as "The Idaho Supreme Court affirmed the decision of the Appellate Court."

No matter what their format, good case briefs share the following elements:

- They use complete sentences.
- They do not overquote from the opinion.
- They do not include unnecessary or distracting citations.
- They do not include the writer's personal opinions.
- They are brief, ideally one page in length.

See Figure 4-8 for a sample case brief, briefing *State v. Boyd,* the case shown as Figure 4-1.

Figure 4-8
Sample Case Brief

State v. Boyd,
595 S.E.2d 697 (N.C. Ct. App. 2004)

Procedural History

Defendant Boyd was convicted of conspiracy to sell a controlled substance but acquitted of the crimes of sale of a controlled substance, contributing to the delinquency of a minor, and employing and using a minor to commit a controlled substance offense. He appealed his conviction and sentence. The Court of Appeals affirmed.

Statement of Facts

Defendant was convicted of conspiracy to sell crack cocaine. The evidence at trial showed that Defendant supplied the cocaine to a minor, Hampton, who actually conducted the sale to undercover police officers. At the close of the State's evidence, Defendant's attorney did not move to dismiss the conspiracy charge but did move to dismiss all other charges. Counsel renewed all motions at the conclusion of all evidence. The motions were denied. The jury convicted Defendant of the conspiracy charge and acquitted him of the remaining charges. In sentencing the Defendant, the trial judge found as an aggravating factor that Defendant involved a person under the age of 16 in the commission of a crime.

Issues

1. May Defendant appeal his conspiracy conviction if he did not make a motion to dismiss the conspiracy charge at trial?
2. If Defendant is acquitted of certain charges relating to a minor, may the minor's age be considered as an aggravating sentencing factor when Defendant is sentenced for conspiring with a minor to sell a controlled substance?

Answers

1. No. A Defendant may not attack on appeal the sufficiency of evidence at trial unless he makes a motion to dismiss at trial.
2. Yes. A trial court may consider any aggravating factors that it finds proved by a preponderance of evidence that are reasonably related to the purposes of sentencing.

Reasoning

North Carolina's rules of appellate procedure provide that to preserve an issue for appeal, a defendant must make a motion to dismiss the action at

Figure 4-8 *(Continued)*

trial. Because defendant's counsel moved to dismiss all charges against Defendant *except* the conspiracy charge at the close of the State's case, at the close of all evidence, he could not renew a nonexistent motion. Thus, the appellate court was precluded from reviewing the merits of Defendant's argument.

If a defendant is acquitted of a crime, it cannot be used as an aggravating sentencing factor. In this case, Defendant was convicted of conspiracy to sell a controlled substance; thus, Defendant and Hampton were conspirators. Moreover, the parties expressly stipulated that Hampton was a minor. Thus, the trial court could consider Hampton's age as an aggravating sentencing factor when sentencing Defendant on the conspiracy count.

Holding

The Court of Appeals affirmed the conviction and sentence.

The preceding brief follows a very standard format. A more thorough brief would include the name of the author of the majority opinion, a reference to how many justices were in the majority and how many dissented (for example, 5-2), a summary of any dissenting and concurring opinions, a summary of each party's contentions and legal arguments, a discussion of social policies furthered by the decision, and a final section including your comments and criticism of the case. In most instances, such a thorough brief is not needed, and the format shown above should suffice for most purposes.

After you have gained experience in case briefing, you may be able to use a technique some experts refer to as *Technicolor briefing,* in which you use colored pens and highlighters to mark sections of cases as you read them. You will photocopy or print the cases you need to brief and annotate the critical sections in the margins. For example, use "PH" to mark the procedural history section, "I" to mark the issue the court is deciding, and so forth. In law school, this technique is usually called *book briefing* because you brief the cases in your casebooks by these notes rather than preparing a separate brief.

***Help Line:** Briefing Cases*

Westlaw provides an interesting and informative article titled *How to Write a Brief* by attorney Dana L. Blatt at its website at http://lawschool.westlaw.com/highcourt/HowToBrief.doc. The article includes tips and pointers on writing various types of briefs and includes sample briefs as well.

Case Brief Assignment

Prepare a brief of the case *Kirk v. Harter*, 188 F.3d 1005 (8th Cir. 1999).

L. Citation Form

	Bluebook (for practitioners)	*ALWD*
United States Supreme Court Cases	*Roe v. Wade*, 410. U.S. 113 (1973).	*Roe v. Wade*, 410. U.S. 113 (1973). (Parallel citations are permitted but disfavored.)
United States Courts of Appeal Cases	*Scorteanu v. INS*, 339 F.3d 407 (6th Cir. 2003).	*Scorteanu v. INS*, 339 F.3d 407 (6th Cir. 2003).
United States District Court Cases	*Trent Partners v. Digital Corp.*, 120 F. Supp. 2d 84 (D. Mass. 1999).	*Trent Partners v. Digital Corp.*, 120 F. Supp. 2d 84 (D. Mass. 1999).
State Court Cases (when parallel citations are required)	*Graniteville Co. v. Williams*, 209 S.C. 112, 39 S.E.2d 202 (1946).	*Graniteville Co. v. Williams*, 209 S.C. 112, 39 S.E.2d 202 (1946).
State Court Cases (when parallel citations are not required)	*Graniteville Co. v. Williams*, 39 S.E.2d 202 (S.C. 1946).	*Graniteville Co. v. Williams*, 39 S.E.2d 202 (S.C. 1946).

***Practice Tip:** Formulating Issues in Case Briefs*

To gain experience in formulating issues for case briefs and other court documents, review the briefs filed with the U.S. Supreme Court and examine the "Questions Presented." The Supreme Court requires all petitions for writs of certiorari and all principal briefs to set forth the questions the Court is asked to review. Examine these questions to sharpen your skills at writing your own issue statements. The briefs may be accessed through the Court's website at http://www.supremecourtus.gov. Select "Merit Briefs."

CyberSites

http://www.uscourts.gov	U.S. Courts provide links to federal courts and information about the federal court system.
http://www.supremecourtus.gov	The website of the United States Supreme Court provides information about the Court, its docket, Court rules, and access to its opinions and to briefs filed with the court.
http://scholar.google.com	Google Scholar offers free and easy access to federal and state court cases. Search by case name or topic.
http://www.loc.gov/law/guide	This site, called Guide to Law Online, provides access to cases from the federal courts as well as links for state cases.
http://www.washlaw.edu	Washburn University School of Law's site offers links to federal and state cases as well as links to numerous excellent law-related sites.
http://www.findlaw.com	FindLaw, one of the best-known legal sites, provides easy access to federal and state cases as well as to a wide variety of other law-related information and links to other sites.
http://www.lawschool.westlaw.com	Westlaw's site for law students offers a guide to briefing cases. Select "Survival Guide" and then "Briefing Cases" or access the site http://lawschool.westlaw.com/highcourt/HowToBrief.doc.

Research Assignment

1. What is the name of the case at 533 F.2d 1106, and what issue does this case deal with, generally?
2. Review volume 957 of P.2d. Which case in this volume construes the meaning of the term "strict elements test"?
3. Review volume 968 S.W.2d. Which case in this volume construes Texas Family Code § 156.301?
4. Give the name of the case and the author of the opinion for the case located at 546 U.S. 1 (2005).
5. a. Give the name of the case at 714 N.E.2d 830.
   b. Give the parallel citation for this case.
   c. Give the date of argument and date of decision for this case.
   d. What does headnote 1 discuss?
6. Give the name of the case at 522 F. Supp. 2d 204 (D.D.C. 2007) and indicate why the U.S. government wished to seize the real property.
7. a. Give the name of the case at 221 F.R.D. 545 (W.D. Wash. 2004).
   b. Describe the defendant.
   c. Use this volume. Which case in this volume construes the phrase "excusable neglect"?
8. Give the parallel citations for the case located at 120 S. Ct. 467.
9. a. Give the name of the case at 255 F.R.D. 151 (D.N.J. 2008).
   b. Describe or identify the defendants.
   c. What New York case is cited near the end of the opinion (in footnote 38)?
10. Locate *Spencer v. OPM*, 95 F. App'x 352 (D. Del. 2004). What two notes or warnings are given before the case name?
11. Give the name of the case located at:
    a. 772 A.2d 1179.
    b. 897 N.E.2d 322.
    c. 133 P.3d 645.
12. Locate the case at 449 F. Supp. 2d 1. How many headnotes are there in this case? Give the name of the case.
13. Locate the case at 125 S. Ct. 551. How does page 176 of the parallel *United States Reports* begin?
14. Locate the case at 163 L. Ed. 2d 429. How does page 119 of the parallel *United States Reports* begin?
15. Locate the case at 98 Cal. Rptr. 2d 431. How does page 903 of the parallel *California Reports* begin?

16. Locate the case at 503 S.E.2d in which the defendant's name is *Spires*.
    a. Give the citation.
    b. Who represented the appellant in this case?
    c. Who was the Chief Judge of the Georgia Court of Appeals during the period of time covered by this volume?
    d. Which case in this volume construes West Virginia Code § 38-3-18?

17. Give the parallel citations for *People v. Coffman*, 34 Cal. 4th 1 (2004).

18. Give the name of the case located at 645 F. Supp. 141 (D. Del. 1986), identify what type of entity the defendant is, and give a brief description of the case.

19. How many headnotes are provided in the case located at 449 F. Supp. 2d 1 (D.D.C. 2006)?

20. Use the *National Reporter Blue Book* (2009 Cumulative Supplement—or newer), and give the parallel citations for the following cases:
    a. 359 N.C. 65.
    b. 280 Kan. 890.
    c. 163 Ohio App. 3d 567.
    d. 349 Md. 419 (use the 2000 Permanent Supplement).

Internet Assignment

1. Access the U.S. Supreme Court website and locate "Opinions," specifically, "2007 Term Opinions of the Court."
    a. Review the case with the docket number 07-290. Give the name of the case.
    b. In which volume of the *United States Reports* will the case be published?
    c. Who dissented in this case?

2. Access the U.S. Supreme Court website, and review the Chief Justice's Year-End Report on the Federal Judiciary for 2008.
    a. Give the percentage of the decrease in total number of case filings in the United States Supreme Court in the 2007 Term.
    b. Did civil filings in the District Courts increase or decrease in 2007? Why?

3. Access the site WashLaw (Washburn University School of Law).
    a. Select "Arizona" and review decisions of the Court of Appeals, Division One. Access the civil cases and review the decision for November 29, 2007 (docket number CV-07-0256). Give the name of the case and briefly give the holding.

b. Select "North Carolina" and review North Carolina Supreme Court opinions for 2008. Locate the case 362 N.C. 514. Give the name of the case and indicate what headnote 7 discusses.

4. Access the site MegaLaw and locate opinions from the Sixth Circuit Court of Appeals. Review the 2007 case assigned docket number 05-6575.
   a. Give the name of the case.
   b. What are the first words printed at the top of this case?
   c. Briefly, why were the defendant police officers granted qualified immunity in this case?

5. Access Google Scholar and search for cases relating to the display of a nativity scene at Christmas.
   a. What is the first case to which you are directed?
   b. How many times has this case been cited?
   c. Access the case. Who delivered the opinion of the Court?

Chapter 5

Locating Cases Through Digests and Annotated Law Reports

Chapter Overview

This chapter completes the discussion of the primary authorities previously introduced (statutes, constitutions, and cases) by explaining the use of digests, which serve as comprehensive casefinders. Additionally, you will be introduced to annotated law reports, which can "speed up" the research process and provide you with an exhaustive treatment of an area of the law. Digests and annotated law reports help you find cases on point.

A. Using Digests to Locate Cases

1. *Introduction*

Although you know that you can locate cases by using a citation or annotated codes (which send you to cases interpreting statutes), some cases do not interpret statutes and thus cannot be found through the use of annotated codes such as U.S.C.A. or U.S.C.S. One way to find cases is through the use of sets of books called *digests*. Digests serve as comprehensive casefinders. They arrange cases by subject matter so that, for example, all of the battery cases are brought together and all of the contracts cases are brought together. These digests do not reprint in full all of the battery cases, however, but rather print a brief one-sentence summary or "digest" of each battery case and then provide you with a citation so you can determine whether to retrieve and read the case. In this way, digests serve as guideposts, which help direct you to the specific cases you need so you can research as efficiently and effectively as possible. Because the digests are written by publishers (primarily West) and are mere summaries of cases, the digest entries cannot be quoted from or relied upon. The cases the digests direct you to, however, will serve as binding authority.

2. *West's* American Digest System

Although there are several varieties of digests, all of them function in a similar manner. Most are published by West, which realized shortly after it introduced its *National Reporter System* that legal professionals needed a method of finding the cases published therein. The most comprehensive digest set published by West is called the *American Digest System*. Once you understand how to use this digest set, you will be able to use all other West digests because they are all organized in the same manner.

The *American Digest System* is an amazingly thorough set of books that aims at citing and digesting every reported case so you can readily locate *all* cases on a given area of law, such as deeds, fraud, or wills.

Almost all West publications show pictures of keys, which inform the reader that the set is a participant in the West digest system, sometimes called the *Key Number System*.

3. *Organization of the* American Digest System

West has categorized all of American case law into various topics. In fact, West has created more than 400 topic names for areas of law (for example, Corporations, Negligence, and Trespass) and has assigned various numbers, called *Key Numbers*, to these areas of law. As an editor at West receives a case from a court, the editor reads the case, divides it into separate issues of law, each of which is represented by a headnote number, and then assigns each of the headnotes one of West's more than 400 topic names and a Key Number (which includes an image of a key and a number). If the case discusses seven areas of law, it will have seven headnotes. If the case discusses 12 areas of law, it will have 12 headnotes. These headnotes are the brief paragraphs that precede the opinion of the court in a published case. Each headnote is thus given a consecutive number, a topic name (for example, Covenants, Insurance, Venue) based on the area of law the headnote deals with, and a Key Number. For example, West might assign the topic name and Key Number **Landlord & Tenant 166** to a case dealing with injury to a tenant's property in leased premises. Every time thereafter that any portion of a case reported in the *National Reporter System* discusses injury to a tenant's property in leased premises, West will create a headnote for the case and assign it the topic name and Key Number **Landlord & Tenant 166.** If a headnote deals with more than one topic, West might assign more than one topic name and Key Number. There are approximately 100,000 Key Numbers used by West in its *Key Number System*. See Figure 4-1 for depictions of keys, topic names, and Key Numbers in a published case.

West then gathers all of the headnotes into the *American Digest System*, allowing researchers to readily find numerous cases from all over the country that deal with the same issue. The *American Digest System* comprises sets of books that each cover ten-year periods called *Decennials*.

Thus, the *Tenth Decennial* (*Parts 1* and *2*) covers the time period 1986-1996, the *Ninth Decennial* (*Parts 1* and *2*) covers the time period 1976-1986, and so forth, back to the *First Decennial*, which covers the time period 1897-1906. Note that West has also created a set of books called the *Century Digest* to cover the time period 1658-1897 (the date coverage of the *First Decennial* commences). The *Century Digest* uses a classification scheme different from the *Key Number System* used in the *Decennials*. It is unlikely that you will use the *Century Digest* very often, if ever, as it digests cases that are very old. Figure 5-1 shows the time period covered by each of the *Decennials*.

As you can see, starting in 1976, West began issuing the *Decennials* in two five-year parts (and recently began issuing Decennials in three parts). This change was brought about by the explosion in case law.

General Digest is the name of the set of books currently in use. As soon as the next appropriate time period is completed, the name of the *General Digest, 12th Series* will likely change to *Twelfth Decennial, Part 1*, and the current set will then be called the *General Digest, 13th Series*.

It is not necessary to memorize the time periods covered by each *Decennial* unit. It is sufficient to understand the general structure of the *Decennial* units: Each *Decennial* covers a ten-year period and each *Decennial* will contain all of the headnotes from all of the units of the *National Reporter System* for its particular ten-year period. In fact, the term "Decennial" may well be a term of art as West has adjusted its publishing schedule to keep up with the rapid growth in the number of published cases.

4. *Locating a Topic and Key Number*

Assume you are asked to research whether a tenant may recover damages from her landlord when the tenant's valuable rug is ruined by rain caused by a leak in the roof at the leased premises. Further assume that you need to find cases from all over the United States on this issue. There are four strategies you can use to locate a topic and Key Number that you can then use to find on-point cases.

a. Descriptive Word Approach

Each of the *Decennial* units includes volumes titled "Descriptive Word Index" and which are usually placed at the end of the respective *Decennial* set. Use the Descriptive Word research approach and look up words in this index that describe your research problem (for example, landlord, tenant, leased premises, and so forth). Use the Descriptive Word Index exactly as you do the indexes for U.S.C.A. and U.S.C.S. as described in Chapter Three. Think of words and phrases that describe the problem you are researching and then look up these words in any Descriptive Word Index. You will be given your topic name (**Landlord & Tenant**) andyour Key Number (**166**).

Figure 5-1
Coverage of Decennial Units

Century Digest	1658-1897
First Decennial	1897-1906
Second Decennial	1907-1916
Third Decennial	1916-1926
Fourth Decennial	1926-1936
Fifth Decennial	1936-1946
Sixth Decennial	1946-1956
Seventh Decennial	1956-1966
Eighth Decennial	1966-1976
Ninth Decennial, Part 1	1976-1981
Ninth Decennial, Part 2	1981-1986
Tenth Decennial, Part 1	1986-1991
Tenth Decennial, Part 2	1991-1996
Eleventh Decennial, Part 1	1996-2001
Eleventh Decennial, Parts 2 and *3*	2001-2004
General Digest, 12th Series	2004-Date

If you have difficulty thinking of words to use, think of synonyms (renter), antonyms (owner), defenses a party might assert (waiver), the type of relief a party might seek (damages, injunctive relief, rescission of the lease), or the cause of action a plaintiff might assert (breach of contract). These should assist you in thinking of words to look up in the index. Just as you have seen with the indexes for U.S.C.A. and U.S.C.S., the Descriptive Word Indexes in the *American Digest System* are very "forgiving." Many topics are indexed under more than one entry, making it easy for you to locate the all-important topic name and Key Number.

When starting a research problem, use the Descriptive Word Index to one of the newer *Decennial* units, such as the *Eleventh Decennial Digest, Parts 1, 2*, or *3*. If you cannot locate a topic name and a Key Number in this *Decennial* unit (perhaps because no cases discussed your particular legal issue during the time period covered by the *Eleventh Decennial Digest, Parts 1, 2*, or *3*), try the *Tenth Decennial Digest*, and so forth.

The Descriptive Word method is the easiest and most reliable way of locating a topic name and a Key Number, and this should be the approach you use until you have become thoroughly familiar with West's *Key Number System*. In fact, West advises that this method of search will generally prove most useful and should always be used first unless the researcher knows a specific topic. See Figure 5-2 for a sample page from the Descriptive Word Index to the *Ninth Decennial Digest, Part 2*, which demonstrates how to locate a topic name and Key Number through the Descriptive Word approach.

Figure 5-2
Sample Page from Descriptive Word Index

43-9th D Pt 2—77

LANDLORD — Guide Word

LANDLORD AND TENANT—Cont'd
GUIDE dogs, waiver of pet restriction inapplicable to dog neither trained nor used as guide dog. **Land & Ten 134(1)**
HABITABILITY. **Land & Ten 125**
Implied warranty—
Coextensive with Residential Rental Agreements Act. **Land & Ten 125(1)**
HEALTH regulations, see this index **Health and Environment**
HEAT, see this index **Heat**
HEAT violation, notice as condition precedent to prosecution. **Health & E 39**
HOLDING over—
Damages—
Landlord's proper measure of damages for tenant's willful holdover. **Land & Ten 144**
Estoppel, effect on. **Land & Ten 62(4)**
Extension by. **Land & Ten 90**
Month to month tenancy. **Land & Ten 115(3)**
Renewal by. **Land & Ten 90**
Rent, amount while holding over. **Land & Ten 200.9**
Sufficiency to create new tenancy. **Land & Ten 90(4)**
Tenancy at sufferance, creation by. **Land & Ten 119(2)**
Tenancy at will, creation by. **Land & Ten 118(4)**
Year-to-year tenancy. **Land & Ten 114(3)**
HOMESTEAD, see this index **Homestead**
HOMICIDE conviction arising from death of tenant's guest—
Due process guarantees. **Const Law 258(3)**
HOTELS—
Duties owed to renter's patrons—
Providing guard for coat rack. **Inn 11(3)**
HUNTING rights. **Land & Ten 134(3)**
HUSBAND and wife—
Lease of community property. **Hus & W 267(3)**
Administration of community. **Hus & W 276(6)**
Separate property of wife, see this index **Separate Estate of Wife**
ICE and snow—
Generally, see this index **Ice and Snow**
ILLUSORY tenancy—
Effect—
Protecting against speculative profiteering by tenants of rent controlled apartment. **Land & Ten 278.4(6)**
Summary proceedings to dispossess, right to maintain. **Land & Ten 298(1)**
ILLUSORY tenants—
Entering into sublease in order to evade rent stabilization requirements. **Land & Ten 200.16**
IMPLIED contracts, see this index **Implied Contracts**
IMPLIED covenants. **Land & Ten 45**
IMPLIED tenancy, see this index **Implied Tenancy**
IMPROVEMENTS. **Land & Ten 150–161**
Actions. **Land & Ten 159**
Claims for. **Land & Ten 223(7)**

LANDLORD AND TENANT—Cont'd
IMPROVEMENTS—Cont'd
Compensation. **Land & Ten 157(6–8)**
Damages for failure to make. **Land & Ten 223(6)**
Lien. **Land & Ten 157(10)**
Ownership in general. **Land & Ten 157(2)**
Reimbursing tenant for repair of boiler made at request of tenant. **Impl & C C 40**
Remedy for failure to make. **Land & Ten 159**
Removal. **Land & Ten 157(4)**
INCOME tax, see this index **Income Tax**
INCUMBRANCES. **Land & Ten 145–149**
Reasonable rent, incumbrances as factor in determining. **Land & Ten 200.25**
INDEMNITY against liability for negligence. **Indem 8.1(2)**
INDORSEMENT, extension or renewal on lease. **Land & Ten 89**
INFANT'S property, lease of. **Infants 44**
INJUNCTION—
Assessing tenants nonrefundable rental fees. **Inj 136(2)**
Communication by tenant by signs or notices—
Free speech. **Const Law 90.1(1)**
Covenants as to use of leased premises. **Inj 62(2)**
Disturbance of possession of tenant. **Land & Ten 132(2)**
Preliminary injunction, tenant's consent to sale of building's air rights. **Inj 136(2)**
Summary proceedings. **Land & Ten 299**
Unlawful detainer, action for. **Land & Ten 290½**
Violation of laws relating to suspension of right of reentry and recovery of possession by landlord. **Land & Ten 278.16**
...**nd & Ten 55(4)**
INJURIES— — Subtopic Heading
...**d & Ten 139(4)**
Dangerous or defective condition. **Land & Ten 162–170**
Mobile home parks, see this index **Trailer Parks or Camps**
Employees of tenant. **Land & Ten 165, 169(5)**
Patrons of lessee—
Liability of lessee. **Land & Ten 167(8)**
Premises. **Land & Ten 140–142**
Eviction. **Land & Ten 176**
Property of tenant. **Land & Ten 166** — Topic Name and Key Number
...trance of trespassers and vandals. **Land & Ten 166(6)**
Property of third persons. **Land & Ten 167(9)**
Reversion. **Land & Ten 55**
Scalding of cleaning woman when steam pipe burst—
Liability of tenant. **Land & Ten 167(2)**
Tenants or occupants. **Land & Ten 164**
INNKEEPERS—
See this index **Innkeepers**

LANDLORD AND TENANT—Cont'd
INNKEEPERS—Cont'd
Membership in metropolitan hotel industry stabilization association. **Inn 2**
INSANE persons, see this index **Mental Health**
INSOLVENCY, termination of lease. **Land & Ten 101½**
INSURANCE—
Covenants to insure. **Land & Ten 156**
Insurable interest. **Insurance 115(4)**
Landlord's liability insurance—
Risks and causes of loss. **Insurance 435.34**
Nature and cause of injury or damage. **Insurance 435.35**
Lessee's good-faith efforts to obtain—
Preventing cancellation of lease. **Land & Ten 103(1)**
Right to proceeds. **Insurance 580(4)**
INTERFERENCE with—
Possession of tenant. **Land & Ten 131–133**
Relationship. **Land & Ten 19**
Use of premises. **Land & Ten 134(4), 172(2)**
INTERVENTION, see this index **Intervention**
INTOXICATING liquors, see this index **Intoxicating Liquors**
INTRUDER—
Lessor's liability for lessee's injuries inflicted by. **Land & Ten 164(1)**
INVALIDITY as affecting action for unlawful detainer. **Land & Ten 290(4)**
JOINT tenants, implied tenancy between. **Land & Ten 8**
JUDGMENT—
Conclusiveness. **Judgm 684**
Recovery of possession, action for. **Land & Ten 285(6)**
Summary proceedings for possession, post
Unlawful detainer, action for. **Land & Ten 291(17)**
JURISDICTION, see this index **Jurisdiction**
...
Justices of the Peace
KEY to leased premises, see this index **Keys**
KNOWLEDGE of defects affecting liability for injuries. **Land & Ten 164(6, 7), 165, 166(10)**
LACHES, affecting rescission of lease. **Land & Ten 34(4)**
LANDLORD'S title, estoppel dependent on. **Land & Ten 62(2)**
LARCENY of property from landlord or tenant, see this index **Larceny**
LEASES. **Land & Ten 20–49**
...
Bankruptcy proceedings. **Bankr 3086–3088**
Farm lease. **Land & Ten 322**
Female tenant's right to possession of apartment though not married to signing tenant—
Civil R 11.5
Land & Ten 43
Nonassignment clauses—
Restraints on alienation, policy against. **Perp 6(17)**
Protection leases—
Nature of. **Mines 56**

b. Topic Approach

Recall that in locating statutes, the topic approach calls for you to bypass the general index at the end of a set of statutes, and go directly to the appropriate title and begin examining the statutes. The topic approach for locating a topic name and a Key Number is exactly the same. Thus, if you were using the topic approach for the landlord–tenant problem described previously, you would bypass the Descriptive Word Index and go immediately to the "L" volume of a *Decennial* unit such as the *Eleventh Decennial Digest*, *Part 1*, and look up the phrase "Landlord and Tenant." Prior to the digest listing of the headnotes (**Landlord & Tenant 1, Landlord & Tenant 2,** and so on), you will be given an overview of the coverage of this topic, Landlord & Tenant, much like a book's table of contents. You can then scan the entries to determine the appropriate Key Number, and proceed to look up and examine the headnotes listed or digested under Landlord & Tenant. See Figure 5-3 for a sample page from the *Ninth Decennial Digest*, *Part 2*, showing a partial list of Key Numbers within the topic **Landlord & Tenant.**

Because West's *American Digest System* has more than 400 topics, the topic method of locating topic names and Key Numbers should be used only after you have become thoroughly familiar with West's Key Number classification system.

c. Table of Cases Approach

As an alternate research approach to the Descriptive Word approach, if you know the name of a case, you can look it up in an alphabetically arranged Table of Cases (which accompanies most *Decennial* units), and you will be given the citation(s) to the case and a list of the topics and Key Numbers under which it has been digested or classified.

d. "Case on Point" Approach

If you have already located a case on point, its headnotes will display applicable topic names and Key Numbers. If one of these headnotes is relevant to your research, you can then use that headnote to locate other similar cases by looking up your topic name and Key Number in the various units of the *Decennial Digest System*. For example, if you decide that the topic name and Key Number **Sentencing and Punishment 98** (see Figure 4-1) is critical to your research, you can simply look up this topic and Key Number in the various units of the *Decennial Digest System* to obtain similar and newer cases. Alternatively, you can sign onto Westlaw and search for other cases classified to your topic name and Key Number.

Figure 5-3
Sample Page from *Ninth Decennial Digest, Part 2*

29 9th D Pt 2—783

LANDLORD & TENANT — Topic name

VII. PREMISES, AND ENJOYMENT AND USE THEREOF.—Cont'd

(D) REPAIRS, INSURANCE, AND IMPROVEMENTS.

⇐150. Right and duty to make repairs in general.
(1). In general.
(2). Duty to rebuild on destruction of property.
(3). Landlord's right of entry to make repairs.
(4). Rights of subtenants.
(5). Right of tenant to repair at landlord's cost.
151. Statutory provisions.
152. Covenants and agreements as to repairs and alterations.
(1). In general.
(2). Consideration for agreement.
(3). Construction and operation of covenants in general.
(4). Nature of repairs included in covenant or agreement.
(5). Duty to rebuild on destruction of property.
(6). Right of landlord to notice that repairs are necessary.
(7). Agreement by landlord to pay for repairs.
(8). Rights and liabilities of assignees and subtenants.
(9). Waiver of claims under or stipulations in covenant or agreement.
(10). Right of tenant to repair and recover cost.
(11). Alterations by tenant.
153. Mode of making repairs.
154. Remedies for failure to make repairs and alterations.
(1). Nature and form of remedy.
(2). Right of action and defenses.
(3). Pleading and evidence.
(4). Damages.
(5). Trial.
155. Maintenance of boundaries and fences.
156. Covenants and agreements as to insurance.
157. Improvements by tenant and covenants therefor.
(1). Covenant by lessee to make improvements.
(2). Ownership of improvements in general.
(4). Right to remove and agreements for removal of improvements.
(5). Forfeiture or waiver of right to remove improvements.
(6). Right to compensation in general.
(7). Covenants and agreements to pay for improvements.
(8). Liabilities of successors of lessor.
(9). Mode of termination of tenancy as affecting right to compensation.
(10). Lien for value of improvements.
(11). Determination of compensation.
(12). Actions for compensation.
158. Improvements by landlord and covenants therefor.
159. Remedies for failure to make improvements.
(1). Actions for breach of tenant's covenant to make improvements.
(2). Actions for breach of landlord's covenant to make improvements.
160. Condition of premises at termination of tenancy.
(1). In general.
(2). Covenants and agreements as to condition of premises on termination of tenancy.
(3). Duty of tenant to rebuild or replace personal property.
(4). Actions for breach of covenant.
161. Personal property on premises at termination of tenancy.
(1). Rights and liabilities as to property on premises in general.
(2). Care of property left on premises by outgoing tenant.
(3). Actions to recover property or value.

(E) INJURIES FROM DANGEROUS OR DEFECTIVE CONDITION.

⇐162. Nature and extent of landlord's duty to tenant.
163. Mutual duties of tenants of different portions of same premises.
164. Injuries to tenants or occupants.
(1). Injuries due to defective or dangerous condition of premises in general.
(2). Injuries due to failure to repair.
(3). Injuries due to negligence in making repairs.
(4). Injuries due to unlighted passageways.
(5). Liability for injuries to subtenant.
(6). Liability of landlord as dependent on knowledge of defects.
(7). Notice to or knowledge of tenant as to defects.
165. Injuries to employé of tenant.
(1). Injuries due to defective or dangerous condition of premises in general.
(2). Injuries due to failure to repair.
(3). Injuries due to unlighted passageway.
(4). Liability of landlord as dependent on knowledge of defects.
(5). Failure to guard dangerous places.
(6). Operation or condition of elevators.
(7). Notice to or knowledge of tenant as to de-

166. Injuries to property of tenant on premises.
(1). Nature and extent of the duties of landlord and tenant respectively.
(2). Injuries due to defective condition of premises in general.
(3). Injuries due to failure to repair.
(4). Injuries due to negligence in making repairs.
(5). Injuries due to defective water pipes or drains.
(6). Injuries due to negligent acts of landlord.
(7). Injuries due to negligence of third persons in general.
(9). Injuries due to negligence of cotenant.
(10). Liability of landlord as dependent on knowledge or notice of defects.

Outline of topics and key numbers listed under "Landlord & Tenant"

(1). Duties of landlord and tenant to third persons.
(2). Injuries due to defective or dangerous condition of premises in general.
(3). Injuries due to failure to repair.
(4). Failure to light or guard dangerous places.
(5). Injuries due to openings, defects, or obstructions in walks or streets.
(6). Injuries caused by fall of snow or ice from roof.
(7). Injuries due to the negligence of tenant.

5. *Using Digests*

Once you have obtained a topic name and a Key Number, such as **Landlord & Tenant 166,** you merely look this up in the various units of the *American Digest System* and you will unlock the door to cases from 1658 until last month, all of which relate to injuries to a tenant's property.

Because the *Decennials* are arranged alphabetically, you simply retrieve the "L" volume in any of the *Decennial* units and look up **"Landlord & Tenant 166."** Topics are arranged in alphabetical order and Key Numbers within those topics are given in numerical order, making it as easy to use the *Decennials* as it is to use a dictionary. At this point, West will do more than merely list or digest the case headnotes in a haphazard fashion. West has carefully arranged the entries, giving you federal cases (from the United States Supreme Court, through cases from the United States Courts of Appeal to the lowest federal courts, the United States District Courts). After all of the federal cases have been digested, you will be given the entries for state court case. Again, West will order and list the states alphabetically, making it easy for you to locate cases from a certain state. West's listing of cases from a state will be in the order of the state's court hierarchy (listing cases from higher courts before those from lower courts) and then in reverse chronological order (listing newer cases before older cases). Consider browsing adjacent Key Numbers to determine if another Key Number may be helpful. See Figure 5-4 for a sample page from the *Ninth Decennial Digest, Part 2,* showing the organization of cases.

In looking up your topic name and Key Number in the *Decennial* units, you should start with the more recent *Decennial* units. If you cannot find the cases you need, proceed to examine earlier *Decennial* units.

6. *Other West Digests*

The *American Digest System* is most useful when conducting comprehensive research, because it covers all federal and state cases to the present time. If you do not need to conduct such thorough research, West has created several specialized digests that will assist you in locating cases from a specific jurisdiction, region, or state, all of which are organized identically to the *American Digest System.* The following specialized digests are kept up to date by annual cumulative pocket parts.

• ***United States Supreme Court Digest.*** This digest provides headnotes and references only to U.S. Supreme Court cases. A Table of Cases is included.

• **Federal Practice Digests.** West has created several digests that serve as casefinders for cases from the federal courts. Each digest covers

Figure 5-4
Sample Page from *Ninth Decennial Digest, Part 2,* Showing Digests of Cases

Note alphabetical arrangement of cases from states and arrangement from higher to lower courts within a state

🔑166. Injuries to property of tenant on premises.

Library references

C.J.S. Landlord and Tenant § 423 et seq.

🔑166(1). Nature and extent of the duties of landlord and tenant respectively.

Cal.App. 1 Dist. 1983. Where lessee of storage space was afforded option, by operator of space, of greater monthly payments under lease with insurance or of purchasing insurance elsewhere, and she was not subjected to an adhesive contract under which she had to accept exculpatory clause or forego lease, storage lease did not involve the public interest so as to render exculpatory clause in lease invalid under Civil Code section providing, inter alia, that all contracts which have as their object to exempt anyone from responsibility for his own fraud or willful injury to person or property of another are against policy of the law. West's Ann.Cal.Civ. Code § 1668.—Cregg v. Minister Ventures, 196 Cal.Rptr. 724, 148 C.A.3d 1107.

Cal.Super. 1982. Apartment building owners and managers had no affirmative duty to secure parking facilities, which they never represented as being protected, merely because they had notice of previous instances of vandalism to parked cars and thus tenant could not recover from owners and managers for destruction by fire of tenant's automobile in building parking area.—Jubert v. Shalom Realty, 185 Cal.Rptr. 641, 135 C.A.3d Supp. 1.

D.C.App. 1983. Exculpatory clause in lease which purported to relieve landlord of liability for personal property damage caused by any source, including defective roofing and plumbing, was ineffective to bar recovery of damages from landlord inasmuch as clause amounted to waiver or modification of tenant's rights under implied warranty of habitability.—George Washington University v. Weintraub, 458 A.2d 43.

Kan. 1982. Landlord, having leased premises in their entirety to tenants, did not have control over portion of premises wherein fire started and had no duty to inspect same, and thus failure of landlord to inspect wiring and failure to discover and correct latent defect on premises could not, as a matter of law, constitute negligence.—Moore v. Muntzel, 642 P.2d 957, 231 Kan. 46.

There were no warranties flowing from landlord to tenants on which liability for fire damage could be predicated.—Id.

La.App. 4 Cir. 1982. Alleged failure of lessee to present evidence of negligence by ultimate building owner or lessor had no effect on her right to recover for loss of personal property destroyed in fire at apartment under statutes which base liability on status, either as owner or lessor, rather than on personal fault. LSA-C.C. arts. 2322, 2695.—Barnes v. Housing Authority of New Orleans, 423 So.2d 750.

Minn.App. 1984. Lease provision exculpating landlords from liability for water damage was not ambiguous, even though contract's reference to "premises" varyingly referred to entire building or to first floor and basement.—Fena v. Wickstrom, 348 N.W.2d 389.

N.Y.A.D. 1982. Where the tenant had notice that water would be turned off in building on a Friday and knew that water would be turned on before he reopened his shop on the following Monday, and where building owner did not have access to tenant's premises, it was tenant's responsibility to be particularly careful in closing all the faucets, and his failure to do so was proximate and sole cause of flooding.—Arthur Richards, Inc. v. 79 Fifth Ave. Co., 450 N.Y.S.2d 13, 88 A.D.2d 517, reversed 455 N.Y.S.2d 596, 57 N.Y.2d 824, 441 N.E.2d 1114.

Pa. 1986. Exculpatory clause in commercial lease agreement relieving lessor of liability for injury or damage to personal property in premises caused by fire in any part of building of which demised premises was a part, was valid and enforceable; the clause did not contravene any policy of the law, commercial lease related entirely to parties' own private affairs, there was no disparity in bargaining power between parties, and clause, as modified, spelled out intention of parties with particularity.—Princeton Sportswear Corp. v. H & M Associates, 507 A.2d 339, 510 Pa. 189, appeal after remand 517 A.2d 963, 358 Pa.Super. 325.

Pa.Super. 1984. Exculpatory clauses in lease were valid and enforceable where lease was commercial lease, there was no disparity in bargaining power between the parties, exculpatory clauses had been reviewed, negotiated and modified by both parties and their counsel, and clauses, as modified, evidenced clear and unambiguous intent to release landlords from liability for damages caused by fire when such fire was not the result of any negligence on landlords' part.—Princeton Sportswear Corp. v. H & M Associates, 484 A.2d 185, 335 Pa.Super. 381, reversed 507 A.2d 339, 510 Pa. 189, appeal after remand 517 A.2d 963, 358 Pa.Super. 325.

Landlords were not liable for damages tenant suffered as result of fire which damaged building's power center and thereby deprived tenant of heat, electricity and water, where under exculpatory clauses in lease, it was clear that landlords were not liable for any property damage caused by fire in any portion of the building of which demised premises was a part unless such fire was caused by landlords' negligence, power center constituted portion of building in which demised premises was a part, and lower court specifically found that landlords' conduct was not tortious.—Id.

🔑166(2). Injuries due to defective condition of premises in general.

C.A.La. 1983. Not every defect in leased premises will serve as a basis for a claim of damages against lessor under Louisiana law; instead, vices and defects must be substantial and of such nature as are likely to cause injury to a reasonably prudent individual. LSA-C.C. art. 2695.—Volkswagen of America, Inc. v. Robertson, 713 F.2d 1151.

D.C.App. 1983. While landlords clearly bear burden of maintaining rented premises in compliance with housing code provisions, liability is not imposed upon landlords for losses arising from all conditions that violate the code.—George Washington University v. Weintraub, 458 A.2d 43.

Fla.App. 1 Dist. 1984. Lessee's complaint, which alleged making of the lease and lessor's covenant to keep the roof in good repair, the undertaking by lessor through services of a roofing contractor to keep the roof in good repair, a breach of that covenant by reason of the roof collapsing during course of repairs due either to defects in the structure or to overloading of the roof by the contractor, and resulting damages to lessee's property, was sufficient to state cause of action against lessor for breach of contract.—Cisu of Florida, Inc. for Use and Benefit of Aetna Cas. and Sur. Co. v. Porter, 457 So.2d 1118.

Ill.App. 1 Dist. 1985. Under common law, landlord is not liable for injury to property of tenant caused by defects in demised premises absent express warranty as to condition of premises or covenant to repair.—Wanland v. Beavers, 86 Ill.Dec. 130, 474 N.E.2d 1327, 130 Ill. App.3d 731.

Ill.App. 1982. Warranty of habitability implied in lease of building does not give rise to a cause of action for permanent injuries or property damage.—Auburn v. Amoco Oil Co., 61 Ill. Dec. 939, 435 N.E.2d 780, 106 Ill.App.3d 60.

La.App. 1 Cir. 1986. Lessee and its property insurer were not required to show negligence on the part of the lessor in order to recover damages resulting from a fire caused by a defect in the premises. LSA-C.C. arts. 2322, 2695.—Great American Surplus Lines Ins. Co. v. Bass, 486 So.2d 789, writ denied 489 So.2d 245.

Even if lessee assumed responsibility for the electricity, lessor was liable for damages resulting from the destruction of the lessee's property due to a fire caused by a defect in the building's electrical system where there was no proof of negligence on the part of the lessee and where the lessor knew or should have known of the defect. LSA-R.S. 9:3221.—Id.

La.App. 3 Cir. 1985. Under LSA-C.C. art. 2695, lessor is liable to lessee for any losses sustained as result of "vice and defects" in premises, provided they did not arise as result of lessee's fault.—Freeman v. Thomas, 472 So.2d 326.

La.App. 3 Cir. 1984. Mere fact that common wall between premises leased for jewelry store purposes and adjacent premises was constructed of sheetrock and thus susceptible to breach by burglars did not render the condition a "vice" under statute so as to render owner lessor liable to lessees for damages arising out of the burglary. LSA-C.C. arts. 2322, 2703.—Hall v. Park Dell Terrace Partnership, 452 So.2d 342.

La.App. 4 Cir. 1985. Tenant's allegation that security services provided by landlord were inadequate did not provide basis for landlord's liability for arson damage, where all security services promised in lease were provided.—U.S. Fidelity and Guar. Ins. Co. v. Burns Intern. Sec. Services, Inc., 468 So.2d 662, writ denied 470 So.2d 882.

Implied warranty of fitness for intended use and freedom from defects, applicable to leased office building, did not extend to fire damage caused by arson, in light of provisions in lease waiving landlord's liability for damage caused by fire or unauthorized persons.—Id.

La.App. 4 Cir. 1984. Clause in lease clearly and unambiguously transferred liability of lessor to lessee for damage caused by leaks in roof, and thus lessor and its managing partner could not be held liable to lessee for damage which occurred when roof of premises failed under the burden of a heavy rainstorm.—St. Paul Fire & Marine Ins. Co. v. French Eighth, 457 So.2d 35, writ denied 462 So.2d 195 and Oreck v. French Eighth, 462 So.2d 195, reconsideration not considered 462 So.2d 1240, two cases.

La.App. 4 Cir. 1983. Tenants of building destroyed by fire were entitled to recover damages from landlord, despite fact that defect in leased premises was alleged not to have been in building in which tenants leased premises, but within the building, owned by same landlord, next door to tenants' building, unless landlord could exculpate himself. LSA-C.C. arts. 660, 2322.—Broome v. Gauthier, 443 So.2d 1127, writ denied 445 So.2d 449.

N.J.Super.A.D. 1982. Exculpatory clause in commercial lease which exempted landlord from liability for damage or injury resulting from carelessness or negligence or improper conduct of landlord or others, but did not exclude liability for damage flowing from defective design and construction of major structural aspects of building, did not immunize landlord from liability for water damage to tenant's computer equipment caused by defective design of roof.—Ultimate Computer Services, Inc. v. Biltmore Realty Co., Inc., 443 A.2d 723, 183 N.J.Super. 144, 30 A.L.R.4th 963.

Where exculpatory clause did not clearly express intention to exclude liability for injuries resulting from improper construction, landlord, in a specific time period similar to the manner in which the *Decennials* each cover a ten-year period:

Federal Digest:	Federal Courts (1754-1938)
Modern Federal Practice Digest:	Federal Courts (1939-1961)
West's Federal Practice Digest 2d:	Federal Courts (1961-1975)
West's Federal Practice Digest 3d:	Federal Courts (1975-1984)
West's Federal Practice Digest 4th:	Federal Courts (1984-Date)

- **Regional Digests.** West has created the following regional digests, which allow researchers to locate cases from a given region: *Atlantic Digest, North Western Digest, Pacific Digest*, and *South Eastern Digest*.
- **State Digests.** West publishes state-specific digests for 47 of the states (Delaware, Nevada, and Utah are excluded) and the District of Columbia, allowing researchers to readily locate cases from a given state when such is sufficient for their research purposes. Cases from the pertinent state are included as well as cases from federal courts that pertain to that state's laws.
- **Other Specialized Digests.** West has created some specialized digests as well, such as the *Bankruptcy Digest*, *Military Justice Digest*, and the *Immigration Law Digest* to cover specialized areas of the law.

7. *Common Features of West's Digests*

a. Uniform Classification

All of West's digests are classified to West's uniform topic name and *Key Number System*. Thus, once a legal issue is assigned the topic name and Key Number **Landlord & Tenant 166,** any later cases that deal with this issue will also be digested under **Landlord & Tenant 166,** whether they appear in a *Decennial* unit, the *Pacific Digest*, or the *Ohio Digest*.

b. Descriptive Word Indexes

All of West's digests include Descriptive Word Indexes arranged in similar fashion that provide you with topic names and Key Numbers, which you then look up in the pertinent digest volumes. The indexes use words describing facts, places, things, and legal principles taken from actual cases.

c. Table of Cases

All of the West digests contain a Table of Cases by plaintiff so you may look up a case by the plaintiff's name and obtain parallel citations and the topic names and Key Numbers under which it has been digested. Some of

Practice Tips: *Using State and Regional Digests*

Because West's classification scheme for its *Key Number System* is uniform throughout the system, the process of locating cases from a state or region is identical to that of locating cases using a *Decennial*.

- Select the appropriate digest (for example, the *Atlantic Digest* or the *New York Digest*). Regional and state digests are usually found near the set of case books they cover.
- When researching, think small. Start with the smallest digest unit that will be helpful to you. For example, when researching Oregon law, start with the *Oregon Digest*. If it is not helpful, then review the *Pacific Digest*, and then the various *Decennial* units.
- Use the Descriptive Word Index to the set to determine your topic name and Key Number.
- Look up your topic name and Key Number in the appropriate volume in your digest set.
- Examine the entries.
- Update, as needed, using pocket parts or supplements, to find more recent cases.

the other digests (generally, the more recent ones) also include a Defendant-Plaintiff Table of Cases, listing the defendant's name first. These tables are usually located after the last volumes in a set.

d. Words and Phrases Volumes

The digest sets contain Words and Phrases volumes, which alphabetically list words and phrases that have been construed by cases. Thus, if you look up the word "conspiracy" in the *Florida Digest, 2d*, you will be given citations to the cases decided in Florida that define or interpret this word.

e. Supplementation

Many of the digests (including the regional and state digests) are kept current by annual cumulative pocket parts and supplemental pamphlets. The *American Digest System*, of course, is supplemented by the *General Digest*. If a pocket part or supplement exists, you must consult it to locate more recent cases and to determine if any new topics have been added. Additionally, the most current information is found in "back of the book" digest pages located in West's reporters (in both the hardbound volumes and their advance sheets). These volumes include "Key Number Digest" sections that catalog headnotes and Key Numbers for all cases in that volume.

Ethics Alert: *Using Digests*

Digests are wonderful sources to find cases; however, you may not cite to them, and you must read the cases to which you are directed. Never quote from or rely on the digest or summary of a case; you must read the case itself and analyze it. Only then may you cite it as authority.

f. Integrated Cross-Referencing

Because West's *Key Number System* is a truly integrated research approach, other West publications will give you topic names and Key Numbers, allowing easy access into the system. For example, as you read about an area of the law in West's encyclopedia *Corpus Juris Secundum*, you will be given the appropriate topic names and Key Numbers so that you can use these to find additional cases. Finally, the *Key Number System* is also used in West's computerized legal research system Westlaw. Thus, this cross-referencing by West continually helps you find all cases on a similar point of law.

8. *Other Digests*

Although West is the largest publisher of digests and while its *Key Number System* provides easy access to all reported cases relating to a particular legal issue, it is not the only publisher of digests. The best known of the non-West digests is the *United States Supreme Court Digest, Lawyer's Edition*, published by LexisNexis. This digest uses its own classification scheme to direct readers to U.S. Supreme Court cases. Use either the descriptive word approach or table of cases approach to access this digest. Because this digest is published by LexisNexis, it provides references to other LexisNexis publications.

There are also a few state digests published by companies other than West. These non-West digests also use their own classification schemes. Nevertheless, the basic system is the same: The researcher identifies topics and uses these to find citations to relevant cases.

B. *American Law Reports*

1. *Introduction*

American Law Reports ("A.L.R.") is a West product that publishes selected appellate court cases from all over the nation as well as comprehensive and objective essays relating to the legal issues raised in those cases. For this reason, A.L.R. forms a logical bridge between the primary sources (statutes, constitutions, and cases) that have been discussed, and the secondary sources (encyclopedias, treatises, and so forth) that will be discussed in the next chapters. A.L.R. combines features of primary sources (in that it publishes cases) with features of secondary sources (in that it publishes essays, called "annotations") that explain and expand upon the issues raised by the cases published in A.L.R.

West lawyer-editors review both state and federal appellate court decisions from all over the country and publish certain selected decisions that they believe are of widespread interest to legal professionals.

The significance of A.L.R. does not lie in the fact that it publishes cases. Many sets of reporters do that; the true value of A.L.R. lies in its scholarly and comprehensive articles (the *annotations*), which comment upon each case A.L.R. elects to publish. In fact, West states that the annotations "exhaustively evaluate every case on that point of law" and are the "most complete method to locate cases and understand that point of law."

If you are researching a certain area of the law and an A.L.R. annotation has been written on your topic, you should immediately retrieve the annotation and view it as "free research," as seldom, if ever, will you have the luxury of being able to devote as much time to an analysis of a legal topic as the A.L.R. editors have in their annotations.

2. *A.L.R. Organization*

A.L.R. is published in eight series and consists of more than 800 volumes:

A.L.R.	This 175-volume set covers federal cases and state appellate court cases decided between 1919-1948.
A.L.R.2d	This 100-volume set covers federal cases and state appellate court cases decided between 1948-1965.
A.L.R.3d	This 100-volume set covers state appellate court cases decided between 1965-1980 and federal cases decided between 1965-1969.
A.L.R.4th	This 90-volume set covers state appellate court cases from 1980-1991.
A.L.R.5th	This 125-volume set covers state appellate court cases from 1992-2005.
A.L.R.6th	This set was introduced in 2005 and covers state appellate court cases from 2005 to date.
A.L.R. Fed.	This 200-volume set was introduced in 1969 and exclusively covers federal cases from 1969-2005.
A.L.R. Fed. 2d	This set covers federal cases from 2005 to date.

A.L.R. is not published in advance sheets, and the first volumes that appear on the library shelves are hardbound.

3. *Features of A.L.R.*

Following are the current features of A.L.R., although not all features are found in the older sets.

- **Cases.** All of the volumes publish contemporary cases illustrating new developments or significant changes in the law. Each volume currently publishes about eight to ten cases. A brief synopsis of the case is provided together with headnotes summarizing the issues in the case.
- **Annotations.** A complete research brief or annotation is provided, analyzing all case law relating to the selected case and its topics. After approximately 1992, the cases analyzed are collected together in the back of each volume, following the annotations.
- **Research References.** A.L.R. will direct you to additional sources relating to the topic under discussion, including law review articles, texts, and encyclopedias. Additionally, you will be given suggestions for drafting electronic search queries so you can find additional information on LexisNexis and Westlaw, the computerized research systems. Finally, you are directed to West topic names and Key Numbers to find other similar cases.
- **Outline and Index.** An article outline is presented that shows how the annotation is organized so you can easily locate the sections of most interest to you. Similarly, an alphabetical index is presented, allowing you to quickly find the sections of the annotation that are most relevant to your research issue.
- **Table of Cases, Laws, and Rules.** Because you may be interested in the way in which certain jurisdictions have treated the topic under discussion, A.L.R. provides a table showing you which sections in the annotation discuss cases and statutes from individual states.
- **Scope Note.** Each annotation begins with a section or note titled "Scope," which briefly describes the matters discussed in the annotation and then refers to earlier annotations discussing the topic that are now superseded.
- **Related Annotations Section.** This section directs you to other A.L.R. annotations that might be of interest.
- **Summary.** Each annotation begins with a concise and useful summary of the entire annotation, setting the stage for the extensive research brief to follow. Additionally, annotations often contain "practice pointers," which provide practical tips on how to handle a case dealing with the topic under discussion.

See Figure 5-5 for features of A.L.R.

Figure 5-5
Sample Pages from A.L.R. Annotation Showing Features of Annotations

ANNOTATION

Annotation analyzes issues raised by leading case

EXHIBITION OF OBSCENE MOTION PICTURES AS NUISANCE

by

Jack W. Shaw, Jr., J.D.

Annotation outline/ scheme shows overall organization of annotation

TOTAL CLIENT-SERVICE LIBRARY® REFERENCES

4 Am Jur 2d, Amusements and Exhibitions § 37; 50 Am Jur 2d, Lewdness, Indecency and Obscenity § 26

18 Am Jur Pl & Pr Forms (Rev ed), Nuisances §§ 1 et seq.

8 Am Jur Proof of Facts 527, Nuisances; 18 Am Jur Proof of Facts 465, Obscenity—Motion Pictures

10 Am Jur Trials 1, Obscenity Litigation

ALR Digests, Amusements, etc. § 1; Indecency, etc. § 3

US L Ed Digests, Amusements, etc. § 1; Indecency, etc. § 1

ALR Quick Index, Amusements, Exhibitions, Shows and Resorts; Indecency, Lewdness, and Obscenity; Motion Pictures; Nuisances

Federal Quick Index, Amusements and Exhibitions; Lewdness, Indecency, and Obscenity; Motion Pictures; Nuisances

TCSL provides references to other helpful sources (no longer, provided)

Consult POCKET PART in this volume for later case service

4. *Finding A.L.R. Annotations*

a. Index or Descriptive Word Approach

A multi-volume alphabetical index called *A.L.R. Index* will direct you to annotations in all A.L.R. volumes. Using this index is similar to using any other—use the descriptive word approach and look up words or phrases that describe the problem you are researching, and you will be directed to the appropriate annotation. Be sure to check the pocket parts located in the back of each volume. See Figure 5-6 for a sample page from the *A.L.R. Index*.

West also provides a one-volume softcover index called *Quick Index*, which is easy to use and directs you to annotations in A.L.R.3d, A.L.R.4th, A.L.R.5th, and A.L.R.6th. The *Quick Index* does not provide as much detail as the multi-volume *A.L.R. Index*, but it is a useful starting place for many research problems. A similar index, the *A.L.R. Federal Quick Index*, will direct you to annotations dealing with federal law collected in A.L.R. Fed. and A.L.R. Fed. 2d.

b. Digest Approach

The A.L.R. Digest, a 20-volume set, organizes the law into more than 400 topics, presented alphabetically. For example, if you look up the word "nuisance" in the A.L.R. Digest, you will be given detailed summaries of the various annotations dealing with this topic. A.L.R.'s digest is "synched" into West's *Key Number System*, so that if you have a Key Number, you can easily locate any companion annotation (and vice versa). The Digest is kept current by annual pocket parts.

c. Miscellaneous Approaches

Many other sets of books refer to A.L.R. annotations. For example, the legal encyclopedia Am. Jur. 2d (discussed in Chapter Six) routinely directs readers to A.L.R. annotations. Similarly, when you update cases to make sure they are still good law by Shepardizing (using LexisNexis) or KeyCiting (using Westlaw), you will be informed whether the case has been published in A.L.R. and whether any A.L.R. annotations mention your case. A.L.R. annotations are also available on LexisNexis and Westlaw.

5. *Updating A.L.R. Annotations*

You must always update any annotation you read to make sure that the annotation remains an accurate interpretation of the law and to find newer cases and annotations relating to the topic you have researched. The process of updating A.L.R. annotations varies, depending on how old the annotation is.

Figure 5-6
Sample Page from *A.L.R. Index*

NUISANCES—Cont'd

Lewdness, indecency, and obscenity —Cont'd
- porno shops or similar places disseminating obscene materials as nuisance, 58 ALR3d 1134

Life tenant's right of action for injury or damage to property, 49 ALR2d 1117

Lights and lighting, casting of light on another's premises as constituting nuisance, 5 ALR2d 705

Limitation of actions, when statute of limitations begins to run as to cause of action for nuisance based on air pollution, 19 ALR4th 456

Liquors, see group Intoxicating liquors in this topic

Litter and debris, what constitutes special injury that entitles private party to maintain action based on public nuisance—modern cases, 71 ALR4th 13

Livestock, see group Animals in this topic

Location, funeral home as private nuisance, 8 ALR4th 324

Loudspeakers
- bells, carillons, and the like as nuisance, 95 ALR3d 1268
- use of phonograph, loud-speaker, or other mechanical or electrical device for broadcasting music, advertising, or sales talk from business premises, as nuisance, 23 ALR2d 1289

Massage parlor as nuisance, 80 ALR3d 1020

Merry-go-round as nuisance, 75 ALR2d 803

Mines and Minerals (this index)

Minors, see group Children in this topic

Motel or hotel as nuisance, 24 ALR2d 571

Motion pictures
- drive-in theater as nuisance, 93 ALR2d 1171
- obscene motion pictures as nuisance, 50 ALR3d 969

Motor vehicles, see group Automobiles in this topic

Moving of buildings on highways as nuisance, 83 ALR2d 478

NUISANCES—Cont'd

Mufflers or similar noise-preventing devices on motor vehicles, aircraft, or boats, validity of public regulation requiring, 49 ALR2d 1202

Municipal corporations
- attractive nuisance doctrine, liability of municipality for injury to children by fire under, 27 ALR2d 1194
- dump, municipal liability for maintenance of public dump as nuisance, 52 ALR2d 1134
- rule of municipal immunity from liability for acts in performance of governmental functions as applicable to personal injury or death as result of, 56 ALR2d 1415
- swimming pools, public swimming pool as a nuisance, 49 ALR3d 652

Music and musicians
- bells, carillons, and the like as nuisance, 95 ALR3d 1268
- drive-in theater or other outdoor dramatic or musical entertainment as nuisance, 93 ALR2d 1171
- use of phonograph, loud-speaker, or other mechanical or electrical device for broadcasting music, advertising, or sales talk from business premises, as nuisance, 23 ALR2d 1289

Neighborhood, see group Residential area or neighborhood in this topic

Noise or sound
- air conditioning, existence of, and relief from, nuisance created by operation of air conditioning or ventilating equipment, 79 ALR3d 320
- bells, carillons, and the like as nuisance, 95 ALR3d 1268
- carwash as nuisance, 4 ALR4th 1308
- coalyard, noise caused by operation of, as nuisance, 8 ALR2d 419
- dogs, keeping of dogs as enjoinable nuisance, 11 ALR3d 1399
- electric generating plant or transformer station as nuisance, 4 ALR3d 902
- special injury, what constitutes special injury that entitles private party to maintain action based on public nuisance—modern cases, 71 ALR4th 13
- windmill as nuisance, 36 ALR4th 1159
- zoo as nuisance, 58 ALR3d 1126

1086 **Consult POCKET PART for Later Annotations**

a. Updating Older A.L.R. Annotations

To update an annotation in A.L.R. (namely, one written between 1919 and 1948), use the *A.L.R. Bluebook of Supplemental Decisions*. To update an annotation in A.L.R.2d (namely, one written between 1948 and 1965), use the *A.L.R.2d Later Case Service*.

b. Updating Newer A.L.R. Annotations

To update any annotation in A.L.R.3d, A.L.R.4th, A.L.R.5th, A.L.R.6th, A.L.R. Fed., and A.L.R. Fed. 2d, check the pocket part in each volume, which will direct you to more recent annotations and more recent cases relating to the topic discussed by your annotation (see Figure 5-7).

To update an annotation, you may also use the Annotation History Table in the last volume of the *A.L.R. Index*. This table will inform you whether the annotation you have been researching has been supplemented with new information or completely superseded by a newer annotation.

Figure 5-7
Updating A.L.R. Annotations

Location of Annotation	*Method of Updating*
A.L.R.	*A.L.R. Bluebook of Supplemental Decisions*
A.L.R.2d	*A.L.R.2d Later Case Service*
A.L.R.3d	Pocket part in each volume
A.L.R.4th	Pocket part in each volume
A.L.R.5th	Pocket part in each volume
A.L.R.6th	Pocket part in each volume
A.L.R. Fed.	Pocket part in each volume
A.L.R. Fed. 2d	Pocket part in each volume

C. Citation Form

Digests are used solely to locate cases. You may never cite to them. You may, however, cite to an A.L.R. annotation.

	Bluebook (for practitioners)	*ALWD*
A.L.R. Annotation	Michael F. Alberti, Annotation, *Validity, Construction, and Application of State Right-to-Work Provisions*, 105 A.L.R.5th 243 (2003).	Michael F. Alberti, *Validity, Construction, and Application of State Right-to-Work Provisions*, 105 A.L.R.5th 243 (2003).

CyberSites

http://www.ll.georgetown.edu/tutorials/index.cfm	Georgetown University Law Library offers a number of tutorials to teach and explain legal research. Select "West Key Numbers" or "American Law Reports" for tutorials on digests and A.L.R.
http://www.bu.edu/lawlibrary/research/guides/guidesatoz.html	Boston University Law Library offers several guides to legal research, including one for the *Key Number System* and one for A.L.R.
http://lexisnexis.com/infopro/zimmermans	"Zimmerman's Research Guide" is provided by LexisNexis and offers descriptions of hundreds of legal topics, including digests and A.L.R.
http://law.scu.edu/library/legal-research-guides.cfm	Santa Clara Law School offers research guides on numerous topics, including the use of digests and A.L.R.

Help Line: *Assistance with A.L.R. Annotations*

The front of each pocket part supplement for the A.L.R. sets provides you with a toll-free telephone number (800-225-7488), which you can call to obtain the most recent information regarding annotations.

Practice Tip: *Use of A.L.R. Annotations*

You may cite to A.L.R. annotations in memos and court documents. Although the annotations are a secondary source, they are credible and well written. A better approach, however, is to allow the A.L.R. annotations to direct you to binding primary authorities that you then cite in your documents.

Research Assignment

1. Use the Table of Cases for the *Eleventh Decennial Digest, Part 1.*
   a. Under which topic and Key Numbers is the case *Nutrasweet Co. v. Venrod Corp.* digested?
   b. Give the citation to the case in which the defendant's name is *Victoria Station Forms, Inc.*
2. Use the Descriptive Word Index to the *Eleventh Decennial Digest, Part 1.*
   a. Which topic and Key Number discuss grants of franchises, in general?
   b. Look up this topic and Key Number in the *Eleventh Decennial Digest, Part 1.* Which 1996 Vermont case discusses this topic?
3. Use the Descriptive Word Index to the *Tenth Decennial Digest, Part 2.*
   a. Which topic and Key Number discuss abandonment of delinquent and dependent children?
   b. Look up this topic and Key Number in the *Tenth Decennial Digest, Part 2.* Which 1993 South Dakota case discusses this general topic?
   c. Which 2000 South Dakota case updates this?
   d. Use Volume 51 of West's *General Digest, 10th Series.* What Pennsylvania Superior Court case updates this topic?
4. Use West's set *Federal Practice Digest, 4th Series.*
   a. Which topic and Key Number discuss criminal liability for blasphemy?
   b. Look up this topic and Key Number. What is the most recent federal case that discusses this topic?
   c. Use the "Words and Phrases" volumes. What 1989 case construes the phrase "cost of labor"? What is its topic and Key Number?
5. Use West's set *United States Supreme Court Digest.*
   a. What is the most recent U.S. Supreme Court case that interprets the phrase "prevailing party"? Give the case name only.
   b. Give the official citation to the case *Davis v. Gray.*
6. Use the *Atlantic Digest, 2d Series.*
   a. Which topic and Key Number discuss drug tests in schools and school districts?
   b. Review the previous topic and Key Number. What is the most recent New Hampshire case that discusses this general area of law?
   c. Which topic and Key Number discuss a mistake as to the victim's age as a defense to the crime of rape?
   d. Review the previous topic and Key Number. What is the most recent New Hampshire case that discusses this topic?

7. Use the Table of Words and Phrases for the *California Digest, 2d Series.*
   a. What case interprets the meaning of the phrase "counterfeit mark"?
   b. Under what topic and Key Number is the case digested?

8. Use the Table of Cases in the *New York Digest, 4th Series*. Under which topics and Key Numbers is the case *Sears v. Country Developers, Inc.* digested?

9. Use the A.L.R. Quick Index and answer the following questions.
   a. Which annotation deals with an owner's or keeper's liability for personal injury or death inflicted by a lion?
   b. Review the previous annotation. What Am. Jur. 2d reference are you directed to that relates to this topic? Review Section 3 of this annotation. What is the most recent Georgia Court of Appeals case discussing absolute or strict liability for keeping wild animals?
   c. Which annotation deals with the liability of a business for a lost or missing hat, purse, wallet, coat, or other property deposited by a customer with the place of business?
   d. Review the previous annotation. Is a restaurant liable for the theft of coats when it fails to warn its customers of frequent thefts? Give your answer and cite a case that supports your answer.

10. Use the A.L.R. Federal Quick Index for A.L.R. Fed. and A.L.R. Fed. 2d.
    a. What annotation deals with the validity of the Drug Paraphernalia Act?
    b. Who is the author of the annotation?
    c. Review Section 6 of the annotation. What is the most recent case from the Fourth Circuit relating to the topic discussed in the annotation?

Internet Assignment

1. Access West's website at http://west.thomson.com.
   a. Locate information about *Minnesota Digest, 2d*.
      (i) What does the "Words and Phrases" volume provide?
      (ii) What does the "Descriptive Word Index" provide?
   b. Locate West's "User Guides," specifically, the Law School User Guide entitled "Using Secondary Sources Quick Reference Guide." How does one search in A.L.R.?

2. Access Georgetown Law Center's website at http://www.ll.georgetown.edu and locate the Research Guide "Using Digests." What is the major function of a digest?
3. Access Santa Clara Law's website at http://law.scu.edu/library and review the Legal Research Guide on A.L.R. How is A.L.R. described?

Legal Research

Secondary Authorities and Special Research Issues

Chapter 6

Secondary Authorities

Chapter Overview

Section I of this text discussed the major primary legal authorities: statutes, constitutions, and cases. Administrative rules and regulations and treaties are discussed in Chapter Seven. Nearly all other sources are secondary authorities. In general, the secondary sources serve to explain, summarize, analyze, and locate primary sources.

If you suspect that a legal question is addressed by a statute, you should begin your research in one of the annotated codes by locating the statute and then examining the case annotations following it to find cases that interpret the statute. Often, however, you may not know where to begin a research project. In these instances, many experts recommend that you start your research projects by using a secondary source.

Remember that primary sources are binding on a court. If on point, these primary authorities must be followed. Secondary authorities lack this mandatory authority. Although often highly respected, secondary authorities are persuasive only. Thus, your research goal is always to locate primary sources. The secondary authorities will assist you in this task.

The secondary authorities discussed in this chapter are those most frequently used:

- Encyclopedias
- Legal periodicals
- Texts and treatises
- Restatements
- Miscellaneous secondary authorities (including attorneys general opinions, legal dictionaries, form books, and jury instructions).

Another important secondary authority, A.L.R., was discussed in Chapter Five.

A. Encyclopedias

1. *Introduction*

Legal encyclopedias function in the same way as any other encyclopedia in that they discuss various topics. *Legal encyclopedias* thus explain legal subjects, in alphabetical order, from abandoned property to zoning. They are easy to use, and they serve as an excellent introduction to an area of the law. In addition to providing summaries of legal topics, encyclopedias direct you to cases through the use of footnotes. Generally, the narrative statements or summaries of legal topics will cover the top half of each page in the set, and the bottom half of each page will provide citations to legal authorities that support the narrative statements of the law.

The treatment of legal topics in encyclopedias is general and somewhat elementary. For this reason, encyclopedias are seldom cited in court documents such as briefs. They are rather most useful for giving you the background you need on a legal topic before reading cases. Moreover, they are *noncritical*, meaning that they explain the law as it *is* and do not provide critical comment or suggest what the law *should be*.

There are three types of encyclopedias: general sets, local sets, and special subject sets.

2. *General or National Encyclopedias*

A *general* or *national encyclopedia* is a set that aims at discussing all American law, civil and criminal, state and federal, substantive and procedural. There are two general or national encyclopedias: *Corpus Juris Secundum* (C.J.S.), published by West, and *American Jurisprudence 2d* (Am. Jur. 2d) previously published by Lawyers Cooperative Publishing Company and now also published by West. These sets are competitive, meaning that they are so similar that it cannot be said which is better; you should research in one or the other, not both. Your choice of which set to use will therefore be based largely on habit or convenience.

a. C.J.S.

As its name indicates (*Corpus Juris Secundum*, meaning "Body of Law Second"), C.J.S. was preceded by an earlier set, *Corpus Juris*, no longer in use. C.J.S. consists of more than 150 dark blue volumes and discusses more than 400 different areas of the law in alphabetical order, making it easy for you to locate discussions on topics such as Assault, Bankruptcy, or Corporations.

C.J.S. is an extremely thorough and comprehensive set. The text is articulately presented and easy to understand. The cases that support the narrative statements are arranged in the footnotes alphabetically by state, so you can readily locate cases from your own jurisdiction. Often, the "leading case" in an area of the law is summarized briefly for you.

Each topic (for example, Contracts) begins with a thorough outline to provide you with quick access to the most pertinent parts of the discussion. Each section within a topic begins with a boldface "Black Letter" summary of the rule discussed in the section so you can quickly determine whether you need to read the section in full. Because C.J.S. is a West publication, all cases are fully referenced to West's *Key Number System*. See Figure 6-1 for a sample page from C.J.S.

b. Am. Jur. 2d

American Jurisprudence 2d (Am. Jur. 2d), the successor set to *American Jurisprudence*, consists of more than 100 green volumes and discusses more than 400 areas of law. Similar to the arrangement of C.J.S., Am. Jur. 2d arranges its topics (or "titles") alphabetically, enabling you to quickly locate the discussion you need. Although C.J.S. historically has aimed at directing you to *all* cases that support any legal principle, Am. Jur. 2d has prided itself on "weeding out" redundant or obsolete cases.

Many of the features of Am. Jur. 2d are similar to those of C.J.S., namely, the narrative statements of the law are clearly and concisely presented, and each topic begins with a complete outline. See Figure 6-2 for a sample page from Am. Jur. 2d.

Am. Jur. 2d features two unique books in its encyclopedia system:

• *Am. Jur. 2d Desk Book*. This book serves as a legal almanac and includes miscellaneous legal and historical information, including the text of the Constitution, organization charts for federal agencies, life expectancy tables, and glossaries of legal terms.

• *Am. Jur. 2d New Topic Service*. The New Topic Service binder includes pamphlets on emerging or evolving areas of the law, including Terrorism, the Americans with Disabilities Act, and Limited Liability Companies. These discussions are later placed within the Am. Jr. 2d hardbound volumes.

c. Features Common to C.J.S. and Am. Jur. 2d

The following features are common to C.J.S. and Am. Jur. 2d:

• **Coverage.** Both sets discuss more than 400 topics of law, arranged alphabetically.

• **Table of Laws and Rules.** Although neither set includes exhaustive coverage of statutes (which would make the sets too voluminous), each does include a volume with a table that directs you to specific sections that discuss or cite federal statutes, rules, and the *Code of Federal Regulations*.

• **Text Treatment.** The narrative statements of the law are similar in both sets. The discussion of the law is clear and straightforward. For this reason, it cannot be said that one set is superior to the other. Moreover, now that Am. Jur. 2d is owned by West, its newer volumes include references to the *Key Number System*.

• **Indexing.** Each set includes a multivolume General Index (located after the last volume on the shelf), and each of the more than 400 topics begins with its own outline, allowing you to quickly locate sections of interest.

Figure 6-1
Sample Page from C.J.S.

§ 182. Abandonment and Nonuser

a. Abandonment in general
b. Nonuser
c. Miscellaneous acts or omissions
d. Operation and effect
e. Evidence

Summary of rule discussed in section to follow

a. Abandonment in General

Trade-marks and trade-names may be lost by abandonment; abandonment requires the concurrence of both an intention to abandon and an act or omission by which such intention is carried into effect.

The title to a trade-mark or trade-name acquired by adoption and user may be lost by an abandonment of such use,[5] although abandonment is not favored.[6] An actual intention permanently to give up the use of a name or mark is necessary to constitute abandonment of it.[7] Abandonment requires the concurrence of both an intention to abandon and an act or omission by which such intention is carried into effect.[8] Abandonment must have been voluntary,[9] and an involuntary deprivation of the use of the name or mark does not in itself constitute abandonment.[10] Failure to affix a trade-mark to goods through inadvertence is not abandonment where no intention to abandon is shown;[11] nor can an undisclosed intention constitute abandonment.[12] Despite the fact that abandonment depends in a large part on the intention of the parties, an ineffective attempt to assign a trade-mark ordinarily results in its abandonment.[13]

b. Nonuser

Nonuser of a trade-name or trade-mark is not of itself an abandonment thereof; however, where intention to abandon is shown by other circumstances and conditions, nonuser is a sufficient act of relinquishment and effectuates the abandonment.

While trade-marks and trade-names may be lost through nonuser,[14] mere disuse, although for a con-

5. U.S.—Greyhound Corp. v. Rothman, D.C.Md., 84 F.Supp. 233, affirmed, C.A., 175 F.2d 893—G. F. Heublin & Bro. v. Bushmill Wine & Products Co., D.C.Pa., 55 F.Supp. 964—Bisceglia Bros. Corp. v. Fruit Industries, D.C.Pa., 20 F.Supp. 564, affirmed, C.C.A., Fruit Industries v. Bisceglia Bros. Corp., 101 F.2d 752, certiorari denied 59 S.Ct. 1043, 307 U.S. 646, 83 L.Ed. 1526.
Ky.—**Corpus Juris cited in** Stratton & Terstegge Co. v. Stiglitz Furnace Co., 81 S.W.2d 1, 4, 258 Ky. 678.
N.Y.—Winthrop Chemical Co. v. Blackman, 268 N.Y.S. 647, 150 Misc. 229.
Wash.—Foss v. Culbertson, 136 P.2d 711, 17 Wash.2d 610—Seattle Street Railway & Municipal Employees Relief Ass'n v. Amalgamated Ass'n of Street Electric Railway & Motor Coach Employees of America, 101 P.2d 338, 3 Wash.2d 520.
63 C.J. p 523 note 17.

6. U.S.—Du Pont Cellophane Co. v. Waxed Products Co., D.C.N.Y., 6 F. Supp. 859, modified on other grounds, C.C.A., 85 F.2d 75, certiorari denied E. I. Dupont De Nemours & Co. v. Waxed Products Co., 57 S.Ct. 194, 299 U.S. 601, 81 L.Ed. 443.

7. Ky.—**Corpus Juris cited in** Stratton & Terstegge Co. v. Stiglitz Furnace Co., 81 S.W.2d 1, 4, 258 Ky. 678.
N.Y.—Neva-Wet Corp. of America v. Never Wet Processing Corp., 13 N.E.2d 775, 277 N.Y. 163.
63 C.J. p 523 note 18.
Letter assuring noncontest
Where plaintiff ordering trade-marked razors from manufacturer sent to lender a letter which consented to manufacturer's pledge of razors as security for loan to manufacturer and which stated that plaintiff would not assert any claims contrary to lender's right to realize on security in event of nonpayment of loan, letter was abandonment of all plaintiff's trade-mark and fair trade rights.—Stahly, Inc. v. M. H. Jacobs Co., C.A.Ill., 183 F.2d 914, certiorari denied 71 S.Ct. 239, 340 U.S. 896, 95 L.Ed. 650.

8. U.S.—E. I. Du Pont De Nemours & Co. v. Celanese Corp. of America, 167 F.2d 484, 35 C.C.P.A., Patents, 1061, 3 A.L.R.2d 1213—Greyhound Corp. v. Rothman, D.C.Md., 84 F. Supp. 233, affirmed, C.A., 175 F.2d 893—Hygienic Products Co. v. Judson Dunaway Corp., D.C.N.H., 81 F. Supp. 935, vacated on other grounds, C.A., 178 F.2d 461, certiorari denied 70 S.Ct. 802, 803, 339 U. S. 948, 94 L.Ed. 1362—Colonial Radio Corp. v. Colonial Television Corp., D.C.N.Y., 78 F.Supp. 546—Coca-Cola Co. v. Dixi-Cola Laboratories, D.C.Md., 31 F.Supp. 835, modified on other grounds, C.C.A., Dixi-Cola Laboratories v. Coca-Cola Co., 117 F.2d 352, certiorari denied Coca-Cola Co. v. Dixi-Cola Laboratories, 62 S.Ct. 60, 314 U.S. 629, 86 L.Ed. 505—Bisceglia Bros. Corp. v. Fruit Industries, D.C.Pa., 20 F. Supp. 564, affirmed, C.C.A., Fruit Industries v. Bisceglia Bros. Corp., 101 F.2d 752, certiorari denied 59 S.Ct. 1043, 307 U.S. 646, 83 L.Ed. 1526—Du Pont Cellophane Co. v. Waxed Products Co., D.C.N.Y., 6 F. Supp. 859, modified on other grounds, C.C.A., 85 F.2d 75, certiorari denied E. I. Dupont De Nemours & Co. v. Waxed Products Co., 57 S.Ct. 194, 299 U.S. 601, 81 L.Ed. 443.
Ky.—Stratton & Terstegge Co. v. Stiglitz Furnace Co., 81 S.W.2d 1, 258 Ky. 678.
Wash.—Foss v. Culbertson, 136 P.2d 711, 17 Wash.2d 610.
63 C.J. p 524 note 19.

9. U.S.—E. I. Du Pont De Nemours & Co. v. Celanese Corp. of America, 167 F.2d 484, 35 C.C.P.A., Patents, 1016, 3 A.L.R. 2d 1213—DuPont Cellophane Co. v. Waxed Products Co., C.C.A.N.Y., 85 F.2d 75, certiorari denied E. I. DuPont De Nemours & Co. v. Waxed Products Co., 57 S.Ct. 194, 299 U.S. 601, 81 L.Ed. 443.

10. U.S.—Fraser v. Williams, D.C. Wis., 61 F.Supp. 763—Reconstruction Finance Corp. v. J. G. Menihan Corp., D.C.N.Y., 28 F.Supp. 920.
Md.—American-Stewart Distillery v. Stewart Distilling Co., 177 A. 473, 168 Md. 212.
Wash.—Washington Barber & Beauty Supply Co. v. Spokane Barbers' & Beauty Supply Co., 18 P.2d 499, 171 Wash. 428.

11. U.S.—Chrysler Corp. v. Trott, Cust. & Pat.App., 83 F.2d 302.

12. Wash.—Olympia Brewing Co. v. Northwest Brewing Co., 35 P.2d 104, 178 Wash. 533.

13. D.C.—Old Charter Distillery Co. v. Ooms, D.C., 73 F.Supp. 539, affirmed Continental Distilling Corp. v. Old Charter Distillery Co., 188 F.2d 614, 88 U.S.App.D.C. 73.

14. U.S.—G. F. Heublin & Bro. v. Bushmill Wine & Products Co., D. C.Pa., 55 F.Supp. 964—Bisceglia Bros. Corp. v. Fruit Industries, D. C.Pa., 20 F.Supp. 564, affirmed, C.C. A., Fruit Industries v. Bisceglia Bros. Corp., 101 F.2d 752, certiorari denied 59 S.Ct. 1043, 307 U.S. 646, 83 L.Ed. 1526.

Figure 6-2
Sample Page from Am. Jur. 2d

§ 242 DRUGS AND CONTROLLED SUBSTANCES 25 Am Jur 2d

2. CONDUCT RELATED TO FILLING OF PRESCRIPTIONS [§§ 242–244]

§ 242. Generally

A pharmacist has a duty to act with due ordinary care and diligence in the compounding and selling of drugs.[93] In this regard, a pharmacist owes his customers a duty to properly[94] and accurately[95] fill prescriptions. A pharmacist is required to assure that the drug prescribed is properly selected and measured.[96] Indeed, a pharmacist is held to a high standard of care in filling prescriptions[97] and dispensing prescription drugs,[98] and may be held liable in tort for any breach of his duty to properly fill prescriptions.[99] Generally, however, a pharmacist will not be held liable for correctly filling a prescription issued by a licensed physician.[1] In addition, a pharmacist who sells a generic drug as a substitute for the drug specifically prescribed, as authorized by statute and a physician's prescription, is not negligent for injuries resulting from an adverse side effect of a generic drug, unless the pharmacist knew that the generic drug is inferior or defective.[2]

§ 243. Mistakes in preparing, filling, or dispensing prescriptions; dispensing drug other than that prescribed

Liability may be imposed on a pharmacists for negligently misfilling a prescription,[3] or negligently dispensing a drug other than that prescribed[4] or requested,[5] when a druggist negligently supplies a drug other than the drug

249, app den (Tenn) 1990 Tenn LEXIS 362.

93. Ferguson v Williams, 101 NC App 265, 399 SE2d 389, review den 328 NC 571, 403 SE2d 510; Dooley v Everett (Tenn App) 805 SW2d 380.

94. Adkins v Mong, 168 Mich App 726, 425 NW2d 151, app den 431 Mich 880.

95. Nichols v Central Merchandise, 16 Kan App 2d 65, 817 P2d 1131, review den 250 Kan 805; McKee v American Home Products Corp., 113 Wash 2d 701, 782 P2d 1045, CCH Prod Liab Rep ¶ 12399.

96. Murphy v E. R. Squibb & Sons, Inc., 40 Cal 3d 672, 221 Cal Rptr 447, 710 P2d 247, CCH Prod Liab Rep ¶ 10818.

97. Adkins v Mong, 168 Mich App 726, 425 NW2d 151, app den 431 Mich 880.

98. French Drug Co. v Jones (Miss) 367 So 2d 431, 3 ALR4th 259.

99. Adkins v Mong, 168 Mich App 726, 425 NW2d 151, app den 431 Mich 880.

1. Adkins v Mong, 168 Mich App 726, 425 NW2d 151, app den 431 Mich 880.
Forms: Answer—Denial of negligence—No breach of duty. 9 Am Jur Pl & Pr Forms (Rev), Drugs, Narcotics, and Poisons, Form 37.

2. Ullman v Grant, 114 Misc 2d 220, 450 NYS2d 955.

3. Boeck v Katz Drug Co., 155 Kan 656, 127 P2d 506.
Annotations: Druggist's civil liability for injuries sustained as result of negligence in incorrectly filling drug prescriptions, 3 ALR4th 270.

Reference to A.L.R. annotation

Forms: Complaint, petition, or declaration—Against pharmacy and pharmacist—Damages resulting from alteration of prescription by pharmacist. 9 Am Jur Pl & Pr Forms (Rev), Drugs, Narcotics, and Poisons, Form 31.1.

4. Stebbins v Concord Wrigley Drugs, Inc., 164 Mich App 204, 416 NW2d 381; Walgreen, Inc. v Knatt (Tex Civ App Beaumont) 506 SW2d 751.
Practice References: 18 Am Jur Proof of Facts 1, Medication Errors.
Forms: Complaint, petition, or declaration—Injuries sustained as result of negligence in filling drug prescription—Filling prescription with drug other than drug prescribed. 9 Am Jur Pl & Pr Forms (Rev), Drugs, Narcotics, and Poisons, Form 31.

Complaint, petition, or declaration—Allegation—Harmful drug supplied in place of harmless drug ordered. 9 Am Jur Pl & Pr Forms (Rev), Drugs, Narcotics, and Poisons, Form 36.

5. Troppi v Scarf, 31 Mich App 240, 187 NW2d 511 (criticized on other grounds by Bushman v Burns Clinic Medical Center, 83 Mich App 453, 268 NW2d 683) and (criticized on other grounds by Rinard v Biczak, 177 Mich

462

• **Scope Notes.** Each topic discussion in both sets begins with a *scope note* or paragraph, which briefly outlines what will be discussed in the topic and what subjects may be discussed elsewhere in the set.

• **Supporting References.** Both sets support their narrative discussions of the law with footnotes that provide citations to cases and other sources. Both sets participate in West's *Key Number system*, and both refer you to numerous other resources, including useful A.L.R. annotations.

• **Updating.** Both sets are updated by annual cumulative pocket parts that supplement the hardbound volumes (with pertinent new cases and statutory changes) and by replacement volumes, when needed.

• **New Media.** Both sets are available in CD-ROM form and on Westlaw. Am. Jur. 2d is also available on LexisNexis.

d. Research Strategies for Using General Encyclopedias

There are four techniques you may use to locate the discussion of an area of law in C.J.S. or Am. Jur. 2d.

• **Descriptive Word Approach.** To use the descriptive word approach, think of words or phrases that describe the issue you are researching. Look up these words in the General Index volumes for C.J.S. and Am. Jur. 2d, and you will be directed to the appropriate topic and section. Read the narrative, review the pocket part, and then select the cases and other resources that you will read in full. See Figure 6-3 for a sample page from an index to Am. Jur. 2d.

Because volumes in the set are replaced as needed, and because the replacement volumes may add new sections and discussion, it is possible that the General Index may send you to a section in an older volume that does not exist in a newer replacement volume. In such a case, check the Correlation Table in the front of each volume; it will convert the old section number to the new section number in the replacement volume.

• **Topic Approach.** Because the more than 400 topics discussed in C.J.S. and Am. Jur. 2d are arranged alphabetically, it is often possible to use the topic approach and successfully locate a discussion of the area of law in which you are interested. To use the topic approach, simply think of the area of law you are researching (for example, Homicide or Trusts) and then retrieve that volume from the shelf. Examine the scope note and the outline of the topic, which will direct you to the appropriate section.

• **Table of Statutes Approach.** Use the Table of Laws and Rules volume for each set to look up specific statutes, administrative regulations, or rules in which you are interested. You will be directed to the appropriate volume, topic, and section.

• **Table of Cases Approach.** C.J.S. includes an alphabetical table of cases so you can readily locate a discussion of a case if you know its name. Am. Jur. 2d does not include a table of cases.

Figure 6-3
Sample Page from General Index Update to Am. Jur. 2d

GENERAL INDEX UPDATE

e. The Am. Jur. Total Client-Service Library

Lawyers Cooperative Publishing Company, the former publisher of Am. Jur. 2d, created a number of other sets of books, which it has referred to as the *Total Client-Service Library* (TCSL), which are now published by West. The books in TCSL are designed to be used with Am. Jur. 2d. Most relate to litigation and trial practice. All of the sets are kept current by the use of pocket parts, which provide new forms, checklists, or other pertinent material. To access these sets, use the descriptive word approach, and look up words that describe your issue in the General Index. You will then be directed to the appropriate volume and page. The four sets that make up TCSL are as follows:

- ***Am. Jur. Proof of Facts.*** This set of more than 130 volumes is designed to assist in the preparation for and proving of facts at trial (civil and criminal). Articles explain how to determine the facts essential to winning a case. *Proof of Facts* provides practical information regarding conducting client interviews, preparing witnesses for trial, conducting discovery, and introducing evidence. Checklists, strategy tips, and practice aids are provided, including sample forms for discovery and diagrams that are suitable for courtroom exhibits.
- ***Am. Jur. Trials.*** This set of more than 100 volumes focuses on trial tactics and strategies. The articles in *Am. Jur. Trials* are written by experienced litigators and provide a step-by-step guide to all aspects of litigation, from the initial client interview, through discovery, to trial and appeals. Specific articles outline the steps to take to prevail in a broad spectrum of litigation, including personal injury, business, and criminal litigation. Checklists, forms, opening statements, and litigation aids and charts are all included. Following are examples of actual topics covered by *Am. Jur. Trials*:

  - Pharmacist Malpractice
  - Stockbroker Liability Litigation
  - Litigating Toxic Mold Cases

- ***Am. Jur. Pleading and Practice Forms Annotated.*** This set of more than 70 volumes includes more than 43,000 forms for every stage of state and federal litigation, including forms for complaints, answers, interrogatories, motions, jury instructions, and orders. Practical checklists are included to remind you of items to include in various forms. References to the *Key Number System* and other West resources are included.
- ***Am. Jur. Legal Forms 2d.*** This set provides forms that are not litigation oriented. These documents are often used in connection with a client's personal or business needs, such as a will, trust, lease, or minutes of a corporate meeting. *Am. Jur. Legal Forms 2d* provides more than 20,000 such forms together with checklists, tips, and advice for preparing the forms and documents. Often, optional or alternative clauses are provided, allowing you to pick and choose clauses to construct the best document for a client.

3. *Local or State Encyclopedias*

a. Introduction

You have seen that C.J.S. and Am. Jur. 2d are general provide a national overview of more than 400 areas of t likely, however, that you may not need such broad cove are interested only in the law for your particular state. you should consult a *local encyclopedia* for your state, *if* Generally, encyclopedias are published only for the more

To determine if an encyclopedia exists for your state, library's card catalog, ask a reference librarian, or simply library stacks devoted to the law of your state. Note th encyclopedias label themselves as "digests."

Most of the local sets are published by West, but a few a by LexisNexis. If your state does not have its own encyclopedia, or Am. Jur. 2d, and research your state's law by locating cas footnotes from your state. See Figure 6-4 for a list of the local en dias and their publishers.

b. Features Common to State Encyclopedias

The following features are common to most state encyclopedias:

- **Coverage.** The discussion of the law presented will relate only to the law of a particular state, and the cases you will be directed to will be from that state and from federal courts interpreting that state's law.
- **Arrangement.** The various topics are arranged alphabetically. The narrative statements of the law are clearly presented, and you will be directed to cases and other authorities through the use of supporting footnotes.
- **Table of Cases.** Many local sets include tables that alphabetically list the cases cited in the set. If you know the name of a case, you can readily locate the discussion of it by using the Table of Cases.

Practice Tips: *Selecting Relevant Cases*

As you read discussions of law in the encyclopedias, you may be presented with numerous case citations in the footnotes. There are some techniques you can use effectively to select cases when time or budget constraints prevent you from examining all cases:

- Select and read cases from your jurisdiction before reading those from other jurisdictions;
- Review newer cases before older cases; and
- Review cases from higher courts before those from lower courts.

Figure 6-4
List of Local Encyclopedias

cyclopedias Published by West

alifornia Jurisprudence, Third
lorida Jurisprudence, Second
Georgia Jurisprudence
Illinois Law and Practice
Indiana Law Encyclopedia
Kentucky Jurisprudence (ceased in 2001)
Maryland Law Encyclopedia
Massachusetts Jurisprudence (ceased in 1998)
Michigan Civil Jurisprudence
Encyclopedia of Mississippi Law (successor to *Grant's Summary of Mississippi Law*)
New York Jurisprudence, Second
Ohio Jurisprudence, Third
Summary of Pennsylvania Jurisprudence, Second
South Carolina Jurisprudence
Texas Jurisprudence, Third

Encyclopedias Published by LexisNexis

Illinois Jurisprudence
Michigan Law and Practice Encyclopedia, Second
Pennsylvania Law Encyclopedia
Tennessee Jurisprudence
Michie's Jurisprudence of Virginia and West Virginia

• **Table of Statutes.** Many state encyclopedias contain a detailed table of statutes, which will direct you to a discussion of a statute in which you are interested. For example, if you are interested in Section 50 of the California Probate Code, simply look this up in the table of statutes and you will be directed to any sections in Cal. Jur. 3d that discuss this statute.

• **Indexing.** Most state encyclopedias have a multivolume general index. Additionally, many encyclopedias provide an individual index or outline of a topic just before the discussion of the topic begins.

• **Supplementation.** State encyclopedias are kept up to date by pocket parts and replacement volumes.

c. Research Strategies for Using State Encyclopedias

The research techniques used to access the state encyclopedias are identical to the techniques used to access the national encyclopedias discussed previously, namely, the descriptive word approach, topic approach, table of statutes approach, and table of cases approach.

4. Special Subject Encyclopedias

The encyclopedias previously discussed, C.J.S., Am. Jur. 2d, and the local encyclopedias, discuss hundreds of areas of the law. There are, however, a few encyclopedias, called *special subject encyclopedias*, that are devoted to just one area of the law. For example, *Fletcher Cyclopedia of the Law of Corporations* includes more than 30 volumes and discusses in depth the law relating to corporations. Check the card catalog at your law library to determine if an encyclopedia exists for a particular subject. Browse the stacks of the library devoted to the topic in which you are interested. Many of these "encyclopedias," however, are more accurately classified as treatises, discussed later in this chapter. Retrieve the index to the set, and use the descriptive word approach to access special subject encyclopedias.

5. Summary of Encyclopedias

Encyclopedias provide excellent introductions to numerous areas of the law. You must remember, however, to read the primary sources you are directed to by the encyclopedias, because these mandatory authorities *must* be followed by courts, and the encyclopedias are merely persuasive authorities. In fact, although encyclopedias are excellent ways to "get your feet wet" and gain background information about a topic, you should not cite to them in a court document or research memorandum unless you can find no other relevant authority, because they are not sufficiently scholarly to serve as the sole support for an argument you advance.

B. Legal Periodicals

1. Introduction

Just as you might subscribe to a periodical publication such as *Sports Illustrated*, law firms and legal professionals subscribe to a variety of publications that are produced on a regular or periodic basis. All *legal periodicals* are secondary sources, although many of them, particularly the law school publications, are very well respected and scholarly. Typically, the legal periodicals direct you to primary authorities through the use of extensive footnotes. Periodicals serve many functions: Some provide extensive analyses of legal topics; some serve to keep practitioners current on recent developments in the law; and others provide practical information relating to issues of interest to legal professionals.

There are four broad categories of legal periodicals: publications of law schools, publications of bar and other associations, specialized publications for those in the legal profession sharing similar interests, and legal newspapers and newsletters.

2. *Law School Publications*

Most law schools produce a periodical publication generally referred to as a *law review*, such as the *Harvard Law Review*, although some title their publications "journals," such as the *Yale Law Journal*. Because the law reviews are published so frequently (three or four times each year), they often provide current analysis of recent cases or legislation. Each issue includes its own table of contents.

The law reviews are published by students who have been selected to write for the law review on the basis of academic distinction or writing skill. Law reviews provide scholarly analysis of legal topics and are routinely cited with approval by courts. They differ greatly from encyclopedias, which are noncritical in their approach and usually focus on merely explaining the law. Law reviews offer a critical approach and often advocate reform in the law.

A law review usually has several sections:

- **Articles.** *Articles* are usually scholarly monographs written by professors, judges, or practicing attorneys. Often exceeding 30 pages in length, an article examines a topic in depth. The topics explored are diverse.
- **Comments or Notes.** *Comments* or *Notes* are generally shorter pieces authored by students.
- **Case Comments/Recent Cases/Recent Developments.** This section is also authored by students and examines the effect of recent cases and new legislation.
- **Book Reviews.** Many law reviews contain a section that reviews books or texts relating to legal issues, such as a book written about antitrust law.

Almost all law schools publish one of these general types of law reviews, that is, a review containing articles on a variety of topics. In addition to these general law reviews, many schools also produce law reviews devoted to a specific area, such as international law or civil rights.

Law reviews are often arranged alphabetically in a law library, so that the *Akron Law Review* is followed by the *Alabama Law Review*, and so forth, making locating a law review easy and efficient.

See Figure 6-5 for a sample cover from a law review.

3. *Bar Association Publications*

Each state has a bar association. The dues paid to the association by its members fund various legal programs as well as the periodical publication of a journal for that state's members of the bar. Some bar associations publish monthly journals, but others publish less frequently. In addition, other legal associations publish periodicals. For example, the *ABA Journal* is a highly professional-looking publication that is sent to members of the American Bar Association each month.

Figure 6-5
Sample Cover from Law Review

Fall 2004 Volume 41 Number 1

CALIFORNIA WESTERN LAW REVIEW

ARTICLE

THE NEW ADR: AGGREGATE DISPUTE RESOLUTION AND *GREEN TREE FINANCIAL CORP. V. BAZZLE*
Imre S. Szalai

ESSAYS

VOICELESS *BILLY BUDD*: MELVILLE'S TRIBUTE TO THE SIXTH AMENDMENT
The Honorable Juan Ramirez, Jr. and Amy D. Ronner

FRANCESCO'S DEVILISH VENUS: NOTATIONS ON THE MATTER OF LEGAL SPACE
Igor Stramignoni

COMMENTS

THE BATTLE OF PIRACY VERSUS PRIVACY: HOW THE RECORDING INDUSTRY ASSOCIATION OF AMERICA (RIAA) IS USING THE DIGITAL MILLENNIUM COPYRIGHT ACT (DMCA) AS ITS WEAPON AGAINST INTERNET USERS' PRIVACY RIGHTS
Jordana Boag

PRISON POWER CORRUPTS ABSOLUTELY: EXPLORING THE PHENOMENON OF PRISON GUARD BRUTALITY AND THE NEED TO DEVELOP A SYSTEM OF ACCOUNTABILITY
Andrea Jacobs

CALIFORNIA'S REGULATION OF NON-CONSENSUAL PRIVATE PROPERTY TOWS: WHY SECTION 22658(L) IS FEDERALLY PREEMPTED
Elisabeth M. W. Trefonas

These publications usually offer a very practical approach to practicing law in a jurisdiction and feature articles on ethics, changes to local court rules, human interest biographies of judges and attorneys, reviews of books and software of interest to legal professionals, and lists of attorneys who have been suspended or disbarred. The articles published in these bar association publications are far more practical in their approach than the academic articles published in law reviews. These journals usually resemble nonlegal publications such as *Newsweek Magazine* in their size and appearance.

Just as there are state bar associations, many local jurisdictions have city or county bar associations, such as the San Diego County Bar Association. Specialized groups may form local associations, such as the Women's Bar Association of the District of Columbia. These associations also produce periodical publications: Some are pamphlets, and others are informal newsletters or flyers. Generally these publications are very practical and informal in approach. Job postings are often included.

Because bar associations tend to focus on practical guidelines for law practice, it is unlikely that you would conduct substantive research using these publications. It is far more likely that you will use these publications to keep you current on legal issues facing your jurisdiction. See Figure 6-6 for a sample cover from a bar association publication.

4. *Specialized Publications*

Just as individuals who are interested in fashion might subscribe to *Vogue*, legal practitioners who have an interest in a specialized area of the law might subscribe to a specialized periodical, such as the *American Bankruptcy Law Journal* or the *Transportation Law Journal* to keep current with developments in these fields.

Similarly, many periodicals are published for individuals who may share common interests, such as the *National Black Law Journal* or the *Women's Rights Law Reporter*. These specialized journals vary in their approach, with some being more analytical and academic and others being more practical.

5. *Legal Newspapers and Newsletters*

In large cities such as New York and Los Angeles, you will find daily legal newspapers such as the *New York Law Journal* and the *Los Angeles Daily Journal*. These newspapers contain the text of recent court cases, publish the court calendar or docket for the courts in that locality, and include articles of interest to legal professionals in that jurisdiction. They usually also include extensive classified advertisements and serve as a useful source of job announcements and vacancies. Some legal newspapers do not restrict their coverage to any locality and are national in scope, such as the *National Law Journal*, which is published weekly.

Figure 6-6
Sample Cover from Bar Association Publication

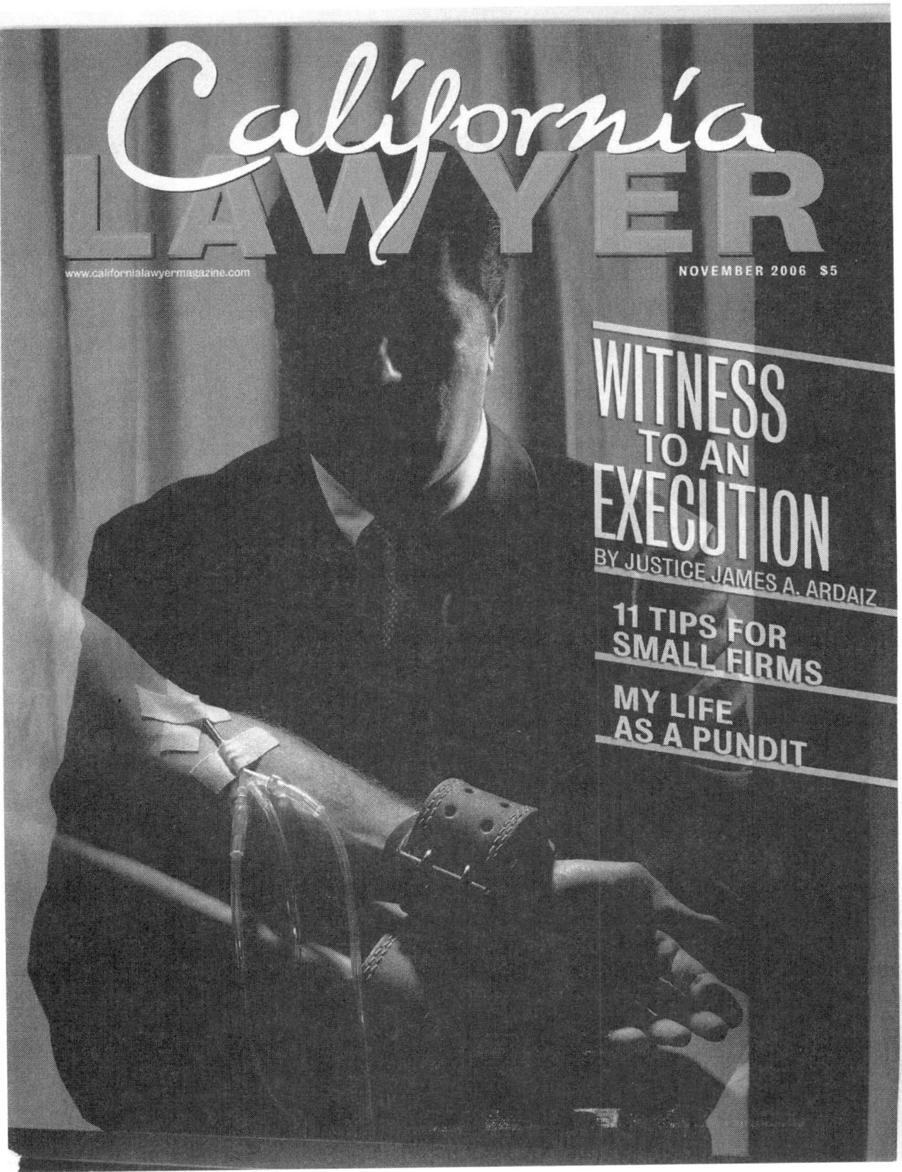

In addition to legal newspapers, more than 2,000 legal and law-related newsletters are published in the United States. Some are one-page bulletins; others are multipage newsletters. Examples are *Jury Trials and Tribulations* (published twice per month and containing summaries of civil jury trials in Florida) and *Bank Bailout Litigation News* (a publication reporting on bank litigation and related matters).

6. *How to Locate Periodical Articles*

Although each issue of any periodical will contain its own table of contents, the best way to locate an article in a periodical publication is to consult one of several published indexes that will direct you to articles published in periodicals. There are several well-known indexes you can use:

a. *Index to Legal Periodicals & Books*

A set of books titled *Index to Legal Periodicals & Books* (I.L.P.) indexes articles published in the United States (and several other common law countries) in more than 1,000 periodicals since 1908. I.L.P. is initially published in softcover monthly pamphlets that are later bound in hardcover volumes.

To locate an article you may use any of the following methods:

• **Subject-Author Approach.** The subject approach calls for you to think of words describing the topic you are interested in, such as bankruptcy or divorce. Look for these words in I.L.P.'s alphabetically arranged Subject and Author Index. You will then be directed to published articles relating to this topic. Alternatively, you may look for articles written by selected authors if you know their names.

• **Table of Cases Approach.** If you wish to read articles that have discussed certain cases, such as *Bush v. Gore*, you can look up this case name in I.L.P.'s Table of Cases (by either the plaintiff's or defendant's name), and you will be directed to periodical articles written about this case.

• **Table of Statutes Approach.** If you are interested in whether any periodical articles have analyzed a particular statute, you can look up the statute in I.L.P.'s Table of Statutes, which will direct you to pertinent articles.

• **Book Review Approach.** If you are looking for a review of a certain book, use I.L.P.'s Book Review Index to be directed to articles that have reviewed the book. See Figure 6-7 for a sample page from I.L.P.

b. *Current Law Index*

Similar to I.L.P., another set of books, titled *Current Law Index*, indexes more than 900 periodical articles from the United States and several other common law countries. Also similar to I.L.P., *Current Law Index* is initially published in monthly softcover pamphlets that are cumulated each quarter and then again at the year's end. To find articles in the *Current Law Index*, you may use the methods discussed previously for

Figure 6-7
Sample Page from *Index to Legal Periodicals & Books*

22 INDEX TO LEGAL PERIODICALS & BOOKS

Coal
The Phasing Constraint: Who May Request Relief and When? J. O. Moreno. *Journal of Transportation Law, Logistics and Policy* v71 no4 p419-33 2004
Coalbed methane
Northern Plains Resource Council v. Fidelity Exploration and Development Co., 325 F.3d 1155 (9th Cir. 2003), cert. denied, 124 S. Ct. 434 (2003). *Environmental Law* v34 no3 p845-8 Summ 2004
Coastal zone
New Zealand
Coastal Management and the Environmental Compensation Challenge. S. Turner. *New Zealand Journal of Environmental Law* v4 p181-200 2000
Coburn, David H.
Rail Construction Cases: Environmental and Other Issues. *Journal of Transportation Law, Logistics and Policy* v71 no4 p379-92 2004
Cochrane, Drew J.
Disability Law in Wisconsin Workplaces. *Wisconsin Lawyer* v77 no10 p8-10, 53-5 O 2004
Codes and codification
History
Special Issue on Comparative Legal History. *The Journal of Legal History* v25 no2 p99-194 Ag 2004
Two Early Codes, the Ten Commandments and the Twelve Tables: Causes and Consequences. A. Watson. *The Journal of Legal History* v25 no2 p129-49 Ag 2004
Canada
Of Codifications, the Uniform Trust Code and Quebec Trusts: Lessons for Common Law Canada? A. Grenon. *Estates Trusts & Pensions Journal* v23 no3 p237-65 Ag 2004
China
Structures of Three Major Civil Code Projets in Today's China. G. Xu. *Tulane European and Civil Law Forum* v19 p37-56 2004
European Union countries
European Code of Contract [Special Issue] *Edinburgh Law Review* v8 Special Issue p I-X, 1-89 2004
Explanatory Note [European Code of Contract: Special Issue] H. McGregor. *Edinburgh Law Review* v8 Special Issue p IX-X 2004
Introduction [European Code of Contract: Special Issue] J. A. D. H. Hope of Craighead. *Edinburgh Law Review* v8 Special Issue p I-VIII 2004
The Optional European Code on the Basis of the Acquis Communautaire—Starting Point and Trends. S. Grundmann. *European Law Journal* v10 no6 p698-711 N 2004
The Politics of a European Civil Code. M. W. Hesselink. *European Law Journal* v10 no6 p675-97 N 2004
France
Thoughts from a Scottish Perspective on the Bicentenary of the French Civil Code. E. Clive. *Edinburgh Law Review* v8 no3 p415-20 S 2004
Great Britain
Codification in England: The Need to Move from an Ideological to a Functional Approach—A Bridge too Far? E. Steiner. *Statute Law Review* v25 no3 p209-22 2004
Louisiana
Interpretations of the Louisiana Civil Codes, 1808-1840: The Failure of the Preliminary Title. T. W. Tucker. *Tulane European and Civil Law Forum* v19 p57-182 2004
Mapping Society Through Law: Louisiana Civil Law Recodified. D. Gruning. *Tulane European and Civil Law Forum* v19 p1-36 2004
Middle East
History
Wrongs and Responsibility in Pre-Roman Law. D. Ibbetson. *The Journal of Legal History* v25 no2 p99-127 Ag 2004
Québec (Province)
German influences
Imported Books, Imported Ideas: Reading European Jurisprudence in Mid-Nineteenth-Century Quebec. E. H. Reiter. *Law and History Review* v22 no3 p445-92 Fall 2004
History
Imported Books, Imported Ideas: Reading European Jurisprudence in Mid-Nineteenth-Century Quebec. E. H. Reiter. *Law and History Review* v22 no3 p445-92 Fall 2004
Scotland
Thoughts from a Scottish Perspective on the Bicentenary of the French Civil Code. E. Clive. *Edinburgh Law Review* v8 no3 p415-20 S 2004
Codicils *See* Wills
Coerced treatment *See* Involuntary treatment
Cogeneration of electric power *See* Electricity
Cohabitation *See* Unmarried couples

Cohen, Adam I.
Rules 33 and 34: Defining E-documents and the Form of Production. Panel Discussion. *Fordham Law Review* v73 no1 p33-51 O 2004
Cohen, Elizabeth J.
The Meaning of 'Forever'. *American Bar Association Journal* v90 p28 N 2004
Cohen, Fred
Silence of the experts. *Trial* v40 no10 p20-2, 24-5, 27-9 O 2004
Cohen, Jerry
The new Massachusetts Business Corporation Act, chapter 127, Acts of 2003. *Massachusetts Law Review* v88 no4 p213-17 S 2004
Colb, Sherry F.
A World without Privacy: Why Property Does Not Define the Limits of the Right against Unreasonable Searches and Seizures. *Michigan Law Review* v102 no5 p889-903 Mr 2004

Entry by author

Collateral estoppel
See also
Res judicata
The U.N. Convention on the Recognition and Enforcement of Foreign Arbitral Awards and Issue Preclusion: A Traditional Collateral Estoppel Determination. S. M. Sudol, student author. *University of Pittsburgh Law Review* v65 no4 p931-50 Summ 2004
Collecting societies (Copyright)
European Union countries
Collective hysteria? A. Hobson. *Copyright World* no143 p15-17 S 2004
Collective bargaining
See also
Employee benefits
Promoting Labour Rights in International Financial Institutions and Trade Regimes. P. Barnacle. *Saskatchewan Law Review* v67 no2 p609-36 2004
Canada
ILO Freedom of Association Principles as Basic Canadian Human Rights: Promises to Keep. K. Norman. *Saskatchewan Law Review* v67 no2 p591-608 2004
"Labour is Not a Commodity": The Supreme Court of Canada and the Freedom of Association. J. Fudge. *Saskatchewan Law Review* v67 no2 p425-52 2004
Collective security *See* International security
Collectivism
Yugoslavia
The Fate of the Yugoslav Model: A Case Against Legal Conformity. K. Medjad. *The American Journal of Comparative Law* v52 no1 p287-319 Wint 2004
College admissions *See* Colleges and universities—Admission
College and university libraries
Exclusion or Efficient Pricing? The "Big Deal" Bundling of Academic Journals. A. S. Edlin, D. L. Rubinfeld. *Antitrust Law Journal* v72 no1 p119-57 2004
College athletics *See* College sports
College sports
With the First Pick in the 2004 NFL Draft, the San Diego Chargers Select . . . ?: A Rule of Reason Analysis of What the National Football League Should Have Argued in Regards to a Challenge of Its Special Draft Eligibility Rules under Section 1 of the Sherman Act. J. M. Ganderson, student author. *University of Miami Business Law Review* v12 no1/2 p1-33 Spr/Summer 2004

Entry by topic

Colleges and universities
See also
Academic freedom
College sports
Colleges and universities—Finance
Fraternities and sororities
Law schools
Does the Tax Law Discriminate against the Majority of American Children?: The Downside of Our Progressive Rate Structure and Unbalanced Incentives for Higher Education. L. B. Snyder. *San Diego Law Review* v41 no3 p1311-35 Summ 2004
Dreaming of an Equal Future for Immigrant Children: Federal and State Initiatives to Improve Undocumented Students' Access to Postsecondary Education. A. Stevenson, student author. *Arizona Law Review* v46 no3 p551-80 Fall 2004
Admission
Litigators and Communities Working Together: Grutter v. Bollinger and the New Civil Rights Movement. M. Massie. *Berkeley Women's Law Journal* v19 no2 p318-23 2004
Finance
Florida
Monetary and Regulatory Hobbling: The Acquisition of Real Property by Public Institutions of Higher Education in Florida. C. L. Zeiner. *University of Miami Business Law Review* v12 no1/2 p103-68 Spr/Summer 2004

I.L.P.: the Subject Approach (locating articles by looking up topics or key words); the Author–Book Title Approach (locating articles by looking up an author's name or finding book reviews by looking up the title of the book); the Table of Cases approach (locating articles by looking up a plaintiff's or defendant's name); and the Table of Statutes approach (locating articles by looking up a statute number or citation).

I.L.P. and *Current Law Index* are usually found in the reference section of a law library.

c. Other Indexes

Although I.L.P. and *Current Law Index* are the most comprehensive indexes because they send you to hundreds of periodicals, there are several other indexes that may assist in your research efforts, including the following:

- ***Index to Foreign Legal Periodicals.*** This index will direct you to periodical articles from countries other than the United States and the British Commonwealth. Access is gained through an alphabetically arranged subject index (in English) or an index by author name.
- ***Index to Periodical Articles Related to Law.*** Remember that I.L.P. and *Current Law Index* will direct you only to legal publications. It is possible, however, that articles related to legal topics may appear in the popular press such as *Time Magazine* or *Wired*. The *Index to Periodical Articles Related to Law* will direct you to such articles through its alphabetically arranged index.

d. Electronic Finding Aids

Because the major print indexes, I.L.P. and *Current Law Index*, are cumulated on a monthly, quarterly, and annual basis, you may need to check several pamphlets and bound volumes to find articles of interest to you. This is somewhat time consuming; therefore, most researchers now use electronic or online versions of these indexes.

- **Legal Periodicals & Books.** The online version of I.L.P. is called "Legal Periodicals & Books." Researching using the online index is much easier than using the conventional print volumes because the online version is completely cumulative. Once you type in the appropriate search terms (topic, author name, and so on), you will be directed to all pertinent articles after 1993.
- **LegalTrac.** LegalTrac is an online index to the articles found in the *Current Law Index* together with articles found in business and general interest periodicals. Many law libraries subscribe to LegalTrac, allowing you desktop computer access, so you can easily search for and locate articles since 1980 by subject matter, author name, and so forth.
- **LexisNexis and Westlaw.** Periodical articles are easily retrieved on both LexisNexis and Westlaw. You may locate articles by their citation (for example, 19 Berkeley Tech. L.J. 104) or by key words and terms. In fact, LexisNexis and Westlaw both include the full text of both I.L.P. and *Current Law Index*.

Help Line: *Research Guides for Secondary Sources*

West offers a number of free publications with instructions on using secondary sources, including encyclopedias and law reviews. Access http://west.thomson.com/support/user-guide/westlaw/law-school.aspx and select the research guide you desire.

- **University Law Review Project.** The University Law Review Project is a free service, available at http://www.lawreview.org, which offers links to hundreds of law reviews and periodicals. The site allows searching for journal articles by key words inserted into a search box. The site also offers direct linking to numerous school law reviews. Thus, if you select *Duke Law Journal*, you will be given access to all of the Duke law review articles since 1997.
- **Law Review Websites.** Most law reviews now have their own websites and post their most recent issues. Some also post the full text of older articles.

C. Texts and Treatises

1. *Introduction*

Texts written by legal scholars that focus on one topic of the law are referred to as *treatises*. Treatises comment on and analyze an area of the law. The authors may be academics or practicing attorneys, and the treatises vary a great deal in scope and depth. A treatise may be a one-volume work on a fairly narrow topic or a multivolume work on a broader topic, such as the 24-volume set *Collier on Bankruptcy, 15th Edition Revised*.

Treatises cover an area of the law in greater depth than encyclopedias. For example, if you were to read all of the C.J.S. treatment on Contracts, you would be presented with approximately 2,000 pages of material. If you were to review the well-known treatise *Williston on Contracts*, you would be presented with more than 30 volumes and approximately 18,000 pages of material. Moreover, the narrative statements found in a treatise are typically more analytical than those found in encyclopedias. Encyclopedias are noncritical summaries of the law, meaning that the information you are given merely summarizes the law relating to that topic. Treatises, however, may be *critical* in the sense that they may criticize current case law and suggest a different approach than courts are currently taking.

One feature treatises share in common with encyclopedias, however, is that they serve as casefinders. The format of most treatises is similar to that of encyclopedias: Narrative discussions of the law are found on the top portion of each page with case citations (and citations to other authorities) located through the use of supporting footnotes on the lower portion of each page.

Although treatises are secondary authorities and are therefore persuasive rather than binding authority, many treatises are highly regarded and are often cited with approval by courts. Thus, you may and should rely on them and quote from them in memoranda and briefs so long as you also have at least one "on point" primary authority to support your position. Following are some tips that suggest that a treatise is highly regarded:

- If the treatise is published in multiple editions (showing wide acceptance and use);
- If court decisions frequently cite a treatise; and
- If the author has produced other writings on this topic.

Also, you may ask your reference librarians for their opinion on the expertise of the author and the treatise's overall reputation in the courts.

To determine whether a treatise exists for an area of the law, check your card catalog (whether conventional or online), which will direct you to the "stack" where the treatise is located; browse the shelves where the books relating to that area of law are maintained and skim the titles; or ask a reference librarian. See Figure 6-8 for a sample page from a treatise.

2. *Common Features of Treatises*

Treatises usually share the following features:

• **Format.** Treatises are essentially expert opinions on one topic of the law. The analysis of the law is presented in narrative form, and readers are usually directed to cases and other authorities through the use of footnotes. Generally, treatise volumes are arranged by chapters and then by sections or paragraphs within those chapters.

• **Index.** An index to the treatise consisting of an alphabetical arrangement of the topics, words, and phrases discussed in the treatise will be located in the last volume of the set or as a separate index volume.

• **Table of Contents.** A table of contents is usually given in the front of each volume, showing how the discussion of this area of law is arranged by chapter.

• **Table of Cases.** Many treatises include an alphabetically arranged table of cases so you may readily locate a discussion of a certain case.

• **Table of Statutes.** Some treatises contain a table of statutes so you can locate the discussion of a certain statute.

• **Appendices.** Many treatises include the entire text of statutes and regulations in an appendix at the end of the set.

• **Updating.** Most treatises are updated by the traditional method of updating law books: an annual cumulative pocket part (or a separate softcover supplement). Other treatises are in looseleaf binders, and the publisher will send replacement pages to provide new information.

Figure 6-8
Sample Page from a Treatise

§ 11:32 Abbreviations

An abbreviation of a descriptive term which still conveys to the buyer the descriptive connotation of the original term will still be held to be descriptive. For example, the mark "B and B" for benedictine and brandy was held descriptive of the ingredients of the product.[1] Further, ALR was held merely descriptive and unregisterable in that members of the electrical industry equate ALR with "aluminum revised," used to describe aluminum wire meeting the revised and upgraded standards of the Underwriter's Laboratories.[2] Other abbreviations held to be descriptive include:

- B-100 was held descriptive of vitamins with 100 milligrams of vitamin B[3]
- V2 was held a descriptive grade designation for vitamin enriched 2 percent butterfat milk[4]
- the letter "O" was held to be descriptive of an orange flavored vodka[4.1]

[Section 11:32]

[1]Martell & Co. v. Societe Anonyme de La Benedictine, 116 F.2d 516, 48 U.S.P.Q. 116 (C.C.P.A. 1941). *See* Automatic Electric, Inc. v. North Electric Mfg. Co., 28 F.2d 979 (6th Cir. 1928); In re General Aniline & Films Corp., 136 U.S.P.Q. 306 (T.T.A.B. 1962); Foremost Dairies, Inc. v. Borden Co., 156 U.S.P.Q. 153 (T.T.A.B. 1967) (HOMO for homogenized milk); Calgon Corp. v. Hooker Chemical Corp., 151 U.S.P.Q. 359 (T.T.A.B. 1966); Spin Physics, Inc. v. Matsushita Electric Industrial Co., 168 U.S.P.Q. 605 (T.T.A.B. 1970) (HPF recognized abbreviation in the trade for "hot-pressed ferrite"). *See also* §§ 12:37-12:40 and 13:20.

[2]Southwire Co. v. Kaiser Aluminum & Chemical Corp., 196 U.S.P.Q. 566 (T.T.A.B. 1977). *See* CPP Ins. Agency, Inc. v. General Motors Corp., 212 U.S.P.Q. 257 (S.D. Cal. 1980) (CPP is recognizable acronym for descriptive term CONSUMER PROTECTION PLAN for supplemental auto repair insurance plan).

[3]Nature's Bounty, Inc. v. Basic Organics, 432 F. Supp. 546, 196 U.S.P.Q. 622 (E.D.N.Y. 1977). *Compare* Nature's Bounty, Inc. v. Super X Drugs Corp., 490 F. Supp. 50, 207 U.S.P.Q. 263 (E.D.N.Y. 1980) (KLB6 held neither generic nor descriptive of food supplement containing kelp, lecithin and vitamin B6).

[4]East Side Jersey Dairy, Inc. v. Jewel Cos., 197 U.S.P.Q. 535 (S.D. Ind. 1977).

[4.1]Star Industries, Inc. v. Bacardi & Co. Ltd. Corp., 71 U.S.P.Q.2d 1026, 2003 WL 23109750 (S.D. N.Y. 2003), aff'd, 412 F.3d 373, 75 U.S.P.Q.2d 1098 (2d Cir. 2005), petition for cert. filed (U.S. Dec. 13, 2005) (no secondary meaning was proven).

3. *Research Strategies for Using Treatises*

To locate information of interest to you in a treatise, use the following standard research methods:

- **Descriptive Word Approach.** Select the word or phrase that describes your issue and look it up in the index, which will then direct you to the appropriate treatise volume and section. For example, if the index directs you to **4:12**, this is a signal for you to retrieve volume 4 and review section 12.
- **Topic Approach.** Review the table of contents for the treatise (check the first volume) and scan the list of chapter titles and subsections, and proceed to the appropriate chapter.
- **Table of Cases/Table of Statutes Approach.** To locate a discussion of a particular case or statute, look up the case name or statute number in the table of cases or table of statutes, respectively, which will direct you to the pertinent volume and section.
- **Other Approaches.** Researchers are often directed to treatises through other sources. For example, if you are reading a pertinent case on an issue and the case relies on a treatise, you should then examine the cited treatise. Similarly, other sources (encyclopedias, periodical articles, and library references found in U.S.C.A. and U.S.C.S.) may direct you to a treatise.

D. Restatements

1. *Introduction*

The *Restatements* are multivolume sets of books on specific topics. They are a product of a group of legal scholars called the American Law Institute (ALI), which was formed in 1923 to restate U.S. case law in a clear and concise manner because the scholars believed case law was uncertain and complex. Membership in ALI is currently limited to 3,000, and individuals are selected for membership in ALI on the basis of their professional accomplishments and their commitment to improving the law. The goal of ALI, to restate American case law in a clear and certain manner, has largely been accomplished due to the authority and repute of the members of ALI.

Restatements do not exist for every area of law but only for selected topics. ALI has several projects in draft status, including a proposed Restatement (Third) of Employment Law. See Figure 6-9 for a chart of Restatements.

Figure 6-9
Chart of Restatements

Topic	*Series*
Agency	First,* Second,* and Third
Conflict of Laws	First* and Second
Contracts	First* and Second
Foreign Relations Law of the United States	Second* and Third
Judgments	First* and Second
Law Governing Lawyers	Third
Property (includes volumes for Landlord & Tenant, Wills and Other Donative Transfers, Mortgages, and Servitudes)	First, Second, and Third
Restitution	First
Suretyship and Guaranty**	Third*
Torts (includes volumes for Restatement (Third) for Apportionment of Liability, Products Liability, and Liability for Physical Harm)	First,* Second, and Third
Trusts (includes volume for Prudent Investor Rule)	First,* Second, and Third
Unfair Competition	Third
(** Replaces superseded Restatement of Security)	(* The original work on this subject is now out of print and has been replaced by the current series.)

2. *Arrangement of Restatements*

Each Restatement typically consists of two to five volumes. Each volume is arranged in chapters, and the chapters are then arranged in titles and numbered sections. Each section states a principle of the law in clear straightforward language printed in bold typeface. These Restatement sections are followed by "Comments" that provide general analysis of the legal principle previously given and "Illustrations" that provide articulately written examples demonstrating the application of the principle. The Reporter's Notes then complete each section by providing general discussion and explanations, together with references to cases that support the Restatement position. See Figure 6-10 for a sample page from Restatement (Second) of Contracts.

Figure 6-10
Sample Page from Restatement (Second) of Contracts

§ 145. Effect of Full Performance

Where the promises in a contract have been fully performed by all parties, the Statute of Frauds does not affect the legal relations of the parties.

Comment:

a. Rationale. The Statute of Frauds renders certain contracts unenforceable by action or defense; it does not forbid the making or performance of such contracts, or authorize their rescission after full performance on both sides. After such full performance, neither party can maintain an action for restitution merely because the contract was unenforceable under the Statute. See § 141. The Statute has no further function to perform, and the legal relations of the parties are the same as if the contract had been enforceable. Compare § 147.

Illustrations:

1. A owes B a debt of $20,000. A's land, worth $10,000, is about to be sold on foreclosure under a mortgage held by C. B contracts to bid in the land and to deduct from A's debt to B $10,000 less the amount B pays. B bids in the land for $6,000. A's debt is reduced by $4,000.

2. At D's request S orally guarantees to C that D will pay a debt D owes to C. On D's failure to pay at maturity, S pays the debt. C's claim against D is discharged, and S has the same rights against D as if S's promise to C had been enforceable.

REPORTER'S NOTE

This Section is based on former § 219. See 3 Williston, Contracts § 528 (3d ed. 1960); 2 Corbin, Contracts § 285 (1950 & Supp. 1971).

Comment a. Illustrations 1 and 2 are based on Illustrations 1 and 2 to former § 219. See Mapes v. Kalva Corp., 68 Ill. App.3d 362, 24 Ill. Dec. 944, 386 N.E.2d 148 (1979); Trimmer v. Short, 492 S.W.2d 179 (Mo. Ct. App. 1973); Scott v. Southern Coach & Body Co., 280 Ala. 670, 197 So.2d 775 (1967); cf. Rice v. Insurance & Bonds, Inc., 366 So.2d 85 (Fla. Dist. Ct. App. 1979).

§ 146. Rights of Competing Transferees of Property

(1) Where a contract to transfer property or a transfer was unenforceable against the transferor under the Statute of Frauds but subsequently becomes enforce-

3. *Research Strategies for Using Restatements*

The easiest way to locate a pertinent Restatement provision is to use the descriptive word approach. Consult the alphabetically arranged index to your Restatement, which is usually found in the last volume of the Restatement set. Look up words or phrases that describe your research problem, and you will be directed to the appropriate section of the Restatement. Alternatively, you may be directed to a pertinent Restatement section in the course of your research; for example, a case you may be reading may refer to a Restatement section. You may also browse through your Restatement's Table of Contents. Finally, you may use the alphabetical Table of Cases (for newer Restatements) to be directed to Restatement sections that have discussed certain cases.

The Restatements are kept current through pocket parts and appendix volumes (which themselves contain pocket parts). The Restatements are available on LexisNexis and Westlaw.

4. *Effect of Restatements*

Because the Restatements are a secondary source, courts are not required to adopt or follow the Restatement positions. Nevertheless, the Restatements have been cited in cases more than 160,000 times. Many legal experts believe the Restatements are the most highly regarded of all of the secondary authorities, and you should freely rely on them and cite to them in your research projects.

E. Miscellaneous Secondary Authorities

Although the most frequently used secondary authorities are A.L.R. annotations, encyclopedias, periodicals, treatises, and Restatements, there are also numerous other secondary authorities that researchers often use. The following are the most commonly used of these other secondary authorities.

1. *Attorneys General Opinions*

The U.S. Attorney General (appointed by the President) is the chief law enforcement official for the government. Each of the 50 states and D.C. also has an attorney general (usually elected by voters). The attorneys general issue written opinions on a variety of topics, including the interpretation of statutes and the duties of government agencies. These *attorneys general opinions* typically are written in response to questions by legislators, the executive branch, or other government officials.

Any large law library in your area will collect the opinions of the U.S. Attorney General and will also have the opinions of your state attorney general. Although attorneys general opinions are secondary authorities, because they are written by the chief legal advisor to the executive branch (whether federal or state) and are usually followed, they are highly persuasive, and you should feel free to cite them in your research projects.

Most sets of opinions of attorneys general will have an index, which you can access by using the descriptive word approach. It is more likely, however, that you will be directed to a pertinent attorney general opinion by another source you are using, such as U.S.C.A., U.S.C.S., or a state annotated code. Similarly, when you update a case by Shepardizing or KeyCiting it, you will be directed to attorneys general opinions that have mentioned your case. Finally, many opinions are now available on the Internet. Almost all states now offer their attorneys general opinions on their respective websites. Access the site of the Office of Legal Counsel at http://www.usdoj.gov/olc/opinions.htm to link to the U.S. Attorney General opinions or to the website of the National Association of Attorneys General at http://www.naag.org/attorneys_general.php to link to your state's attorneys general opinions.

2. Words and Phrases

West's multivolume set *Words and Phrases* will direct you to cases that have interpreted words, terms, or phrases. Arranged alphabetically, the set is as easy to use as any dictionary. Once you look up the word or phrase in which you are interested, you will be directed to any cases in which this word has been judicially defined or interpreted. *Words and Phrases* contains no narrative treatment but rather focuses exclusively on helping you locate cases by providing a brief summary of the cases that interpret a certain word and then giving you the case citation. Be sure to review the pocket part in each volume to determine if newer cases have interpreted or construed the word you are reviewing.

3. *Legal Dictionaries and Thesauri*

A *legal dictionary* will give you the spelling, pronunciation, and meaning of a legal word or phrase such as "en banc" or "abatement." In some instances you will be directed to a case or secondary authority in which the word was defined. The best known of the legal dictionaries is *Black's Law Dictionary* (9th ed. 2009). *Black's* not only includes more than 45,000 definitions, but also includes West Key Numbers and provides a table of common legal abbreviations, definitions of legal maxims, and many other useful features. *Black's* differs from *Words and Phrases* in that the coverage of *Words and Phrases* is limited to words and phrases that have been defined in cases; *Black's* defines words whether they have been the subject of court interpretation or not.

A *legal thesaurus* provides synonyms and antonyms for legal words and terms. For example, if you wish to find another word for "abandon," a thesaurus will suggest "forsake," "abdicate," "retract," and other terms. One of the best known of the legal thesauri is *Burton's Legal Thesaurus* by William C. Burton, which provides more than 8,000 terms, synonyms, and definitions. Dictionaries and thesauri are found in the reference section of your law library.

A recent trend is publication of glossaries of legal terms on the Internet. For example, the website Law.com offers a legal dictionary at http://dictionary.law.com. Although these online glossaries are not particularly comprehensive, they may be helpful in providing you with a quick understanding of a legal term or Latin phrase.

4. *Legal Directories*

a. Introduction

A *legal directory* is simply a list of lawyers. Some law directories, such as the highly regarded *Martindale-Hubbell Law Directory*, aim at listing all lawyers admitted to any jurisdiction. Other directories are more limited in scope and may list only those lawyers in a certain city or locality. Law directories are usually kept in the reference section of a law library.

b. *Martindale-Hubbell Law Directory*

The best-known law directory in the United States is *Martindale-Hubbell Law Directory*, in existence for more than a century. At present, nearly all major U.S. law firms pay to be listed in *Martindale-Hubbell*. The set is published annually in hardbound volumes and is organized alphabetically by state. For example, Volume 1 covers the states Alabama, Alaska, Arizona, and Arkansas. Within each state listing, law firms and attorneys are identified alphabetically by city name and then by law firm or attorney name. Each firm that has an entry will list its attorneys and provide brief biographical information about them. Moreover, the firm's address, phone number, website, representative clients, and practice areas will be noted. By reviewing *Martindale-Hubbell*, you may be able to target your résumé to a law firm that focuses on a field of law in which you are interested. Legal professionals also use *Martindale-Hubbell* to refer clients to other firms if a conflict of interest arises or if a firm cannot represent a client. See Figure 6-11 for a sample page from the *Martindale-Hubbell Law Directory*.

Martindale-Hubbell also offers State Digests, which provide a brief overview of some of the laws of all 50 states. Although *Martindale-Hubbell* will not include all of the laws of these jurisdictions, it will provide a summary of some of the more common laws of each state. Thus, for example, you will be able to determine the fees for creating a corporation in each state, residency requirements to obtain a divorce, and so forth. The State Digests are arranged alphabetically, from Alabama to Wyoming. Since 2007, the State Digests are no longer available in print and are available only on CD-ROM.

Figure 6-11
Sample Page from *Martindale-Hubbell Law Directory*

DRATH, CLIFFORD, MURPHY, WENNERHOLM & HAGEN

A PROFESSIONAL CORPORATION

1999 HARRISON STREET, SUITE 1900

OAKLAND, CALIFORNIA 94612-3578

Telephone: 510-287-4000

Telefax: 510-287-4050

Email: dcmwh@msn.com

San Diego, California Office: 600 B Street, Suite 1550. Telephone: 619-595-3060. Fax: 619-595-3066.

Areas of practice

Civil Litigation with an emphasis in the fields of insurance and self-insured defense, insurance coverage analysis, construction, employment, environmental, products liability, personal injury and professional liability defense.

FIRM PROFILE: Drath, Clifford, Murphy, Wennerholm & Hagen is a Martindale-Hubbell Bar Register of Preeminent Lawyers firm.

JOHN M. DRATH, born Portland, Oregon, November 14, 1944; admitted to bar, 1970, California; 1971, Colorado; 1993, Montana. *Education:* University of Washington (B.A., 1965); University of San Francisco (J.D., 1969). *Member:* State Bar of California; Association of Defense Counsel, Northern California (President, 1992-1993); Defense Research Institute; American Board of Trial Advocates; Federation of Insurance and Corporate Counsel. ***PRACTICE AREAS:*** Professional Liability Defense; Personal Injury Defense; Insurance Coverage; Bad Faith Defense; Complex Litigation. ***Email:*** dcmwh@msn.com

RICK J. MURPHY, born San Francisco, California, March 26, 1951; admitted to bar, 1976, California. *Education:* University of California at Davis (B.A., cum laude, 1973); University of Santa Clara School of Law (J.D., cum laude, 1976). *Member:* State Bar of California; Association of Defense Counsel; American Board of Trial Advocates. ***PRACTICE AREAS:*** Insurance Defense; Accident and Personal Injury; Business Litigation. ***Email:*** dcmwh@msn.com

TRACI E. WENNERHOLM, born Los Angeles, California, July 13, 1960; admitted to bar, 1985, California. *Education:* University of California at Riverside (B.A., 1982); Hastings College of the Law, University of California (J.D., 1985). *Member:* State Bar of California; Association of Defense Counsel; Defense Research Institute. ***PRACTICE AREAS:*** Construction Law; Personal Injury Defense; Asbestos Defense. ***Email:*** dcmwh@msn.com

DAVID F. BEACH, born Jackson, Michigan, March 31, 1955; admitted to bar, 1980, California. *Education:* College of San Mateo (A.A., 1975); University of California at Berkeley (B.S., 1977); University of San Diego (J.D., magna cum laude, 1980). *Member:* State Bar of California; American Arbitration Association; Association of Defense Counsel; Defense Research Institute. ***PRACTICE AREAS:*** Personal Injury Defense; Insurance Coverage; Construction Litigation; Asbestos Litigation. ***Email:*** dcmwh@msn.com

GRETCHEN W. LATIMER, born Berkeley, California, August 8, 1965; admitted to bar, 1992, California. *Education:* University of Puget Sound (B.A., 1987), Seattle University (J.D., 1992). *Member:* San Francisco Bar Association; Contra Costa County Bar Association. ***PRACTICE AREAS:*** Construction Defect; Insurance Defense. ***Email:*** dcmwh@msn.com

Representative clients

REPRESENTATIVE CLIENTS: Allstate Insurance Co.; American Equities Insurance Co.; American States Insurance Co.; Cooper Industries; First Financial Insurance Company; First Mercury Syndicate; Motors Insurance Co.; Nationwide Insurance Co.; Nautilus Insurance Co.; National General Insurance Co.; Northbrook Insurance Co.; Preferred Risk Mutual Insurance Co.; Scottsdale Insurance Co.; Super Computer, Inc,; TOPA Insurance Co.; USS-POSCO Industries, USX Corporation; Unicare Insurance Co.; Willis Corroon.

(For complete Biographical Data on Additional Personnel, see Professional Biographies at San Diego, California)

The set also includes three volumes titled *International Law Directory* that profile lawyers and law firms from more than 160 countries and provide summaries or digests of the laws of more than 80 countries. Finally, the set also provides the text of several treaties, some of the better-known Uniform Acts, the Model Rules of Professional Conduct for attorneys, and other useful information.

All of the attorney information found in the conventional print volumes of *Martindale-Hubbell* can also be located on the Internet at http://www.martindale.com. The site provides free access to comprehensive listings of one million lawyers and law firms around the world (including those in private, corporate, or government practice). Searching is easily accomplished by lawyer name, firm name, location, or law school attended. Another excellent free legal directory on the Internet is provided by FindLaw, West's legal website. Access http://legalrecords.findlaw.com/ss/search_index.jsp to search for attorneys by name or practice area. *Martindale-Hubbell* is available on LexisNexis; Westlaw offers its own legal directories.

5. *Form Books*

Much of a legal professional's time is spent drafting documents. Some documents are litigation related, such as complaints or answers, whereas others are transaction related, such as a partnership agreement. *Form books* help practitioners get a jump start on drafting these documents by providing sample forms. Most sets of form books are multivolume sets with an alphabetically arranged index that allows you to use the descriptive word approach to locate desired forms. Most sets are annotated, meaning that you will be referred to cases that have approved or supported language used in the form. Moreover, many form books provide analysis and commentary on use of the forms and practical aids such as checklists, suggesting items to consider in drafting a certain type of document. Thus, although the form books themselves are practice aids, they include secondary authority references and commentary. Most form books are kept current by pocket parts.

In addition to the form books described previously as part of the Am. Jur. Total Client-Service Library (see Section A.2.e), some of the better-known form books include the following:

- ***Bender's Forms of Discovery.*** This set, by publisher Matthew Bender (part of LexisNexis), provides forms related solely to discovery matters and includes forms for interrogatories, requests for production of documents, depositions, and other discovery devices for both federal and state practice.
- ***Bender's Federal Practice Forms.*** This multivolume set provides litigation forms for use in federal practice, both civil and criminal.
- ***Current Legal Forms with Tax Analysis.*** This set by Jacob Rabkin and Mark H. Johnson is a 34-volume set of forms for every area of law practice (except criminal law and litigation).

Figure 6-12
Sample Page from Virginia Forms—Criminal Procedure

No. 9-1002. Order Allowing Attorney to Withdraw.

ORDER ALLOWING ATTORNEY TO WITHDRAW

This matter came on this ___ day of _______, 1998, to be heard on the motion of Hope N. Pray, counsel, for leave to withdraw as counsel of record for Daniel Dissatisfied.

Daniel Dissatisfied being present in person in court, the Court heard statements by counsel and defendant.

The Court finding there being good cause and it being proper so to do, it is hereby ORDERED that Hope N. Pray is relieved as counsel of record for Daniel Dissatisfied.

It is further ORDERED that the next attorney on the court-appointed list be assigned this case.

Enter: ____________________
Judge

Date: ____________________

I ask for this:

____
Hope N. Pray

Seen and Agreed:

____
Daniel Dissatisfied

Note: Rules of the Supreme Court of Virginia, Virginia Code of Professional Responsibility, DR 2-108 as to termination representation.

Ethics Alert: Using Form Books and Metadata

Drafting a legal form requires more than finding a good form and then filling in the blanks. You are required to research the area of law and then modify any preprinted form to comply with the law. Use an annotated form book; it will direct you to primary authorities that endorse use of the language given in the form and provide additional critical references. Because the law changes frequently, using an outmoded form from one of your form files may be malpractice.

In addition, documents created at law firms often contain *metadata*, or information describing the history, management, and tracking of an electronically created document. For example, if you change the name "Smith" in an older contract that you are now drafting for "Jones," metadata enables a reader to discover that the document was originally prepared for Smith. Metadata also reveals who received documents, comments, and deletions made during the drafting process, sequences of changes, delays in sending a document, and other critical information. Many law firms now use sophisticated "scrubbing" programs to eliminate metadata and protect confidential client information. Check your law firm's policies on metadata mining and scrubbing, and be scrupulous about maintaining confidential client information.

Many publishers produce sets of form books devoted strictly to forms for use in one state. For example, a set commonly used in California for business or transactional matters is Matthew Bender's *California Legal Forms: Transaction Guide*. Treatises often provide forms as well. See Figure 6-12 for a sample page from a form book.

Finally, the Internet offers thousands of legal forms. As with many offerings on the Internet, however, it is unknown who authored the forms or whether they have been subjected to the rigorous review that accompanies print publications. Thus, they should be used with extreme caution, although they may serve as a useful starting place. Better forms may be found on a state's official website. For example, all states now provide comprehensive forms for organizing, maintaining, and dissolving business entities such as corporations. Similarly, many courts now offer free forms on their websites, and these are highly reliable.

To locate form books, check the card catalog in your law library, browse the shelves, or consult your law librarian. When you locate a pertinent set, use the descriptive word approach to locate appropriate forms, and be sure to check any pocket parts.

Form books provide an excellent starting point for drafting legal documents; however, do not view drafting documents as merely an exercise in finding a form and then "filling in the blanks." Carefully review the form to ensure it is appropriate for the document you are preparing. Revise the form if needed.

6. *Uniform Laws*

A group of more than 300 practicing attorneys, judges, law professors, and other legal scholars form the National Conference of Commissioners on Uniform State Laws, which meets on an annual basis to draft proposed legislation on various areas of the law in which national uniformity is desirable. These proposed laws, called *uniform laws* or *uniform acts*, are then presented to the legislatures of the various states with the hope and expectation that the legislature will pass the Conference's version of the law. No uniform law is effective until a state legislature specifically enacts it. Some states will adopt the uniform act "as is." Other states may reject the act, and others may revise the act, adding certain provisions and omitting others. Thus, although the goal of the Conference is to produce a statute that will be uniform from state to state, the end result is a statute that nearly always has some variation from state to state.

The Conference has approved more than 250 uniform laws, ranging from perhaps the best known, the Uniform Commercial Code (relating to commercial practices and sales), which has been adopted in whole or in part by every state, to the Uniform Adoption Act, to the Uniform Partnership Act.

The Conference and other organizations also draft proposed legislation known as *Model Acts*, which serve as a source to which states can look for guidance in drafting their own laws and which are seldom enacted in their entirety. Uniform laws, however, are intended to be adopted exactly as written.

To locate the text of the uniform laws, use West's *Uniform Laws Annotated* (U.L.A.), which includes the text of all uniform laws (arranged by general subject matter), the comments of the drafters explaining the purpose of each uniform law, a list of the states that have adopted each particular uniform law, brief descriptions of how various states have modified the uniform law, and other resources. See Figure 6-13 for a sample page from this set. To locate specific uniform laws, you may scan the spines of the volumes or use the *Uniform Laws Annotated Directory of Acts*, a pamphlet that lists all uniform laws alphabetically and directs you to a uniform law's location in U.L.A. Additionally, some of the more widely adopted uniform laws are printed in *Martindale-Hubbell*. The text of all uniform laws is available on Westlaw and many are available on LexisNexis. Finally, the uniform laws are available on the Internet on the website of the Conference at http://www.nccusl.org. The text of uniform laws is given, along with a summary of each act and legislative facts about the adoption of an act in the various states.

Remember that uniform laws are secondary authorities, but once a uniform law is adopted by a state legislature, it is a primary authority like any other statute, and it can be located in your state's code. If another state has adopted the same uniform law, its interpretation of that law may be persuasive (but not binding) to a court interpreting your state's uniform law.

Figure 6-13
Sample Page from *Uniform Laws Annotated*

INTESTATE SUCCESSION—WILLS § 2-102

wife which listed as a possible heir the illegitimate child of appellant. In re Raso's Estate, Fla.App.1976, 332 So.2d 78.

Trial court abused its discretion in denying appellant's motion to vacate default judgment where appellant properly alleged excusable neglect for her failure to timely respond to petition for determination of heirs and where appellant properly alleged a meritorious defense. Id.

Section 2-102. [Share of the Spouse.]

The intestate share of the surviving spouse is:

(1) if there is no surviving issue or parent of the decedent, the entire intestate estate;

(2) if there is no surviving issue but the decedent is survived by a parent or parents, the first [$50,000], plus one-half of the balance of the intestate estate;

(3) if there are surviving issue all of whom are issue of the surviving spouse also, the first [$50,000], plus one-half of the balance of the intestate estate;

(4) if there are surviving issue one or more of whom are not issue of the surviving spouse, one-half of the intestate estate.

COMMENT

This section gives the surviving spouse a larger share than most existing statutes on descent and distribution. In doing so, it reflects the desires of most married persons, who almost always leave all of a moderate estate or at least one-half of a larger estate to the surviving spouse when a will is executed. A husband or wife who desires to leave the surviving spouse less than the share provided by this section may do so by executing a will, subject of course to possible election by the surviving spouse to take an elective share of one-third under Part 2 of this Article. Moreover, in the small estate (less than $50,000 after homestead allowance, exempt property, and allowances) the surviving spouse is given the entire estate if there are only children who are issue of both the decedent and the surviving spouse; the result is to avoid protective proceedings as to property otherwise passing to their minor children.

See Section 2-802 for the definition of spouse which controls for purposes of intestate succession.

Law Review Commentaries

How the family fares. Donald L. Robertson. 37 Ohio S.L.J. 264 (1976).

Modern Wills Act. John T. Gaubatz. 31 U.Miami L.Rev. 497 (1977).

Probate change. 20 Boston Bar J. No. 11, p. 6 (1976).

59

7. *Looseleaf Services*

Looseleaf services are sets of ringed binders with individual looseleaf sheets of paper, which are easily removed and replaced. The looseleaf services are a variety of treatise, and many are devoted to rules and regulations promulgated by our federal agencies, such as the service titled *Communications Regulations*. The looseleaf services usually include primary authorities (such as cases, statutes, and administrative regulations) as well as secondary authorities (such as commentary and discussion of the topic and recent developments). Generally, looseleaf services function as "finding" tools in that they provide general background information about a topic of the law and then direct you to relevant primary authorities. Use the descriptive word approach, and look up words in the alphabetically arranged index to be directed to the appropriate volume and paragraph or section in the set. Looseleaf services are discussed further in Chapter Seven.

8. *Jury Instructions*

At the end of a trial, when a judge "charges" a jury by providing it with instructions for reaching a decision, the judge relies on form or pattern *jury instructions*, which are usually drafted by legal scholars or bar associations to make sure the instructions given to a jury are accurate and understandable. Many sets of jury instructions not only provide the actual text of an instruction but also follow it with commentary directing you to cases, statutes, and other authorities that support the language used in the instruction. Both the commentary and the instructions themselves are excellent research tools. For example, if you were writing a memorandum on a contract matter and needed to list the elements of a cause of action for breach of contract, a jury instruction will likely set them forth, as follows:

> Ladies and Gentlemen, if you find from your consideration of all the evidence that there was an agreement between the parties, that the parties were legally capable of entering into the agreement, that the defendant without justification or excuse breached the agreement, and that this breach was the cause of damage to the plaintiff, then you should find the defendant liable for breach of contract.

Thus, jury instructions serve to provide a quick summary of the key elements of many areas of the law, including contracts, fraud, negligence, and so forth.

To locate jury instructions, check the card catalog at your law library. Nearly every state has its own sets of jury instructions for civil and criminal cases, and many states make them available on the Internet (use Table T.1 of *The Bluebook* to locate your state's judicial website). Similarly, many of the federal courts also post jury instructions on their websites. Use http://www.uscourts.gov to link to all federal courts. If there is no set of jury instructions specific to your state, consult *Am. Jur. Pleading and Practice Forms, Annotated*. For federal cases, consult *Modern Federal Jury Instructions*. See Figure 6-14 for a sample jury instruction.

Figure 6-14
Sample Jury Instruction

7.19 LIABILITY OF MUNICIPALITY

If you find that Plaintiff has proved [these things] [any of his claims] by a preponderance of the evidence, you must consider whether [*Municipality*] is also liable to Plaintiff. [*Municipality*] is not responsible simply because it employed [*Officer*]. [*Municipality*] is liable if Plaintiff proves by a preponderance of the evidence that Defendant's conduct was a result of its official policy.

Committee Comments

a. **Authority:** *See Monell v. City of New York Dep't of Soc. Svcs.*, 436 U.S. 658, 690-691 (1978).

b. **Usage:** In a case involving a single constitutional claim, the Committee suggests that courts use this instruction in conjunction with the relevant elements instruction. In a case involving multiple constitutional claims, the Committee suggests that courts use this instruction separately after the jury has been instructed on the elements of each individual claim.

F. Summary of Secondary Authorities

All of the sources discussed in this chapter are secondary authorities, meaning that although you may refer to these sources and cite them in memoranda and briefs, courts are not required to follow them. Although secondary authorities are often highly reputable, they remain persuasive at best and lack the force of the primary authorities of cases, constitutions, statutes, and administrative regulations.

Remember that some of the secondary authorities such as Restatements and law review articles are highly regarded and often cited, whereas others, such as encyclopedias, are viewed as elementary in approach and are seldom cited. One of the best indications of the strength of a secondary source is found in Rule 1.4(i) of *The Bluebook*, which provides a hierarchical order when string-citing numerous secondary authorities. *ALWD* Rule 45 is similar.

All of the secondary sources do an excellent job of providing commentary on the law and typically direct you to the primary authorities that you should rely on and cite in your memoranda and briefs. A summary of the secondary sources is provided in Figure 6-15.

Figure 6-15
Chart of Secondary Authorities

Secondary Authority	Overview	Identification of Sets	Supplementation	Research Techniques	Use Notes
A.L.R. Annotations	Thorough articles or "annotations" on various legal topics	Multivolume sets	Annual cumulative pocket parts	Descriptive word approach	A.L.R. annotations are very well respected.
Encyclopedias	Alphabetically arranged narrative statements of hundreds of legal topics, supported by cases and other authorities in footnotes	General sets are C.J.S. and Am. Jur. 2d; about 15 states have their own local sets; some specialized sets exist	Annual cumulative pocket parts	Descriptive word approach; Topic approach	Good introductory information but somewhat elementary in their approach.
Legal Periodicals	Publications produced on a periodic basis on a variety of topics	Law school publications; bar association publications; special interest publications; and newspapers	No supplementation	*Index to Legal Periodicals & Books*; *Current Law Index*; online indices	Law reviews are often scholarly and well respected; other periodicals are more practical.

Figure 6-15 *(Continued)*

Secondary Authority	Overview	Identification of Sets	Supplementation	Research Techniques	Use Notes
Texts and Treatises	Texts written by scholars on one topic that analyze cases and statutes	Multivolume sets include thorough and often critical analysis.	Annual cumulative pocket parts; new pages; or softcover supplements	Descriptive word approach; topic approach; table of cases or statutes approach	Many treatises are highly regarded.
Restatements	Statements of the law in clear language	Multivolume sets on selected areas of the law, such as trusts	Appendix volumes with pocket parts	Descriptive word approach; topic approach	Restatements are highly authoritative.
Attorneys General Opinions	Written opinions by U.S. attorney general and state attorneys general on various topics	Multivolume sets	No supplementation; each volume is complete	Descriptive word approach; references from other sources; online access	Attorneys general opinions are strongly persuasive and highly respected.
Words and Phrases	Set providing references to cases that have interpreted words or phrases	Multivolume set	Annual pocket parts	Alphabetical approach	Useful in locating cases interpreting words or phrases.

Figure 6-15 *(Continued)*

Secondary Authority	Overview	Identification of Sets	Supplementation	Research Techniques	Use Notes
Dictionaries	Books providing definitions of legal words and phrases	One-volume alphabetical arrangements of words and phrases	No supplementation; each volume is complete	Alphabetical approach	Useful in determining meaning of a word or phrase.
Directories	Lists of lawyers	Usually multi-volume sets; *Martindale-Hubbell* includes useful features such as uniform laws	New set or volume issued annually	Alphabetical approach by state, city, firm, and attorney's name	Used to locate attorneys and law firms.
Form Books	Sets of books with standard forms to help in drafting documents	Multivolume sets of books	Pocket parts	Descriptive word approach; topic approach	Used primarily to assist in preparing documents; never cited.
Uniform Laws	Drafts of statutes proposed by legal scholars for certain areas of the law	Multivolume set, *Uniform Laws Annotated,* containing text of uniform laws, commentary, references to other sources, etc.	Pocket parts and supplements	Use *Uniform Laws Annotated Directory of Acts* to locate a uniform law; available online	Cases interpreting a uniform law (even those from another state) may be highly persuasive in your state if your state has also adopted the uniform law.

Figure 6-15 *(Continued)*

Secondary Authority	Overview	Identification of Sets	Supplementation	Research Techniques	Use Notes
Looseleaf Services	Type of treatise devoted to one area of law	Multivolume sets of ringed binders	Replacement pages	Descriptive word approach	Services provide a thorough overview of an area of law.
Jury Instructions	Sets of books containing instructions for charging the jury in civil and criminal trials as well as commentary and annotations	One-volume or multivolume sets specific to federal courts, one state, or general in nature	Pocket parts	Descriptive word approach	Useful in obtaining a "snapshot" of an area of the law, although seldom cited in research projects.

G. Citation Form

You will never cite to some of the secondary authorities discussed in this chapter, namely, *Words and Phrases*, legal directories, or form books. Other secondary sources are cited as follows:

	Bluebook (for practitioners)	*ALWD*
Encyclopedias	79 C.J.S. *Insurance* § 281 (2000). 38 Am. Jur. 2d *Guaranty* § 29 (1999).	79 C.J.S. *Insurance* § 281 (2000). 38 Am. Jur. 2d *Guaranty* § 29 (1999).
Periodicals	Sharon Dolovich, *State Punishment and Private Prisons*, 55 Duke L.J. 437 (2005).	Sharon Dolovich, *State Punishment and Private Prisons*, 55 Duke L.J. 437 (2005).
Treatises	3 J. Thomas McCarthy, *McCarthy on Trademarks and Unfair Competition* § 9:12 (4th ed. 1996).	J. Thomas McCarthy, *McCarthy on Trademarks and Unfair Competition* vol. 3, § 19:12 (4th ed., West 1996).
Restatements	Restatement (Second) of Contracts § 101 (1981).	*Restatement (Second) of Contracts* § 101 (1981).
United States Attorneys General Opinions	43 Op. Att'y Gen. 369 (1982).	43 Op. Atty. Gen. 369 (1982).
Dictionaries	*Black's Law Dictionary* 781 (9th ed. 2009).	*Black's Law Dictionary* 781 (Bryan A. Garner ed., 9th ed., West 2009).
Uniform Laws	Unif. P'ship Act § 103, 7A U.L.A. 119 (2002).	Unif. Partn. Act § 103, 7A U.L.A. 119 (2002).
Looseleaf Services	*In re Stevens Textiles Co.*, 4 Bankr. L. Rep. (CCH) ¶ 16,041 (Bankr. D.N.J. Mar. 10, 2003).	*In re Stevens Textiles Co.*, 4 Bankr. L. Rep. (CCH) ¶ 16,041 (Bankr. D.N.J. Mar. 10, 2003).
Jury Instructions	2 John S. Siffert, *Modern Federal Jury Instructions* § 12.04 (1984).	John S. Siffert, *Modern Federal Jury Instructions* vol. 2, § 12.04 (Matthew Bender 1984).

CyberSites

http://www.law.harvard.edu/library/research/guides/index.html	Harvard Law School offers a number of useful Research Guides that provide research tips for using encyclopedias, treatises, Restatements, and other secondary authorities.
http://www.ll.georgetown.edu/tutorials	Georgetown Law Center offers several Research Guides for using secondary sources, including periodicals, encyclopedias, treatises, and other authorities.
http://www.lawreview.org	The University Law Review Project, a coalition of legal educators, provides links to hundreds of law reviews, legal periodicals, and newsletters. Search by key words, topics, and specific journal names.
http://www.hg.org/journals.html	The website HG.org is a comprehensive law and government portal with links to hundreds of periodicals.
http://www.ali.org	The website of the American Law Institute lists the Restatements in print and discusses Restatements in the drafting or revising process.
http://usdoj.gov/olc/opinions.htm	The Department of Justice provides access to opinions of the U.S. Attorney General. Search by year and topic.
http://www.naag.org	The National Association of Attorneys General provides direct links to each state's website for its attorney general, where opinions may be located.
http://dictionary.law.com/	LawCom offers a law dictionary at its site.
http://www.martindale.com	LexisNexis offers a searchable directory of more than one million lawyers and law firms.
http://www.megalaw.com	MegaLaw offers a wide variety of legal materials and forms. Select "Legal Forms."
http://www.allaboutforms.com	AllAboutForms offers hundreds of legal forms.
http://www.nccusl.org	The website of the National Conference of Commissioners on Uniform State Laws provides the text of all final uniform laws and information about and legislative status of uniform laws.
http://www.llrx.com/columns/reference19.htm	An article entitled "What is the Law? Finding Jury Instructions" provides links to several sets of jury instructions.

Research Assignment

1. Use Am. Jur. 2d.
   a. Which title and sections generally deal with invasion of a deceased person's or decedent's privacy?
   b. Review the sections to which you are directed. Do actions for the violation of the right to privacy generally survive the allegedly invaded party's death? Answer the question and cite a federal case that supports your answer.

2. Use Am. Jur. 2d.
   a. Which title and section deal with the defense of entrapment in an action for burglary?
   b. Review this section. Which Illinois Supreme Court case held that if a person who will be affected by the burglary or his authorized agent induces another to commit the offense, entrapment may be a defense to a prosecution for burglary?

3. Use C.J.S.
   a. Use the Table of Cases. Under which topic and section is the case *Trani v. Anchor Hocking Glass Corp.* discussed?
   b. Which topic and section discuss the claiming of a reward by claimants acting in concert?
   c. Read the section for your previous answer. May a reward be apportioned to a party whose participation was of little consequence? How will a reward be distributed among two or more claimants? What case governs your answer?
   d. Give a short summary of the definition of "larceny."

4. Use *Am. Jur. Proof of Facts (3d)*.
   a. Give the citation to an article relating to unnecessary surgery, namely, for an unnecessary hysterectomy.
   b. Review the article. What does section 37 provide (with regard to damages for lost earnings)?
   c. Who authored this article?
   d. Review section 3. How many women undergo hysterectomies each year?

5. Use *Index to Legal Periodicals & Books* (volume 102, number 1).
   a. Cite an article written by David Baxter in 2007 relating to asylum law.
   b. Cite an article written in 2008 relating to spying spouses in divorce cases.
   c. Cite an article published in Fall 2007 about a case in which the plaintiff's name is *Nike, Inc.*

6. Use the Subject Index for *Current Law Index* for 2007 (volume 28, part A) and give the title and author of an article relating to California's grandparent visitation law.

7. Give the title and author of the article located at 109 Colum. L. Rev. 237.

8. Use *Callman on Unfair Competition, Trademarks and Monopolies*.
   a. What section discusses "puffing"?
   b. Review the first section to which you are directed.
      (i) Does the law of unfair competition forbid puffing?
      (ii) Is a claim by a manufacturer that its ice cream maker is "better" than competing ice cream makers actionable? Answer the question and cite a case that supports your answer.
   c. What section of the treatise discusses *Doud v. Hodge*, 146 F. Supp. 887 (N.D. Ill. 1956)?

9. Use the treatise *Federal Practice and Procedure* (by Wright and Miller).
   a. What section discusses vacating or setting aside default judgments as being within the discretion of the court?
   b. Review the section to which you are directed. Why is considerable weight given to the district trial judge's decision on the motion?
   c. What case supports your previous answer?

10. Use Restatement (Second) of Contracts.
    a. If an offer does not specify a time when it must be accepted, when must it be accepted? What section supports your answer?
    b. Review the illustrations for the previous section. Assume that A publishes an offer of a reward for information leading to the arrest and conviction of the person guilty of a specified murder, and B, intending to obtain the reward, gives the requested information a year after publication of the offer. Is acceptance timely?

11. Use Restatement (Third) of Unfair Competition.
    a. What section discusses the difference between laches and acquiescence in trademark infringement?
    b. Review the section to which you are directed. What is the difference between laches and acquiescence?
    c. What 2000 District of Minnesota case held that the plaintiff was barred by laches in pursuing trademark protection?

12. Use West's set *Words and Phrases*. Which Massachusetts case(s) construes the meaning of the phrase "direct estoppel"? Give case name(s) only.

13. Use *Black's Law Dictionary* (9th ed. 2009).
    a. What is the definition given for "business trust"?
    b. To what topic and key number relating to this definition are you directed?

c. What does the legal maxim *non omne damnum inducit injuriam* mean?

14. Use the most current volumes of *Martindale-Hubbell Law Directory*.
    a. William H. Gammon is an attorney with the Raleigh, North Carolina, law firm Nelson Mullins Riley & Scarborough, LLP. Where and when did he receive his J.D. degree?
    b. An attorney named Gianluigi Santoro is with the Rome, Italy, law firm Meranda & Pagliaro. Where did he receive his education?
    c. What is the age requirement in Sweden to adopt a person?
    d. Review the ABA Model Rules of Professional Conduct. What does section 1.5 discuss with regard to prohibited contingent fees?

15. Use *Am. Jur. Pleadings and Practice Forms Annotated*.
    a. Which form provides a petition or application for inspection of a corporation's stockholders' list (to enlist additional stockholders for a derivative action)?
    b. Review the complaint to which you are directed. Briefly, what does Paragraph 7 allege?
    c. Which form provides a complaint (by a surviving spouse against the estate of a deceased spouse) to set aside an antenuptial or prenuptial agreement on the ground of mistake, nondisclosure, undue influence, etc.?
    d. Review the complaint to which you are directed. Briefly, what does Paragraph 15 allege?

16. Use *Am. Jur. Legal Forms (2d)*.
    a. Which form(s) relates to royalties based on a business franchise's sales?
    b. Which form provides a definition of "gross sales"?

17. Use *Uniform Laws Annotated* (West's Master Edition).
    a. Has Kentucky adopted the Uniform Marriage and Divorce Act of 1970 (as amended in 1971 and 1973)?
    b. If so, give the citation to Kentucky's statute.
    c. Review the Uniform Marriage and Divorce Act. What is the general topic of section 306?
    d. Review section 306. Generally, are the terms of a separation agreement (set forth in a decree) between parties to a marriage enforceable by contempt? Give your answer and indicate the specific subsection that governs your answer.

18. Locate 43 Op. Att'y Gen. 212.
    a. What is the general subject matter of this opinion?
    b. Who requested the opinion?
    c. Who authored the opinion?
    d. What was the conclusion reached in the opinion?

19. Use *Federal Criminal Jury Instructions* (2d ed.) by Josephine R. Potuto, et al.
    a. Which instruction is used to instruct a jury on the crime of bank embezzlement?
    b. Review the comments to the instruction. Must the defendant act with the motive of injuring the bank to be guilty of the offense of bank embezzlement?

Internet Assignment

1. Access Harvard Law School Law Library's website at http://www.law.harvard.edu/library. Review the Research Guide for A.L.R. and Legal Encyclopedias. When are A.L.R. and legal encyclopedias useful sources?
2. Access the University Law Review Project at http://www.lawreview.org. Select "General Law Reviews" and then "Arizona Law Review." Locate the 2008 article published in Volume 50, Number 2, and written by Jane C. Ginsburg. What is the title of this article and who is the author?
3. Access the Washington & Lee Law School study on the most cited legal periodicals at http://lawlib.edu/LJ/index.asp. Sort or select by rank and review the total number of citations to journals from federal and state court cases for 2008. In 2008, what were the top four most-cited periodicals by courts and how often were they cited?
4. Access the site of the American Law Institute at http://www.ali.org, and review ALI's Annual Report for 2004. Review the table that indicates how many times published cases cite to the Restatements. How many times was each of the following Restatements cited: Property? Torts? Trusts?
5. Access the website for the Department of Justice Office of Legal Counsel and review the Opinions and Memoranda for 2008. Which Memorandum Opinion was issued on July 24, 2008? Who requested the opinion? Who signed it?
6. Access West's website at http://www.west.thomson.com. Using the "Search" box, search for *Words and Phrases*. Review the product information about this set, specifically its "Summary of Contents." In which volume would the word "immunity" be construed?
7. Use the law dictionary at http://dictionary.law.com. What is the definition of "nolo contendere"?

8. Access LexisNexis's Lawyer Locator at http://www.martindale.com. Catherine G. O'Sullivan is a U.S. government attorney. For which division does she work and from what school did she receive her J.D. degree?

9. Access the website of the National Conference of Commissioners on Uniform State Laws and review the Uniform Limited Liability Company Act (Revised). Under Section 803, do the following activities constitute transacting business by a foreign limited liability company: Bringing a lawsuit? Having its meetings?

10. Access the California Civil Jury Instructions (released by the Judicial Council of California). What does Instruction 105 provide?

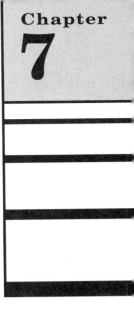

Special Research Issues

Chapter Overview

Most legal research problems can be solved by examining and analyzing the conventional primary and secondary authorities. There are, however, a few types of legal research tasks that lie outside those usual approaches and that involve sources arranged and published differently from other sources. Some are primary authorities (executive orders, administrative regulations, treaties, and municipal ordinances, and any cases interpreting the same) and others are secondary sources (legislative histories, some executive materials, and commentary on any topic). This chapter will examine these special research issues and will provide basic information on legislative histories, executive materials, administrative law, international law, and municipal law research.

A. Legislative History

1. *Introduction to Federal Legislative History Research*

If a statute you are researching is unclear, adverse to the position you wish to advocate, or lacks cases interpreting it, you may wish to examine the various documents that reflect the activity of the legislature that enacted the statute to help you determine the intent of the legislature. This process is referred to as preparing or compiling a *legislative history*.

Although a well-constructed argument relating to a legislative history may be instructive to a court, a court is not required to adopt an interpretation of a statute based on the legislature's intent in enacting the law. In fact, many courts dislike legislative history arguments, and will examine the legislative history of a statute only if the meaning of a statute is not clear or "plain" from a reading of it. Supreme Court Justice Scalia is a vehement opponent of the use of legislative history, noting in 2008 that it is the Court's job to read statutes, not to write them.

Alternatively, you may be monitoring a piece of legislation as it progresses in order to better assist clients or your employer. You may wish to review Chapter Three, which discusses the process by which legislation is enacted.

Review the following published guides, all available on the Internet, for background on legislative histories, the process of compiling one, and links to other sources:

- Carol D. Davis, *Tracking Current Federal Legislation and Regulations: A Guide to Basic Sources*, http://www.fas.org/sgp/crs/98-461.pdf (last updated Jan. 13, 2005).
- Richard J. McKinney & Ellen A. Sweet, Law Librarians' Society of Washington, D.C., Inc., *Federal Legislative History Research: A Practitioner's Guide to Compiling the Documents and Sifting for Legislative Intent*, http://www.llsdc.org/Fed-Leg-Hist (last revised Jan. 2008).
- Law Librarians' Society of Washington, D.C., Inc., *Legislative Sourcebook* (with numerous links to legislative history sources and guides), http://www.llsdc.org/sourcebook (last revised Feb. 2009).
- University of Michigan Documents Center, *Legislative Histories—United States Congress*, Mar. 2007, http://www.lib.umich.edu/govdocs/legishis.html.

2. *Documents Used in Compiling a Federal Legislative History*

The documents that you might analyze in compiling a legislative history are as follows:

- **Bill Versions.** By examining the various versions of a bill as it passed through Congress, you may be able to draw some inferences about Congress's intent. Additionally, the bill may include a preamble or introductory section explaining its intent and purpose.
- **Transcripts of Committee Hearings.** When individuals testify before congressional committees, their testimony is recorded and transcribed in booklet form. Many courts view this testimony with skepticism because although some of those testifying are neutral parties, others are well-paid lobbyists.
- **Committee Reports and Prints.** After the committee concludes its hearings, it will issue a report with its recommendations and its reasons therefor. Committee reports are viewed as considerably more credible than transcripts of committee hearings.
- **Debates.** If debate is held on a bill, the remarks of the speakers are published in the *Congressional Record*, a publication prepared for each day that Congress is in session. These remarks may reflect the intent of the legislature when it enacted a statute.

3. *The Process of Compiling a Federal Legislative History*

Researchers often struggle in compiling a legislative history because the documents are diverse and are seldom located together. You may need to search many sources. This is often true because a statute may have been enacted one year and then amended on several occasions thereafter, and you may need to compile a legislative history for each version of the statute. Do not be shy asking reference librarians for help; they are well aware that few researchers are familiar with the many sources used. There are, however, several steps you can take to gather the documents you need:

• **Locating a Public Law Number.** After you read a statute, you will be given historical notes about the enactment of a statute. For example, immediately following a statute in U.S.C.A., you will see the following information:

> Jan. 2, 1975, Pub. L. 93-596, § 1, Oct. 22, 1999, 88 Stat. 1949. (See Figure 3-2.)

Thus, U.S.C.A. gives you the public law number of your statute (namely, Public Law 93d Congress, 596th law), the date of its enactment, and its citation in *United States Statutes at Large*. For newer statutes, West also refers you to its publication *United States Code Congressional and Administrative News Service* (USCCAN), a monthly pamphlet that includes public laws, legislative history for selected bills, some committee reports, presidential signing statements, and other material. Once you have a public law number, you can access USCCAN and many other sources.

• **Using USCCAN.** Once you have a public law number, access USCCAN's Table of Legislative History (called Table 4) and look up your public law number. Table 4 will give you the original bill number (for example, H.R. 289), references to committee reports to examine, and dates of any debates. USCCAN also provides you with official committee reports, conference reports, statements by legislative leaders on major bills that explain the background and purpose of the legislation, and presidential signing statements. Read these materials to determine legislative intent.

• **Using *Congressional Information Service.*** *Congressional Information Service* (CIS), part of the LexisNexis family, is published in monthly pamphlets that are ultimately cumulated in three bound volumes for each year. Many experts consider CIS the most thorough and useful source for compiling a legislative history. Each CIS yearly set includes a comprehensive index, allowing you to access documents through several methods: by subject matter (for example, environment or social security); by name of any witness who testified at committee hearings; by bill number; and by name of committee chairperson. The CIS Index will then direct you to the appropriate pages in its Annual Abstracts volume, which contains summaries or "abstracts" of the bill as introduced, the testimony at committee hearings, the committee reports, and the dates of debate, so you can read the debates in the *Congressional Record*. Review these Abstracts to determine which documents you should examine in full. Additionally, you can use CIS's annual volume, titled *CIS Annual Legislative Histories*, arranged by public law number. By looking up your public law number, you will be directed to a brief summary of the law and references to the documents you need (including House and Senate Reports, committee hearing transcripts, and debates).

4. *Using Electronic Sources and the Internet to Compile a Legislative History*

Using LexisNexis, Westlaw, THOMAS (Congress's database), or GPO Access, you can usually find the documents you need by searching by bill number or key words and then linking to the pertinent documents.

- **LexisNexis.** After logging on to LexisNexis, select the database or "Library" called "Legislation & Politics" and then select "U.S. Congress." You can search by Congress number (such as the 109th Congress), bill number, public law number, topic of the legislation, and so forth. You will then be linked to the full text of the bill, selected hearing transcripts, committee reports, and the *Congressional Record*. You may also select "Legislative Histories" for full "prepackaged" legislative histories for selected statutes (usually those of widespread public interest, such as the Americans with Disabilities Act).
- **Westlaw.** Westlaw also offers compiled, full legislative histories for some statutes of public interest, such as the USA Patriot Act. After you log on, select the pertinent database. For example, Billcast (enter "BC") provides information on current bills in Congress. "BC-OLD" provides information on public bills introduced in previous congressional sessions. Additionally, when viewing a statute on the Westlaw screen, you may click on and select "Graphical Statutes," which will show you the timeline for your statute and allow you to link to previous versions of the statute, conference reports, the *Congressional Record,* and other pertinent legislative materials. Graphical Statutes is available for all federal statutes and for selected states, including California, New York, Texas, and other larger jurisdictions. This feature allows nearly instantaneous access to legislative history documents
- **THOMAS.** Unlike LexisNexis and Westlaw, which are fee-based services, THOMAS (http://thomas.loc.gov) is a free service provided by the Library of Congress. THOMAS (named for Thomas Jefferson) offers a wealth of information, including historical documents such as the Constitution, House and Senate directories, committee schedules, and links to other legislative agencies. More important, THOMAS offers easy access to many documents of legislative history. When you access THOMAS you may search by key words (for example, "Patent Reform Act"), bill number (for example, 109-31), or public law number. You will then be given access to the exact text of the bill or public law, a summary of

it, and its status (such as when it was introduced or referred to a committee). You can search within multiple Congresses in a single search, making it easier for you to locate legislative materials when you do not know in which congressional session legislation was introduced. Once you locate the bill you are interested in, you will be directed by hyperlinks to committee reports, the *Congressional Record* (since 1989), and other documents.

• **GPO Access.** The Government Printing Office offers numerous official publications through its comprehensive website called *GPO Access* at http://www.gpoaccess.gov. Congressional bills, transcripts of hearings, committee publications, and the *Congressional Record* are available. Searching is easily done by bill number, public law number, key words, or U.S.C. citation.

5. *Alternative Methods of Obtaining Legislative History for Federal Statutes*

There are several alternative approaches you can use to obtain a legislative history, including the following:

• **Compiled Legislative Histories.** A *compiled legislative history* is a "prepackaged" legislative history, namely, one that has already been compiled for the statute in which you are interested. Generally, compiled legislative histories exist for legislation that is well known or of public importance. USCCAN, LexisNexis, and Westlaw all offer several compiled legislative histories, especially for significant legislation.

• **Commercial Services.** There are several commercial companies that will assist you in obtaining documents or in monitoring legislation. Check your local phone book or local legal directory to obtain information about private companies that will obtain government documents for you for a fee. Following are two well-known companies:

- BNA Plus is located in Washington, D.C. Call (800) 372-1033 or visit http://www.bna.com/products/docs.htm.
- Legislative Intent Service will obtain either federal or state legislative histories. Call (800) 666-1917 or visit http://www.legintent.com.

• **Reference Assistance.** Law librarians are well aware of the complex nature of gathering the documents needed to compile a legislative history and will not be surprised if you ask for help. Some law libraries provide worksheets for you to use that provide a step-by-step approach and clear instructions for compiling a legislative history.

• **Congressional Assistance.** Members of Congress employ office staff and assistants whose job it is to respond to requests for information by constituents. Call the office of your congressional representative and ask for copies of the bill, the committee reports, or other pertinent materials. Check the House and Senate rosters in THOMAS to locate your representative. If you have a bill number, call (202) 226-5200 (House

Practice Tip: *Legislative History Research in Three Easy Steps*

There are many places for you to locate the documents that make up a legislative history. Consider simplifying the process by following these three steps:

1. Obtain a public law number by looking at the end of your statute in U.S.C.A. or U.S.C.S.
2. Look up the public law number (or a key word or phase related to the statute) in THOMAS at http://thomas.loc.gov.
3. Read and analyze the pertinent documents, linking to other related documents as needed.

For information on conducting legislative history research, access LexisNexis's site at http://support.lexisnexis.com/lawschool/record.asp?ArticleID=lexiscom_leghist.

of Representatives) or (202) 225-1772 (Senate). To learn how to obtain a bill number, review the article "How to find bill numbers" provided by the U.S. Senate at http://www.senate.gov/reference/common/faq/how_to_numbers.htm.

• **Law Reviews and Annotations.** A law review article or A.L.R. annotation may provide a thorough analysis of a statute you are researching and already may have examined the bill, committee hearing transcripts, committee reports, and debates. To determine if an article or annotation discusses your statute, Shepardize or KeyCite it (see Chapter Eleven). Alternatively, examine the "Table of Laws, Rules and Regulations" in A.L.R.'s Index to Annotations, which will direct you to A.L.R. annotations that cite or analyze statutes.

• **Web-based Tutorials.** A number of websites offer guidance and tutorials on conducting legislative history research for federal statutes. View the following sites:

- Boston College Law Library's Federal Legislative Histories: http://www.bc.edu/schools/law/library/research/researchguides.html (select "Federal Legislative Histories").
- Chicago-Kent College of Law's Federal Legislative History: http://library.kentlaw.edu/tutorials/Leghist%20Tutorial/Intro.htm.
- The Law Librarians' Society of Washington, D.C.'s Federal Legislative History *Legislative Source Book*: http://www.llsdc.org/sourcebook.
- The University of Washington School of Law: http://lib.law.washington.edu/ref/fedlegishist.html.

6. *State Legislative Histories*

a. The Process of Compiling a State Legislative History

The process of compiling a legislative history for a state statute is substantially similar to that for federal statutes. Unfortunately, collecting the actual documents involved can be frustrating because many of them are not published, and some are available only at the state capitol.

Just as is the case with federal statutes, after you read a state statute, carefully examine the historical notes following it to determine the derivation of the statute. For example, you may be presented with information such as the following:

Derivation Stats. 2001, c. 141, p. 621

This would indicate the statute was enacted in 2001 and was initially published at Chapter 141 of the state's session laws and can be found at page 621 of the 2001 session laws.

Consult your law librarian to determine if a legislative service exists for your state. If it does, it will operate similarly to USCCAN or CIS in that it will provide you with a bill number for your statute and information about the committee that considered the bill.

Once you have a bill number or the name of the committee that considered the bill, you can contact the committee staff and ask for copies of the pertinent documents. Although the bill and its versions will likely be available, many states do not maintain transcripts of committee hearings, committee reports, or debates.

To determine what documents are available in your state, consult the following: William H. Manz, *Guide to State Legislation, Legislative History, and Administrative Materials* (7th ed. 2008), which provides a state-by-state outline of the legislative and administrative documents available in all U.S. jurisdictions.

b. Alternative Methods of Obtaining Legislative History for State Statutes

Because of the difficulties in compiling state legislative histories, you may find that the following alternative methods of legislative history research are the most effective.

- **Compiled Legislative Histories.** Some well-known state statutes may already have been the subject of a legislative history. Consult your law librarian.
- **Commercial Services.** There may be private companies that will perform state legislative history research for you. Because many of the documents are available only at the state capitol, these private companies are often located in a state's capital city. To determine if such a company

exists, check with a reference librarian, consult a directory of legal services, contact directory information at the capital city, or contact an attorneys' service. The following fee-based commercial service provides state legislative history information and documents: StateNet, 2101 K St., Sacramento, CA 95816 (800) 726-4566 (http://www.statenet.com).

• **Web-Based Tutorials.** Several websites will greatly assist you in compiling state legislative histories. Following are some of the best:

- Cornell University Library's site (http://www.library.cornell.edu/olinuris/ref/statedocs.html) provides a research guide to finding state legislation.
- Indiana University's website (http://www.law.indiana.edu/lawlibrary/research/guides/statelegislative/index.shtml) links to each state's legislative history materials.
- The Law Librarians' Legislative Source Book (http://llsdc.org/state-leg) links to state legislative bodies, laws, and regulations.
- The National Conference of State Legislatures (http://www.ncsl.org) is a gateway to state legislative sites, allowing direct linking to the legislative website in each state.

• **LexisNexis and Westlaw.** Both LexisNexis and Westlaw provide bill text and bill tracking for all U.S. jurisdictions.

• **Reference Assistance.** Ask your law librarian for assistance or to determine if a worksheet or checklist is available to assist in compiling a legislative history.

• **Law Reviews and Annotations.** Shepardize or KeyCite the statute you are researching to determine if it has been the subject of any law review article, A.L.R. annotation, or attorney general opinion.

7. *Tracking Pending Legislation*

You may need to monitor pending legislation for clients who must keep abreast of emerging laws that could affect their organizations. Following are some sources that will help you track pending legislation:

• A conventional print source entitled *CCH Congressional Index* describes action on a bill and provides weekly updates on pending legislation.

• LexisNexis's service called "Congressional" provides bill tracking. Similarly, its service called "Alerts" will provide you with monthly, weekly, daily, or more frequent updates on legislation you are monitoring.

• Westlaw also provides bill tracking through its database called "Netscan Legislative History." Its clipping service, WestClip, delivers periodic updates to your email account about legislation you are tracking.

• THOMAS does not provide automatic alerts to you regarding changes in legislative status, but by routinely checking the status and summary of a bill, you can monitor its progress.

• StateNet, the commercial service described earlier, provides bill tracking and email alerts.

• Many states now automatically provide email updates on pending legislation. For example, California provides a bill status updating service that sends you an email to alert you to actions affecting the legislation you are monitoring. The free tracking service is located at http://www.leginfo.ca.gov.

Ethics Alert: *Tracking Legislation*

If a client retains your firm to monitor pending legislation that affects the client, you have an ethical duty to monitor the legislation on a periodic basis and notify the client of the progress of the legislation. Because legislation tracking is so easily accomplished, and you can readily arrange to have status updates delivered to your email account, it will be legal malpractice to "drop the ball" when you are tracking pending legislation.

B. Executive Materials

The executive branch issues certain directives and documents that affect all of us, although they are of varying legal effect.

1. *Proclamations*

A *proclamation* is a presidential statement that may or may not have legal effect. Proclamations are often issued for ceremonial or public awareness reasons. For example, Presidential Proclamation No. 6459 declared a certain week to be Lyme Disease Awareness Week. See Figure 7-1 for a sample Presidential Proclamation. Proclamations often have no legal effect because they do not command or prohibit any action, although some proclamations, such as President Lincoln's Emancipation Proclamation, have legal effect. You can locate proclamations in a variety of sources:

- USCCAN.
- *Federal Register*, the daily newspaper published by the Office of the Federal Register.
- Title 3 of the *Code of Federal Regulations*.
- *Daily Compilation of Presidential Documents* (formerly named the *Weekly Compilation of Presidential Documents*), available both in print and online through GPO Access at http://www.gpoaccess.gov.
- LexisNexis and Westlaw.

Figure 7-1
Sample Presidential Proclamation

Administration of Barack H. Obama, 2009

Proclamation 8350—Irish-American Heritage Month, 2009
March 2, 2009

Even before the birth of our Nation, the sons and daughters of Erin departed their homes in search of liberty and a more hopeful future. As these early pioneers left familiar lands, they carried with them the rich traditions of home. This March we honor their journey and their lasting contributions to the history and culture of the United States.

Following the colonial migrations, the United States enjoyed the greatest influx of Irish during the 1840s as Ireland suffered the Great Famine. Hungry but hopeful, poor but perseverant, Irish-Americans seized the opportunity to work hard, enjoy success, and pursue the American Dream.

Many took on the difficult work of constructing America's infrastructure. Others assumed positions of leadership. Among those leaders were signers of the Declaration of Independence and Presidents of the United States. Still others enjoyed great success and influence in the arts and literature. From social activists to business leaders, athletes to clergy, and first responders to soldiers, distinguished Irish-Americans have made indelible contributions to our national identity.

Today, tens of millions of Irish-Americans can look back with pride on the legacy of their forebears. Irish-Americans are integral to the rich fabric of the United States, and we are grateful for their service and contributions.

Now, Therefore, I, Barack Obama, President of the United States of America, by virtue of the authority vested in me by the Constitution and laws of the United States, do hereby proclaim March 2009 as Irish-American Heritage Month. I encourage all Americans to observe this month with appropriate ceremonies, programs, and activities.

In Witness Whereof, I have hereunto set my hand this second day of March, in the year of our Lord two thousand nine, and of the Independence of the United States of America the two hundred and thirty-third.

BARACK OBAMA

[Filed with the Office of the Federal Register, 11:15 a.m., March 4, 2009]

NOTE: This proclamation was published in the *Federal Register* on March 5.

Categories: Proclamations : Irish-American Heritage Month.

Subjects: Irish-American Heritage Month.

DCPD Number: DCPD200900116.

2. *Executive Orders*

Executive orders are declarations issued by the President to direct government officials and agencies. These executive orders have the force of law (unless a court rules otherwise) and require no action by Congress. Thus, they are primary authority. An example of an executive order is Executive Order No. 13354 for the establishment of a National Counterterrorism Center. Executive orders may be located in the same sources as proclamations.

One of the best sources for materials relating to the executive branch is a set of books entitled *Daily Compilation of Presidential Documents*. This publication includes a wide variety of presidential materials, including addresses and remarks, appointments and nominations, interviews with news media, and executive orders and proclamations.

The *Daily Compilation* is available in print form (use the alphabetically arranged index) and is available for free online from GPO Access (a service of the Government Printing Office). Documents since 1993 are available, and you may search by proclamation or executive order number or by key words. Access http://www.gpoaccess.gov.

C. Administrative Law

1. *Introduction*

To keep up with the demands of modern society, Congress has delegated certain tasks to agencies, each created to administer a body of law. For example, the use of airwaves to communicate information by radio led to the creation of the Federal Communications Commission. Note that agencies have different titles, with some being referred to as "Administrations," some referred to as "Boards," and others as "Agencies," and so forth. Agency heads and staffers are individuals with expertise in the area of law that the agency regulates.

Note that whereas the product of a legislature is a "law" or "statute," the product of an administrative agency is a *rule* or *regulation*, which terms are synonymous. Thus, rules of administrative agencies are primary authorities (as are cases interpreting administrative law issues). Rules or regulations are issued by an agency to carry out its policies. Violation of a rule or regulation may subject one to punishment just as can violation of a statute. Administrative agencies are often referred to as *regulatory bodies* because their function is to regulate a body of law. The statutes that create agencies and set forth their powers are called *enabling statutes*. Some agencies, such as the Internal Revenue Service, issue advisory opinions, which opinions generally state whether they are legally binding.

2. *Publication of Federal Administrative Law*

For any rule or regulation to be effective, it must be published in the *Federal Register*, a pamphlet that is published weekdays and distributed by the U.S. Government Printing Office. The *Federal Register* includes proposed, interim, and final rules. It does more than merely recite the language of the agency rules. It provides a summary of the regulation, its effective date, a person to contact for further information, and background material relating to the regulation. See Figure 7-2 for a sample page from the *Federal Register*.

The *Federal Register* includes about 80,000 pages each year, making research a difficult task. Thus, just as our federal statutes that are originally published in *United States Statutes at Large* are better organized or codified into the 50 titles of the *United States Code*, so also has the *Federal Register* been codified to enable researchers to access administrative materials. In fact, the *Federal Register* has been codified in 50 titles in a set called *Code of Federal Regulations* (C.F.R.). These 50 titles represent the areas subject to federal regulation and roughly correspond to the 50 titles of U.S.C. For example, Title 29 of both U.S.C. and C.F.R. is "Labor." Each of the 50 titles in C.F.R. is divided into chapters, which chapters are further subdivided into "parts" and sections covering specific regulatory areas. For example, 9 C.F.R. § 352.1(k) defines "exotic animals."

C.F.R. is a softcover set revised annually with one-fourth of the volumes in the set issued on a quarterly basis. Thus, revision of the set is staggered throughout the calendar year. Each year the softcover volumes of C.F.R. are issued in a color different from the previous year (although Title 3, containing various presidential materials, is always white or black). See Figure 7-3 for a sample page from C.F.R.

3. *Research Techniques for Administrative Law*

a. C.F.R. Indexes

C.F.R. contains an Index volume entitled *C.F.R. Index and Finding Aids*. This one-volume Index is revised annually and can be accessed by subject matter (pesticides, shellfish) or by the name of the agency (Nuclear Regulatory Commission). The Index will direct you to the pertinent title and part of C.F.R. There is also a separate Index for each of the 50 titles of C.F.R. located immediately after the last part of each of the 50 titles. See Figure 7-4 for a sample page from the C.F.R. Index.

West also publishes a separate Index to C.F.R. called *West's Code of Federal Regulations, General Index*, which is designed to provide access to C.F.R. by subject matter (for example, port safety) or by geographic location (for example, Appalachia or Boston). You will be directed to a title and part of C.F.R.

The National Archives and Records Administration also provides indexes to the *Federal Register* and C.F.R. online at http://www.archives.gov.

b. *Code of Federal Regulations Annotated*

West publishes a set entitled *Code of Federal Regulations Annotated*, which is arranged identically to C.F.R. and includes all C.F.R. regulations. In addition, however, the set includes references to law reviews and other authorities and annotations to cases interpreting C.F.R. provisions so that you may easily find authorities interpreting and construing C.F.R. provisions that you are researching.

c. *Federal Register Index*

Because C.F.R. is issued annually, it will not contain newly promulgated rules and regulations, which are published in the *Federal Register*. To access the *Federal Register*, use the *Federal Register Index*, which is issued monthly in cumulative form. Thus, the *Federal Register Index* for May contains all of the information for the previous months. Entries in this Index are arranged alphabetically by agency (Agriculture Department, Air Force Department, and so forth).

4. *Updating C.F.R. Regulations*

Because agency rules and regulations are revised so frequently, you must always check the status of any regulation you have found. Updating C.F.R. regulations is a two-step process.

a. *List of C.F.R. Sections Affected*

To update any regulation, consult the publication *List of C.F.R. Sections Affected* ("LSA"). LSA is a monthly softcover cumulative publication designed to notify researchers of changes to any C.F.R. regulation. It also publishes new and proposed regulations. By looking up the C.F.R. title and section you are researching, you will be provided a short explanation such as "revised" and then directed to the appropriate page of the *Federal Register* where the amendatory language is found. See Figure 7-5 for a sample page from LSA.

b. C.F.R. Parts Affected

After you have used LSA (which will update the regulation only through the end of last month), you must further check a regulation by determining its status as of today's date. This is accomplished by reviewing the section titled "Reader Aids" at the back of the most recent issue of the

Figure 7-2
Sample Page from *Federal Register*

62446

Proposed Rules

Federal Register
Vol. 73, No. 204
Tuesday, October 21, 2008

This section of the FEDERAL REGISTER contains notices to the public of the proposed issuance of rules and regulations. The purpose of these notices is to give interested persons an opportunity to participate in the rule making prior to the adoption of the final rules.

DEPARTMENT OF AGRICULTURE

Grain Inspection, Packers and Stockyards Administration

7 CFR Part 800

RIN 0580–AB00

USDA's Role in Differentiating Grain Inputs for Ethanol Production and Standardizing Testing of Co-Products of Ethanol Production

AGENCY: Grain Inspection, Packers and Stockyards Administration, USDA.

ACTION: Withdrawal of advance notice of proposed rulemaking.

SUMMARY: The Grain Inspection, Packers and Stockyards Administration (GIPSA) published an advance notice of proposed rulemaking (ANPR) in the **Federal Register** on July 20, 2007 (72 FR 39762), inviting comments from interest persons regarding the appropriate government role in differentiating grain attributes for ethanol conversion, as well as standardizing the testing of co-products of ethanol production. The original notice provided an opportunity for interested parties to comment until September 18, 2007. In response to a request from the grain industry, on October 5, 2007 (72 FR 56945), we reopened the comment period until December 4, 2007, to provide interested parties with additional time in which to comment. The commenters overwhelmingly agreed that GIPSA should not intervene in standardizing testing of ethanol inputs and outputs. Accordingly, we will not initiate any rulemaking action at this time related to the matters presented in the ANPR.

FOR FURTHER INFORMATION CONTACT: Ross D. Heiman at USDA, GIPSA, FGIS, Market and Program Analysis Staff, Beacon Facility, STOP 1404, P.O. Box 419205, Kansas City, Missouri 64141; Telephone (816) 823–2580; Fax Number (816) 823–4644; e-mail *Ross.D.Heiman@usda.gov*.

SUPPLEMENTARY INFORMATION: We published an ANPR in the **Federal Register** on July 20, 2007, inviting comments from interested persons regarding the appropriate government role in differentiating grain attributes for ethanol conversion, as well as standardizing the testing of co-products of ethanol production. The initial comment period closed on September 18, 2007, but due to a request from the National Grain and Feed Association, the closing date for comments was extended through December 4, 2007, as published in the **Federal Register**.

We received 29 comments from individuals and organizations across the marketing chain. Overall, respondents do not want GIPSA to assist in the revision of existing definitions for ethanol co-products, establish standards for the co-products, or offer standardized tests for grain going into ethanol production or the resulting co-products, with one exception. Some commenters recommended that GIPSA's expertise in verifying the performance of commercial test kits might be applied to the marketing of the co-products. Commenters presented an overriding theme that the perceived needs of the ethanol industry will be best met by the various industry participants. One final observation was a recurring comment that the ethanol industry is relatively young, and because of this youth, GIPSA involvement (i.e., standardizing testing of ethanol inputs and outputs) may hinder its progress.

In view of the comments received, we will not initiate any rulemaking action related to the matters presented in the ANPR. We will continue to monitor developments and remain actively engaged with the ethanol and co-products markets and will support the industry, as appropriate, in its efforts to successfully market ethanol co-products.

Authority: (7 CFR 71–87k).

Randall D. Jones,
Acting Administrator, Grain Inspection, Packers and Stockyards Administration.

[FR Doc. E8–24946 Filed 10–20–08; 8:45 am]

BILLING CODE 3410–KD–P

DEPARTMENT OF AGRICULTURE

Grain Inspection, Packers and Stockyards Administration

7 CFR Part 810

RIN 0580–AA96

United States Standards for Soybeans

AGENCY: Grain Inspection, Packers and Stockyards Administration, USDA.

ACTION: Withdrawal of advance notice of proposed rulemaking.

SUMMARY: On May 1, 2007, the Grain Inspection, Packers and Stockyards Administration (GIPSA) published an advance notice of proposed rulemaking (ANPR) in the **Federal Register** seeking public comment on the effectiveness of the soybean standards. We asked for input on factors used in the current standards and grading procedures, whether changes in soybean processing practices and technology merited changes in the standards, and whether any other changes were needed to ensure that the standards remain relevant to market needs. Because the comments that we received did not indicate a consensus concerning changes to the standards, we will not proceed with rulemaking in this matter.

FOR FURTHER INFORMATION CONTACT: Ross D. Heiman at USDA, GIPSA, FGIS, Market and Program Analysis Staff, Suite 180, STOP 1404, 6501 Beacon Drive, Kansas City, Missouri 64133; Telephone (816) 823–2580; Fax Number (816) 823–4644; e-mail *Ross.D.Heiman@usda.gov*.

SUPPLEMENTARY INFORMATION: GIPSA published an advance notice of proposed rulemaking (ANPR) in the **Federal Register** on May 1, 2007 (72 FR 23775), initiating a review of the United States Standards for Soybeans to determine their effectiveness and responsiveness to current grain industry needs. The original notice provided an opportunity for interested parties to comment until July 2, 2007. In response to a request from the soybean industry, on July 20, 2007 (72 FR 39764), GIPSA reopened the comment period until August 20, 2007, to provide interested parties with additional time in which to comment. We received 17 comments from producers, handlers, international associations and companies, and an academic. The comments that we

Figure 7-3
Sample Page from C.F.R.

anywhere in its labeling, the term must be qualified by describing the cosmetic benefit provided by the sunscreen ingredient.

(b) The qualifying information required under paragraph (a) of this section shall appear prominently and conspicuously at least once in the labeling in conjunction with the term "sunscreen" or other similar sun protection terminology used in the labeling. For example: "Contains a sunscreen—to protect product color."

[64 FR 27693, May 21, 1999]

PART 701—COSMETIC LABELING

Subpart A—General Provisions

Subpart B—Package Form

Subpart C—Labeling of Specific Ingredients

AUTHORITY: 21 U.S.C. 321, 352, 361, 362, 363, 371, 374; 15 U.S.C. 1454, 1455.

SOURCE: 39 FR 10056, Mar. 15, 1974, unless otherwise noted.

Subpart A—General Provisions

§701.1 Misbranding.

(a) Among representations in labeling of a cosmetic which render such cosmetic misbranded is a false or misleading representation with respect to another cosmetic or a food, drug, or device.

(b) The labeling of a cosmetic which contains two or more ingredients may be misleading by reason (among other reasons) of the designation of such cosmetic in such labeling by a name which includes or suggests the name of one or more but not all such ingredients, even though the names of all such ingredients are stated elsewhere in the labeling.

§701.2 Form of stating labeling requirements.

(a) A word, statement, or other information required by or under authority of the Act to appear on the label may lack that prominence and conspicuousness required by section 602(c) of the Act by reason (among other reasons) of:

(1) The failure of such word, statement, or information to appear on the part or panel of the label which is presented or displayed under customary conditions of purchase;

(2) The failure of such word, statement, or information to appear on two or more parts or panels of the label, each of which has sufficient space therefor, and each of which is so designed as to render it likely to be, under customary conditions of purchase, the part or panel displayed;

(3) The failure of the label to extend over the area of the container or package available for such extension, so as to provide sufficient label space for the prominent placing of such word, statement, or information;

(4) Insufficiency of label space (for the prominent placing of such word, statement, or information) resulting from the use of label space for any word, statement, design, or device which is not required by or under authority of the Act to appear on the label;

(5) Insufficiency of label space (for the prominent placing of such word, statement, or information) resulting from the use of label space to give materially greater conspicuousness to any other word, statement, or information, or to any design or device;

(6) Smallness or style of type in which such word, statement, or information appears, insufficient background contrast, obscuring designs or vignettes, or crowding with other written, printed, or graphic matter.

(b)(1) All words, statements, and other information required by or under authority of the Act to appear on the

Figure 7-4
Sample Page from C.F.R. Index

Reference to C.F.R. title and part

Help Line: *GPO Access*

Users needing assistance with GPO Access may access its Contact Center for access to highly trained specialists. Call toll free at (866) 512-1800 or send an email to ContactCenter@gpo.gov.

Federal Register. Each issue of the *Federal Register* includes a section within "Reader Aids" titled "C.F.R. Parts Affected," which will inform you of any changes to any C.F.R. regulations for the period after the most recent issue of LSA. If you do not locate any entries for your C.F.R. title and part in either LSA or C.F.R. Parts Affected, this means there are no revisions to your regulation during the period covered.

5. *Electronic and Online Methods of Administrative Law Research*

LexisNexis and Westlaw, the fee-based computer research services, both include the full text of the *Federal Register* and C.F.R. in their easy-to-use and search databases. Updating is accomplished by a click of the keystroke to access Shepard's or KeyCite, respectively.

Free access to both the *Federal Register* and C.F.R. are now provided by the Government Printing Office at its GPO Access website (http://www.gpoaccess.gov). Searching can be easily done by key words, agency names, citation, or by browsing tables of contents or volumes.

Updating a C.F.R. regulation you locate online at GPO Access is readily accomplished. Select "List of C.F.R. Sections Affected" and enter your C.F.R. section in the search box. Then access "Current List of CFR Parts Affected" and view the list of parts affected to see if your specific C.F.R. citation has been revised or revoked. If so, access the pertinent page within C.F.R. to review the amendments, changes, or proposed rules that affect your C.F.R. provision. In addition, the GPO Access website offers e-cfr, an electronic service that updates the *Code of Federal Regulations* on a daily basis.

6. *Agency Decisions*

In addition to issuing rules and regulations, administrative agencies interpret and enforce their rules and regulations through the process of issuing decisions. For example, if the Federal Communications Commission alleges that a broadcaster has violated one of its rules, it will hold a hearing and issue a decision relating to this matter. The agency hearing is somewhat less formal than a trial conducted in a courtroom, but its purpose is the same: to determine facts and render a decision. There is no jury, and the individual who conducts the proceeding (called an *adjudication*) is an *administrative law judge* ("ALJ") who is an expert in this field. Alternatively, the agency can prosecute violators in court, often by referring the matter to the Department of Justice for prosecution.

Figure 7-5
Sample Page from LSA

DECEMBER 2008 73

CHANGES APRIL 1, 2008 THROUGH DECEMBER 31, 2008

655.750 (a), (b)(1)(i) and (2) revised 19949
655.760 Introductory text added 19950
655.800—655.855 (Subpart I) Heading revised...............................19950
655.1102 Amended 78068
655.1112 (c)(2) revised 78068
656 Authority citation revised........78068
656.3 Amended 78068
656.15 (a) amended; (f) removed; (g) redesignated as new (f)........78068
656.40 (a), (b) introductory text, (c), (g), (h) and (i) revised 78068
656.41 Revised 78069

Chapter IX—Office of the Assistant Secretary for Veterans' Employment and Training, Department of Labor (Parts 1000—1099)

1002 Appendix correctly revised 63632
1010 Added 78142

Proposed Rules:

220...44946
404...........20564, 22871, 33745, 35100, 40997, 47103, 50260, 51963, 66563, 66564, 76573
405...66563
408 ....33745, 51963
416...........20564, 33745, 35100, 40997, 50260, 51963, 66563, 66564, 74663
422 ....33745, 51963
501...35102
641...47770
655...29942
656...29942
1010 48086

TITLE 21—FOOD AND DRUGS

Chapter I—Food and Drug Administration, Department of Health and Human Services (Parts 1—1299)

1.276—1.285 (Subpart I) Revised; eff. 5-6-09 66402
2.125 (e)(2)(v) removed 69552
16 Technical correction..................54314
16.1 (b)(2) amended...............49942, 51919
17.1 (c) through (g) redesignated as (e) through (i); new (c) and (d) added 66752
17.2 Revised 66752
101 Technical correction 66754
Uniform compliance date............74349
101.72 Revised; eff. 1-1-10 56486
101.80 Regulation at 72 FR 52789 confirmed 30301
101.81 (c)(2)(iii)(C) revised; (c)(2)(iii)(D) added 23953
Regulation at 73 FR 9947 confirmed....................................47829
111.75 (c)(3) correctly revised..........27727
179.26 (b) table amended 49603
189.5 (a)(1) revised; (e) added; interim 20793
201.66 Regulation at 73 FR 403 confirmed 63897
203.3 (q) revised..............................59500
203.22 (h) and (i) added....................59500
205.3 (h) revised 59501
208.20 Regulation at 73 FR 404 confirmed 63897
209 Regulation at 73 FR 404 confirmed.......................................63897
210 Technical correction 63361
210.2 (c) added 40462
210.3 Regulation at 72 FR 68068 withdrawn 18440
(b)(6) revised..................................51931
211 Technical correction 63361
211.48 Regulation at 72 FR 68068 withdrawn 18440
211.67 Regulation at 72 FR 68068 withdrawn 18440
(a) revised.....................................51931
211.68 Regulation at 72 FR 68068 withdrawn 18440
(c) added 51932
211.72 Regulation at 72 FR 68068 withdrawn 18440
Revised..51932
211.82 Regulation at 72 FR 68069 withdrawn 18440
(b) revised.....................................51932
211.84 Regulation at 72 FR 68069 withdrawn 18440
(c)(1), (d)(3) and (6) revised 51932
211.94 Regulation at 72 FR 68069 withdrawn 18440
(c) revised.....................................51932
211.101 Regulation at 72 FR 68069 withdrawn 18440
(c) and (d) revised 51932

The decisions rendered by the agencies will be published so you may access and review them. There is no one set of books containing the decisions of all of the agencies; however, the Government Printing Office publishes sets containing decisions for many agencies. Table T.1 of *The Bluebook* and Appendix 8 of *ALWD* identify more than 30 official administrative publications, such as *Interstate Commerce Commission Reports*. Although these publications are official, they lack a uniform approach. The indexes are often difficult to use, and updating can be sporadic. Thus, private publishers such as CCH, BNA, and Matthew Bender have published easy-to-use sets that report agency decisions. Typically, these sets are in looseleaf format (see Chapter Six), and decisions are located through alphabetically arranged Tables of Cases or through the subject matter index for the set, which will direct you to a narrative discussion followed by annotations to cases. To locate the actual case, use the citation given in the annotation. These cases are often published in separate bound volumes that contain both agency and court decisions. Table T.15 of *The Bluebook* identifies more than 100 of these services, such as *Aviation Cases* and *Environmental Law Reporter*.

Many cases can also be accessed through Washburn University School of Law's website at http://www.washlaw.edu/doclaw/executive 5m.html#arms.

7. *Federal Cases Reviewing Agency Decisions*

A party who is dissatisfied with an ALJ's decision may appeal the matter to the federal courts. Because a "trial" has already occurred at the agency itself, the aggrieved party typically appeals the agency decision to the appropriate U.S. Court of Appeals, usually the Court of Appeals for the District of Columbia, bypassing the United States District Courts, which function as federal trial courts. Further appeal may be made to the United States Supreme Court, assuming certiorari is granted. See Figure 7-6 for a chart showing the appeal process for most federal agency decisions. In some cases (for example, those heard by the Social Security Administration), a party who is dissatisfied with an ALJ's decision may file a civil suit in a federal district court. Statutes governing the agency will specify a forum for review.

To locate federal cases that have reviewed agency decisions, use the standard sources you would use to locate federal cases on any topic: digests and annotations. For federal court cases, use West's *Federal Practice Digests*; to locate annotations, use A.L.R. Fed.

If using LexisNexis or Westlaw, you can also Shepardize or KeyCite the agency decision to be referred to other cases that affect or mention the agency decision.

Finally, many agencies post their decisions on their websites. For example, when you access the site of the National Labor Relations Board (http://www.nlrb.gov), you can immediately link to decisions and search by key word.

Figure 7-6
Appeal of Typical Agency Decision

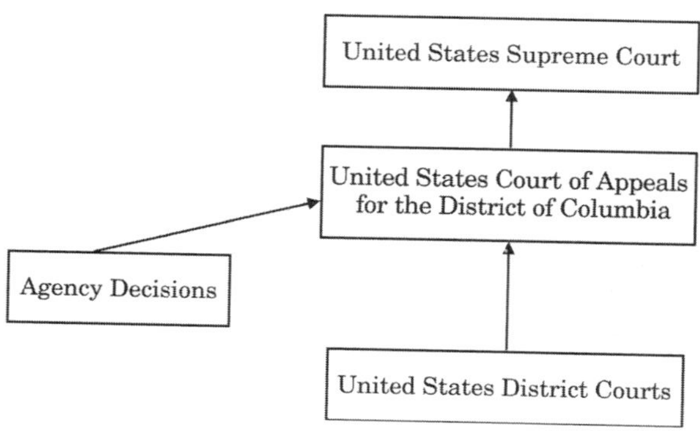

8. *State Administrative Law*

There are agencies in most states, the actions and activities of which often parallel federal agencies. For example, one of the better-known federal agencies, the Occupational Safety and Health Administration (OSHA), is patterned after the California Division of Occupational Safety and Health. Although the federal OSHA agency regulates health and safety measures on a national basis, the state safety and health agency may impose additional standards for ensuring that work environments in California are safe. Similarly, many state agencies issue regulations for the practice of certain occupations in the state, such as standards for cosmetologists and real estate agents.

Some states, usually the more populous ones, publish their agency's rules and regulations similarly to the publication of administrative law at the federal level, that is, in separate sets of books devoted solely to agency regulations and titled "Administrative Codes." These sets are generally accessed through their alphabetically arranged indexes.

You may also find that after you read a statute in a state code, you are referred to an administrative regulation in the cross-references or library references that follow the statute. In other instances, in the course of reading a case or a local encyclopedia, you may come across a reference to an administrative regulation. In any of these events, carefully review the administrative regulation, because it is typically subject to strict compliance.

Some state agencies issue decisions. With the exception of tax and unemployment compensation decisions, these are rarely published. Some agencies, however, publish newsletters or other publications that briefly review and summarize their decisions and other activities. These newsletters may be available by subscription, at your law library, or through the agency itself.

Practice Tips: *Administrative Law Research*

- For a tutorial on conducting administrative law research, access the following site: http://lib.law.washington.edu/ref/adminus.html.
- For a complete overview of all federal administrative agencies, consult *The United States Government Manual*, which identifies principal officials of each agency, and gives a brief history of each agency, organization charts, and other pertinent information. The *Manual* is now provided free online by the Government Printing Office at GPO Access's website at http://www.gpoaccess.gov/gmanual.

Both LexisNexis and Westlaw offer state agency rules and some state agency decisions. Agency rules and decisions may also be available for free on the Internet. Access either of the following sites:

- Washburn University School of Law: http://www.washlaw.edu. Select your state's name from the list provided.
- Florida State University: http://www.law.fsu.edu/library/admin/admin5.html. Select your state's name from the list provided.

D. International Law

1. *Introduction*

International law is broadly defined as the law pertaining to relations among sovereign nations. One often hears that there are two branches of international law: public and private. *Public international law* is what we typically view as international law: the conduct and regulation of nations. *Private international law* is an older and more archaic term, used primarily in Europe to describe an area of law more properly classified as "conflict of laws," pertaining to which jurisdiction's law would apply to a given transaction or event. Many contracts include a choice of law clause that specifies what country's law applies in a dispute and where venue will lie.

Although it is true that international law is a specialized field of law and that most legal professionals will not be involved in this practice area, with more and more companies "going global" and the Internet allowing worldwide communication and commerce, you should become sufficiently familiar with international law sources and research procedures so that, if needed, you can adequately perform a basic research task in this field.

2. *Sources of International Law*

International law is derived from four sources:

- International conventions (for example, treaties), which set forth rules for conduct expressly recognized and voluntarily agreed to by signatory nations;
- International custom, namely, some general practice accepted as law or believed to be obligatory;
- General principles of law accepted by civilized nations; and
- Judicial decisions and the teachings of international law experts.

Note that both treaties and judicial decisions interpreting international law are primary law, whereas any commentary about international law is a secondary authority.

3. *Overview of International Law Research Procedure*

If you are presented with an international law research task, you should use the following procedure unless you know the exact source for the answer to your problem.

- "Get your feet wet" by reading some background information relating to your issue and familiarizing yourself with the area of law;
- Determine whether a treaty covers your issue and provides a definitive answer to your question (if so, read the treaty and then determine if it is still in force); and
- Read analytical commentary and cases interpreting any treaty.

To follow this research process, you need to know which sources to consult. The following sections of the chapter will introduce you to the sets of books you should consult to perform your research.

4. *Basic Texts and Sources*

Law libraries usually collect all international law materials together. Browse the shelves and become familiar with the library's collection. Three of the better-known general texts and guides relating to international law are as follows:

Claire M. Germain, *Germain's Transnational Law Research: A Guide for Attorneys* (1991)
Green H. Hackworth, *Digest of International Law* (1940-1944)
Marjorie M. Whiteman, *Digest of International Law* (1963)

These texts provide excellent information on international law. In many ways, they resemble special subject encyclopedias in that they are multivolume sets that contain articulate narrative statements of the law and citations to cases and other authorities that are located in footnotes. There may also be specialized treatises for your topic. (For example, a multivolume set exists that covers only issues relating to the North American Free Trade Agreement.)

Also, consult Restatement (Third) Foreign Relations Law of the United States. This Restatement focuses on international law and is an excellent starting place for international law research because it provides general information on international law; international agreements; and international jurisdiction, judgments, and remedies. The Restatement will also provide you with citations to cases that have interpreted treaties.

Finally, consult the *American Journal of International Law*, a quarterly periodical that contains analytical articles relating to various international law topics. Use the index for the set or use any of the indexes to periodicals discussed in Chapter Six.

5. *Treaties*

a. Introduction

Treaties, which are formal agreements, may be *bilateral* (between two parties) or *multilateral* (among several parties). Some treaties have ended wars, others have resolved boundary disputes, and still others deal with trade or economic issues. One type of treaty is referred to as a *convention* and usually relates to a formal multilateral agreement with numerous parties.

Although treaties may have been signed and agreed to by representatives of the countries involved, they are not effective until they are ratified or officially approved by each government. In the United States, treaties are initiated by the executive branch and then negotiated by individuals selected by the President, often foreign service officers employed by the Department of State. They are entered into by the President with the "advice and consent" of the Senate, namely, by two-thirds approval by the Senate (although one type of international agreement, an *executive agreement*, is entered into with a foreign nation by the President acting without Senate approval).

Because treaties are expressly stated by the U.S. Constitution to be the "supreme law of the land," they are primary law.

b. Sources for Treaties

- **Pre-Ratification.** During the time between signing of a treaty and approval by the Senate, treaties can be located in a series entitled *Senate Treaty Documents*, which is available in conventional print form through *Congressional Information Service* (CIS) *Index* or through the

Help Line: *Treaty Assistance*

The Department of State offers excellent information about U.S. Treaties. If help is needed, call the Treaty Desk at (202) 647-1345 or send an email asking for assistance to treatyoffice@state.gov.

Senate's Treaty Page online at http://www.senate.gov/pagelayout/legislative/d_three_sections_with_teasers/treaties.htm.

• **Post-Ratification.** Since 1945, all treaties and executive agreements to which the United States is a party are published as pamphlets in a set titled *Treaties and Other International Acts Series* ("TIAS"). Since 1950, these pamphlets are then published in hardbound volumes titled *United States Treaties and Other International Agreements* ("UST"). To locate treaties in either of these sets, use the index *United States Treaties and Other International Agreements Cumulative Index*. You may locate a treaty by country name or by its topic.

Another collection of treaties is the *United Nations Treaty Series* ("UNTS"), which publishes treaties filed with the United Nations. Thus, this set collects numerous treaties to which the United States is not a party. A cumulative index to UNTS provides easy access by country name or treaty topic.

• **LexisNexis and Westlaw.** Treaties are available on both LexisNexis and Westlaw. Searching is easily accomplished by treaty citation, country name, or key words and phrases. Once a treaty is located it is easily updated to ensure it is still in force.

• **Internet Access.** Many treaties are now available on the Internet. Use the following sources:

- United States Senate Treaty Page. Access the Senate site http://www.senate.gov/pagelayout/legislative/d_three_sections_with_teasers/treaties.htm for the text of treaties received or approved by the Senate and information on action taken by the Senate.
- THOMAS provides treaty information since approximately 1968 (although the full text of treaties is not provided). You may search by treaty number, key word or phrase, or the type of treaty. Access the site http://thomas.loc.gov/home/treaties/treaties.html.
- GPO Access provides many recent treaty documents at its site at http://www.gpoaccess.gov/serialset/cdocuments/index.html. You may search by key word or treaty number. You will then be given a summary of the treaty and its full text.
- The United Nations website is primarily a fee-based site, but some treaties (and information on the status of certain treaties) are available for free viewing at http://www.un.org.

- The Global Legal Information Network provided by the Library of Congress at http://www.glin.gov is a public database of the official texts of laws, regulations, cases, and other sources from more than 50 countries. You may search by country, topic, or date.

c. Determining the Current Status of Treaties

In many instances, treaties themselves specify the date until when they will be in force. For example, a treaty might state, "The treaty enters into force 30 days after ratification and remains in force for a period of 10 years and continues in force thereafter unless terminated by either party by giving one year's written notice to the other."

Perhaps the easiest way to determine whether a treaty involving the United States is still in force is to access the Office of the Legal Adviser of the State Department at http://www.state.gov/s/l/treaty/treaties, which provides access to *Treaties in Force*, an annual publication that identifies all of the treaties and executive agreements still in force. *Treaties in Force* is easy to use because it is organized by country and topic.

d. Interpreting Treaties

To assist you in interpreting treaties, use both secondary and primary sources. For secondary sources that have construed treaties, review the digests and the *American Journal of International Law* described previously. To locate primary sources, for example, cases that have interpreted treaties, check the following sources:

- ***Shepard's Federal Statute Citations.*** Look up the volume and page of your treaty citation in the print volumes of this Shepard's set, and you will be directed to cases and A.L.R. annotations that have mentioned or interpreted your treaty.
- **U.S.C.S.** U.S.C.S. contains a separate volume titled "Notes to Uncodified Laws and Treaties," which will provide you with annotations to judicial decisions interpreting treaties.

Once you have located cases construing your treaty, be sure to Shepardize or KeyCite these cases to ensure they are still good law and to help you locate additional pertinent materials.

A hotly debated issue is the use and citation of foreign law by American courts, specifically, the U.S. Supreme Court. Some justices are strong supporters of the use of foreign law, and three recent U.S. Supreme Court cases have cited foreign law or intentional conventions. Other justices are vehemently opposed to the use of foreign law.

Practice Tip: *International Law Research*

For tutorials on conducting international law research, access either of the following sites:

- http://www.asil.org/resource/treaty1.htm and
- http://www.bc.edu/schools/law/library/meta-elements/pdf/researchguides/treaties.pdf

6. International Tribunals

There are a variety of methods available to nations to resolve disputes. One country may agree to act as an informal mediator in a dispute between two countries. Additionally, the Permanent Court of Arbitration was established in 1899 at The Hague, Holland's royal city, to offer mediation, arbitration, and fact-finding to disputant countries. The *International Court of Justice* (often called the *World Court*) is also located at The Hague and is one of the six major organs of the United Nations. Any United Nations member may bring a dispute before the Court, which renders its decision by majority vote of its 15 judges. Its decisions are reported in a set of books titled *Reports of Judgments, Advisory Opinions and Orders*. In many instances, its decisions are ignored by an offending nation. There is no uniform method of enforcing the World Court's decision. The United Nations itself has no permanent police force to resolve international conflicts or sustain peace and will send peacekeepers when 9 of 15 Security Council members decide and the affected countries agree (although a peacekeeping proposal will fail if any one of the five permanent members of the United Nations, including the United States, votes against it).

7. International Organizations

There are thousands of international organizations. The best known is the United Nations, established in 1945 and located in New York City. The United Nations now has 192 member nations, including its original 51 member nations, which includes the United States. Its website at http://www.un.org offers invaluable information about the organization, its members, and its programs.

Other well-known international organizations include the following:

- The Organization of American States, composed of 35 North, Central, and South American nations, Caribbean nations, and the United States;
- The African Union, an association of 53 African nations;

- NATO (North Atlantic Treaty Organization), a military alliance of 26 countries from Europe and North America;
- The European Union, composed of 27 democratic European countries; and
- The G20 (formerly known as the "G8"), an unofficial forum consisting of the major industrial nations that meets annually to discuss global economic issues.

E. Municipal Law

1. *Introduction and Terminology*

A client's question about whether horses may be kept on his or her property or the height and type of fence required around the perimeter of a swimming pool is answered by conducting municipal or local legal research.

Most municipalities operate under a document called a *charter*, which functions as the municipality's constitution, setting forth the powers and activities in which the municipality may engage. Local laws are usually called *ordinances* rather than statutes. The local governing body may be a city council, board of supervisors, a county executive, aldermen, or other legislative body.

After municipal ordinances are enacted, they are typically organized or "codified" so that all of the zoning ordinances are brought together, all of the animal control ordinances are brought together, and so forth, into the city's or county's code.

2. *Municipal Research Materials and Procedure*

One of the most difficult tasks in performing municipal research is finding a current version of a city or county code. The law library in your area will usually maintain the codes for the surrounding municipalities. You can also check your public library or the appropriate government office (for example, the city hall, city clerk's office, county counsel's office, and so on).

Once you have found the code for your municipality, the research techniques used to locate ordinances are identical to the research techniques used to locate federal or state statutes, namely, the descriptive word or topic approaches.

Municipal codes are usually maintained in looseleaf binders that contain all of the municipality's ordinances organized by topic, such as business regulations, elections, and fire procedures. Use the index at the end of the binder just as you would any other index. Think of words that describe your research issue, look them up in the alphabetically arranged index, and you will be directed to the appropriate ordinance.

Alternatively, you can examine the code's table of contents, usually placed at the front of the binder, and scan the list of topics.

3. *Interpretation of Municipal Ordinances*

Few municipal codes are annotated. Thus, after you read the pertinent ordinance, you are seldom directed to cases interpreting this ordinance. In fact, ordinances are rarely interpreted by court cases. Thus, conducting research on municipal law can be difficult. Perhaps the best way to locate cases interpreting ordinances is through LexisNexis or Westlaw. Type the name or number of your ordinance in the search box and you will be directed to any cases that have mentioned the provision in which you are interested. Additionally, West publishes a multivolume set titled *Ordinance Law Annotations*, which directs you to cases that interpret or apply ordinances. The set is arranged by topic (demonstrations and parades, street vendors, and so forth) and provides digests or brief summaries of cases that have interpreted ordinances relating to these topics. *Ordinance Law Annotations* is available in conventional hardbound volumes and on Westlaw.

4. *Municipal Research on the Internet*

Hundreds of city and county municipal codes are now available on the Internet. Following are some of the best sites to locate municipal codes on the Internet:

- Municipal Code Corporation (http://www.municode.com) provides codes for more than 1,600 local governments. Select a state, a locality, and then search by key words or by reviewing an index or chapter.
- The Seattle Public Library's website (http://www.spl.org/default.asp?pageID=collection_municodes) provides links to city and county codes throughout the nation.
- LexisNexis Municipal Codes Web Library (http://www.bpcnet.com) provides links to numerous codes from all over the country. Searching can be done by key words or by viewing chapter headings.

F. Citation Form

Legal Materials	Bluebook *(for practitioners)*	*ALWD*
Legislative Materials	• H.R. 104, 109th Cong. § 2 (2005).	• H.R. 104, 109th Cong. § 2 (Jan. 4, 2005).
	• H.R. Rep. No. 108-796, pt. 1, at 7 (2004), *as reprinted in* 2004 U.S.C.C.A.N. 1390, 1395.	• H.R. Rpt. 108-796 at 7 (Dec. 7, 2004).
	• *The Methamphetamine Remediation Research Act of 2005: Hearing on H.R. 042 Before the H. Comm. on Science*, 109th Cong. 7 (2005) (statement of Mr. Gary Howard, Sheriff, Tioga County, New York).	• H.R. Comm. on Sci., *The Methamphetamine Remediation Research Act of 2005: Hearing on H.R. 042*, 109th Cong. 7 (Mar. 3, 2005) (statement of Mr. Gary Howard, Sheriff, Tioga County, New York).
	• 151 Cong. Rec. H11, 462-463 (daily ed. May 25, 2006) (statement of Rep. Sherwood Boehlert).	• 151 Cong. Rec. H11462-63 (daily ed. May 25, 2006) (statement of Rep. Sherwood Boehlert).
Presidential Materials	• Proclamation No. 8107, 3 C.F.R. 8 (Feb. 26, 2007), *reprinted in* 3 U.S.C. § 469 (Supp. I. 2007).	• Exec. Procl. 8107, 3 C.F.R. 8 (2007) (reprinted in 3 U.S.C. § 469 (Supp. 2007)).
	• Exec. Order No. 7125, 3 C.F.R. 477 (1981-1985), *reprinted in* 3 U.S.C. § 297 (2006).	• Exec. Or. 7125, 3 C.F.R. 477 (2003) (reprinted in 3 U.S.C. § 297 (2006)).

Legal Materials	Bluebook *(for practitioners)*	*ALWD*
Administrative Materials	• DNA-Sample Collection and Biological Evidence Preservation in the Federal Jurisdiction, 73 Fed. Reg. 74,932, 74,935 (Dec. 10, 2008) (to be codified at 28 C.F.R. pt. 28). • Homeland Security, 6 C.F.R. § 5.1 (2006).	• DNA-Sample Collection and Biological Evidence Preservation in the Federal Jurisdiction, 73 Fed. Reg. 74,932, 74,935 (Dec. 10, 2008) (to be codified at 28 C.F.R. pt. 28). • Homeland Security, 6 C.F.R. § 5.1 (2006).
International Materials	• Protocol Relating to the Madrid Agreement Concerning the International Registration of Marks art. 4, Nov. 2, 2003, 114 Stat. 2875, 41 I.L.M. 1520. • Convention on Nuclear Proliferation, U.S.-Can., art. 14, Nov. 20, 2000, 46 U.S.T. 107, 109.	• *Protocol Relating to the Madrid Agreement Concerning the International Registration of Marks* art. 4 (Nov. 2, 2003), 114 Stat. 2875. • *Convention on Nuclear Proliferation* art. 14 (Nov. 20, 2000), 46 U.S.T. 107, 109.
Municipal Materials	• Balt., Md., Code § 7-10 (1998).	• Balt. City Code (Md.) § 7-10 (1998).

CyberSites

http://www.gpoaccess.gov	GPO Access offers access to the *Federal Register*, C.F.R., public laws, executive materials, and a wide variety of legislative materials, and treaties.
http://thomas.loc.gov	THOMAS offers the text of bills, public laws, committee information, the *Congressional Record*, and treaties.
http://lib.law.washington.edu/ref/adminus.html	The University of Washington School of Law provides an excellent tutorial on conducting administrative law research.
http://www.llsdc.org/Fed-Leg-Hist	Consult this excellent guide for information on compiling a federal legislative history.
http://www.law.indiana.edu/lawlibrary/research/guides/statelegislative/index.shtml	Access this website to link to state legislative history information.
http://www.un.org	The website of the United Nations offers the text of some treaties and a glossary of treaty terms.
http://www2.lib.uchicago.edu/~llou/forintlaw.html	Access this site for an excellent primer on conducting international law research on the Internet with links to treaties and websites of major international organizations.
http://www.state.gov/s/l	The State Department provides links to treaty actions and the current edition of *Treaties in Force*.
http://www.municode.com	Municipal Code Corporation provides the text of numerous municipal codes.

Research Assignment

1. Use the CIS Annual Index for 2008.
   a. What public law relates to the extension of the Parole Commission programs?
   b. Locate the CIS "Legislative History" volume for this public law.
      (i) When was it approved?
      (ii) What was its designation in the Senate?
      (iii) On what days did debate occur?

2. Use the CIS Annual Index for 2007.
   a. For what piece of legislation did Nancy Grace testify?
   b. Review the CIS Abstracts volume for 2007. On what date did Ms. Grace testify?
   c. Who is Ms. Grace?

3. Use *United States Code Congressional and Administrative News*.
   a. To what topic does Public Law 110-177 relate?
   b. Use Table 4 for the 100th Congress, 1st Session. Locate the following information relating to the preceding act.
      (i) Give the House Bill Number.
      (ii) Give the date on which the bill was passed by the House.
      (iii) Give the date on which the bill was passed by the Senate.
      (iv) Give the date on which the bill was approved.

4. Review the legislative history in *United States Code Congressional and Administrative News* for the Public Law identified in Question 3.
   a. According to House Report 110-218, page 14, how much will it cost to implement this legislation over the 2008-2012 time period?
   b. What volume of the *Congressional Record* includes debates and information relating to this legislation?

5. Review the *Congressional Record* for September 21, 2004.
   a. Who offered the prayer in the Senate?
   b. Who called the Senate to order on September 21, 2004?
   c. In this same volume, review the information for the House of Representatives for September 23, 2004, relating to the "Pledge Protection Act of 2004" (H.R. 2028). Review the voting tallies. Did the legislation pass?

6. Use the most recent C.F.R. Index and Finding Aids volume.
   a. What C.F.R. title and part deal with promotion, research, and consumer information for popcorn?
   b. Review this part. What is the definition of "popcorn"?
   c. What specific section provides this definition?

7. Use the Topical Index (for Wages-Hours) for *CCH Labor Law Reporter*.
   a. What paragraph generally deals with paid holidays under the Fair Labor Standards Act?
   b. Review this paragraph. What case held that absent any contractual obligation, a newspaper publisher did not have to count unworked Thanksgiving and Christmas holidays as hours worked for overtime purposes? Give case name only.

8. Review the case at 2006-07 CCH *NLRB Decisions* ¶ 17,430.
   a. What is the name of this case?
   b. Was it a violation of the National Labor Relations Act for the employer to inform employees that it would be futile to support unionization?
   c. What amended remedy was awarded to the employees?

9. Use the Case Table in *CCH Federal Securities Law Reporter*.
   a. Give the citation for *Hunt v. Robinson*.
   b. Review this case. According to this case, what is the fundamental purpose of the Securities Exchange Act of 1934?

10. Use *Weekly Compilation of Presidential Documents* for the week ending Friday, March 4, 2005.
    a. Who received a posthumous Congressional Gold Medal?
    b. Review the "Interviews with the News Media" at the CIA on March 3, 2005. What did the President say about Syria?

11. Use the Cumulative Index, Volume 40, for volumes 2151-2200 for the United Nations Treaty Series. Find the treaty that deals with friendship and cooperation between Turkey and Bulgaria.
    a. Where and when was the agreement signed?
    b. Once you locate the date of signature, use the Chronological Index in the front of this volume to locate the citation to the treaty in the United Nations Treaty Series. Locate and review the treaty.
       (i) How long was the treaty to last?
       (ii) What does Article III provide?

12. Use the Cumulative Index, Volume 42, for volumes 2251-2300 of the United Nations Treaty Series and find the agreement between Japan and the United States concerning an international observer scheme for whaling operations. Once you locate the date of signature, use the Chronological Index in the front of this volume to locate the citation to the original agreement in the United Nations Treaty Series.
    a. Give the citation to this treaty.
    b. Where and when was the original agreement signed?
    c. Locate the extension of the agreement. Who signed the extension of the agreement for each party?
    d. How long is the extension effective?

13. Use Moore's *Digest of International Law*.
    a. What volume and page discuss the issuance of passports only to citizens of the United States?
    b. Review this section. What act expressly forbids issuance of a passport to any person not a citizen of the United States?

14. Use Whiteman's *Digest of International Law*.
    a. What volumes and pages deal with piracy as a crime against the law of nations?
    b. Review the first reference to which you are directed. If members of a crew revolt and convert a ship and its goods to their own use, has piracy been committed?
    c. Continue reviewing the information in this section relating to the 1958 Convention on the High Seas. What does Article 14 provide?

15. Use U.S. Treaties and Other International Agreements.
    a. What is the general subject matter of 35 U.S.T. 4968 (T.I.A.S. 10979)?
    b. Who signed this agreement for the United States?
    c. When did this agreement enter into force?

Internet Assignment

1. Access the website for GPO Access and select "Congressional Record." Review the Senate Recorded Votes for Thursday, March 5, 2009 (for S. 85). How many yea and nay votes were recorded on the amendment being considered?

2. Access the website THOMAS. Locate H.R. 1106 introduced in the 111th Congress. What is the title of this bill, and what House Resolutions are related to it?

3. Access the website for GPO Access and select "Code of Federal Regulations." Browse Title 21, part 216. Why were the listed drugs withdrawn or removed from the market?

4. Access the website for GPO Access and select "Presidential Materials."
    a. Using the *Daily Compilation of Presidential Documents*, locate President Obama's first proclamation (dated January 20, 2009). What is its title?
    b. Using the *Weekly Compilation of Presidential Documents*, locate Executive Order 12,333, dated July 30, 2009. What is its title?
    c. What is the subject matter of Presidential Proclamation No. 8403?

5. Access http://www.washlaw.edu and select "Colorado." Review the Code of Colorado Regulations.
   a. Review the list of Colorado departments and agencies. For how long is an initial real estate license issued?
   b. Review the information regarding license qualifications. How many hours of instruction must one have to obtain an initial license?
6. Access the State Department's Treaty Affairs Office at http://www.state.gov/s/l. Select "Treaty Affairs" and then "Treaties in Force." Select the treaties in force in 2007. Review Belgium's bilateral treaty on extradition. When was it signed? When did it enter into force? What is its citation?
7. Access the website of the United Nations and review the Glossary of treaty terms, within the U.N. Treaty Collection section. Generally, what is an "exchange of notes/letters"?
8. Access http://www.municode.com and select "Online Library." Locate the El Paso, Texas, Code of Ordinances. May a person maintain a lynx in his or her home in the city of El Paso? Answer the question and give the citation to the sections that govern your answer.

Legal Research

Using Electronic and Computer Resources

Chapter 8

The Digital Library: LexisNexis, Westlaw, and Non-Print Research Tools

Chapter Overview

Legal research can be accomplished by means other than using the conventional sources of bound books and journals. There are several new technologies that allow you to conduct research efficiently and accurately. This chapter introduces you to the digital library, primarily computer-assisted legal research. Legal research using the Internet is discussed in Chapter Nine. Being a competent researcher requires use and familiarity with all media, including traditional print courses, computer systems, and the Internet to find the best answer to a legal question in the most efficient manner and at the lowest cost to the client.

A. Introduction to Computer-Assisted Legal Research

1. *LexisNexis and Westlaw*

There are two major competing computer-assisted research services: *LexisNexis* (for simplicity, referred to as "Lexis" in this chapter and also commonly known as Lexis in practice) and *Westlaw*. These research systems provide access to a tremendous variety of cases, statutes, administrative regulations, and numerous other authorities that a law firm or other employer may not otherwise be able to afford. The more familiar you become with Lexis or Westlaw, the more efficient you will be at locating the information you need. Lexis and Westlaw operate in essentially the same manner; most users, however, eventually develop a preference for one or the other. Because both services contain substantially the same materials, it is impossible to declare than one service is superior to the other. The one that is "best" is the one that is best for you.

Each service consists of thousands of databases. The databases include cases, statutes, administrative regulations, hundreds of secondary sources, and other materials for you to access. In general, research using Lexis and Westlaw is highly similar. Both allow easy retrieval of cases, statutes, and other materials when you already have a citation. You merely type the citation into an open field and click on "Go" or a similar button. When you do not have a citation, you will usually access the appropriate database (such as selecting federal cases or Ohio cases) and then formulate a search question by using *Boolean searching* (a search method using symbols, word fragments, and numbers, rather than plain English) or by using plain English, usually called "natural language."

It is important to have a basic understanding of the two computerized legal research systems; however, the best way to learn how to perform computerized legal research is to do it. There is no substitute for "hands-on" experience. Lexis and Westlaw both offer training courses and written materials describing their systems. Often a complete tutorial package is available, consisting of written descriptions of the systems as well as CD-ROMs to demonstrate use of the system. Contact:

LexisNexis	West, A Thomson Reuters Business
9443 Springboro Pike Dayton, OH 45342	610 Opperman Drive Eagan, MN 55123
24-hour toll-free customer service: 1 (800) 543-6862 http://www.lexisnexis.com/support/training	24-hour toll-free customer service: 1 (800) Westlaw http://west.thomson.com

Ethics Alert: *Computer Literacy*

Legal professionals are ethically bound to provide competent representation to clients. This duty is broad enough to require that you be sufficiently familiar with conventional *and* electronic research techniques such that you can make an accurate determination as to which sources will yield the best results at the lowest cost for the client. Neither conventional research nor computer-assisted legal research should be used exclusively. Effective researchers use a combination of the two methods and employ selectivity to determine which method is best for a given task.

2. *Getting Started Using Lexis or Westlaw*

Getting started usually requires you to sign on to Lexis or Westlaw with your identification number and password assigned to you by your school or employer. When performing research on the job, you will usually enter a client name or number so that the client can be billed for the time spent conducting the research. In most firms, legal professionals have desktop computer access to Lexis, Westlaw, or both.

The first screen presented to you after sign on usually allows you to retrieve a document or case (if you know the citation), check a citation (either through *Shepard's Citations* or KeyCite), or construct a search if you do not have a citation.

3. *Boolean Searching*

You will find that computers are extremely literal. They will not search for cases containing the word "collision" if you search for "collide." Thus, a method called *Boolean searching* allows you to use words, symbols, numbers, and connectors (collectively, often called *Terms and Connectors*) to overcome the literalness of the computer. For example, Lexis and Westlaw both use an exclamation point (!) to substitute for any number of additional letters at the end of a word. Thus "colli!" will locate "collide," "collision," "colliding," and so forth. Of course, words such as "collie" will also be located, so use the symbols carefully. Both Lexis and Westlaw also offer publications that explain the use of their search symbols, numbers, and connectors. See Figure 8-9 at the end of this chapter for a chart of Lexis and Westlaw Terms and Connectors.

These symbols and connectors help you narrow your search and make it more manageable. If you merely entered "first amendment," Lexis and Westlaw would retrieve thousands of documents containing this phrase. A more effective search would be "first amendment /50 free! and press": This instructs Lexis and Westlaw to locate only those documents that contain the phrase "first amendment" within 50 words of the words "freedom" or "free" and "press."

4. *Plain English Searching*

Recognizing that many individuals find working with Boolean connectors awkward, Lexis provides "Natural Language" and Westlaw offers "WIN" (an acronym for "Westlaw Is Natural," now more frequently called "Natural Language") to allow you to enter your issue in plain English or natural language and eliminate the need for symbols, numbers, and connectors. Thus, you could enter in a search question such as "May unmarried or single individuals adopt children?"

Construct your searches before you sign on so that you work efficiently and do not incur excessive costs. Draft some sample queries and search terms. Although using natural language is easier when constructing queries, Boolean searching usually produces more precise results.

B. Lexis

1. *Getting Started*

Lexis's database consists of a series of *sources* (sometimes called *libraries*)—materials relating to particular areas of law, such as the source titled "GENFED," which contains cases, statutes, and materials relating to federal legal topics. Within each source are "files." For

> ***Practice Tips:** Boolean or Plain English Searching? Westlaw's Suggestions*
>
> **Use Boolean searching when:**
>
> - You are searching for particular terms;
> - You are searching for a particular document; or
> - You are searching for all documents containing specific information, such as all cases classified under a particular topic name and Key Number.
>
> **Use plain English or natural language searching when:**
>
> - You are researching broad concepts; or
> - You are a new or infrequent computer user, or you are unfamiliar with Boolean terms and connectors.

example, the GENFED source contains separate "files" for cases from the U.S. Supreme Court, cases from the Courts of Appeal, and other federal materials. In fact, Lexis provides more than 40,000 sources, including cases, statutes, forms, treatises, the Restatements, encyclopedias, dictionaries, jury instructions, and much more. For a searchable directory of Lexis's sources, access the following site: http://w3.nexis.com/sources.

After you log on at http://www.lexis.com, the first screen provides various research options at the top of your screen, including the following:

- **Search.** The "Search" tab at the top of your screen is divided into four subtabs:
  - Search "by Source" is a frequently used starting point and allows you to select a source you want to search (for example, federal cases or state cases) before you enter your search terms. In most instances, when you first access Lexis, this "by Source" screen is preselected for you as your starting point.
  - Search "by Topic or Headnote" allows you to select the topic you wish to research and then customize the sources and jurisdictions in which to conduct your research or elect to view all headnotes relating to a particular topic.
  - Search "by Guided Search Form" lists several broad categories (for example, "States Legal" and "Law Reviews"). When you select a category, you will then be given a search box and a guided form that has several recommended sources already identified for you.
  - Search "by Dot Command" should be used when you know the Lexis library and file name of the source you wish to research (for example, "GENFED").
- **Research Tasks.** Selecting the "Research Tasks" tab identifies more than 20 practice areas (for example, Bankruptcy or Patents). When you select an area of the law, for example, "Patents," you will then be provided a list of patent materials such as treatises, cases, news, and legal developments within which to search further.
- **Get a Document.** Use the "Get a Document" tab when you know the citation to a case, statute, law review, or other authority. Type your citation in the open field (for example, 14 p3d 890) and click "Get." You need not use correct citation form.
- ***Shepard's.*** Use this feature to Shepardize your authorities (primarily, to ensure your primary authorities are still good law).

(See Figure 8-1.)

Figure 8-1
Lexis "Search by Source" Screen

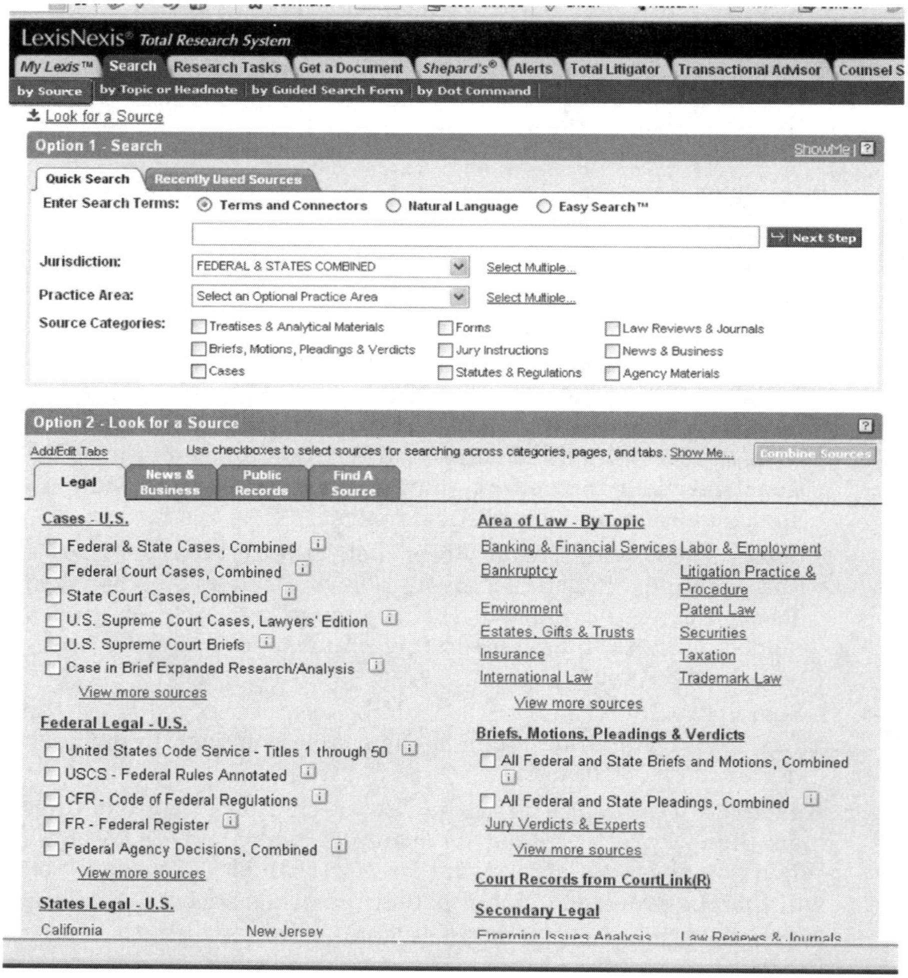

2. *Constructing a Search*

There are three ways to search for materials on Lexis if you do not have a citation: the traditional search using Boolean connectors (which Lexis calls "Terms and Connectors"), the newer plain English search method called "Natural Language" (formerly called "Freestyle"), or Lexis's new Easy Search, a search method similar to popular Internet searching.

a. Boolean Searching

Most experts agree that Boolean searching provides more targeted results than plain English searching. Following are some tips for constructing a search query using terms and connectors on Lexis:

- **Lowercase Letters.** Lexis is not sensitive to capital letters (unless you specify such in your search request). Thus, for basic searching, use lowercase letters.
- **Singulars, Possessives, and Plurals.** Forms of singular, possessives, and plurals are automatically found if they are regular forms. Thus, a search for "tenant" will produce results for "tenants" and "tenant's" but a search for "foot" will not find "feet."
- **Universal Symbols.** Lexis offers some *universal symbols* or "wildcards" to help you expand your search:

  - An *asterisk* (*) replaces single letters within words. Thus, "m*m" will find "man" or "men" and "anders*n" will find "andersen" or "anderson."
  - An *exclamation point* (!) replaces any ending to a word. Thus, "sec!" finds "security," "securities," "secure," and so forth.

Figure 8-2
Lexis Natural Language Search Screen

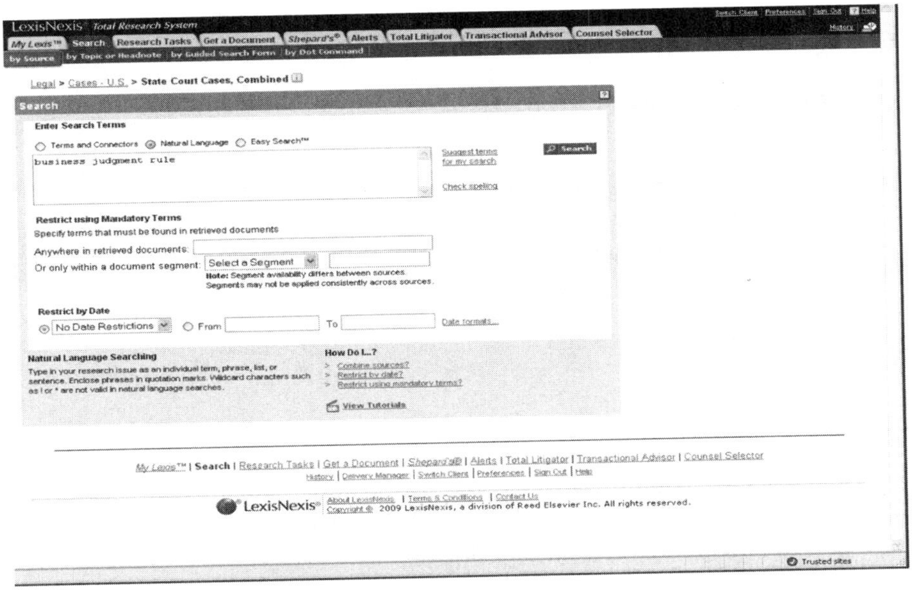

- **Connectors.** *Connectors* help you locate needed documents and narrow your search. Following are the most commonly used connectors:

  - **Or.** A search for "teacher or student" will locate documents containing either or both of these words.
  - **And.** A search for "negligence and doctor" will locate documents only if they contain both these terms.
  - **w/n.** The connector "w/n" instructs Lexis to find documents that contain words appearing within a specified number(n) of words of each other. Thus, a search for "tenant w/50 evict" locates documents in which the words "tenant" and "evict" appear within 50 words of each other.
  - **w/s and w/p.** The connector "w/s" finds words in the same sentence and "w/p" finds words in the same paragraph. Thus, a search for "alter w/s ego" (or "alter w/p ego") locates documents in which the words "alter" and "ego" appear in the same sentence or paragraph, respectively.

Lexis offers other connectors as well; they are described in Lexis's marketing materials and on its website at http://web.lexis.com/help/research/gh_search.asp#TermsConnectors. Multiple connectors may be used in one search request. (See Figure 8-9 at the end of this chapter.)

Constructing a proper search is the most important part of computerized legal research and requires thought and planning. Draft your search query before you sign on and begin incurring charges.

If your search does not produce sufficient results (or perhaps produces too many documents), you may modify your search. Simply type "m."

b. Plain English Searching

Because many individuals find working with terms and connectors awkward, Lexis allows you to use plain English through its Natural Language feature. First, you must select a Source (such as federal cases). Type your words or phrases into the open field. For example, you could type, "What is the term of a design patent" and select the open circle marked "Natural Language." Click "Search" and modify as needed. Use the "Suggest Terms" tab to see a list of words that can be included in your search. (See Figure 8-2.)

c. Easy Search

Lexis's new service, *Easy Search*, is a quick search method, which is used similarly to Internet search engines such as Google. Users simply enter their search terms in the open search box without using either Terms and Connectors or Natural Language.

To use this service, click on the "Search" tab, then choose a legal source (for example, federal codes) from the menu, and then select "Easy Search." Type your search terms in the open field and click "Search." Just as you search using Google or another Internet search engine, you may search by phrase ("business judgment rule"), citation (520 us 10), or other relevant terms. As they are by Google, results are ranked by their relevance. (See Figure 8-3.)

Figure 8-3
Lexis Easy Search Screen

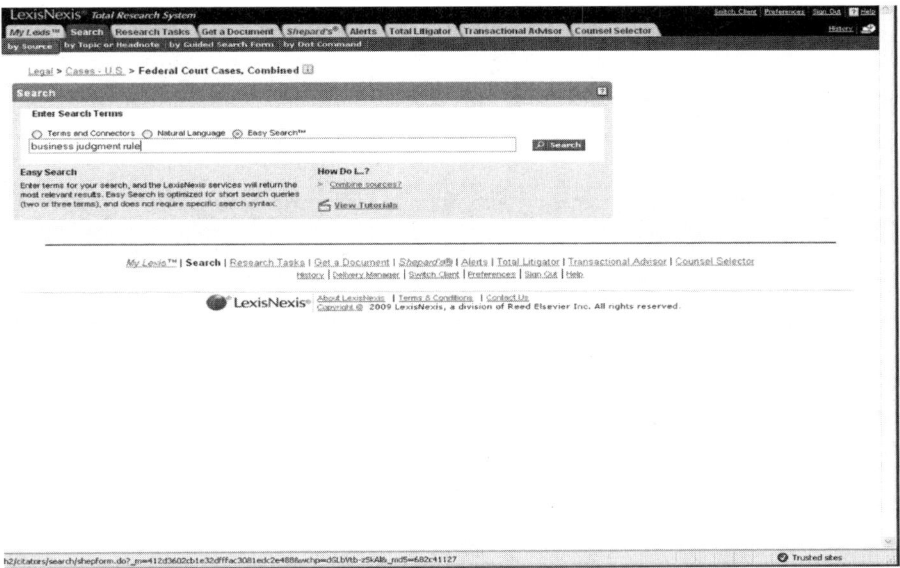

d. Display of Search Results

If your search produces numerous documents, you can weed out irrelevant ones by using the following techniques when reviewing your search results:

- **KWIC.** Use the command "KWIC" to highlight your search terms and the 25 words on either side of your search terms so you can review at a glance the portion of the case or document of most interest to you.
- **FULL.** Select "Full" to display the full text of the document containing your search terms.
- **CITE.** When you select "Cite," Lexis displays the citations to documents containing your search terms.

Once the search results are on screen, you may move back and forth between documents. (See Figure 8-4.)

3. *Specialized Searches*

a. Searching for Statutes and Constitutions

• **By Citation.** If you know the precise citation for a federal or state statute or constitution, click the "Get a Document" tab. Type your citation (such as 35 uscs 101) in the open field and click "Get." After reviewing the statute, you can browse through preceding and consecutive sections. You can also review the case annotations following your citation, just as you would in the print version of U.S.C.S.

Figure 8-4
Viewing Lexis Results

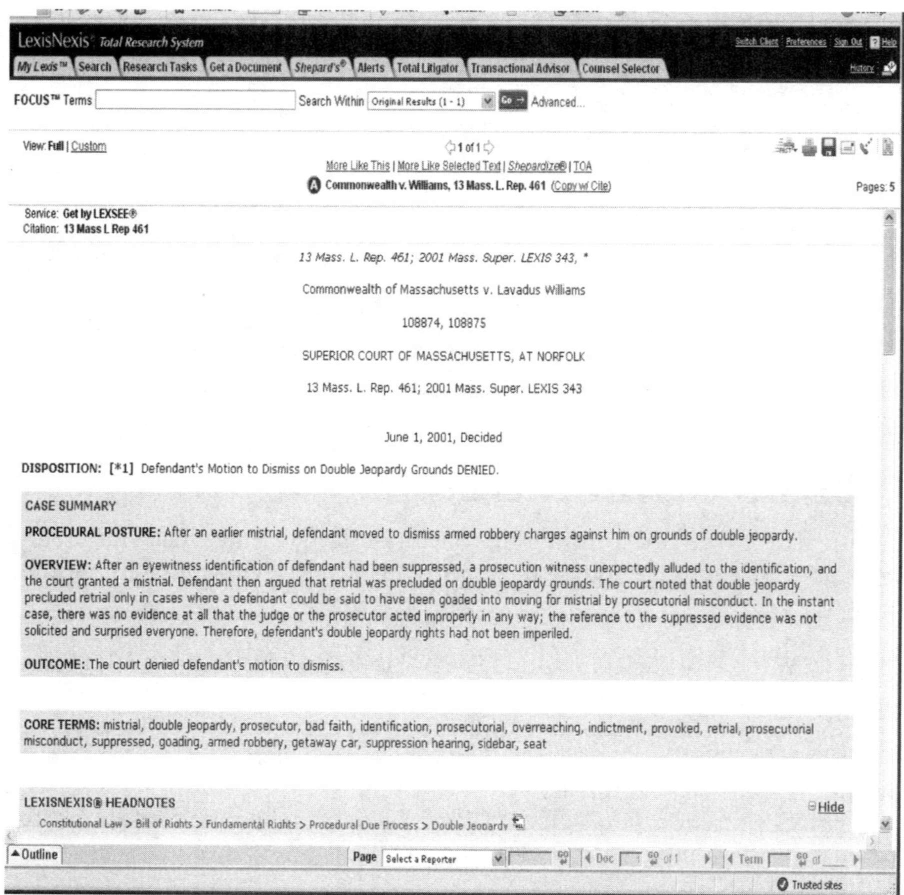

• **By Topic.** When you do not know a statute or constitutional citation, you must select a library or source (such as "States—Legal" and then "Ohio Statutes"). You may browse various titles within the Ohio code or you may construct a search using Terms and Connectors or Natural Language, as described previously.

b. Searching for Cases

• **By Citation.** If you know a case citation, use the "Get a Document" feature and type your citation (such as 430 us 128 or 222 s ct 1) in the open field. Lexis includes star paging to inform you of the page number you would be on if you were reading the case in the other sets that report U.S. Supreme Court cases.

• **By Party Name.** If you know a plaintiff's or defendant's name, click the "Get a Document" tab and then the "Party Name" tab. Type the party's name in the open field and select "Search."

• **By Topic.** When you do not have a citation, use the Search tab and the subtab "Search by Topic or Headnote" or "Search by Guided Search Form," as discussed previously.

c. Searching for Administrative and Legislative Materials

• **By Citation.** If you know the citation to a C.F.R. provision, the *Federal Register*, or a public law number, use the "Get a Document" feature and type your citation (for example, 29 cfr 401.1).

• **By Topic.** If you do not have a citation, select "Search" at the top of your screen and then select the source you desire (for example, "CFR"). Type your terms or connectors, use Natural Language or Easy Search in the open field, and select "Search."

• **Legislative History.** Lexis offers several compiled legislative histories. Select "Legal," then "Federal Legal—U.S.," and then "Legislative History Materials."

d. Searching for Law Reviews and Journals

• **By Citation.** Use the "Get a Document" feature if you know the citation to a law review or journal article.

• **By Topic.** When you do not have a citation, use the "Search by Guided Search Form" tab.

• **By Law Reviews.** Select the "Search by Source" tab at the top of the toolbar and then select "Law Reviews & Journals" and type your key terms in the open field. Click "Search." Alternatively, you may select specific journals in which to conduct your research.

e. Searching for Secondary Authorities

You may search for secondary authorities by selecting the tab "Search" and then the subtab "by Source" from the toolbar and then clicking on "Secondary Legal," and then selecting the specific secondary source desired, such as "A.L.R." or "Area of Law Treatises." Alternatively, you may select the tab "Research Tasks" at the top of the toolbar, and then select a desired area of law (for example, Bankruptcy or Insurance) to be directed to a list of selected sources.

4. Shepardizing

As will be discussed in Chapter Eleven, Lexis makes it easy to verify that your cases, statutes, and other primary authorities are still valid. To do so, you may click the Shepard's tab, type your citation in the open field, and click "Check." Alternatively, when you are viewing a case or statute on the screen, watch for the "signal indicators" on the screen. For example, a red circle is a warning that your case has been subject to some negative treatment (such as being reversed). A yellow triangle indicates caution, meaning that your case has been criticized or limited.

5. Other Lexis Features

Lexis offers numerous features to make your research efficient and accurate.

- **Hyperlinking.** As you read a case, statute, or other authority on the screen, references to other cases or authorities are hyperlinked, allowing you to jump to these other documents by merely placing your cursor on the item displayed.
- **Total Litigator.** Lexis's new Total Litigator feature offers a wealth of tools for litigation, including tips on creating a discovery plan, help for drafting documents, links to court briefs, and more.
- **Alerts.** By selecting the Alerts tab, you can save a search and schedule it to run again in the future so you can receive updates by email.
- **Practitioner's Toolbox.** When federal statutes or statutes from selected states are displayed on the screen, a Practitioner's Toolbox will appear on the right side of the screen, directing you to the history of the statute and related helpful research resources.
- **Focus.** Lexis's "Focus" feature looks for additional terms in your search results. Thus, when you are viewing a case or other result, select "Focus" at the top of the page, type additional terms in the open field, and click "Focus."

• **Segment Searching.** Lexis allows you to restrict your search using segments. For example, you can select "dissent" or "court" to narrow your research. You can also use date restrictions to locate cases before or after a certain date. A menu allows you to select your desired time period.

• **More Like This.** This feature allows you to find other cases or authorities similar to the one you have identified as relevant to your research. Simply highlight the desired text and click "More Like Selected Text" and then "Search."

• **50 State Surveys.** This feature allows you to compare and contrast legislation and regulations from all states on various topics. For example, if you need to determine the requirements for forming a limited liability company in each state, the 50 State Surveys feature provides links to all states' relevant statutes in an easy-to-read spreadsheet format.

• **Briefs and Records.** As you view a case on your screen, look for a link to "Briefs," so you can review the briefs and arguments filed by the attorneys involved in the displayed case. You can also search for briefs by Terms and Connectors or Natural Language. These briefs may give you ideas for drafting your own briefs and memoranda. Briefs are not offered for all cases.

• **Live Help.** Lexis offers researchers the ability to send email questions asking for help from Lexis's customer support. Real-time chat support provides immediate help and assistance.

• **Affiliated Services.** Lexis offers numerous complementary services. For example, "Company Dossier" provides business information on more than 35 million companies worldwide, including company overviews, financial reports, and more. The "Academic" service offers documents from nearly 6,000 legal, medical, and business publications.

6. *Quick Review of Lexis*

To use Lexis:

a. Establish your Internet connection and access http://www.lexis.com.

b. Sign on by typing in your Lexis user number, identification number, or password.

c. Type in the client or billing number.

d. If you know a citation to a case, statute, or other authority, select "Get a Document" at the top of your screen, enter the citation, and click "Get."

e. Use one of the four Search tabs when you are unsure where to start your legal research. Click on topics until you reach the most relevant topic, select a jurisdiction, type key words into the search boxes (using Terms and Connectors, Natural Language, or

Easy Search), and click "Search" to access relevant cases, treatises, and other materials. Examine the results and Shepardize all primary authorities.

C. Westlaw

1. *Getting Started*

The information in Westlaw is contained in *databases* (analogous to Lexis's "sources") and *files*. Westlaw includes more than 16,000 databases, more than 1 billion public records, more than 6,800 news and business publications, and more than 700 law reviews. Within each database there may be several files. For example, within the database called "Federal Materials" are files for federal cases and federal statutes. You can access Westlaw through the Internet at http://www.westlaw.com. After you enter your password and client identification, the first screen (see Figure 8-5) will provide you with several shortcut choices, including the following:

- **Find by Citation.** "Find by Citation" allows you to find a case, statute, or other document by its citation. Type your citation (such as 11 p3d 105) and click "Go."

Figure 8-5
Westlaw Resources Screen

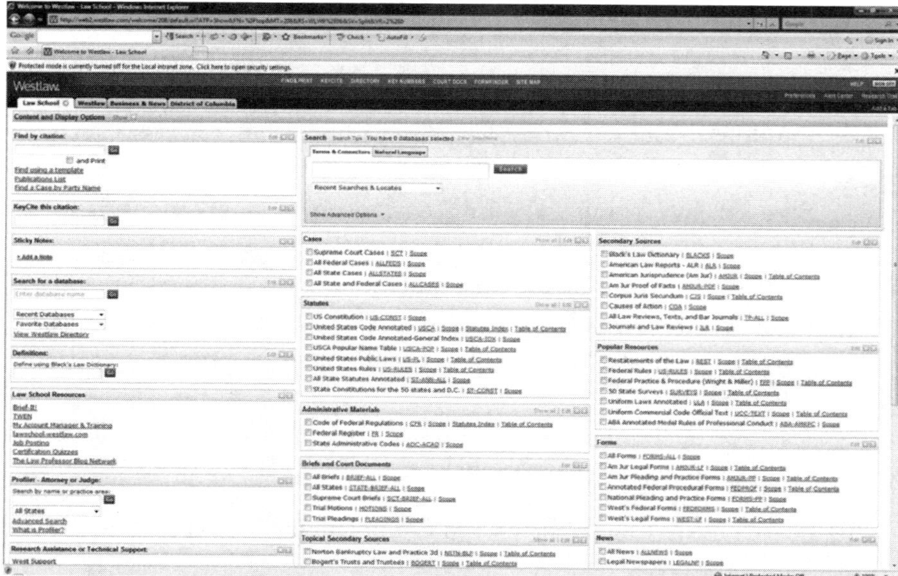

Figure 8-6
Westlaw Directory Search Screen

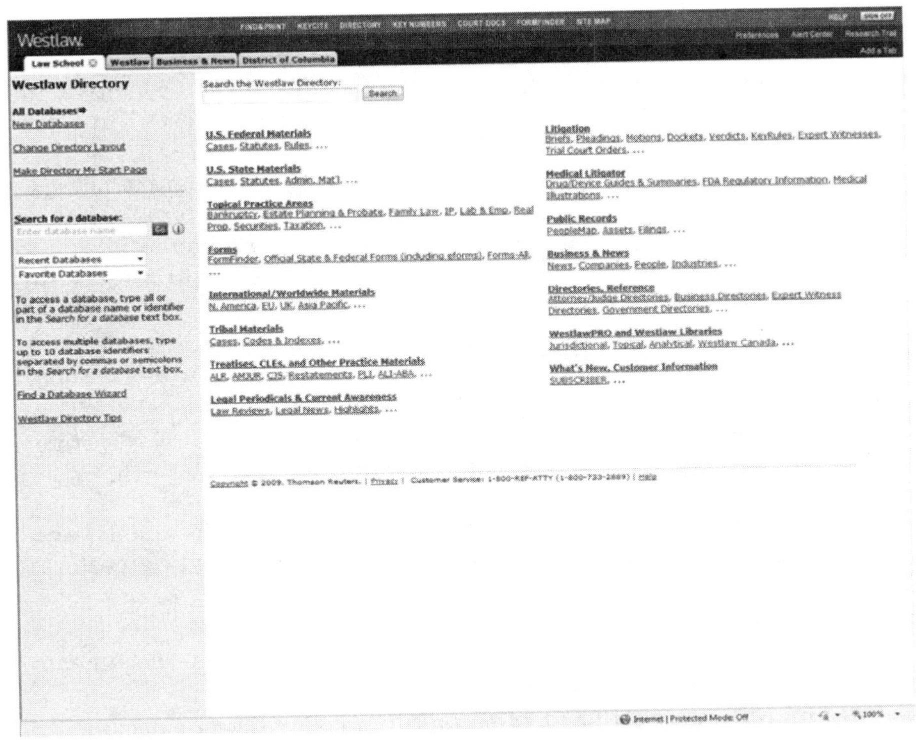

• **KeyCite.** KeyCite allows you to enter a citation and ensure your authority is still valid (analogous to Shepardizing on Lexis).

• **Search for a Database.** This feature allows you to enter a database identifier (such as "ALLFEDS" for all federal cases) and access that database for searching.

• **Resources.** Westlaw's first screen allows you to select a number of resources, including cases, statutes, the Restatements, C.F.R., Am. Jur. 2d, and so on, and then begin your search by entering words into the search box displayed (using Terms and Connectors or Natural Language).

• **Directory.** If you do not know where to begin, select "Directory" at the top of the screen toolbar for access to Westlaw's list of databases. You can then click and select your desired resource. (See Figure 8-6.)

2. *Constructing a Search*

If you do not have a citation, you must construct a search or formulate a *query*. As soon as you access a database, Westlaw will prompt you to enter your query. You may search by Terms and Connectors or Natural Language.

a. Boolean Searching

Following are some tips for constructing a search query using Terms and Connectors on Westlaw. Note that many of these are either similar or identical to the Lexis Terms and Connectors. (See Figure 8-9.)

• **Lowercase Letters.** Like Lexis, Westlaw is not sensitive to capital letters (unless you specify such in your search request). Thus, for basic searching, use lowercase letters.

• **Singulars, Possessives, and Plurals.** Forms of singular, possessives, and plurals are automatically found if they are regular forms. Thus, a search for "patent" will produce results for "patents" and "patent's."

• **Universal Symbols.** Westlaw offers some universal symbols to help you expand your search:

- An *asterisk* (*) replaces single letters within words. Thus, "franchis*r" will retrieve franchisor and franchiser.
- An *exclamation point* (!) replaces any ending to a word. Thus, "valu!" will retrieve value, valued, valuation, and so forth.

• **Connectors.** Connectors help you locate needed documents and narrow your search. Following are the most commonly used connectors:

- **Or.** In Westlaw, the "or" connector is represented by a single space. Thus, a search for "landlord lessor" will locate documents containing either or both of these words.
- **And (&).** A search for "landlord & covenant" will locate documents only if they contain both these terms.
- **/n.** The connector "/n" instructs Westlaw to find documents that contain words appearing within a specified number(n) of words of each other. Thus, a search for "rescission /25 contract agreement" locates documents in which the word "rescission" appears within 25 words of the term "contract" or "agreement."
- **/s and /p.** The connector "/s" finds words in the same sentence, and "/p" finds words in the same paragraph. Thus, a search for "patent /s infringement" (or "patent /p infringement") locates documents in which the words "patent" and "infringement" appear in the same sentence or paragraph, respectively.

Westlaw offers other connectors as well; they are described in Westlaw's User Guide "Westlaw Quick Reference Guide: Getting Started on Westlaw," available at http://west.thomson.com (select "Customer Support" and then "User Guides"). The most commonly used terms and connectors are also displayed on the screen on which you construct your query, allowing you to pick and choose the connectors desired. Multiple connectors may be used in one search request.

Constructing a proper search is the most important part of computerized legal research because a poorly constructed search query will produce too few or too many documents. Remember to draft your search query before you sign on and costs are assessed.

If your search does not produce sufficient results (or else produces too many documents), you may edit your search. Select "Edit Search" at the top of the screen, and modify your search by adding additional terms and connectors.

b. Plain English Searching

Just as Lexis allows searching by plain English, so does Westlaw. When you select a database, and the search box is displayed, simply click on "Natural Language." A new search box is given, into which you type your query in plain English. You may narrow your search by excluding or requiring certain words, and you are given prompts to add related terms. (See Figure 8-7.)

c. Database Wizard

Just as Lexis's Search tabs help you find the right sources, Westlaw's *Database Wizard* walks you through the process of picking the right database to meet your research needs. After you select the tab "Directory," select "Find a Database Wizard." You will be asked a series of questions about what you are trying to find, and the "Wizard" will help you select the right database by continually narrowing your options.

Figure 8-7
Westlaw Sample Query Screen

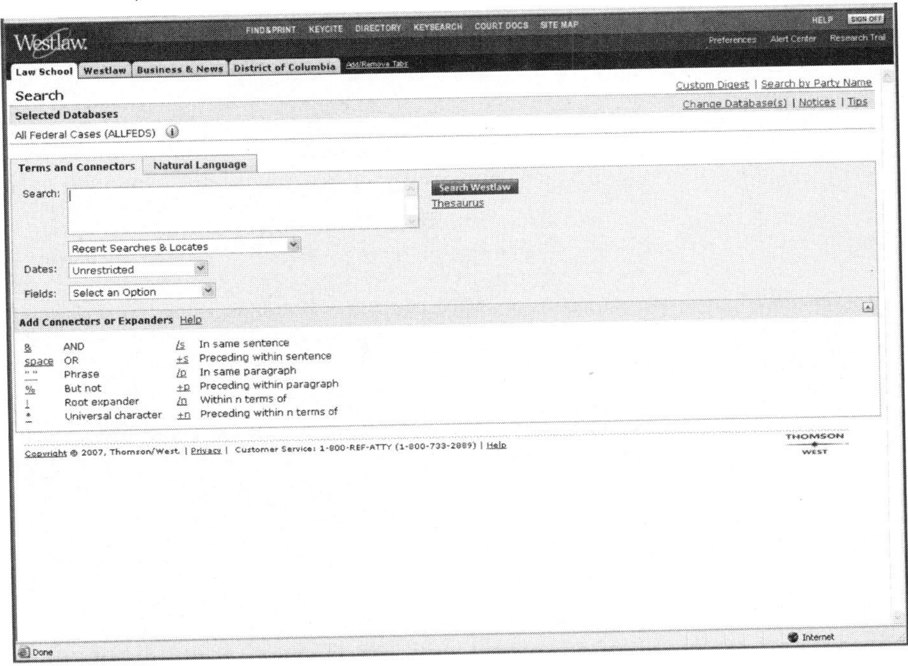

d. Display of Search Results

Once your search results are shown on your Westlaw screen, there are several methods you can use to browse the materials to determine if they are on point. On the left side of the screen, citations to cases that respond to your query will be listed with your search terms (For example, "patent infringement") banded in yellow. Select as desired. Also on the side of the screen, the "Results Plus" feature displays additional sources that may be of help, such as references to A.L.R. annotations or articles in *Am. Jur. Proof of Facts*. (See Figure 8-8.)

When you select the full text of a case, you can select "Locate in Result" from the menu on the screen and type in terms you wish to find in the document. Thus, you can type in "damages" and Westlaw will locate any use of that word in the case or document being displayed. Cases include the same features as in West's conventional print volumes, meaning that headnotes and topic names and Key Numbers are given.

Figure 8-8
Viewing Westlaw Results

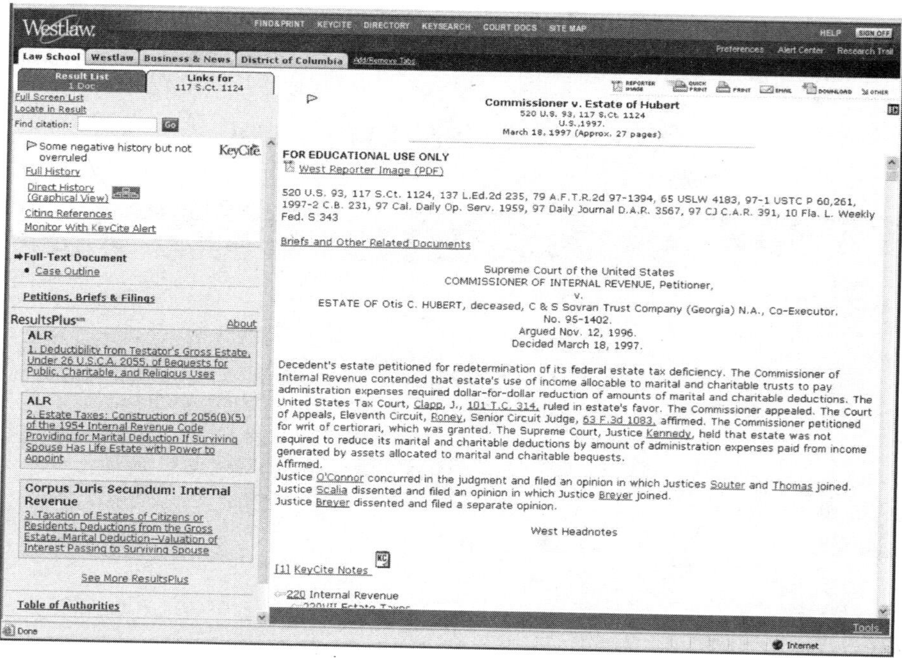

3. *Specialized Searches*

a. Searching for Statutes and Constitutions

• **By Citation.** If you know the citation to a statute or a constitution, select the tab "Find by Citation," type the citation in the search box (for example, 17 usca 109), and click "Go." You will be given the statute, library references, and annotations.

• **By Topic.** If you do not have a citation, select a database. For example, for federal statutes, select the database "USC" or "USCA." You will then need to decide whether you will search by Terms and Connectors or Natural Language. Type your search in the search box and click "Search." Westlaw's recently added feature "Statutes Results Plus" provides links to other sources (cases, other statutes, administrative code references, and legislative history documents) that discuss your statute. You will also be informed if pending legislation might affect your statute.

b. Searching for Cases

• **By Citation.** If you know a case citation, use the "Find by Citation" tab, enter your citation in the search box (for example, 520 us 788), and click "Go."

• **By Topic.** If you do not have a citation, select an appropriate database, such as all federal cases, cases from the First Circuit, or cases from Texas, and then formulate your query by using Terms and Connectors or Natural Language.

- Remember to use "ResultsPlus" to expand your research efforts. References to additional sources such as A.L.R. annotations are automatically displayed on the screen with your search results when you conduct case law research on Westlaw.
- Westlaw includes star paging to inform you of the page number you would be on if you were reading the case in parallel sets for the case.
- A new feature is the display of cases on Westlaw's screen exactly the way they appear in a printed book. If the note "West Reporter Image PDF" is shown on the screen, you may select this to view your case same easy-to-read, dual-column format you're used to seeing in print reporters.

c. Searching for Administrative and Legislative Materials

• **By Citation.** If you know the citation to a provision in either C.F.R. or the *Federal Register*, you may enter it in the "Find by Citation" search box.

• **By Topic.** You can search through the C.F.R., the *Federal Register*, and other sources by accessing the pertinent database from your first search screen and then entering your search query in the search box, using either Terms and Connectors or Natural Language. Alternatively, by selecting "Directory" from the top toolbar, you can select "Topical Practice Areas" and then select the field in which you are interested, such as "Energy Law."

- **Legislative History.** Westlaw also includes numerous legislative history documents, including bills, the *Congressional Record*, and compiled legislative histories for certain statutes. Select "Directory" from the toolbar and then "U.S. Federal Materials" and then "Legislative History" (or "Arnold & Porter Collection—Legislative Histories") for numerous compiled legislative histories.

d. Searching for Law Reviews and Journals

When you sign onto Westlaw, the first screen displays the entry "Journals and Law Reviews." Once you select that database, you then enter your search query using Terms and Connectors or Natural Language. Alternatively, you may enter an author's name or title of article, or you may enter a citation to a law review article in the "Find by Citation" box. You may also select "Directory" from the top toolbar and then select "Law Reviews," allowing you to search within specifically named law reviews and journals.

e. Searching for Secondary Authorities

When you sign onto Westlaw, a category titled "Secondary Sources" allows you to search through a number of secondary sources, including encyclopedias, A.L.R., and other secondary sources. Alternatively, select "Directory" from the top toolbar, and then review the various sources listed, including "Treatises," "Directories, Reference," and others. Select the database you wish to search and proceed to enter your query.

4. *KeyCiting*

To update and validate your primary authorities when using Westlaw, use its service called "KeyCite." The service and process is highly similar to Shepardizing using Lexis. Westlaw's first screen provides a search box titled "KeyCite this Citation." Enter your citation into the search box, click "Go," and view your results. Alternatively, when you are viewing a case or statute on the screen, watch for the "signal indicators" on the screen. For example, a red flag signals strong negative history, and a yellow flag indicates caution. KeyCiting is discussed in detail in Chapter Eleven.

5. *Other Westlaw Features*

Like Lexis, Westlaw offers a number of added features to make legal research easy and efficient, including the following:

- **Hyperlinking.** As you read through various authorities, references to other authorities will appear in a bright blue color as hyperlinks, which allow you to click and be immediately transported to them. For example, many cases displayed on the screen include a hyperlink to "Briefs and Other Related Documents," allowing you to retrieve and review the briefs submitted by the parties to the case.
- **Clipping Service.** WestClip and Alert are electronic clipping services that allow you to monitor topics of interest to you and provide you with automatic email notification when there are changes affecting the cases or statutes in which you are interested.
- **Database Wizard.** To help you select the right database for your search, Westlaw's Database Wizard provides questions and prompts and then suggests the most appropriate database for your use.
- **Key Numbers.** Select "Key Numbers" at the top of the Westlaw toolbar and you can then browse various topics and subtopics. You can enter descriptive terms into the open search box to locate topic names and Key Numbers, or you may browse various digest topics to locate topic names and Key Numbers so you can find numerous cases dealing with the same area of the law.
- **Field Searching.** Like Lexis, Westlaw allows you to retrieve only part of a document or to view documents by name or date. After you select a database, you can restrict your search to search by court, date, judge, attorney, or other fields. For example, if your query is "landlord tenant /20 default da (aft 1990)" Westlaw will search for cases decided after 1990 containing the words "landlord" or "tenant" within 20 words of the term "default." Drop-down menus help you select fields and dates.
- **Graphical Display of Direct History for Cases.** A recently added Westlaw feature shows you the direct history of your case in an easy-to-understand flowchart format. For example, you would be shown in graphical format, using arrows, how your case progressed from trial, through its initial appeal, when certiorari was granted, and then what the United States Supreme Court held. You may easily link to the court briefs and motions filed at each level of the case's history.
- **Graphical Display of Timelines for Statutes.** West now displays timelines for federal statutes and some state statutes, allowing you to link to prior versions of your statute and to relevant legislative history (such as committee reports and testimony, public laws, the *Congressional Record*, and more).

• **50 State Surveys.** Like Lexis, Westlaw gives access to all 50 states' statutes on more than 250 state and regulatory topics. For example, if you wished to know the requirements in all 50 states to form a corporation, the 50 State Survey feature would list, alphabetically, all applicable statutes from all states, thus allowing you to find and compare statutes all over the nation.

• **Briefs and Records.** Like Lexis, Westlaw also provides access to briefs and petitions filed in many cases. As you view your case on the screen, look for a link to "Briefs." You can also search for briefs and other court filings by Terms and Connectors or Natural Language or link to them when you KeyCite your cases.

• **Live Help.** Like Lexis, Westlaw offers researchers the opportunity to initiate real-time chat to ask for help and assistance. Simply click the "Help" tab, type in your question, and press "Send." Customer support will respond to your question in moments.

• **Affiliated Services.** Westlaw offers several affiliated services, including the following: "Business Information and News," a comprehensive collection of more than 8,000 news and business magazines, newspapers, and other sources; FormFinder, which helps you draft forms; and Westlaw Litigator, a complete service for legal professionals engaged in litigation, affording access to jury instructions, court briefs and records, motions, experts, and more.

6. *WestlawNext*

In Spring 2010, West introduced a new electronic research system called WestlawNext. Generally, WestlawNext mimics the ease of use of Google's search engine. Researchers who use WestlawNext will no longer have to choose a specific database before conducting a search (which often presents problems to researchers who may not know where to begin a search). A single search box presented on a clean, uncluttered screen asks WestlawNext researchers to enter "search terms, citations, databases, anything." The results presented are ranked in their order of relevance, across multiple databases. For example, when searching on Westlaw, once might select a database of federal cases. A search query is entered, and results presented, of course, are limited to a list of federal cases. A user of WestlawNext, however, enters search terms in plain English in a search box, and results presented would include cases, statutes, A.L.R. annotations, and numerous other relevant resources.

Users can highlight portions of the results shown on screen and add notes and comments, for example, a note to "include this case in my brief." Research results can be dragged into folders for quick access later. Once you view a case, it is marked with an eyeglasses icon to remind you that you have already looked at the case. If a case has negative history, that history is shown on the screen with the case (currently, using Westlaw, one is presented with a yellow flag and must then click on the flag to determine the nature of the negative history). As of the time of the writing of this text, WestlawNext coexists with Westlaw and promises to

Help Line: Lexis and Westlaw Interactive Tutorials

Lexis and Westlaw both offer free online interactive training and tutorials (as well as useful print products) to help you learn to use their services.

- **Lexis.** For interactive training, access http://www.lexisnexis.com/infopro/training. Take a tour of Lexis at http://web.lexis.com/help/multimedia/tour.htm. Print materials may be viewed and downloaded at http://www.lexisnexis.com/literature.
- **Westlaw.** For interactive training, access http://west.thomson.com/support/training/default.aspx. For user guides and reference materials, access http://west.thomson.com/westlaw/guides.
- **Georgetown University Law Center.** Georgetown offers tutorials on performing research using Lexis and Westlaw at http://www.ll.georgetown.edu/tutorials/index.cfm.

be a highly user-friendly addition to electronic research. Users who wish access to the new WestlawNext must pay a subscription fee in addition to the fee they pay for Westlaw.

D. Final Pointers on Computer-Assisted Legal Research

1. *When to Use Lexis or Westlaw*

Some tasks are best performed by using conventional print research tools, whereas others are best performed by using Lexis or Westlaw. Still other tasks might call for you to blend both methods of research. Knowing which method to use requires an analysis of many factors, including the complexity of your task, the costs involved, and time constraints. Many instructors urge students to first become familiar with the conventional print tools before becoming too wedded to computer-assisted legal research. Strong skills in manual legal research provide a good foundation for using Lexis and Westlaw more effectively.

Use conventional print sources when:

- You need to "get your feet wet" and get some background about an area of the law.
- You need a thorough and comprehensive analysis of an area of the law, such as that provided by a treatise.

- You are having difficulty formulating research queries for Lexis or Westlaw because you are unfamiliar with the issue you are researching.
- It would be more cost-effective and easier to use traditional print sources to get a quick answer to a question than to incur costs by using Lexis or Westlaw.

Use computer-assisted legal research when:

- You already have a citation to a known case or other authority.
- You are looking for cases involving a known party, attorney, or judge.
- The area of law is new or evolving.
- You are looking for the most current information available.
- You are validating your primary authorities (by Shepardizing or KeyCiting).

Computer-assisted legal research is a valuable tool. The services provide rapid access to a wide range of materials that no law firm could afford to purchase or shelve. Nevertheless, computer-assisted legal research may be expensive and will produce useful results only if you understand how to make the systems work effectively for you. This takes practice and experience. Legal research is not as easy as merely inserting some words into a query box. Effective researchers use a combination of computer-assisted legal research and conventional research techniques to obtain the best results for clients.

2. *New Developments in Lexis and Westlaw*

Lexis and Westlaw continually add new materials and work to make their services affordable, attractive, and easy to use for legal professionals. Lexis has therefore launched "LexisOne Community" (http://www.lexisone.com), which offers free access to some legal materials, including recent federal and state cases, forms, and other materials. To access older cases or to Shepardize, the user must switch to Lexis and pay a fee. Westlaw now offers a "pay as you go" research plan called "Westlaw by Credit Card," allowing you to access some of its databases on an "as needed" basis without a formal subscription, paying by credit card.

Some Lexis and Westlaw materials are also available in wireless electronic formats, accessible through personal digital assistants, such as BlackBerrys. Both Lexis and Westlaw offer cases, statutes, and validating (through Shepardizing or KeyCiting), thus allowing legal professionals on the run immediate access to many materials.

3. *Limitations of Computer-Assisted Legal Research*

Following are some limitations of computer-assisted legal research:

- **Literalness.** Computers are extremely literal. Thus, a search for "teacher" will not produce results including "instructor." Construct your search query carefully before you sign on and begin incurring costs.
- **Cost.** There are numerous pricing variations for Lexis and Westlaw. Large law firms pay flat rates, allowing unlimited use of Lexis and Westlaw by their legal professionals. Hourly pricing can range from $10 to $800 per hour, depending on the files accessed and the time of day the service is used, with higher fees charged during peak hours.
- **Database Limitations.** There are some limitations to the Lexis and Westlaw databases. For example, both provide the *Federal Register*, but only since 1980. Similarly, both provide the *Congressional Record*, but only since about 1985. To determine the date limitations of publications and materials, consult Lexis's and Westlaw's database lists at the following sites, respectively: http://w3.nexis.com/sources and http://directory.westlaw.com/?tf=90&tc=11.

E. Other Competitors in Electronic Research

Although Lexis and Westlaw are the acknowledged giants in the field of computer-assisted legal research, a number of other companies offer access on a fee basis to legal materials through the Internet. Most charge moderate fees and appeal to small firms and sole practitioners. Some cater to government users.

- **Loislaw.** (http://www.loislaw.com). Loislaw, a service of Wolters Kluwer, offers case law, statutes, constitutions, administrative law, court rules, and more for all states and the federal courts. Loislaw offers a more comprehensive database than most of the other services described in this section, including all federal and state primary materials as well as treatise and forms libraries for a wide variety of secondary sources, such as estate planning and family law. Moreover, Loislaw offers *GlobalCite*, a service similar to Shepardizing, which refers you to cases that mention or discuss the case you are researching. Searching may be done either through Boolean connectors or through a "find" feature if you know a citation. Low monthly flat fees are charged.
- **VersusLaw.** (http://www.versuslaw.com). VersusLaw provides access to federal and state cases, statutes, and other legal sources for as low as $14 per month.

• **JuriSearch.** (http://www.jurisearch.com). JuriSearch offers primarily California and Florida materials for moderate fees.

• **PACER.** (http://pacer.psc.uscourts.gov). Public Access to Court Electronic Records or PACER, a service of the U.S. Judiciary, allows users to obtain case and docket information from all federal courts. The PACER system offers electronic access to a listing of all parties and participants in cases, documents filed for certain cases, case status, and other useful information. For example, if you wish to review Lehman Brothers' bankruptcy filings, you may access the court files and review all documents filed in the matter. The fee is presently $0.08 per page, whether pages are viewed, printed, or downloaded.

• **Google Scholar** (http://scholar.google.com). The newest competitor in the field of electronic case searching is Google Scholar, launched in late 2009. Google Scholar allows searchers free and easy access to both federal and state court cases. Some articles are also provided. Searching may be done by case name or by topic. Although the service does not provide access to statutes, some experts have commented that Google Scholar poses a serious competitive risk to Lexis and Westlaw.

F. Non-Print Research Tools

In addition to computer-assisted legal research, there are some other non-print tools that legal researchers should know how to use: microforms, sound recordings, videocassettes, and CD-ROMs.

1. *Microforms*

a. Types of Microforms

Microforms are based on the principle of microphotography: Images are reduced and placed on rolls or sheets of film. A microfilm reader is then used to review the images recorded on the film. The readers resemble a television screen and are usually equipped with printers so you may obtain a photocopy of the material being viewed. There are three main types of microform:

• **Microfilm.** *Microfilm* is a reel of film (usually 16 or 35 millimeters) that is threaded into a reader. Although microfilm saves storage space, it has not been widely used for legal materials. It is, however, often used for government records, bank records, newspapers, and other materials. Many counties preserve their land records on microfilm. The image shown on the screen is often fuzzy, and the prints reproduced are also often difficult to read.

• **Microfiche.** *Microfiche* is a microform displayed on a thin transparent celluloid flat sheet rather than on a roll of film. Each sheet of microfiche may contain images of up to 400 pages. Probably the best-known use of microfiche for legal research is LexisNexis's *Congressional Bills, Resolutions, & Laws on Microfiche*, used to compile legislative histories. Many law libraries maintain their legislative history materials on microfiche.

- **Ultrafiche.** *Ultrafiche* is a type of microfiche with a high reduction ratio. As many as 1,800 pages of text can be held on a single sheet of ultrafiche. West has reproduced many volumes of its *National Reporter System* in ultrafiche, with each sheet replacing one hardbound volume.

b. Summary of Microforms

All microforms save storage space. Although their use for nonlegal purposes has been broad, their role in legal research has never really taken hold. A notable exception is that microfiche is used for the materials making up a legislative history. To determine what materials are published in microform, consult *Guide to Microforms in Print*, an alphabetical list of more than 200,000 books, journals, and other materials currently available in microform. Ask your law librarian what materials are available in microform at your law library.

2. *Sound Recordings and Videocassettes*

Many continuing legal education programs are offered for those in the legal profession. Professionals may attend the seminars or programs in person or may usually purchase a sound recording, videocassette, or CD-ROM of the program. Law firms often use video for mock trials, helping to sharpen attorneys' skills as well as point out certain characteristics of client witnesses that may bear on credibility. Some firms use videotape presentations to introduce clients to certain routine matters, such as providing clients with basic information about having a deposition taken or the trial process. Videotapes are often used at trials to show the jury an accident scene or in criminal prosecutions to show occurrence of the crime itself (such as bank robbery or shoplifting).

3. *CD-ROMs*

CD-ROMs are highly efficient storage media; they may contain more than 200,000 pages of text. CD-ROMs have generally replaced the earlier technology of floppy disks. Many legal materials are available in CD-ROM form, including *Martindale-Hubbell Law Directory*. The disks need to be replaced annually. LexisNexis and Westlaw both make cases, statutes, and practice guides available on CD-ROM. One disc can take the place of several bound volumes. For example, West's *Atlantic Reporter, 2d Series* is available on seven discs. Searching is easy, making it efficient to locate cases by citation, party name, key words, or other elements. The CD can be used with a portable laptop computer and small printer, enabling legal professionals to perform valuable research at home or while traveling. Their use at trial can be extremely valuable. If adverse counsel cites an unfamiliar case, you can insert a CD and locate the case. Because discs containing new cases and statutes must be purchased, most publishers issue new discs (for a fee) and take back old ones at periodic intervals. The cost for CD-ROM products is about the same as for their print counterparts. High-speed wireless Internet access to legal materials using laptops and devices such as iPhones may make using CD-ROMs for legal materials a relic of the past.

G. Citation Form

	Bluebook (for practitioners)	***ALWD***
Lexis Case	*Smith v. Jones*, No. 05-233, 2006 U.S. App. LEXIS 19334, at *3 (1st Cir. May 15, 2006).	*Smith v. Jones*, 2006 U.S. App. LEXIS 05-233 at *3 (1st Cir. May 15, 2006).
Westlaw Case	*Allen v. Bailey*, No. 05-CV-310, 2006 WL 12656, at *2 (S.D.N.Y. June 10, 2006).	*Allen v. Bailey*, 2005 WL 12656 at *2 (S.D.N.Y. June 10, 2006).
Videotape	Videotape: Shepardizing Made Easy (Shepard's/ McGraw-Hill, Inc. 1994) (on file with Georgetown Law Center).	*Shepardizing Made Easy* (Shepard's/ McGraw-Hill, Inc. 1994) (videotape).

Figure 8-9
Comparison of Selected Lexis and Westlaw Terms and Connectors

Lexis Term, Connector, or Symbol	Westlaw Term, Connector, or Symbol	Function	Example	Retrieves documents
!	!	Retrieves words with variant endings	*lend!*	with the words "lender," "lending," etc.

Lexis Term, Connector, or Symbol	Westlaw Term, Connector, or Symbol	Function	Example	Retrieves documents
*	*	Replaces one or more characters	*m*n*	with the word "man" or "men"
and	&	Locates two search terms in a document	*Probate and damages* (Lexis); *probate & damages* Westlaw)	containing both "probate" and "damages"
or	Either "or" or a space between two words	Locates documents with either or both words	*Teacher or professor* Lexis); *teacher professor* (Westlaw)	containing either "teacher" or "professor" or both
W/n	/n	Locates documents with one word within a number of words of the other	*patent w/10 infringement* (Lexis); *patent /10 infringement* (Westlaw)	containing the word "patent" within ten words of the word "infringement"
w/p	/p	Locates documents with two terms in the same paragraph	*Wrongful w/p death* (Lexis); *wrongful /p death* (Westlaw)	containing the words "wrongful" and "death" in the same paragraph
w/s	/s	Locates documents with two terms in the same sentence	*Wrongful w/s death* (Lexis); *wrongful /s death* (Westlaw)	containing the words "wrongful" and "death" in the same sentence
And not	But not or %	Excludes documents with certain terms	*Patent and not accounting* (Lexis); *patent % accounting* (Westlaw)	containing the term "patent" but not the word "accounting"

Lexis Term, Connector, or Symbol	Westlaw Term, Connector, or Symbol	Function	Example	Retrieves documents
" "	" "	Locates documents in the same order as they appear in quotation marks	*"all elements rule"*	containing the phrase "all elements rule"
At least		Term must appear a certain number of times	atleast4RICO	containing the term "RICO" at least four times

CyberSites

http://www.lexis.com	LexisNexis's home page; select "Products & Services" to learn more about Lexis's features and offerings. Numerous tips and resources are provided.
http://www.westlaw.com	Westlaw's home page allows you to point and click to review its databases, learn about training options, and view its helpful User Guides.

Research Assignment for Lexis

1. Select "Get a Document" and "Get by Citation." Retrieve the case located at 545 U.S. 308.
   a. What is the Lexis citation?
   b. What are the first words on page 313 of this case?
   c. Select and click on the yellow triangle shown for this case. What does the yellow triangle mean? How many times has the case been distinguished by later cases?
2. Select "Search" at the top of the toolbar and then select the topic "Trademark Law." Select "Federal Trademark, Unfair Competition & Trade Secret" cases relating to the Red Cross.
   a. Retrieve the 1946 U.S. Supreme Court case. What is the name of the case?
   b. Review the "Case Summary" for this case. What was the "Outcome" of this case?
   c. Select and click on the green cross icon shown for this case. What does this icon mean? Is there any subsequent appellate history for this case?
3. Select "Get a Document" and "Get by Citation." Retrieve the case located at 250 F. Supp. 2d 1094.
   a. What is the name of this case?
   b. Select "More Like This" and then "Search." What is the first case you are directed to?
   c. Return to your original case at 250 F. Supp. 1094. Select "Shepardize." Identify the two categories of citing references that *Shepard's* indicates.
4. Select "Get a Document" and "Get by Citation." Enter 18 U.S.C.S. § 1302.
   a. What does this statute relate to, generally?
   b. What text are you directed to?
   c. Review the annotations for this statute. Must a person be conscious of depositing the information in the mail and know that the circular he is mailing relates to chance? Give your answer and cite the case that supports your answer.
   d. Review "Practitioner's Toolbox" for this statute. Select "History." When was the most recent amendment to this statute and what was its public law number?
5. Select "Search" on the toolbar. In the search box, use Natural Language and locate the Virginia statute relating to the statute of limitations for wrongful death.
   a. Give the citation for this statute.
   b. What is the statute of limitations?

6. Select "Get a Document" and then "Party Name" and locate a U.S. Supreme Court case in which the defendant's name is *Grokster*.
   a. What is the citation for this case?
   b. How many pages long is this case?
   c. When was certiorari granted for this case?
   d. What is the Lexis citation for this case?

7. Select "Search" on the toolbar and select "Search by Topic or Headnote." Explore the legal topic of "Education Law" and select "Right to Education." Select Oregon state cases. What case held that a school district did not deny a four-and-one-half-year-old child free, appropriate education by denying her speech therapy?

8. Select "Get a Document" and then "Docket Number." Locate the case from the U.S. Supreme Court with the docket number 05-83.
   a. What case are you directed to?
   b. Retrieve this case and then Shepardize it. What 2008 *Notre Dame Law Review* article are you directed to?
   c. Retrieve the article. Who wrote the article? Where is your case cited in the article?

9. Select "Search" from the toolbar and then "Secondary Legal" and then "Law Reviews & Journals." Use Natural Language and locate U.S. articles relating to the Protect America Act.
   a. What 2008 *Texas Review of Law and Politics* are you directed to?
   b. Review page 48 of this law review article. How many judges sit on the Foreign Intelligence Surveillance Court?

10. Select "Search by Source" and then "Find a Source." Locate the source titled "A Dictionary of Modern Legal Usage." Briefly, what is a "debenture"?

11. Select "Search by Topic or Headnote" and then "Family Law." Review Colorado's corporate statutes relating to corporate name reservations.
    a. What Colorado statute are you directed to?
    b. Review the statute. For how long is a name reservation valid?

Research Assignment for Westlaw

1. At the initial Westlaw screen, in the "Find by citation" box, enter 23 P.3d 117.
   a. What is the name of this case?
   b. How many pages long is the case?
   c. Select "Results Plus." What A.L.R. annotation are you directed to?
2. At the initial Westlaw screen, select *Black's Law Dictionary.*
   a. Give the first definition for "collateral estoppel."
   b. What topic and Key Numbers are you referred to?
3. Select "Directory" and continue selecting the appropriate databases to search Minnesota state court cases. Use Natural Language and develop a query to locate cases from Minnesota dealing with the liability of corporate directors for errors in their business judgment.
   a. What 2008 Minnesota Supreme Court case are you directed to?
   b. Retrieve this case. On the left side of the screen, select "Table of Authorities." How many cases are cited in this 2008 Minnesota case?
   c. Return to the case. Select "Results Plus." Select the A.L.R. annotation. What Eighth Circuit Court of Appeals case is cited in the A.L.R. annotation?
   d. Return to the case. What KeyCite icon is displayed?
4. Select the appropriate database for federal statutes. Using Natural Language, locate the federal statute relating to the death of an inventor.
   a. What is the first statute you are directed to?
   b. Select this statute. Give the citation to the Am. Jur. 2d article that comments on this statute.
   c. Select this Am. Jur. section. What happens if an inventor dies after making a patent application but before a patent is granted?
5. Select the appropriate databases to use the U.S.C.A. Popular Name Table.
   a. Give the citation to the most recent act named for Ryan White.
   b. Review the Act. Generally, what does the Act deal with?
6. Locate the case published at 549 U.S. 225.
   a. What is the name of the case?
   b. What parallel citation is given?
   c. How does page 235 of the case begin?

d. On the left side of the screen, select "Case Outline." Which four sections of the case are you given?
e. Select "Direct History (Graphical View)." When was certiorari granted for this case and what was the case's citation in the lower circuit court of appeals?
f. Return to the case located at 549 U.S. 225. At the left side of the screen, select "Petitions, Briefs & Filings." Review the Petition for Writ of Certiorari filed by counsel for the petitioner.
   (i) What is the first question presented for review?
   (ii) Review the Table of Authorities in the brief. Select *Melo v. Hafer*. Select or click on this case. What KeyCite icon is displayed?
   (iii) Select the KeyCite icon. What case declined to follow *Melo v. Hafer*?
   (iv) How many green stars are displayed?
   (v) Review the KeyCite box at the left of the screen. What summary is provided for you relating to the current status of this case as good law?

7. Locate the case published at 889 So. 2d 457. Click on the authoring judge's name. Give the judge's full name and his telephone number.

8. Select "Directory," and select "Administrative & Executive Materials" within the "U.S. State Materials" database. Locate the attorney general opinions for Illinois. Using Natural Language, search for opinions relating to whether written reports by a therapist are "records" under the Confidentiality Act.
   a. Select the opinion from March 2000. To whom was the opinion addressed?
   b. What Illinois statute was construed in the opinion?

9. Select "Directory" and then "Litigation." Select "Jury Verdicts, Settlements & Judgments" and then "Georgia Jury Verdicts Combined." Using Natural Language, retrieve information relating to dentist malpractice for liability for infection after tooth extractions (decided within the last three years). Select the April 2008 case relating to this topic.
   a. What was the verdict?
   b. Who was the defendant's expert?

10. Select "Directory" from the toolbar and then A.L.R. Using Natural Language, locate annotations relating to liability for keeping domestic animals (such as dogs) as constituting a nuisance. Select the annotation published in 90 A.L.R.5th.
   a. What Arkansas case is discussed in this annotation?
   b. Review this Arkansas case. Briefly, what did it hold?

11. At the initial Westlaw screen, select "Find a case by party name." Locate the 2005 U.S. Supreme Court case in which the defendant's

name is *Jacoway*. Retrieve this case and review "Direct History (Graphical View)." When did the U.S. Supreme Court grant certiorari for this case?

12. Locate 18 U.S.C.A. § 152.
    a. What does this statute relate to, generally?
    b. Review the annotations following the statute. Is a defendant's claim for back wages "property" as defined by the statute? Give your answer and cite the best case supporting your answer.

13. Select "Key Numbers" from the toolbar. Select "Intellectual property" as your topic and the Second Circuit as your jurisdiction. In the "Search for Key Numbers" box, search for cases relating to immoral and scandalous trademarks.
    a. What is the first Key Number that appears in the yellow banded "Trademarks" section?
    b. Select this Key Number. What 1999 case are you directed to?
    c. Review the case. Who was the defendant?

14. Select "Key Numbers" from the toolbar. Select "West Key Number Digest Outline." Select "Divorce" and expand the topic. Indicate what key symbol has been assigned to the topic of payment of alimony or allowance.

15. At the initial Westlaw screen, select "Find a case by party name." How many U.S. Supreme Court cases are there in which a party's name is *Josey*?

16. Select "Find by citation" and locate the case designated 2005 WL 1715689.
    a. What is the name of this case?
    b. Was this case reported in the *Federal Supplement*?

17. Locate the most recent U.S. Supreme Court memorandum opinion in 2005 relating to Theresa Marie Schiavo. Give the citation.

18. Locate the most recent U.S. Supreme Court case *Slaughter v. Oklahoma* relating to an application for a stay of execution.
    a. Was the petition for certiorari granted or denied?
    b. Use "Direct History (Graphical View)" and locate the earliest case. When did the jury return its verdict against Mr. Slaughter?

Internet Assignment

1. Access Lexis's Searchable Directory of Online Sources at http://w3.nexis.com/sources. Select "Regions of Coverage" and determine the coverage of South Carolina Attorney General Opinions and Florida Courts of Appeal cases.
2. Access LexisONE at http://www.lexisone.com and review "About LexisONE Community." What coverage is offered for free case law?
3. Access Westlaw's Database Directory at http://directory.westlaw.com/tf=90&tc=11. Give the appropriate database identifier for the Pacific Reporter. Select "Federal Materials" and then "Arnold & Porter Collection—Legislative Histories." What is the database identifier for the legislative history for the Family and Medical Leave Act of 1993?
4. Access Westlaw's site for its User Guides at http://west.thomson.com/support/user-guide/westlaw/default.aspx. Select "Westlaw—General Materials" and then "Getting Started on Westlaw."
   a. What does Westlaw's feature "Research Trail" provide you?
   b. How can you retrieve a case if you are unsure of its citation format?

Chapter 9

E-Research: Legal Research Using the Internet

Chapter Overview

The best legal researchers know how to use a combination of conventional research methods with computerized and electronic methods to achieve results. Although one need not be a computer guru to satisfy the duty to perform legal research competently, legal professionals should be sufficiently proficient in using the Internet that they can quickly find a case or statute. This chapter provides some tips and strategies on conducting legal research on the Internet as well as some cautionary notes about over-relying on the Internet. The chapter also provides the "best of the best" sites for various legal research tasks, as well as some sites for non-legal research.

A. Introduction

Today's legal professionals have at their fingertips vast amounts of information that is free and available 24 hours each day. Until just recently, a researcher wanting to review a newly issued Supreme Court decision had only two options: drive to a law library or subscribe to a fee-based service such as LexisNexis or Westlaw. The advent of the Internet has dramatically changed legal research, allowing professional immediate access to cases, statutes, federal regulations, forms, legislative materials, and much more. In some instances, cases are posted by courts (including the Supreme Court), to the Internet within hours after their release. The good news is that there is a vast array of legal materials available for your use; the bad news is that the information is so voluminous that making sense of the materials offered can be difficult and confusing.

Legal professionals typically use the Internet for the following purposes:

- **Communication.** Legal professionals use the Internet to communicate with each other and with clients. Through email, clients can be kept informed of the progress of their cases. Legal professionals can subscribe to listservs or newsgroups and automatically receive newsletters and bulletins to keep current in their fields of interest.
- **Court Filings.** Many courts and agencies require or permit documents and motions to be filed electronically with the court. Electronic filing allows courts to verify immediately page limit and word count requirements.
- **Marketing.** The American Bar Association reports that all law firms with 50 or more attorneys have a website, which is a marketing brochure about the firm that is published electronically rather than in print form. The site typically describes the firm, its professionals, its locations, and may provide articles or newsletters on legal topics. State bar ethics codes regulate advertising. Thus, firms need to ensure that their websites are in compliance with those regulations.
- **Commerce.** Legal professionals can order books, publications, and other materials from publishers and other vendors.
- **Education.** Legal professionals can take continuing education classes online and subscribe to educational newsletters and other informative materials.
- **Research.** Legal professionals can use the Internet to conduct research, including legal research. One can quickly determine an adversary's address, a client's exact corporate name, find a case, review a journal, and track legislation. This chapter will focus on use of the Internet to conduct legal research.

The general duty of competence imposed on legal professionals to have a sufficient level of competence to represent their clients is broad enough to require competence in new and emerging technologies, including the Internet. A recent law review article has declared that "[t]he lawyer in the twenty-first century who does not effectively use the Internet for legal research may fall short of the minimal standards of professional competence and be potentially liable for malpractice." Lawrence Duncan MacLachlan, *Gandy Dancers on the Web: How the Internet Has Raised the Bar on Lawyers' Professional Responsibility to Research and Know the Law*, 13 Geo. J. Legal Ethics 607, 607 (2000). Moreover, employers and clients are increasingly technologically proficient and will justifiably expect their legal team to be equally proficient, so that clients can be kept informed of the status of their matters by email, relevant cases can be sent electronically to co-counsel, documents can be filed electronically with courts, and others in the firm can access a client's files.

Not only is there a nearly overwhelming amount of information available on the Internet, the technology continues to develop rapidly. For example, attorneys can now retrieve and Shepardize or KeyCite cases and statutes on their handheld BlackBerry devices and smart phones.

Why use the Internet rather than LexisNexis or Westlaw? Although search strategies using LexisNexis and Westlaw are generally more focused and produce more targeted results, these services are fee-based. The Internet offers free legal research 24/7; LexisNexis and Westlaw, however, have far more complete databases. Moreover, there is no way to check the validity of a case you locate on the Internet, whereas you can Shepardize or KeyCite the cases you read on LexisNexis or Westlaw, respectively. Nevertheless, the Internet can be extremely helpful in allowing you to check the accuracy of a quotation or citation or to obtain background information on a legal topic. Opinions posted by the courts themselves, of course, are highly reliable.

There is, of course, some danger in relying too much on the Internet, primarily because not all legal materials are available online. Nevertheless, learning good Internet research techniques will save you a great deal of time. Internet legal research should complement your other research techniques—namely, conventional book research and research using LexisNexis and Westlaw.

B. Conducting Legal Research Online

1. Getting Started

To begin searching on the Internet, open your browser (for example, Internet Explorer), or, if you have a dial-up connection, double-click on the icon that identifies your Internet service provider (for example, AOL). Type a URL (such as http://www.sec.gov) into the address box at the top of your browser window or enter a word or phrase in the search box that appears when you access AOL, your Internet service provider, or a search engine.

Many researchers begin with a general-purpose search engine. Some of the better-known ones are as follows:

- AltaVista (http://www.altavista.com)
- Ask (http://www.ask.com)
- Google (http://www.google.com)
- Bing (www.bing.com)
- Yahoo! (http://www.yahoo.com)

Consider using one of these sites as your home page so that when you access the Internet, you see the same page layout every time. Google is generally considered to be the world's largest search engine. With its references to more than 8 billion websites and its ranking of results by relevance, Google is arguably the most popular of all search engines. In fact, its search engine is so intuitive that you can enter a statute citation such as "17 usc 106" into its search box and be referred directly to 17 U.S.C. § 106. You can also now install Google on your toolbar so that you may do a Google search at any time from any website (access http://toolbar.google.com/T4 and follow the directions).

Note that although most Internet addresses begin with "http://www" you may not need to type in the initial "http" information. Most browsers (software that helps access and review information on the Internet, such as Netscape or Internet Explorer) are configured to recognize "www" by itself. Similarly, in most instances, the Internet is not "case sensitive," meaning that you can usually type in either upper- or lowercase letters and they will be recognized.

2. *Using a Good Start Page*

There is probably no better tip for conducting legal research on the Internet than to always begin your project with one good *start page*. Your start page should be reliable and easy to use, and it should be formatted in a user-friendly manner so that you can easily read the print and locate needed information without confusing graphics, pictures, and distracting scrolling advertisements or pop-ups. The advantage of always beginning at the same place or start page is that you will quickly become comfortable and familiar with the page, and it will serve as an excellent jumping-off place for your research tasks.

Although there are many start pages from which you can begin your research, following are five well-known legal favorites:

- **Cornell Law School's Legal Information Institute** (http://www.law.cornell.edu). The Legal Information Institute is one of the best-known legal sites. It offers overviews of legal topics such as bankruptcy and corporations and allows direct linking to federal and state cases, statutes, court rules, and administrative regulations. The site is highly respected and credible.
- **Washburn University School of Law** (http://www.washlaw.edu). This site alphabetically lists legal materials, courts, and states, making it very easy to locate material of interest. Because it is a site offered by an education institution, it is highly regarded.
- **FindLaw** (http://www.findlaw.com). FindLaw is an extremely well-known legal site (now owned by West). It directs users to a vast array of legal materials, including cases, statutes, forms, reference materials, and legal periodicals. Links to numerous sources of interest to legal professionals are provided, including links to state bar associations, special links for law students, links to help locate attorneys, and numerous other helpful sources. See Figure 9-1.

Figure 9-1
Home Page for FindLaw

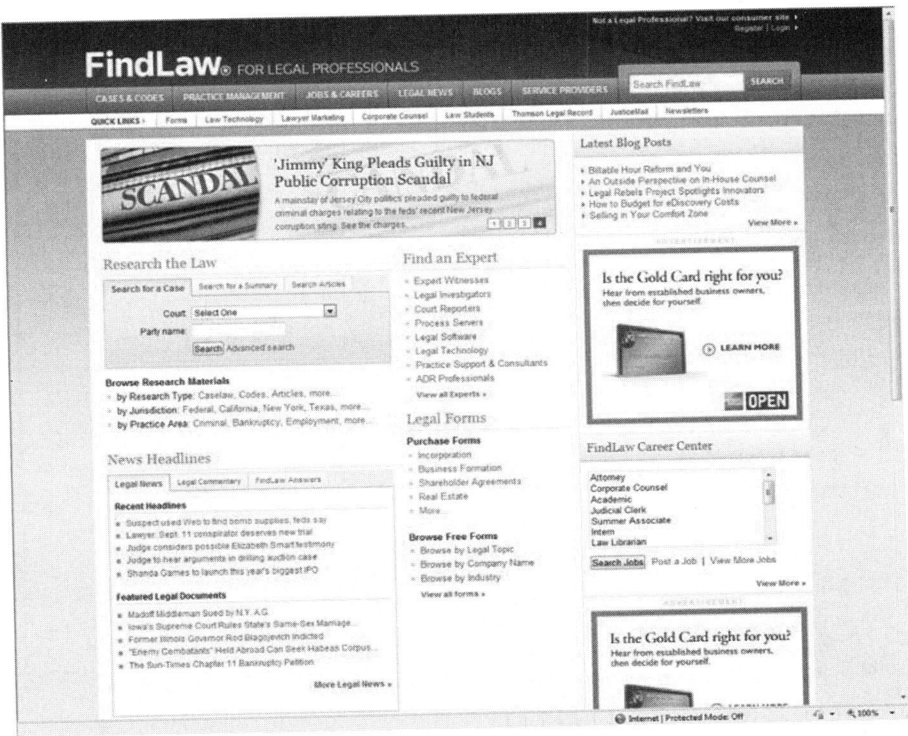

• **MegaLaw** (http://www.megalaw.com). Like FindLaw, MegaLaw is a commercial site offering links to thousands of useful law-related sites. The site is easy to navigate and offers ready access to federal and state cases, statutes, court rules, legal forms, and more. See Figure 9-2.

• **CataLaw** (http://www.catalaw.com/catalaw.shtml). CataLaw is an Internet catalog of worldwide law on the Internet. This thorough metaindex allows you to search by Topic, Region, or "Extras" (such as searching for information on experts or law libraries).

Once you choose a start page that you are comfortable with, begin your research task with this page and progress from there. After some time, you may encounter other sites that are of more use to you. If you are a beginner in Internet legal research, however, this method of consistently beginning any Internet legal research task with your "one good start page" is the best way to gain expertise on the Internet.

Figure 9-2
Home Page for MegaLaw

Practice Tip: *Using the Internet to Impress Clients*

Use the Internet as a tool to track clients' stock prices, determine the weather at the client's headquarters, and obtain basic information about a client's business. Read the press releases issued by clients, and then comment on them when you next speak with the client. Clients will be pleased and flattered that you took the time and effort to do some homework about their business, location, future plans, and financial status.

3. *Strategies and Tips for Internet Legal Research*

It is far easier to get distracted when researching on the Internet than when researching using conventional print volumes. A site piques your interest, so you click on it. When you access that site, another link looks promising, and you click on it. Before you know it, you have drifted far afield from your original topic. The vast amount of information on the Internet is a constant source of diversion and distraction. Staying focused is a continuing campaign.

Following are some tips and strategies to help ensure that your Internet research is as efficient and effective as possible:

- **Understand Ranking.** When you enter a term in a search box and a list of relevant sites is given, the sites are usually listed or ranked in order of how many times your term (for example, "insider trading") appears on the site, even in coded or hidden form. Thus, the first site listed is not necessarily the best; it is merely the one that uses or displays the term "insider trading" most often. Some sites, however, most notably Google, list the most relevant and useful sites first, making research easy and productive.
- **Take Notes.** Rather than jumping from site to site, jot down the sites that look promising and visit them later. Stay focused on the task at hand.
- **Use Bookmarks.** When you determine that there are certain sites that you continually visit or that provide useful information, "bookmark" them or add them to your "favorites" list so that you can readily link to them.
- **Avoid Reading the Screen.** Do not spend too much time reading screens. Reading material on a computer screen is often tiring and causes eye strain. If an article or case appears promising, print it and read it in hard copy form.
- **Never Rely Completely on the Internet.** Although the Internet provides some excellent information and is often the easiest and cheapest way to find a case or statute, it is not a substitute for a law library. Relying solely on the Internet for legal research will result in a research project that lacks in-depth analysis. Many unpublished cases find their way onto the Internet. No one edits out the "dog" cases. Some state courts prohibit citations to unpublished decisions. Thus, exercise care.
- **Be Aware of Gaps in Information.** Whereas a law library and LexisNexis and Westlaw offer all federal court cases, some sites offer only more recent lower federal court opinions.
- **Review Materials.** Retrieving a case is not the same as analyzing it. Locating a case or statute is just the beginning of a research task. Cases and secondary authorities that interpret the statute must be analyzed.
- **Subscribe to a Listserv.** Consider subscribing or signing up to receive news bulletins or updates from a law-related website or listserv. You will be emailed daily or periodic updates on topics of interest to you.
- **Consider Disclaimers.** Review the disclaimer section of a website. It will tell you the limitations of the site and will usually indicate if you are permitted to reproduce the material on the site. Unless otherwise indicated, material on a private, educational, or commercial website is protected by copyright law, and you cannot reproduce it without permission. The "gov" sites, however, publish materials in the public domain, and material on these sites is freely available for printing, using, or other purposes.

4. Assessing the Credibility of Websites

Much of the material that appears on the Internet appears authoritative and reliable; however, many sites are not subject to the rigorous fact checking and editing of their print counterparts. Authors who publish in print form are often the acknowledged experts in their field. On the Internet, it is nearly impossible to judge credibility. Articles often fail to identify an author or date. Contributors to listservs or newsgroups are anonymous. Consider the following factors in evaluating the credibility of websites:

- **Domain Name.** Examine the domain name in the website (specifically, examine the ending, such as "com" or "org"). Some sites are considered more reliable than others. For example, the "gov" (government) sites are probably most authoritative, followed by the "edu" (educational) sites. If the domain name shows it is a commercial site (through the use of "com" or sometimes "org"), its content may be influenced by its owner or publisher. Review advertising on commercial sites to determine if there is bias. Consider whether the purpose of the site is to generate revenue. On the other hand, many law firm websites end in "com," and articles posted on the firm website are highly reliable and authoritative.
- **Currency.** Articles posted on the Internet may become quickly stale. Examine the site to determine if material has been recently updated. If hyperlinks connect you to "cancelled" or "unavailable" websites, this is another sign that the site is not current.
- **Author.** A tilde (~) in a web address indicates that the author is an individual rather than an institution. Well-known experts usually like to be paid for their work; thus, "free" articles on the Internet may not be authored by the best-known experts in the field. Check the author's qualifications. Does the author include contact information? Reliable authors often encourage readers to contact them.
- **Appearance.** Review the overall look and feel of the site. If the site is amateurish or accompanied by cartoons and humorous graphics, this may be a sign that its content is not serious.
- **Errors.** If you locate even one error in content (such as incorrect citation form or out of date fee schedules), it may well signal that other errors exist. Similarly, errors in grammar, spelling, and punctuation are signs that the material was not subject to thorough editing and review.
- **Attribution and References.** Quotations and statistics should be attributed to their source (and, ideally, there should be hyperlinks to the original source). Most reliable sites include references and hyperlinks to other resources to allow their users to obtain additional information.
- **Richness of Content.** Review a few other websites to compare their content and to serve as a double-check of the accuracy and depth of analysis of your site.

Never rely exclusively on the Internet for an answer to a legal question. Although the Internet provides some excellent information and is often the easiest and cheapest way to find a case or statute, it is not a substitute for a law library. Moreover, there are gaps in information available on the Internet. Whereas law libraries, LexisNexis, and Westlaw offer all federal court cases, the Internet presently offers only all the United States Supreme Court cases; lower federal cases are often available only for the past several years. Thus, research on the Internet cannot be a substitute for research using conventional print sources, LexisNexis, or Westlaw. Moreover, cases on the Internet do not include useful editorial enhancements, such as headnotes or key numbers. The Internet, however, is an excellent tool for locating a parallel citation or quickly answering questions such as "What is the statute of limitations for breach of contract actions in Iowa?" or "What is the definition of 'work for hire' in the Copyright Act?" To complete a research project you will need to supplement your Internet legal research efforts with conventional research methods, with computerized legal research services, or both.

C. Best Internet Legal Research Sites

At the end of each chapter in this text, pertinent websites have been given to assist you in your research efforts. There are hundreds of websites available, so many that research using the Internet can seem overwhelming. For example, federal cases can be located through at least ten different websites. This section of this chapter will give you brief descriptions of some of the best sites for legal research.

Ethics Alert: *Avoiding Copyright Infringement*

Be careful not to fall into the trap of thinking that everything on the Internet is in the public domain and can be used without permission. Whereas all federal and nearly all state materials are in the public domain and can be freely used, an article posted on the Internet is generally given the same protection against copyright infringement as its print counterpart. Thus, avoid excessive quoting from Internet sources unless attribution is given or permission is received. In many instances, you can directly email the author of an article and ask for permission to reproduce the material. Look at the site to see if the author has granted permissionto reprint and use.

1. *Best Sites for Locating Cases*

http://www.supremecourtus.gov	The U.S. Supreme Court site allows searching by party name, citation, or docket number and provides the text of its cases, its rules, schedules of arguments, and access to briefs filed with the Court.
http://www.uscourts.gov	This is the U.S. federal courts home page and gateway to federal courts and their opinions, briefs, and rules.
http://scholar.google.com	Google Scholar allows free and easy access to federal and state cases. Searching is done by case name or topic.
http://www.law.cornell.edu	Cornell's site offers access to federal and state cases (availability of state cases varies from state to state).
http://www.findlaw.com	This site offers access to federal cases and links for each state (availability of state cases varies from state to state).

2. *Best Sites for Locating Statutes*

http://www.law.cornell.edu	Cornell's site offers access to all federal and state statutes.
http://www.findlaw.com/casecode/uscodes	FindLaw's site offers access to all federal and state statutes.
http://www.megalaw.com	MegaLaw's site offers direct access to federal and state statutes.
http://www.nccusl.org	The website of the National Conference of Commissioners on Uniform State Laws offers the text of uniform laws.

3. *Best Sites for Government Materials*

Generally, whenever you have a problem or question relating to a government agency, the best place to start is with the agency's website. Most federal (and state) agencies offer excellent information, forms, and links to other resources. You can usually "guess" the website address for government agencies. For example, the website of the Federal Trade Commission is http://www.ftc.gov. Following are some useful sites for locating federal and state government materials.

http://www.usa.gov	The U.S. government's official web portal (formerly called "FirstGov") is a gateway to all government information, including federal executive, legislative, and judicial materials, information about agencies, and links to state government home pages.
http://thomas.loc.gov	THOMAS offers United States legislative information, bills, voting records, public laws, and other legislative information. See Figure 9-3.
http://www.gpoaccess.gov	GPO Access provides direct links to the Code of Federal Regulations, the Federal Register, presidential materials, and other government materials.
http://www.fedworld.gov	FedWorld is an excellent guide to federal government resources and offers links to top government websites.

4. *Best Sites for Locating Forms*

http://www.washlaw.edu	Select "LawForms."
http://www.megalaw.com	Select "Legal Forms."
http://www.lectlaw.com	Select "Legal Forms" for litigation, business, corporations, and other forms.
http://www.allaboutforms.com	All About Forms provides more than 2,000 free legal forms.

5. *Best Specialty Sites*

Note that two sites provide extensive and reliable coverage of numerous law topics:

- Cornell Law School's site entitled "Legal Information Institute" (http://www.law.cornell.edu) offers information on more than 100 topics, including bankruptcy, criminal law, and employment law. Select the topic of interest.
- MegaLaw's site (http://www.megalaw.com) offers information on many legal topics. Select "Law Topic Pages" to review more than 230 law topics from aboriginal law to zoning law.

Figure 9-3
Home Page of THOMAS

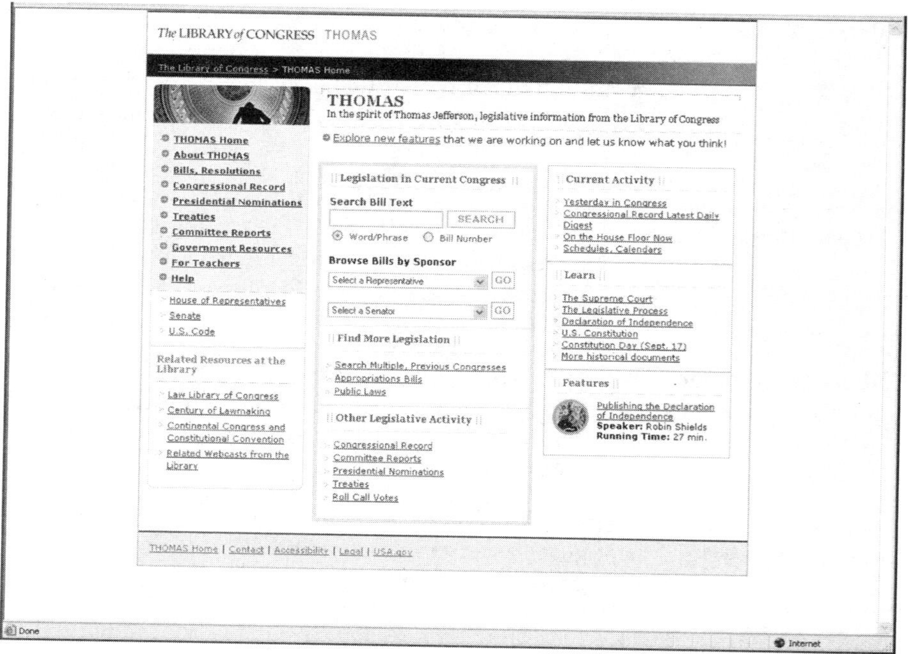

Following are some sites for specialized legal topics:

Americans with Disabilities Act Site	
http://www.ada.gov	The home page for ADA offers information and links relating to the ADA.
Attorney and Ethics Sites	
http://www.abanet.org/cpr	The ABA's Center for Professional Responsibility offers ethics resources.
http://www.martindalehubbell.com	Martindale-Hubbell offers a directory of lawyers.
http://www.law.cornell.edu/ethics	Cornell's American Legal Ethics Library offers links to ethics materials for most states.
http://www.legalethics.com	This comprehensive site provides ethics information relating to the use of technology by legal professionals.

Corporate, Business, and Securities Sites	
http://www.sec.gov	The Securities and Exchange Commission's website offers the full text of filings made by public companies, links to securities laws, and more.
http://securities.stanford.edu	This site provides extensive securities law materials and information.
http://www.hoovers.com	Profiles of more than 25 million companies are provided by Hoover's.
http://www.nass.org	The website of the National Association of Secretaries of State offers direct links to each state's corporations or business division for access to state forms, filing fees, and more.
http://www.megalaw.com/top/corporate.php	Numerous corporate links, including links to text of laws and recent cases, are provided by MegaLaw.
Environmental Sites	
http://www.epa.gov	The website of the Environmental Protection Agency offers excellent environmental-related information.
http://www.megalaw.com/top/environmental.php	MegaLaw's Environmental Law Center provides links to numerous sites of interest.
Intellectual Property Sites	
http://www.uspto.gov	The United States Patent and Trademark Office's site offers the text of statutes, general overviews of patent and trademark procedure and law, and a fully searchable database, allowing one to search for patents and trademarks.
http://www.copyright.gov	The Copyright Office site offers forms, detailed information on copyright law, and links to other valuable resources.
http://www.ipmall.fplc.edu	Pierce Law Center's "IP Mall" provides in-depth coverage of intellectual property law and numerous links to other sites and resources.

International Law Sites	
http://www.un.org	The United Nations website offers a variety of international materials and information.
http://www.wipo.org	The World Intellectual Property Organization site offers the text of various treaties and other valuable information.
Legal Research and Writing Sites	
http://www.ll.georgetown.edu/research/browse_topic.cfm?85	Georgetown Law Center's guides and tutorials describe legal research methods.
http://ualr.edu/cmbarger	This site provides research, writing, and advocacy resources and links.
http://www.gpoaccess.gov/stylemanual/index.html	The U.S. Government Printing Office Style Manual is the authoritative guide to writing, grammar, spelling, and so forth.
http://press-pubs.uchicago.edu/garner	This site offers exercises and information on writing from expert Bryan A. Garner.
Legal Reference Materials Sites	
http://www.usa.gov	USA.gov (previously called FirstGov) is the government's portal to a wide variety of materials, including both federal and state materials.
http://www.lexisnexis.com/infopro/zimmerman	Zimmerman's Research Guide offers an A to Z list of legal topics with thorough and articulate explanations.
http://dictionary.law.com	Use this site for a legal dictionary, searchable by word or phrase.
Tax Sites	
http://www.irs.gov	Website of the Internal Revenue Service, providing information, forms, and links to other resources.
http://www.taxprophet.com	Valuable information and links to other tax sites are provided.

6. *Best Non-Legal Sites*

Although it is critical to have a repertory of law-related sites at your fingertips, you also need to be familiar with some basic information sites, so you can determine the weather in the city where tomorrow's deposition will be taken, directions to the client's office, or the last price at which the client's stock was sold. Following are some basic information and reference sites.

http://www.dictionary.com	A dictionary and thesaurus are offered at this site.
http://www.bartleby.com	Bartleby features dictionaries, *Bartlett's Familiar Quotations,* and many reference materials.
http://www.refdesk.com	This excellent all-purpose site offers links for news, encyclopedia information, weather around the world, stock ticker symbols and much more.
http://www.usps.com	Obtain zip codes at this site.
http://maps.google.com	Obtain maps and directions to a location at this site.
http://www.2docstock.com/res-travel.html	Access travel resources, including currency converter, maps, local time around the world, weather information, and more.
http://www.weather.com	Obtain weather in any city.

7. *Listservs, Newsgroups, Blawgs, and Apps*

Listservs, newsgroups, and law-related weblogs (called *blawgs*) help legal professionals share information and keep current on cutting-edge legal issues. Technically, *listservs* are different from newsgroups in that listservs operate through email. For example, a listserv system automatically sends everyone on the mailing list a message at the same time. In a *newsgroup*, anyone with an Internet connection may view the messages, post their own, or reply to other messages. A blawg is an online journal or weblog related to legal topics. Following are some excellent websites:

http://newsletters.findlaw.com	FindLaw allows you to subscribe to daily or weekly newsletters so you will be notified by email of breaking legal news and recently released cases.
http://www.blawg.com	BLAWG will link you to well-known legal blawgs, including May It Please The Court, a weblog of legal news.

Help Line: *Maintaining Your Calendar*

Most legal professionals routinely calendar dates for responding to pleadings or motions, filing clients' reports with the SEC, and other time-sensitive matters. Use the website Time and Date (http://www.timeanddate.com) to calculate due dates, the duration between two dates, and more. Thus, if a report must be filed with the SEC within 45 days after a certain event, this site will provide mistake-free calculations.

http://abajournal.com/blawgs	The ABA provides a list of more than 100 law-related blawgs.

One of the newest tech-related developments is the creation of various applications or "apps" that can be used with iPhones, BlackBerrys, and other similar devices. Some of these apps include databases for the Federal Rules of Civil Procedure, U.S. Constitution, tax and other federal laws, federal regulations, *Black's Law Dictionary*, and various state statutes, all accessible anytime and anywhere. Other apps available to legal professionals include those that calculate court deadlines, apps for time and billing entries, and case management tools.

D. Cautionary Notes on Internet Legal Research

Many beginning researchers confuse locating information on the Internet with researching. Retrieving a case is not the same as analyzing it. Locating a statute or a case is just the beginning of a research task: Cases that interpret the statute must be analyzed; treatises and Restatements should be reviewed; and periodicals and other materials should be consulted.

Moreover, because much of the material that appears on the Internet is anonymous you cannot assess the credibility or expertise of the author. Just as you would not take medical advice from a stranger on a street corner, you should not take legal advice from strangers on an Internet corner. Similarly, much material is undated; thus, you cannot tell if it is current or outdated.

There are obviously tremendously valuable research materials on the Internet, particularly the U.S.C., the C.F.R., state statutes, and federal and state court cases. Note that all of these materials share one thing in common: They are all materials in the public domain. The well-known legal publishers, such as West and LexisNexis, have not posted their valuable databases on the Internet, and you should not expect that these materials will be made available for free.

Finally, always consider that even the most reputable-seeming sites can be subject to abuse. The CIA and Department of Justice's websites have both been hacked. Thus, at any given moment, the materials you review on the Internet may be false (or stale).

As long as you remember these cautionary notes, the Internet remains a valuable and efficient tool for beginning many research projects; however, it can never be a substitute for a full in-depth analysis of legal materials, such as those you would find in a law library or through the computer research services such as LexisNexis and Westlaw. See Figure 9-4 for a chart comparing the pros and cons of Internet research.

Figure 9-4
Internet Research Pros and Cons

Pro	*Con*
Access to Internet sources is available 24/7, from anywhere in the world.	The glut of materials on the Internet can make finding the right source like finding a needle in a haystack. Some websites disappear without a trace.
The Internet provides free access to a wide array of legal materials.	Many unpublished cases find their way onto the Internet. Some state courts prohibit citations to unpublished decisions. Thus, look for the words "published" or "unpublished" at the beginning of a case.
Email, chat rooms, and news group postings allow you to ask colleagues for assistance and information.	The responders to your requests for information are usually anonymous; thus, you cannot assess their reliability or expertise.
The Internet provides access to many private materials. For example, many law students have posted case briefs and research memos on the Internet and invited others to use them. Similarly, law firms often publish informative articles on legal topics.	Accessing the law is far different from understanding and analyzing it. Once again, whereas law firm authors are generally reliable, other authors are unknown and unproved.

Pro	*Con*
Office space for library books and binders is expensive. The Internet stores incredible amounts of information at no cost.	Reading materials in print form is far easier than reading matter on a screen. Internet materials are seldom professionally proofread and edited as are their print counterparts.

E. Citation Form

As discussed in the next chapter, generally, *The Bluebook* and *ALWD* require the use and citation of traditional printed sources unless the information is not available in printed form. Rule 18 of *The Bluebook* and *ALWD* Rules 38-42 provide numerous rules for citing to the Internet, some of which are quite complicated.

	Bluebook *(for practitioners)*	*ALWD*
Article Available in Print and on the Internet	Clarisa Long, *Dilution*, 106 Colum. L. Rev. 1029 (2006), *available at* http://www.columbialawreview.org/articles/index.cfm?article_id=817.	Clarissa Long, *Dilution,* 106 Colum. L. Rev. 1029 (2006) (available at http://www.columbialawreview.org/articles/index.cfm?article_id=817).
Article Available Solely on the Internet	Mark Lemley, *Theft of Trade Secrets* (1998), http://www.fr.com/news/articledetail.cfm?articleid=105.	Mark Lemley, *Theft of Trade Secrets* (1998), http://www.fr.com/news/articledetail.cfm?articleid=105.

Internet Assignment

1. Access the website USA.gov and select "A-Z Agency Index." Select the Mine Safety and Health Administration.
   a. When was the Bureau of Mines created?
   b. Where is the Mine Safety and Health Administration headquartered?
2. Access the website http://www.washlaw.edu and search for "Organizational Chart." In which branch of government is the Office of Technology Assessment?
3. Access Cornell's Legal Information Institute and review the Federal Rules of Civil Procedure. Generally, how many interrogatories may one party serve on another? What rule governs your answer?
4. Access the website of the U.S. Supreme Court. Review Rule 33 of the Rules of the Supreme Court. In what text must booklets submitted to the Court be printed? What size type must be used?
5. Access Hoover's and locate information about Polo Ralph Lauren.
   a. What is the company's stock ticker symbol, and on what exchange is its stock traded?
   b. Who is the company's President?
   c. Where is the company located?
6. Access the website of the Social Security Administration and locate the information about FOIA (Freedom of Information Act). Review Section V of the 2008 Annual Report. How many FOIA requests did the agency receive?
7. Access the website of the Securities and Exchange Commission. Select "Search for Company Filings."
   a. Use Ralph Lauren's ticker symbol and locate its annual report, Form 10-K, filed on May 28, 2008. Review page one. What is the par value of the company's common stock?
   b. Review Nike Inc.'s annual report, Form 10-K, filed July 28, 2008. Review Item 1 ("Business"). How many total retail stores does the company operate in the United States?

Section

IV

Legal Research

Citing and Validating the Authorities

Chapter 10

Legal Citation Form

Chapter Overview

All legal professionals must know how to cite legal authorities. This chapter discusses *The Bluebook* and *ALWD*, the best-known guides to citation form, and provides examples of citation form for both primary and secondary authorities. Note that although numerous examples of citations are provided in this chapter, most are fictitious and are provided solely for the purpose of illustrating citation rules. *Bluebook* citation form will be addressed first, followed by *ALWD* formats. References to *Bluebook* and *ALWD* rules are given in parentheses.

A. Introduction to Citation Form

A critical part of the writing process in many legal documents is citing authorities. Every legal assertion made in a document must be supported by legal authority. These supporting authorities appear as *citations* in your document. Citations must appear in a standard and consistent format so that any reader will be able to retrieve the legal authority you cite and verify that you have accurately represented the status of the law. Because these citations communicate information to readers, it is essential that legal professionals use the same "language" or citation form. When you present a persuasive argument, you do not want to distract the reader by using incorrect citation form.

Newcomers to the legal field often inquire what will happen if citations are incorrect in a brief or other document. Citation errors have an effect similar to an egregious spelling error: They cause a loss of respect for the author and make readers question the integrity and analysis of an argument.

B. Citation Manuals

Citation manuals provide the rules for citing legal authorities. There are two primary guides to citation form in the United States:

• *Bluebook.* The oldest and best-known system of citation is found in *The Bluebook: A Uniform System of Citation* (Columbia Law Review Ass'n et al. eds., 18th ed. 2005) ("*The Bluebook*"). *The Bluebook* is complex, and its rules are often poorly worded. It provides few examples. Nevertheless, because most judges and practicing professionals were taught to use *The Bluebook* for citation form, at present it is the most commonly used citation manual. Generally, unless you are specifically directed to use some other system of citation rules, follow *The Bluebook*.

• *ALWD.* In 2000, the Association of Legal Writing Directors and Professor Darby Dickerson introduced an alternative to *The Bluebook*: ALWD & Darby Dickerson, *ALWD Citation Manual* (3d ed., Aspen Publishers 2006). Called *ALWD* (pronounced "all wood"), this citation system was intended to provide an easy-to-learn and user-friendly alternative to *The Bluebook*, and its presentation and numerous examples do make it easier to use. At the same time, in many instances, the *ALWD* format is identical to *Bluebook* format. There are, however, several differences.

Although there are other guides to citation form, the most notable of which is the *Chicago Manual of Legal Citation* (2d ed. 2000), usually referred to as the *Maroonbook*, and used primarily in the Chicago metropolitan area, *The Bluebook* is probably the best-known system at this time, although *ALWD* continues to attract a great deal of interest because of its sensible rules and approach. Follow your school, firm, or office practice. Note, however, that if local citation rules exist for a court or jurisdiction, they must be followed and will supersede any citation system. For example, California requires the use of either a specific manual published by West, the *California Style Manual* (4th ed. 2000), or *The Bluebook* in citing cases. Cal. R. Ct. 1.200. See Figure 10-1 for a chart showing some differences between *The Bluebook* and *ALWD* rules.

C. *The Bluebook*

1. Introduction

It would be unnecessarily time-consuming to read *The Bluebook*; however, you should still become familiar with its overall arrangement and read at least the Bluepages section in the front of the book. Also, review the tables at the back of *The Bluebook* and glance at its alphabetically arranged index. Flag the pages and tables you will refer to most frequently.

Figure 10-1
Some Differences Between *The Bluebook* and *ALWD*

	Bluebook	ALWD
Typeface	Large and small capitals are used in law review footnotes; practitioners never use large and small capitals.	Large and small capitals are never used.
U.S. Supreme Court Cases	*Bluebook* does not allow parallel citations.	*ALWD* allows (but does not prefer) parallel citations.
Abbreviations in Case Names	Some abbreviations in case names given in Table T.6 differ from *ALWD* abbreviations. For example, *Bluebook* uses "Ass'n" and "P'ship."	Some abbreviations in case names given in Appendix 3 differ from *Bluebook* abbreviations. For example, *ALWD* uses "Assn." and "Partn."
United States as a Party	Present plaintiff or defendant as *United States*.	Present plaintiff or defendant as *U.S.*
Lexis or Westlaw Cases	Include docket number.	Docket number need not be included.
Pinpoints for Page Spans	Always retain last two digits, but omit repetitious digits as in "937-39."	Option is given to drop repetitious digits or retain them, as in "937-39" or "937-939."
Multiple Statutes	Do not use *et seq.* for a span of statutes.	The use of et seq. is "not encouraged" for a span of statutes.
Treatises and Dictionaries	• The publisher name is not included. • The volume number is given as the first element.	• The publisher name is given in the parenthetical. • The volume number is given after the title.
A.L.R. Annotations	The word "Annotation" is included in the citation.	The word "Annotation" is not included.

Figure 10-1 *(Continued)*

	Bluebook	ALWD
Signals	• There are commas within and after *See, e.g.*, when used before citations. • Separate different types of signals with a period.	• There are no commas within or after *See e.g.* when used before citations. • Separate different types of signals with a semicolon.
String Citing	Treat all federal courts of appeal as one court and all district courts as one court and list in reverse chronological order.	Order cases from the federal courts of appeal by ordinal and then in reverse chronological order; order cases from the district courts alphabetically and then in reverse chronological order.
Quotations	Block indent any quotation of 50 or more words.	Block indent quotations of 50 or more words or any quotation that exceeds 4 lines of text.

2. *Typeface Conventions*

The Bluebook uses two different citation formats. The citation form used by those writing law review journal articles is different from that used by practitioners in that LARGE AND SMALL CAPITAL LETTERS are used. Practitioners do not use large and small caps. Thus, perhaps the single most important fact you should know about *The Bluebook* is that almost all of the examples given in its white pages show how to cite authorities as if you were writing a journal article or law review article; the Bluepages, however, show a different format for practitioners. Thus, law students must learn a different format when they enter law firm practice.

The three most significant differences in the way citations are presented in law reviews and by practitioners are as follows:

• **Typeface.** Journal articles, author names, titles of books, and names of periodicals are presented in LARGE AND SMALL CAPS. Practitioners never use large and small caps.

Example for citing a treatise in a law review or journal article:

1 J. THOMAS MCCARTHY, MCCARTHY ON TRADEMARKS AND UNFAIR COMPETITION § 3:1 (4th ed. 1997).

Example for citing a treatise in a practitioner's court brief or other document:

1 J. Thomas McCarthy, *McCarthy on Trademarks and Unfair Competition* § 3:1 (4th ed. 1997).

Do not become confused and assume that because an example appears in the body of *The Bluebook* that it is correct. It may well be correct—but only for law review footnotes. Practitioners must always check the Bluepages and the inside back cover of *The Bluebook*, and adapt the typeface for use in a court document or legal memorandum. Remember that practitioners never use large and small capitals. One of the nice advantages of *ALWD* is that it eliminates this odd distinction between large and small capitals and ordinary type and requires only the use of "ordinary" typeface.

• **Location of Citations.** *The Bluebook* states that citations in journal articles appear in footnotes and that practitioners place their citations in the text of a document rather than in footnotes (Bluepages ("B") 13). This rule may be an oversimplification; many practitioners place citations in footnotes in their court briefs.

• **Presentation of Case Names.** Practitioners always underscore or italicize case names. There are no exceptions to this rule for practitioners. However, when full case names appear in journal articles, they are neither underscored nor italicized (although short form case names are italicized in journal articles).

D. *Bluebook* Citation Rules and Examples for Primary Authorities

Unless otherwise noted, all *Bluebook* citation examples in this chapter are in the form used by practitioners rather than in the form used for law review articles. Thus, large and small capital letters are not used.

Practice Tip: *Citation Form*

In citing legal authorities, do not rely on the way books and cases refer to themselves. For example, every volume of U.S.C.A. includes an instruction similar to the following: "Cite This Book Thus: 42 U.S.C.A. §1220." This form is incorrect according to *The Bluebook* and *ALWD*, however, which provide the following correct form: 42 U.S.C.A. §1220 (West 1994) (with a space after the section symbol and a date). Similarly, many courts in California use the incorrect abbreviation "C.A." rather than the correct abbreviation "Cal. Ct. App." to refer to cases from the California appellate courts.

You should therefore always rely on the appropriate *Bluebook* or *ALWD* rules rather than the citation forms you may observe in books or case reports or on LexisNexis or Westlaw screens, which are often more intent on saving space than on complying with *TheBluebook* or *ALWD*.

1. *Cases*

a. Introduction

A typical case citation includes the following elements:

- Case name;
- References to set(s) of reports that publishes the case and the page on which the case begins;
- A parenthetical that includes the court and jurisdiction (if not apparent from the name of the set) and the year of decision; and
- Subsequent history of the case, if any. (R.10.1)

Thus, a typical citation to a Florida case is as follows:

Smith v. Gregory, 675 So. 2d 119 (Fla. 2001).

b. Case Names

(1) General Principles

The Bluebook provides numerous rules regarding case names in citations. Carefully review Bluepages B5.1 and Rule 10 in *The Bluebook* for a full discussion of these rules. Some of the more common guidelines you should be aware of are as follows:

• Case names may be <u>underscored</u> or *italicized* (B2; B13). Follow your firm or office practice. Select one method and be consistent. When underscoring, use a solid unbroken line, as in <u>Hendrix v. Hamilton.</u>

• If there are several plaintiffs and defendants, list only the first one on each side (B5.1.1(i) and R.10.2.1(a)). Do not use *et al.* to signal that other parties exist.

Correct: *Smith v. Martinez*
Incorrect: *Smith and Jacobsen v. Martinez, Klein, and O'Brien*
Incorrect: *Smith v. Martinez, et al.*

• Omit first names or initials for parties (although retain full corporate or business names). Use surnames only (B5.1.1(ii) and R.10.2.1(g)).

Correct: *Smith v. Martinez*
Correct: *Smith v. Ralph Lauren Ltd.*
Incorrect: *Ellen Smith v. T.J. Martinez*

• When underscoring, underscore the period in words such as "Inc.," "Co.," or "Corp." When italicizing, make sure to italicize this final period.

Correct: *Bailey v. Nike Inc.*
Incorrect: *Bailey v. McDonald's Corp*.

• The comma that follows a case name is neither underscored nor italicized (B5.1.1).

Correct: *Young v. Talbot*,
Incorrect: *Young v. Talbot,*

• Omit words describing a party's status, such as "plaintiff," "trustee," or "executor" (R.10.2.1(e)).

Correct: *Harrison v. Kendall*
Incorrect: *Harrison, Plaintiff, v. Kendall, Trustee*

• If a party is known by a widely known acronym (WHO) or initialism (FDA), you may use it without periods (R.6.1(b)).

Preferred: *Willis v. FBI* *Simmons v. SEC*
Disfavored: *Willis v. F.B.I.* *Simmons v. S.E.C.*

• Do not abbreviate "United States" in a case name if it is the entire name of a party (R.10.2.2).

Correct: *United States v. Reynolds*
Correct: *Lee v. U.S. Dep't of Justice*
Incorrect: *U.S. v. Reynolds* *U.S.A. v. Reynolds*

• Generally, omit prepositional phrases of location (R.10.2.1(f)).

Correct: In *Brown v. Board of Education*, 347 U.S. 483 (1954), the Court held that a system of school segregation based on race violates the Equal Protection Clause of the Fourteenth Amendment.
Incorrect: In *Brown v. Board of Education of Topeka, Kansas*, 347 U.S. 483 (1954), the Court held that . . .

• The abbreviation for "versus" in a citation is a lowercase "v" followed by a period. Note, however, that "vs." is often used in pleadings and court documents.

Correct: *Garcia v. Walker*
Incorrect: *Garcia vs. Walker*

(2) *Abbreviations in Case Names (B5.1.1(v) and R.10.2.1(c))*

Because case names can be long, learning when you can abbreviate words in case names will save you time and effort. Unfortunately, the rules regarding abbreviating words in case names are awkwardly phrased and located in *The Bluebook*. Which words may be abbreviated in a citation depends on the location and use of the citation.

• If your citation appears as part of a textual sentence (meaning that the citation is needed to make sense of the sentence), then you may abbreviate only widely known acronyms and initialisms (such as FBI) and the following commonly known and widely recognized words:

&	Ass'n	Bros.	Co.	Corp.	Inc.	Ltd.	No.

If one of these eight words begins a party's name, do not abbreviate it.

• If your citation "stands alone" (rather than appearing as part of a textual sentence), you may abbreviate any of the nearly 170 words in Table T.6 of *The Bluebook* even if it is the first word of a party's name.

Examples:

- According to *Harrison Manufacturing & Equipment Inc. v. Southern Mutual Co.*, 430 U.S. 655 (1995), trademarks can be abandoned through nonuse.

  Explanation: Because the citation appears as part of a textual sentence, abbreviate only "&," "Inc.," and "Co."
- Trademarks can be abandoned through nonuse. *Harrison Mfg. & Equip. Inc. v. S. Mut. Co.*, 430 U.S. 655 (1995).

  Explanation: Because the citation "stands alone," you may abbreviate any of the words in Table T.6.

Until 2000, *The Bluebook* strictly prohibited abbreviation of the first word in a party's name. This rule changed in 2000 in the Seventeenth Edition, and remains in existence in the Eighteenth Edition. Many law firms and practitioners dislike this rule and continue to follow the prior rule by never abbreviating the first word in a party's name.

c. Citation Form for State Court Cases

Prior to 1996, *The Bluebook* required that when citing state court cases, in every instance, all parallel citations should be given, with the official citation given first, followed by the unofficial citation(s). The current Eighteenth Edition of *The Bluebook* rule is as follows:

• If court rules require parallel citations, you must give them (typically giving the official citation first, followed by the unofficial citation(s)).

• Unless court rules require parallel citations, cite solely to the regional reporter (for example, P.2d or N.W.2d) and give a reference to the state and to the deciding court parenthetically, using Table T.1 of *The Bluebook* to construct your abbreviation. (See B5.1.3 and Rules 10.3.1 and 10.4.)

Examples:

- *Samson Corp. v. Bailey*, 302 S.C. 118, 671 S.E.2d 909 (1990). This form is used when a court rule requires parallel citations.
- *Samson Corp. v. Bailey*, 671 S.E.2d 909 (S.C. 1990). This form is used in any instance other than when a court rule requires parallel citations.

You do not need to include the name of the court in the parenthetical if the court that decided the case is the highest court of the state. For example, *Bluebook* Table T.1 tells us that "S.C." indicates a case from the South Carolina Supreme Court. Thus, no further information is needed in the date parenthetical in the previous example. However, for cases from the lower courts, the rule is different. Examine the following example:

- *Taylor v. Fletcher*, 304 N.W.2d 18 (Mich. Ct. App. 1981).

Because we cannot tell which court decided the case from the reference to "N.W.2d," we must include the deciding court in the parenthetical with the date (as shown in Table T.1 of *The Bluebook*).

Remember that more than 20 states no longer publish their cases officially. For cases from these states (decided after the date the official set was discontinued), the correct citation form will refer the reader only to the regional reporter and will include information about the court that decided the case in the date parenthetical, as follows: *Lee v. Lee*, 704 P.2d 119 (Wyo. 2001). To determine which states no longer publish officially, see Figure 4-2 of this text, or review Table T.1 of *The Bluebook* or Appendix 1 of *ALWD*.

d. Citation Form for Federal Cases (B5.1.3; Table T.1)

- **United States Supreme Court Cases.**

Cite to U.S. If the case has not yet been published in U.S., cite to S. Ct., L. Ed., or U.S.L.W., in that order of preference. Do not give a parallel citation.

Example: *Johnson v. Ruiz*, 514 U.S. 118 (1995).

- **Cases from the United States Courts of Appeal.**

Cite to F., F.2d, or F.3d. You *must* include a reference to the circuit that decided the case in the parenthetical with the date.

Example: *Garrison v. Monroe*, 145 F.3d 901 (4th Cir. 1999).

- **Cases from the United States District Courts.**

Cite to F. Supp. or F. Supp. 2d. You *must* include a reference to the particular district court that decided the case in the parenthetical with the date. See Figure 2-2 for abbreviations for our 94 district courts.

Example: *Ryan v. Arne*, 32 F. Supp. 2d 18 (E.D. Va. 1998).

e. Subsequent and Prior History (B5.1.5; R.10.7)

- **Subsequent History.** When a decision is cited in full, give the entire subsequent history. You may, however, omit denials of certiorari or other similar discretionary appeals, unless the decision is less than two years old or the denial is particularly relevant. This rule relating to omitting denials of certiorari is new since 1996, and has often been criticized. Many attorneys believe that denial of certiorari is always relevant and therefore should always be included. You will be given the subsequent history of your case when you Shepardize or KeyCite (see Chapter Eleven). Then, use Table T.8 of *The Bluebook* to find the appropriate abbreviation for the history of your case. Give the subsequent history after your full citation, as follows:

Examples: *Fraley v. Carson*, 890 F. Supp. 114 (E.D. Va. 1996), *rev'd*, 13 F.3d 114 (4th Cir. 1998).

Halliwell v. Vance, 150 F.3d 120 (3d Cir. 2009), *cert. denied*, 430 U.S. 899 (2010).

• **Prior History.** Give the prior history of your case only if it is relevant to the point for which you are citing your case.

f. Spacing in Citations (R.6.1(a))

Follow these three rules to determine spacing in citations:

- Adjacent single capitals are placed next to each other with no spaces. For purposes of this rule, the abbreviations for 2d, 3d, 4th, 5th, and so forth are viewed as single capital letters.

  Correct: P.2d
  S.E.2d
  U.S.
  F.3d
  A.L.R.5th

- Multiple-letter abbreviations are preceded and followed by spaces.

  Correct: Cal. App. 2d
  So. 2d
  F. Supp. 2d
  Fed. R. Civ. P. 56(c)

- Be careful with the names of periodicals. Consult *Bluebook* Table T.13 and mimic the spacing shown.

Correct:	B.C. L. Rev.	N.Y.U. L. Rev.
Incorrect:	B.C.L. Rev.	N.Y.U.L. Rev.

Do not use superscripts (such as 1st or 4th). Set ordinals (such as 1st or 4th) and numerals "on line" (so they will be consistent with the presentations of 2d and 3d). (See R.6.2(b).)

2. *Statutes*

a. Federal Statutes (B6; R.12)

Recall that our federal statutes are published in three sets: U.S.C. (the official set), and U.S.C.A. and U.S.C.S. (the unofficial sets). Cite to U.S.C. whenever possible, giving the title number, the name of the set, and the section number. *The Bluebook* also requires a parenthetical giving the year of the code and the publisher name, if you cite to an unofficial set.

Examples: 17 U.S.C. § 109 (2006).
17 U.S.C.A. § 109 (West 2003).
17 U.S.C.S. § 109 (LexisNexis 2003).

Note that the "year of the code" is not the date the statute was enacted, but the year that appears on the spine of the volume, the year that appears on the title page, or the latest copyright year (in that order of preference). If your statute is found in a pocket part or softcover supplement, indicate such as follows: 42 U.S.C.A. § 2331(a) (West. Supp. 2008).

b. State Statutes

Use Table T.1 of *The Bluebook* for instructions on citing each state's statutes. Most states have numbered statutes, with no specifically named titles.

Examples: Ariz. Rev. Stat. Ann. § 10-120 (2003).
Fla. Stat. § 607.0101 (2004).

A few states (including California, Maryland, New York, and Texas) have specific names for their statutes.

Examples: Cal. Fam. Code § 1204 (West 2001).
N.Y. Educ. Law § 3220 (McKinney 2000).

c. Notes on Citing Statutes

- Practitioners almost always omit the parenthetical following the statute.
- Follow the section symbol (§) with a space (R.6.2(c)).
- The section symbol should be used in a stand-alone citation (R.12.9). Never start a sentence with the section symbol. Use the word "Section."
- Unless you are referring to a provision of the *United States Code*, use the word "section" in text (rather than using the symbol §).
- When citing more than one section, use two section symbols (§§) and give inclusive numbers. Do not use "*et seq.*," and do not drop

any repetitious digits (R.3.3(b)). Note that "*et seq.*" is shown in italics in *The Bluebook*.

Correct: 35 U.S.C. §§ 101-105 (2006).
Incorrect: 35 U.S.C. §§ 101-05 (2006).

3. Court and Other Rules (B6.1.3; R.12.8.3)

Examples: Fed. R. Civ. P. 56(c).
Fed. R. Evid. 109.
Sup. Ct. R. 33(a).

4. Constitutions (B7; R.11)

Cite constitutional provisions that are currently in force without a date.

Examples: U.S. Const. amend. VI.
U.S. Const. art. I, § 8.
Cal. Const. art. XX.

5. Administrative Regulations (B6.1.4; R.14)

Examples: 15 C.F.R. § 12.203 (2008).
Indian Trust Management Reform, 71 Fed. Reg. 45,173 (Aug. 8, 2006).

E. *Bluebook* Citation Form for Secondary Authorities

Examples for citations for secondary authorities will be discussed in the order in which those authorities were discussed in Chapters Five and Six.

1. A.L.R. Annotations (R.16.6.6)

Example: Deborah F. Buckman, Annotation, *Intellectual Property Rights in Video, Electronic, and Computer Games*, 7 A.L.R. Fed. 2d 269 (2005).

2. *Encyclopedias (B8; R.15.8)*

Examples: 23 C.J.S. *Indemnity* § 24 (1998).
7 Am. Jur. 2d *Agency* § 14 (1994).

3. *Periodicals (B9; R.16)*

Following are some notes on citing periodicals and journal articles:

- Note that the form for citing periodical articles differs when the author is a student. (See Rule 16.6.2.)
- Give the author's name as he or she does in the publication.
- If there are two authors, list both in the order in which they appear on the title page, and separate the names with an ampersand (&).
- If there are more than two authors, either identify the first author's name followed by the signal "et al." or else list all of the authors.
- Do not abbreviate words or omit any articles in the title.
- Italicize or underscore the title of the article.
- Note that there is a comma following the title of the article.
- Use Table T.13 to determine the abbreviations for periodical titles, remembering that the format for citing journal articles in law review footnotes uses large and small capitals whereas practitioners do not use large and small capitals.

Example: Sharon Dolovich, *State Punishment and Private Prisons*, 55 Duke L.J. 437 (2005).

4. *Texts and Treatises (B8; R.15)*

Following are some notes on citing books, texts, and treatises:

- Follow the rules for author names given above for periodical articles.
- Do not place a comma after the title of the book or text.
- If citing to anything other than the first edition of the text, indicate as such in the parenthetical with the date.
- Remember that the book title will appear in large and small capitals when it is cited in a journal article, but will not when it is cited by practitioners.

Example: 2 Melvin F. Jager, *Trade Secrets Law* § 104 (2d ed. 2005).

5. Restatements (B6.1.3; R.12.8.5)

Example: Restatement (Second) of Contracts § 104 (1995).

6. Attorneys General Opinions (R.14.4)

Example: 62 Op. Att'y Gen. 109 (1994).

7. Dictionaries (B8.1; R.15.8)

Example: *Black's Law Dictionary* 891 (9th ed. 2009).

8. Uniform Laws (B6.1.3; R.12.8.4)

Examples: U.C.C. § 2-316 (1977).
Unif. P'ship Act § 402 (amended 1997), 8 U.L.A. 18 (2001).

9. Looseleaf Services (R.19)

Example: *SEC v. Edwards*, 85 Fed. Sec. L. Rep. (CCH) ¶ 92,656 (Fed. Cir. July 10, 2004).

Help Line: *The Online* Bluebook

The Bluebook is now available online at http://www.legalbluebook.com. The fee-based online version of *The Bluebook* allows some interesting and convenient features, including the following:

- Online searching makes it easy to locate needed information. You can search by key word or phrase to find sections of *The Bluebook* of interest to you.
- Just as you can mark up your print copy of your *Bluebook*, you can add notes and bookmarks to your online *Bluebook*.

Additionally, there are several video tours and features you can use to familiarize yourself with the online *Bluebook*.
The website also offers two interesting new features:

- The site now provides "Blue Tips," which is similar to an FAQ section and answers questions frequently asked about *The Bluebook*.
- The site provides an "Errata" section, which identifies minor corrections and edits made to *The Bluebook*.

F. *ALWD* Citation Rules and Examples for Primary Authorities

Remember that *ALWD* makes no distinction between the typeface used by practitioners and that used in law review or article journals, so all of its examples are acceptable for those writing law review articles and for practitioners.

1. *Cases (R.12)*

a. Introduction

ALWD rules for citing cases are nearly identical to those of *The Bluebook*. In fact, there are only three major differences for cases published in print form:

• **Information About Divisions for State Court Cases.** *ALWD* Rule 12.6(b) generally requires that when you cite a state case, you must include available information about departments, districts, or divisions that decided the case. *The Bluebook* generally does not permit this information.

- *ALWD*: *Holt v. Holt*, 14 S.W.3d 887 (Ark. App. Div. IV 2000).
- *Bluebook*: *Holt v. Holt*, 14 S.W.3d 887 (Ark. Ct. App. 2000).

• **Abbreviations in Case Names.** *ALWD* Rule 12.2(e) provides that you may abbreviate any word in a case name when the citation appears as a stand-alone clause or sentence, and that it is "traditional" to spell out all words in a case name when it appears in text. This approach is a bit more permissive than that of *The Bluebook*, which requires that you spell out all words in a case name when it appears in text (except words such as "Inc." and "Corp.") and that you abbreviate words in a case name in a stand-alone citation.

• **General Abbreviations.** The abbreviations used in *ALWD* and *The Bluebook* vary. For example, *The Bluebook* abbreviates the word "Association" as "Ass'n," whereas *ALWD* uses "Assn." Similarly, *The Bluebook* generally requires that when the United States is a party to a case, the case name must read "United States," while *ALWD* (R.12.2(g)) provides that the case name must read "U.S." as in *U.S. v. Dana*. Finally, abbreviations for names of courts vary. For example, *Bluebook* Table T.1 shows "Alaska Ct. App." for the Alaska Court of Appeals while *ALWD* Appendix 1 shows this as "Alaska App."

b. Federal Cases

ALWD's formats for federal cases are identical to those in *The Bluebook* (although *ALWD* permits, but does not favor, using all parallel cites for U.S. Supreme Court cases).

c. State Cases

ALWD's rules for state cases are identical to those in *The Bluebook*, namely, follow all local rules for citing cases, and in the absence of any rules, cite only to West's regional reporter, and indicate parenthetically the year of decision and the court that decided the case. Thus, give parallel citations only when required by local rules. Use *ALWD*'s Appendix 1 to determine the appropriate abbreviation for state courts.

d. Subsequent and Prior History (R.12.8; R.12.9)

ALWD's rules relating to subsequent and prior history are nearly identical to those of *The Bluebook*. Thus, you must include subsequent history for the cases you cite, although you may omit denials of certiorari unless the cited case is less than two years old or the denial is particularly important. Prior history need not be included.

e. Spacing in Citations (R.2.2)

ALWD's spacing rules are identical to those found in *The Bluebook*:

- Close up all adjacent single capitals, and treat ordinals as single capitals (as in U.S. and N.W.2d).
- Place spaces on either side of multiple letter abbreviations (as in F. Supp. 2d).
- In legal periodicals, set the abbreviations for an institution or geographical entity apart from other capital letters (as in N.M. L. Rev.). Use *ALWD*'s Appendix 5 for examples of periodical names.

2. *Statutes (R.14)*

a. Federal Statutes

The presentation of federal statutes is the same in *ALWD* as it is in *The Bluebook*. The rules requiring you to include a date parenthetical for federal statutes and the name of the publisher for the unofficial sets (U.S.C.A. and U.S.C.S.) are also identical, although *The Bluebook* uses "LexisNexis" and *ALWD* uses "Lexis." Remember that almost all practitioners omit the parenthetical following the section number of the statute.

Examples: 18 U.S.C. § 1889 (2006).
18 U.S.C.A. § 1889 (West 2003).
18 U.S.C.S. § 1889 (Lexis 2002).

Additionally, whereas *The Bluebook* flatly prohibits the use of "*et seq.*" to indicate a span of statutes, *ALWD* merely discourages it (but does allow it). Moreover, while *The Bluebook* shows "*et seq.*" in italics (R.3.3(b)), *ALWD* does not. (*ALWD* R.6.6(d)).

b. State Statutes

Appendix 1 of *ALWD* provides the format for each state's statutes. These are highly similar or identical in form to those shown in Table T.1 of *The Bluebook*.

Examples: Cal. Evid. Code Ann. § 5102 (West 2004).
Fla. Stat. § 607.0101 (2003).
Mich. Comp. Laws § 450.1101 (2004).

3. *Court and Other Rules (R.17)*

Examples: Fed. R. Civ. P. 12(b)(6).
Fed. R. Evid. 501.
S. Ct. R. 17.

4. *Constitutions (R.13)*

Examples: U.S. Const. amend. IX.
U.S. Const. art. III, § 8.
Cal. Const. art. XXII.

5. *Administrative Regulations (R.19)*

Examples: 28 C.F.R. § 43.201 (2008).
Suspension of Community Eligibility, 70 Fed. Reg. 16,964 (Jan 10, 2005).

G. *ALWD* Citation Rules and Examples for Secondary Authorities

Most of the *ALWD* rules for citing secondary authorities are identical to those for *The Bluebook*. Following are examples for the most often cited secondary authorities. An asterisk (*) following an example indicates that the format is identical for both *ALWD* and *The Bluebook*.

1. *A.L.R. Annotations (R.24)*

Example: David J. Marchitelli, *Causes of Action Governed by Limitations Period in UCC § 2-725*, 49 A.L.R.5th 1 (1997).

2. *Encyclopedias (R.26)*

Examples: 77A C.J.S. *Sales* § 377 (1996).*
93 Am. Jur. 2d *Trials* § 16 (2004).*

3. *Periodical Materials (R.23)*

Example: Jane S. Schacter, *Sexual Orientation, Social Change, and the Courts*, 54 Drake L. Rev. 303 (2006).*

4. *Texts and Treatises (R.22)*

A key difference in the way citations for treatises are presented under *ALWD* rules is that *ALWD* requires that the publisher of the treatise be identified in the parenthetical with the date. Also, the location of the volume number for a multivolume set is different in *ALWD* from *The Bluebook*.

Example: Homer H. Clark, *Clark's The Law of Domestic Relations in the United States* vol. 2, § 104 (2d ed., West 1987).

5. *Restatements (R.27)*

Example: *Restatement (Second) of Torts* § 201 (1997).

6. *Attorneys General Opinion (R.19.7)*

Example: 43 Op. Atty. Gen. 387 (1965).

7. *Dictionaries (R.25)*

Example: *Black's Law Dictionary* 584 (Bryan A. Garner ed., 9th ed., West 2009).

8. *Uniform Laws (R.27.4)*

Examples: U.C.C. § 2-316 (1977).*

Unif. Partn. Act § 402 (amended 1997), 8 U.L.A. 18 (2001).

Ethics Alert: _Finding Local Rules_

Both *Bluebook* and *ALWD* provide that any local rules relating to citation form will "trump" or supersede their rules. Thus, you have an ethical obligation to find and follow these local rules. To find specialized local citation rules:

- Access the website http://www.uscourts.gov for links to all federal court websites, which usually post their local rules.
- Review each state's judicial website, identified in Table T.1 of *The Bluebook*, for state and local rules.
- Review *The Bluebook*'s Bluepages Table BT.2, which identifies court rules relating to citation form.
- Review Appendix 2 of *ALWD* for a discussion of local rules relating to citation form.
- Call the clerk of the court to which you are submitting a document, and inquire whether any local rules dictate the form for citations.
- Consult a law librarian.

9. Looseleaf Services (R.28)

Examples: *SEC v. Edwards*, 85 Fed. Sec. L. Rep. (CCH) ¶ 92,656 (Fed. Cir. July 10, 2004).*

H. Special Citation Issues (*Bluebook* and *ALWD*)

1. Introduction

Citations do not exist alone. They appear as part of sentences that must be correctly punctuated, as support for quotations, and together with certain signals that give readers information about the level of support the citation provides for the assertion you have made. This section of the chapter addresses special citation issues such as punctuation, quotations, signals, and short form citations you may use when you have cited an authority in full and wish to refer to it again later. *Bluebook* examples provided will be shown in the form used by legal practitioners (rather than in the form used for law review journal articles).

2. *Punctuation (*Bluebook *B2 and R.1.1;* ALWD *R.43)*

There are three punctuation marks that may follow a citation: a period, a comma, or a semicolon.

- Use a period to follow a citation when it supports (or contradicts) the entire previous sentence.

Example: An individual may obtain court review after a final decision of the Commissioner of Social Security. *Sims v. Apfel*, 530 U.S. 103, 109 (2000).

- Use commas to surround a citation when it appears as a clause within a sentence, namely, when it supports (or contradicts) only part of the previous sentence.

Example: Although an individual may obtain court review after a final decision of the Commissioner of Social Security, *Sims v. Apfel*, 530 U.S. 103, 109 (2000), review may not be sought unless the individual has exhausted all administrative remedies, *Weinberger v. Salfi*, 422 U.S. 749, 755 (1975).

- Use a semicolon to follow a citation when the citation appears in a *string* of other citations. (*Bluebook* B4.5 and Rule 1.4; *ALWD* Rule 45). Sometimes legal writers cite more than one authority in support of a proposition. When citations appear in a string, however, they must be ordered in a strict hierarchy. *The Bluebook* (but not *ALWD*) allows the reader to place the most helpful citation first. Except in this situation, list citations in the following order (see Figure 10-1 and *Bluebook* and *ALWD* for complete instructions and list):
  - Constitutions (list federal Constitution first, then state constitutions, alphabetically by state);
  - Statutes (list federal statutes first by order of U.S.C. title, then state statutes alphabetically by state);
  - Cases (list federal cases first, ordering by United States Supreme Court, then United States Courts of Appeal, then United States District Courts, then state cases, alphabetically by state and from highest court to lowest court, and then listing newer cases before older ones);
  - Secondary authorities (in the order listed by *The Bluebook* and *ALWD*).

Example: If a claimant fails to request review from the Social Security Appeals Council, there may be no judicial review. 42 U.S.C. § 401 (2006); *Bowen v. New York*, 476 U.S. 467, 473 (1986); *Weinberger v. Salfi*, 422 U.S. 749, 757 (1975); 20 C.F.R. § 404.900 (1999).

*3. Quotations (*Bluebook *B12 and R.5;* ALWD *R.5 and R.47)*

a. Introduction to Pinpoints

You must always indicate the exact page a quotation appears on (generally called a *pinpoint* or *pincite*, or occasionally a *jump cite*). Moreover, as a courtesy to your reader, you must include a pinpoint even when you paraphrase material. If parallel citations are given, you must indicate the pinpoint for all sources. Per *The Bluebook*, if your quotation spans more than one page, provide the inclusive page numbers but separate them by a hyphen; retain the last two digits but omit any other repetitious digits.

> ***Example:*** "Divorce ends tenancy by the entirety." *Craft v. Craft*, 535 U.S. 274, 282-83 (2002).

ALWD allows you to either keep all of the digits or drop repetitious digits, so long as two digits are retained.

b. Indicating Quotations in Text

The rules for showing quotations are nearly identical in *The Bluebook* and *ALWD*: Indent longer quotations (those that are 50 words or more) and do not use quotation marks for such longer quotes. These indented quotations are usually called *block quotations*, and they should be fully justified. Place shorter quotations (those of fewer than 50 words) in the narrative portion of the text, using quotation marks, and always placing commas and periods inside the quotation marks. *ALWD* allows writers to indent quotations if they contain 50 words or more or if they exceed four lines of text.

c. Altering Quotations and Using Ellipses (*Bluebook* R.5.2 and 5.3; *ALWD* R.48 and 49)

Use brackets to show a minor addition to or omission from a quotation.

> ***Example:*** "Failure to produce evidence within a party's [exclusive] control raises the presumption that it would operate against him." *Long v. Earle*, 269 N.W. 577, 581 (Mich. 1936).

Use an ellipsis to show an omission from the middle or end of a quotation.

> ***Examples:*** "The Court of Appeals found that large [political] contributions are intended to . . . gain special treatment." *McConnell v. FEC*, 540 U.S. 93, 119 (2003).
>
> "The appellant's statements permitted the inference that he was prepared to use his weapon . . . ." *Monroe v. Fisher*, 538 U.S. 19, 26 (2002).

4. *Citation Signals (*Bluebook *B4 and R.1.2;* ALWD *R.44)*

Legal writers often use certain *citation signals* as a shorthand method of indicating to the reader the manner in which an authority supports or contradicts an assertion. Thus, *The Bluebook* provides that the signal *see* is placed before a citation when the citation clearly supports the proposition.

> ***Example:*** Language in a statute must be read in context. *See Hibbs v. Wynn*, 542 U.S. 88, 101 (2004).

Do not use any signal when your cited authority directly states the proposition, is the source of a quotation, or identifies an authority referred to in the text.

> ***Example:*** "An assessment is closely tied to the collection of a tax." *Hibbs v. Wynn*, 542 U.S. 88, 101 (2004).

The signals can be very confusing, and often there are only very subtle shadings of difference between one signal and another. Some of the signals have shifted their meanings from one edition of *The Bluebook* to another. Moreover, there are subtle differences in the presentation and meaning of the signals depending on whether you are following *The Bluebook* or *ALWD*. For example, *The Bluebook* follows the signal *e.g.* with a comma, whereas *ALWD* does not. These signals are often used more in academic legal writing, such as law review articles, than in court briefs and legal memoranda. Carefully review *Bluebook* Rule 1.2 and *ALWD* Rule 44 for the use, meaning, and presentation of these signals.

5. *Short Form Citations*

Once you have cited an authority in full, to save time you may use a short form when you refer to it again later in your writing.

a. Use of *Id.* (*Bluebook* R.4.1; *ALWD* R.11.3)

The citation short form *id.* sends your reader to the immediately preceding authority, whether it is a case, statute, or any other legal authority. *Id.* may appear capitalized or it may begin with a lowercase "i" if it is part of a citation clause or sentence. Underscore or italicize the period in *id.*

Example: Title X of the Public Health Service Act provides federal funding for family-planning services. *Rust v. Sullivan*, 500 U.S. 173, 179 (1991). When language in a federal statute is ambiguous, courts typically defer to the expertise of the agency charged with administering the statute. *Id.* at 186.

Follow these tips when using *id.*:

- Use *id.* alone when directing a reader to the exact source/page/section/paragraph as the preceding citation. Use "*id.* plus" the change to send the reader to a different page or paragraph.

  First reference: *Avco Corp. v. Machinists*, 390 U.S. 557, 560 (1968).

  Second reference: *Id.* at 561.

- *The Bluebook* prohibits the use of the word "at" before a section or paragraph symbol. (Note that *ALWD* allows the word "at" before a symbol.)

  First reference: Susan Gray, *Due Process* § 101 (3d ed. 2001).

  Second reference: *Id.* § 207.

- When giving parallel citations, *id.* replaces only the official citation. The regional reporter must be repeated.

  First reference: *Causey v. Whittig*, 321 Mo. 358, 360, 11 S.W.2d 11, 13 (1928).

  Second reference: *Id.* at 369, 11 S.W.2d at 24.

- *Id.* may be used to refer to an immediately preceding authority only if there is one citation in the previous reference.

b. Use of *Supra* (*Bluebook* B8.2, B9.2, and R.4.2; *ALWD* R.11.4)

Supra means "above" and is used to direct a reader to a preceding (but not immediately preceding) authority. *The Bluebook* and *ALWD* both prohibit the use of *supra* for primary authorities, such as cases, statutes, and most legislative materials. Thus, *supra* is most frequently used as a short form for books, law review articles, and other materials with an author's name.

First citation:	Stephen Faberman, *Special Relationships, Schools, and the Fifth Circuit*, 35 B.C. L. Rev. 97, 105 (1993).
Intervening citation:	45 U.S.C. § 2442 (2006).
Supra citation:	Faberman, *supra*, at 114.

Infra (meaning "below") directs a reader to a later citation and is not commonly used in legal writing, although it is often used in indexes to sets of books such as U.S.C.A.

c. Short Forms for Cases (*Bluebook* B5.2 and R.10.9; *ALWD* R.12.21)

Assume your full citation is *Hoyme v. Brakken*, 677 N.W.2d 233, 235 (Wis. 1999). Once you have given this full citation, you may use any of the following short forms, so long as the reader will be able to locate readily the earlier full citation:

- *Hoyme*, 677 N.W.2d at 236.
- 677 N.W.2d at 236. (Note that you should use the plaintiff's name unless doing so would cause confusion.)
- *Id.* at 236.

d. Short Forms for Statutes (*Bluebook* B6.2(b) and R.12.9; *ALWD* R.14.6)

Once you have given a full citation to a statute, you may later use any short form that clearly identifies the statute.

First reference:	Ohio Rev. Code Ann. § 1701.01 (West 1990).
Later references:	Ohio Rev. Code Ann. § 1701.01. *Id.* § 1701.01. (Note that *ALWD* would show this as "*Id.* at § 1701.01.")

6. *Neutral Citation Format (*Bluebook* R.10.3.3;* ALWD *R.12.16)*

Current citation rules mandate citation to conventional print forms, the majority of which are published by West, requiring legal professionals to purchase West sets even though cases and other materials are easy and inexpensive to access on the Internet. Thus, many legal professionals and consumers advocate the implementation of what is usually referred to as a neutral, public domain, or universal citation system, meaning that the citation looks the same whether the reader has accessed the case by

Help Line: *Online Citation Primer*

Professor Peter W. Martin of Cornell Law School has published an online guide to citation form entitled *Introduction to Basic Legal Citation* (rev. 2007) for both *The Bluebook* and *ALWD*. The guide provides information on the purpose of legal citations, examples for nearly all citation formats, and a table of state-specific citations, giving examples for cases, statutes, and regulations for all 50 states and the District of Columbia.

The website address is as follows: http://www.law.cornell.edu/citation. Consider "bookmarking" this valuable site as one of your favorite sites. Use it as a "backup" or to confirm the accuracy of your citations.

Caveat: Although this site is excellent and provides great examples, always use *The Bluebook* or *ALWD* as the final authority. Nevertheless, this website will provide you with a wealth of valuable information and numerous examples of citation form.

conventional print format, through LexisNexis or Westlaw, or on the Internet. Generally, the neutral citation includes the case name, year of decision, the state's two-character postal code, the court abbreviation (unless the court is the state's highest court), the sequential number of the decision, and, if a parallel citation is available, it must be given. A pinpoint paragraph rather than a pinpoint page is given.

Use neutral citations when required by local rules. As of the writing of this text, the following states have adopted a neutral citation format: Arizona, Colorado, Louisiana, Maine, Mississippi, Montana, New Mexico, North Dakota, Ohio, Oklahoma, South Dakota, Utah, Wisconsin, and Wyoming.

The following example tells the reader that the case *Renville v. Taylor* was the 217th case decided by the highest court in North Dakota in 2007, and the reader is specifically directed to paragraph 14 in that case. The remaining part of the citation is a parallel citation to West's *Northwestern Reporter, Second Series*.

Example: *Renville v. Taylor*, 2000 ND 217, ¶14, 607 N.W.2d 109, 114.

The website of the American Bar Association (http://www.abanet.org/tech/ltrc/research/citation/home.html) provides additional information on jurisdictions that have adopted a neutral format. There is a great deal of discrepancy among the adopting states as to spacing and punctuation in the citations, so carefully follow the examples you are given by local rules, Table T.1 of *The Bluebook*, and Appendix 2 of *ALWD*.

7. *Capitalization Rules* (Bluebook *R.8;* ALWD *R.3.3)*

The Bluebook and *ALWD* both offer guidance on capitalizing certain words, including the following:

- **Act.** Capitalize "act" when you refer to a specific legislative act, such as "the Act," when referring to the United States Trademark Act.
- **Circuit.** Capitalize "circuit" only when used with a circuit number, as in "the Fifth Circuit held that . . . ."
- **Court.** Capitalize "court":
  - When naming a court in full, as in "The California Supreme Court held":
  - When referring to the United States Supreme Court;
  - When referring to the court to which a document is submitted, as in "Plaintiff respectfully requests this Court grant her motion."
- **Party Designations.** Capitalize "plaintiff," "defendant," and so forth when referring to a party in the pending case, as in "Defendant in this action moved for a change of venue."
- **Federal.** Capitalize "federal" only when it precedes a capitalized word, as in "the Federal Elections Commission." Do not capitalize "federal" in phrases such as "the federal government."
- **State.** Capitalize "state" when it is part of the full title of the state, as in "State of Ohio" or when the state is a party to the litigation, as in "The State has argued . . . ."

8. *Electronic Sources* (Bluebook *R.18;* ALWD *R.38-42)*

The Bluebook and *ALWD* both disfavor citing electronic sources, such as LexisNexis, Westlaw, or the Internet. Follow these three rules:

- You may cite to an electronic source alone only if the information is not available in traditional print form, or the source cannot be located because it is so obscure that it is practically unavailable. Only in these two narrow instances should citation be made to an electronic source alone. (See Chapter Eight for LexisNexis and Westlaw examples.)
- You may add an electronic source as a parallel citation if it will help readers access the information more readily.

Example: *Bluebook* example: *Hillside Dairy Inc. v. Lyons*, 539 U.S. 59 (2003), *available at* http://supreme.justia.com/us/539/59/index.html.

ALWD example: *Hillside Dairy Inc. v. Lyons*, 539 U.S. 59 (2003) (available at http://supreme.justia.com/us/539/59/index.html).

- If a source does not exist in conventional print format or on LexisNexis or Westlaw, you may cite solely to the Internet. *The Bluebook* instructs that you use other *Bluebook* rules for guidance, so that articles on the Internet are cited similarly to periodical articles, dictionary definitions found on the Internet are cited similarly to *Black's Law Dictionary*, and so forth. *ALWD* provides numerous specific formats in Rules 38-42.

Example: *Bluebook* example: Vicki L. Gregory, *UCITA: What Does It Mean for Libraries?*, 25 Online 1, ¶ 3 (2001), http://www.infotoday.com/online/OL2001/gregory1_01.html.

ALWD example: Vicki L. Gregory, *UCITA: What Does It Mean for Libraries?*, 25 Online 1, ¶ 3 (2001), http//www.infotoday.com/online/OL2001/gregory1_01.html.

- You may need to cite to cases that have not been selected for publication, in which instance you will need to cite to either LexisNexis or Westlaw. Follow *Bluebook* B5.1.3 and R.18 and *ALWD* R.12.12.

Examples: *Bluebook* examples: *United States v. Carlton*, No. 00-4429, 2001 WL 739246, at *2 (4th Cir. July 2, 2001).

Brown v. Ford Motor Co., No. 99-2513, 2001 U.S. App. LEXIS 4539, at *4 (4th Cir. Mar. 23, 2001).

ALWD examples: *U.S. v. Carlton*, 2001 WL 739246 at *2 (4th Cir. July 2, 2001).

Brown v. Ford Motor Co., 2001 U.S. App. LEXIS 4539 at *4 (4th Cir. Mar. 23, 2001).

9. *Electronic Assistance for Citation Form*

Neither LexisNexis nor Westlaw can perfectly format citations according to either *The Bluebook* or *ALWD*; however, both services offer resources that provide some citation assistance (see Chapter Eleven). LexisNexis's product, StyleCheck (formerly known as CiteRite) checks your citations against *Bluebook* or California rules. Although it is unclear whether StyleCheck can understand all of the idiosyncrasies of citation form, it will notify you of improper underscoring or italicization, missing parallel cites, or improper punctuation. Another Lexis product, BriefCheck, automatically collects the case and law review citations in your brief, verifies them through *Shepard's* to ensure they are still good law, and checks your quotations for errors. Similarly, Westlaw's KeyCite service (see Chapter Eleven) also provides citation verification information, such as a correct case name and parallel citations.

West offers CiteAdvisor, which can build a table of authorities and suggest correct citation format in either *Bluebook* or *ALWD* format. In addition, a company called Cite-R-Us.com has recently introduced Citrus, its fee-based software program that automatically generates citations in correct *Bluebook* form (see http://www.cite-r-us.com). Although all of these programs are helpful, none of them can determine when you should use a signal, when you should include a parenthetical, and other similar decisions that require the use of discretion and an understanding of *Bluebook* and *ALWD* principles.

CyberSites

http://www.legalbluebook.com	*The Bluebook's* website provides an overview of changes to the Eighteenth Edition, asks for comments and corrections, and provides introductory material about *The Bluebook*.
http://www.alwd.org	The website of the Association of Legal Writing Directors offers information about *ALWD*, updates to *ALWD*, explanations of citation rules, and a list of schools that have adopted *ALWD* as their citation manual.
http://www.law.cornell.edu/citation	Professor Peter W. Martin provides examples and explanations of *Bluebook* and *ALWD* citation forms.
http://lexisnexis.com/icw	LexisNexis offers an "interactive citation workstation" allowing users to quiz themselves on both *Bluebook* and *ALWD* citation formats.
http://www.abanet.org/tech/ltrc/research/citation/home.html	The ABA's website has information devoted to neutral or universal citation form.

Citation Form Assignment

There is at least one thing wrong with each fictitious citation below. Correct the citations using the current edition of *The Bluebook* or *ALWD*. You may need to supply missing information such as dates. Punctuation is not needed after the citations. Assume you are preparing a memorandum in your office and, unless otherwise indicated, assume that the citations appear in textual sentences rather than as stand-alone citations. There is no need to include "pinpoints," unless otherwise directed.

1. H. Douglas Connell v. Nora Brown, a 2005 North Carolina Supreme Court case found in volume 540 at page 668 of the relevant reporter.
2. Automobile Dealers Association v. American Machinists, Incorporated, a 2003 Michigan Supreme Court case located at volume 684 at page 432 of the relevant reporter.
3. Cynthia G. Reynolds v. Marina N. Diaz, a 2001 case from the Massachusetts Appeals Court, located in volume 590 of the relevant reporter, page 1101, with quoted material on pages 1115-1118.
4. Lawson Brothers versus Federal Trade Commission, a 2006 U.S. Supreme Court case, located at volume 540 United States Reports 336, 201 Supreme Court Reporter 510, and 199 Lawyers' Edition (Second Series) page 990.
5. Scott Crawford versus Ann and Harvey Nelson, 301 Federal Reporter, Third Series, page 24, Eighth Circuit, 2005.
6. USA v. Susan Davies, Trustee, 301 Federal Supplement, Second Series, page 499, decided in the District Court for the Eastern District of Virginia in 2003.
7. Kyle Smith and John Day versus Flashpoint Incorporated, a 2006 United States Supreme Court case.
8. Title 42, Section 1122 of the United States Code.
9. Title 35, Section 165 of the United States Code Annotated.
10. Title 47, Sections 190 through 198 of the United States Code Service.
11. California Insurance Code Section 6606.
12. Georgia Code Annotated section 10-42-101.
13. Fourth Amendment to the U.S. Constitution.
14. Page 790 of the current edition of Black's Law Dictionary.
15. Section 13 of the Restatement of Torts, Second.

16. An article authored by Thomas M. Price and Donna F. Brock, entitled "Assessing Punitive Damages in Malpractice Actions," published in volume 35 of the New York University Law Review, at page 606, with a quotation appearing on the first page of the article.

17. Volume 3, Section 31:12 of the third edition of the treatise authored by Miles H. Carter entitled "Federal Rules Practices and Procedures" (2006).

18. Assume the following case is cited on page one of a brief submitted to an Oregon court requiring parallel citations: Alan Griffin v. T.G. Mayer, 562 Oregon Reports, Court of Appeals, page 23 (2004). Give the correct citation.

19. Assume the immediately preceding case is cited on page two of the brief (and that there are no intervening citations). Give the correct citation.

20. Correct the following citation. "Punitive damages must bear a reasonable relationship to actual damages." Consolidated Chemicals Inc. v. Western Fidelity and Insurance Federation, 301 Federal Reporter, Third Series, page 303 (Second Circuit 2003).

21. Assume that the immediately preceding case was affirmed at 503 U.S. 110 in 2004. Give the correct citation.

Memorandum Assignment

There are numerous errors in the fictitious citations in the following brief memorandum. Correct citation errors using the current edition of *The Bluebook* or *ALWD*. You may need to supply missing information.

A limited liability company ("LLC") is a relatively new form of business entity. Limited liability companies were first recognized in Wyoming. WY. Stats. § 12-34-502. After 1988 when the Internal Revenue Service issued a ruling indicating that LLCs would be taxed as partnerships, all other jurisdictions soon enacted statutes recognizing these entities. Conrad S. Ciccotello and Terry Grant, "Professionals as Commercial Institutions: An Analysis of Evolving Organizational Forms," 7 Journal of Legal Studies 1.

Limited liability companies are creatures of statute and can be formed only by compliance with state statutes. Limited liability companies offer full protection to their members from personal liability, whether that liability arises in tort or contract. 3 Andrew S. Talbott, "Limited Liability Companies" Section 1:14 (second edition 1999). Moreover, all states but Wyoming allow a one-person LLC, thereby allowing sole proprietors to convert to the LLC form and achieve protection from personal liability. ID. at Section 1:23.

Although LLCs protect their members against personal liability that arises in tort, that shield of protection can be pierced if a member participates in a wrongful act, supervises an LLC member who engages in a wrongful act, or knows about a wrongful act and fails to take reasonable action to stop it. See e.g. *Thomas v. Henry Brothers Construction LLC*, 201 P. 3rd 118, 130-133 (California S. Ct. 2001). Nevertheless, because liability is usually imposed only for some intentional or gross misconduct, the LLC remains an attractive form of business, particularly for professionals such as doctors, lawyers, and accountants. Ciccotello, at 21.

The LLC may be managed either by its members or by appointed managers. See e.g., Cal. Corps. Code Section 1302. One disadvantage, however, of most LLC statutes is that they require unanimous approval of members to admit a new person to the LLC (unless the LLC operating agreement provides otherwise). See e.g., Wisconsin Statute § 23.101.

In sum, the LLC is an attractive form of business entity because it provides protection from personal liability for its members coupled with a flexible management style. Thus, it has been widely adopted by professionals such as doctors, lawyers, and accountants. Ciccotello, at 22.

Internet Assignment

1. Access the site of the Citation Formats Committee of the American Association of Law Libraries at http://www.aallnet.org/committee/citation. How did Arizona implement its neutral citation form rule?

2. Review the Universal Citation Guide, Second Edition, at http://www.aallnet.org/committee/citation. Show the recommended citation form for *Smith v. Jones*, the 1998 Wisconsin case displayed.

3. Access the ABA Legal Technology Resource Center at http://www.abanet.org/tech/ltrc/research/citation/home.html. Access the 2003 House of Delegates resolution relating to citation form. Briefly, what did the resolution recommend?

4. Access the website for *The Bluebook* and review "Blue Tips."
   a. Generally, how should a citation to a plurality opinion be treated?
   b. Is "at" used in short citations to the U.S. Constitution?

5. Access the website of the Association for Legal Writing Directors at http://www.alwd.org. Select "ALWD Citation Manual Resources" and then "Third Edition Resources."
   a. Review the information on Rule 22 relating to citing books and treatises. How should you treat a book written by three or more authors?
   b. Review the information on Rule 14 relating to citing statutes. What are the first three most common mistakes made in citing statutes?

6. Access the website "Introduction to Basic Legal Citation" provided by Professor Peter W. Martin of Cornell Law School. Review the information about How to Cite Statutes. Review Section 2-320. What example is provided?

Chapter 11

Updating and Validating Your Research

Chapter Overview

Before you may cite any primary authority in any document you prepare, you must ensure it is still "good law." This is an inflexible rule of legal research. Updating and validating your authorities can be conducted manually (using a set of books called *Shepard's Citations*) or electronically on LexisNexis (using *Shepard's Citations*) or Westlaw (using its system called *KeyCite*). Previously, when everyone used the conventional print sources, the process was always called *Shepardizing*; this term is often used today to describe the process of ensuring your authorities are still valid, whether one uses *Shepard's* sources or West's KeyCite.

A. Using *Shepard's* in Print Form to Shepardize Cases

1. *Introduction*

Few people validate their authorities manually—using print rather than electronic sources—because validating electronically is quicker and provides more current information. In fact, most law firms no longer subscribe to *Shepard's* in print, relying exclusively on electronic updating. Nevertheless, a thorough grounding in the way the conventional print versions of *Shepard's* work will enhance your understanding of the techniques and value of online updating.

There is a set of *Shepard's Citations* for each set of case reports. Thus, for example, there are sets called *Shepard's Arizona Citations*, *Shepard's Atlantic Reporter Citations*, and *Shepard's United States Citations* (covering United States Supreme Court cases).

A set of *Shepard's* usually consists of two or three hardbound volumes (always a deep maroon color) and one or two softcover advance sheets. To be sure that you have all of the volumes of *Shepard's* you need, look at the most recent softcover supplement. The front of each supplement displays a notice labeled "What Your Library Should Contain," which lists the volumes of *Shepard's* you will need to complete your task.

2. *Locating* Shepard's *References to Your Case*

Assume the case you are Shepardizing is *People v. Briceno*, 99 P.3d 1007 (Cal. 2004). Because this is a case published in the *Pacific Reporter*, you will need to locate the volumes of *Shepard's Pacific Reporter Citations*. Open the first volume in the set and scan the upper corners of each page looking for a reference to **Vol. 99**, the volume of the *Pacific Reporter, Third Series,* in which *Briceno* is reported. This process is similar to looking at the guide words in the upper corners of each page in a dictionary or telephone directory to determine which page will contain the word or name you need.

When you have located the page or pages for **Vol. 99**, scan this page looking for the black boldfaced typed reference **–1007–**, because this is the page on which *Briceno* begins (see Figure 11-1). There are three possibilities.

• **No Reference.** It is possible that there is no reference at all to **–1007–**. Lack of a reference to your page is an indication that during the period of time covered by that volume of *Shepard's*, no case or other authority mentioned *Briceno* in any manner. If this occurs, proceed to examine the next *Shepard's* volume, and so forth.

• **References in Parentheses.** Citations or references appearing in parentheses immediately below **–1007–** are parallel citations for *Briceno*. The first time a volume of *Shepard's* mentions your case, you will be given parallel citations (assuming they exist). This is an easy and efficient way of locating parallel citations.

• **References Not in Parentheses.** Citations listed below **–1007–** that do not appear in parentheses are references to the history and treatment of *Briceno* as it has traveled through the courts and to sources that have mentioned, discussed, or commented on *Briceno*.

3. *Analysis of* Shepard's *References*

a. Abbreviations

You may have already observed that the presentation of citations in *Shepard's* is not in *Bluebook* or *ALWD* format. In fact, the citations givenyou by *Shepard's* have a uniquely cramped appearance, such as follows:

Figure 11-1
Sample Page from *Shepard's Pacific Reporter Citations*

PACIFIC REPORTER, 3d SERIES (California Cases) Vol. 101

39CaR3d158
41CaR3d389
j 114P3d815
Cir. 2
d 402FS2d440
Cir. 5
f 2006USApp [LX1066
f 163FedAppx [308
39SFR1045
104McL1407

Vol. 96

—30—
People v Coffman and Marlow
2004
cc 17CaR3d825
cc 96P3d126
2006Cal LX [5392
2006Cal LX [5867
20CaR3d365
22CaR3d24
24CaR3d[74]657
25CaR3d349
25CaR3d713
26CaR3d43
26CaR3d884
29CaR3d599
30CaR3d531
31CaR3d[149] [147
32CaR3d[25]48
32CaR3d[14]251
32CaR3d[26]914
33CaR3d527
37CaR3d[51]127
37CaR3d[52]127
37CaR3d[49]131
38CaR3d126
f 38CaR3d130
38CaR3d171
e 39CaR3d451
40CaR3d147
41CaR3d615
f 42CaR3d45
42CaR3d305
101P3d976
106P3d1001
107P3d823
108P3d217
114P3d773
115P3d[149]460
116P3d[25]515
116P3d[142]517
117P3d[26]608
118P3d560
126P3d962
f 126P3d965
126P3d999
129P3d345
131P3d1014
f 132P3d247
Cir. 9
2006USDist [LX10612
2006USDist [LX13546
92VaL327

—126—
People v Marlow
2004
US cert den
544US953
US cert den
161LE532
US cert den
125SC1706
cc 17CaR3d710
cc 96P3d30

—141—
In re Marriage of Harris
2004
2006CalApp [LX471
29CaR3d247
34CaR3d[3]484
37CaR3d[5]318
37CaR3d[6]318
37CaR3d[3]458
38CaR3d[3]21
f 38CaR3d618
e 38CaR3d618
d 38CaR3d902
39CaR3d793
112P3d634
f 121P3d298
f 127P3d34
e 127P3d34
129P3d5
36GGU121
38LoyL1871
78SCL1529

—170—
People v Haley
2004
~ 23CaR3d401
26CaR3d15
41CaR3d614
f 41CaR3d651
108P3d194
131P3d1013
f 131P3d1044

—194—
Sav-On Drug Stores, Inc. v Superior Court
2004
26CaR3d339
#f 26CaR3d339
29CaR3d416
32CaR3d487
~ 32CaR3d496
34CaR3d[5]576
34CaR3d[2]584
34CaR3d[5]587
35CaR3d[2]100
f 35CaR3d[2]270
35CaR3d[2]270
35CaR3d[7]270
35CaR3d[1]679
113P3d95
116P3d1166
~ 116P3d1173
Cir. 9
2006USDist [LX9010
2006USDist [LX26778

—496—
Claxton v Waters
2004
j 36CaR3d340
37CaR3d[4]212
j 123P3d614

—507—
People v Barker
2004
20CaR3d364
#f 20CaR3d365
20CaR3d500
24CaR3d265
f 24CaR3d268
25CaR3d105
26CaR3d372
26CaR3d883
28CaR3d659
34CaR3d656
38CaR3d633
39CaR3d827
111P3d932
120P3d1050
127P3d48
129P3d34

Vol. 98

—876—
People v Williams
2004
d 28CaR3d10
j 28CaR3d20
d 110P3d1223
j 110P3d1232

Vol. 99

—500—
Stockett v Association of Cal. Water Agencies Joint Powers Ins. Authority
2004
2006CalApp [LX717
25CaR3d57
Cir. 9
2005USDist [LX26941
2005USDist [LX27375
2006USDist [LX6838
f 2006USDist [LX26651
2006USDist [LX28446

—505—
People v Turner
2004
30CaR3d551
32CaR3d42
32CaR3d[11]889
33CaR3d[11]32
33CaR3d433
39CaR3d892
41CaR3d336
114P3d790
116P3d510
117P3d[11]587
117P3d[11]649
118P3d481
131P3d414

—1007—
People v Briceno
2004
22CaR3d277
22CaR3d421
22CaR3d852
f 22CaR3d853
j 30CaR3d579
33CaR3d[2]635
34CaR3d16
f 34CaR3d[10]17
f 34CaR3d18
36CaR3d[3]454
j 39CaR3d188
j 114P3d813

—1015—
McClung v Employment Development Dept.
2004
j 22CaR3d530
25CaR3d[21]456
25CaR3d[6]508
25CaR3d[18]508
26CaR3d535
26CaR3d[3]633
30CaR3d11
36CaR3d548
d 36CaR3d549
f 37CaR3d[1]28
37CaR3d[2]28
37CaR3d[8]29
37CaR3d[11]29
37CaR3d[14]29
38CaR3d502
f 40CaR3d645
j 102P3d914
32WSR155

Vol. 100

—870—
People v Seel
2004
2006Cal LX [6173

Vol. 101

—140—
Graham v DaimlerChrysler Corp.
2004
2006CalApp [LX728
2006CalApp [LX789
2006CalApp [LX801
19CaR3d322
f 21CaR3d375
j 21CaR3d377
23CaR3d470
24CaR3d820
24CaR3d879
25CaR3d523
30CaR3d206
33CaR3d273
33CaR3d[1]281
33CaR3d[2]281
33CaR3d[13]281
f 33CaR3d283
33CaR3d[11]284
33CaR3d779
33CaR3d[1]822
37CaR3d[9]553
37CaR3d[11]645
38CaR3d[11]29
38CaR3d[19]65
38CaR3d[21]65
39CaR3d560
39CaR3d793
40CaR3d220
41CaR3d561
d 41CaR3d566
104P3d827
106P3d316
129P3d5
129P3d407
Cir. 9
f 2005USDist [LX36806
2005USDist [LX40142
f 373FS2d1032
d 407FS2d1122
q 407FS2d1123
42SDL1295

—174—
Tipton-Whittingham v City of Los Angeles
2004
2006CalApp [LX789
j 21CaR3d362
33CaR3d273
33CaR3d[3]282
f 33CaR3d283
33CaR3d[7]283
33CaR3d[2]285
39CaR3d793
41CaR3d566
129P3d5
Cir. 9
d 2005USDist [LX40142
373FS2d1033

—478—
People v Ramos
2004
US cert den
163LE108
US cert den
126SC91
31CaR3d[14]506
31CaR3d[15]506
32CaR3d[26]866
33CaR3d544
35CaR3d787
36CaR3d776
f 36CaR3d777
115P3d[14]1162
115P3d[15]1162
117P3d[26]568
118P3d575
122P3d991
f 124P3d377

—509—
People v San Nicolas
2004
US cert den
163LE79
US cert den
126SC46
29CaR3d849
30CaR3d706
32CaR3d522

Continued

461

331FS716 (interpreted as 331 F. Supp. 716).

Because *Shepard's* is tasked with presenting so much information as efficiently as possible, it has developed its own "shorthand" references for cases and other legal authorities. You will quickly learn how to correctly interpret the *Shepard's* references. If you have any difficulty, each volume of *Shepard's* contains a Table of Abbreviations decoding its abbreviations.

b. History References

Shepard's will provide you with the subsequent history of your case, meaning you will be informed how your case has been dealt with as it has progressed through the courts. Thus, you will be informed whether your case has been affirmed or reversed, whether certiorari was denied, and so forth. *Shepard's* provides you with this information, called *history references*, relating to the later history of your case by means of an identifying letter placed immediately before the citation. Most of the letters are easy to understand. For example, "a" means "affirmed"; "r" means "reversed"; and "m" means "modified." If you have difficulty understanding the meaning of a history letter, locate the Table of Abbreviations in each *Shepard's* volume.

c. Treatment References

Shepard's will not only tell you how your case has been dealt with by higher courts, but will also refer you to every other case as well as selected law reviews, annotations, and other authorities that discuss or even mention your case in passing. These sources, called *treatment references*, have been thoroughly analyzed, and *Shepard's* will inform you specifically how your case has been treated by these other sources, namely, whether it was followed by a later case, mentioned in a dissenting opinion, or criticized or questioned by a later authority. Some of the most common treatment abbreviations are as follows: "c" (for "criticized"); "d" (for "distinguished"); "e" (for "explained"); "f" (for "followed"); "o" (for "overruled"); and "q" (for "questioned").

Shepard's provides you with this information by means of an identifying letter placed immediately before the reference. Once again, most of the letters are easy to interpret, but if you have difficulty interpreting the letters, check the Table of Abbreviations in each *Shepard's* volume.

Pay careful attention in examining the treatment of your case. If the case you are relying upon is continually being questioned or criticized, you may wish to reevaluate your research strategies and attempt to locate a case that is more authoritative.

The absence of an identifying letter before a citation reference means that the later case merely mentions your case in passing or in a string cite, and there was no significant analysis of your case.

Practice Tip: History and Treatment

The difference between the *history* of a case and the *treatment* of it is readily illustrated by comparing *reversed* (relating to the history of a case) with *overruled* (relating to the treatment of a case). A reversal refers to the later treatment of your case by a higher court discussing that very case. An overruling refers to how a case is treated by some entirely different case, perhaps years later. For example, *Brown v. Board of Education*, 347 U.S. 483 (1954), overruled the much earlier case of *Plessy v. Ferguson*, 163 U.S. 539 (1896).

4. Arrangement of Later Case References

When *Shepard's* lists the cases that mention your case, it arranges the references in chronological order so you are first sent to earlier cases mentioning your case and then to more recent cases. Thus, although *Shepard's* does not provide dates for the cases it lists, you can easily select more recent cases. Also, *Shepard's* references are precise; they direct you to the very page within a case on which your case is being discussed, rather than directing you to the first page of a case. Finally, *Shepard's* will arrange the cases by jurisdiction, when relevant, grouping together entries by circuit or state so you can readily locate cases from a specific jurisdiction that discuss your case.

5. References to Headnotes

Recall that when a case is reviewed by editors at a publishing company, they will assign headnote numbers for each legal issue in a case. It is possible that you are relying on only a portion of a case in a brief or other document you have written. Assume, for example, that you are relying on headnote 1 of *Briceno*. *Shepard's* will not only provide you with information relating to the treatment by later cases of *Briceno*, but will also focus on the cases that have discussed specific headnotes of this case.

These references are accomplished by small elevated or superscript numbers placed immediately after the case citation given to you by *Shepard's*. For example, when Shepardizing *Briceno*, you observe that one of the *Shepard's* entries is 33CaR3d^{2}635 (see Figure 11-1). This indicates that page 635 of volume 33 of the *California Reporter, Third Series,* discusses the point of law discussed in headnote 2 of *Briceno*. This feature of *Shepard's* allows you readily to locate later cases discussing the specific points of law discussed in your case.

Also, if you discover that only headnote 4 of *Briceno* has been criticized or questioned, and you are relying solely on the point of law discussed in headnote 1 of *Briceno*, you may be able to bypass those references with elevated numbers other than "1." If a case is listed without an elevated number, this indicates that the later case discusses your case only in a general fashion.

6. *References to Sources Other Than Cases*

In addition to validating the case you rely on, *Shepard's* will direct you to a wide variety of other sources that mention or discuss your case. Thus, *Shepard's* functions as a finding tool to expand your research efforts by sending you to a variety of sources, including the following: attorneys general opinions, law review articles, and A.L.R. annotations.

See Figure 11-2 for steps in Shepardizing cases using the print volumes of *Shepard's*.

Figure 11-2
Steps in Shepardizing a Case Using Print Sources

- Locate the volumes of *Shepard's* you need (state *Shepard's*, regional *Shepard's*, or federal case *Shepard's*).
- Examine the front cover of the most recent issue of *Shepard's* and read the box labeled "What Your Library Should Contain." Make sure you have all of the volumes needed.
- Select the volumes of *Shepard's* that contain citations to cases decided after your case was decided.
- Examine the upper right and left corners of the pages in *Shepard's* to locate the volume number of the case you are Shepardizing.
- Scan down the page looking for the bold page number identical to the page on which your case begins.
- Carefully examine the entries listed, paying particular attention to the parallel citation, the history of the case as it progressed through the court system, its treatment by later cases, and any other sources, such as annotations and law review articles that cite your case.
- If desired, verify that you are Shepardizing correctly by checking one or two cites listed by *Shepard's* to ensure your case is, in fact, mentioned by these cites.
- Repeat, as needed, in other volumes of *Shepard's*.
- Examine and analyze troublesome entries, including later cases that criticize or question your case.

7. *FAQs: Using* Shepard's *and Analyzing Negative Letters*

Following are some of the most frequently asked questions relating to the Shepardizing process:

Question: Must I read every case or source mentioned by *Shepard's*?

Answer: You must certainly read any reference with a "negative" letter, such as "overruled." However, if you are pleased with your research project, you believe the cases you have cited clearly and articulately support the arguments you have made, and Shepardizing reveals no negative treatment, your task is complete. On the other hand, if the issue you are researching is an uncertain area of the law or a newly emerging legal topic, read some of the later cases identified in *Shepard's* to obtain better insight.

Question: How can I use *Shepard's* to find better or newer cases?

Answer: If you are not entirely pleased with the cases you have located, or the cases are a bit older than you would prefer, use *Shepard's* as a research tool to locate newer cases, cases from higher courts, or cases that more persuasively explain a legal issue. Look for "f" for "followed" or "e" for "explained" and read these cases.

Question: What should I do if my Shepardizing reveals a "negative" letter?

Answer: In all instances, retrieve and read the cases that have been assigned any negative letters; however, understand that it is possible that only a portion of your case has been limited or overruled and that the remainder is still authoritative. Carefully examine the elevated numbers to be sure that the part of the case you rely on (and not some other part or headnote) is, in fact, negatively treated.

Question: My case has two parallel citations—which do I Shepardize?

Answer: For state cases with parallel citations, most legal professionals Shepardize in the companion *Shepard's* for their cases. Thus, if you read a case in the *Kansas Reports*, Shepardize it in *Shepard's Kansas Citations* (rather than *Shepard's Pacific Reporter Citations*). This procedure will enable you to most effectively use the elevated (superscript) numbers given by *Shepard's* to pinpoint later discussion of the headnotes from your case. It is not necessary to Shepardize both parallel citations; if your case has received negative treatment, *Shepard's* will inform you of such, no matter what set you use.

Question: When should I Shepardize?

Answer: When to Shepardize is left to your discretion. Consider Shepardizing fairly early in your research process for two reasons:

- To eliminate the possibility of discovering that a key case has been overruled or reversed, causing a last-minute crisis; and
- To locate other valuable research leads to develop your argument.

Some researchers Shepardize almost concurrently with performing legal research. In any event, you must Shepardize before any document with citations is filed with a court or given to your supervising attorney, a client, or the adverse party.

Question: How many volumes do I use when I Shepardize?

Answer: When you first learn to Shepardize, use all volumes. As you gain familiarity with the process, you will notice that the spines of the *Shepard's* volumes are marked with volume numbers or dates, and you need not Shepardize for any date before your case was decided. Remember, however, that the volumes of *Shepard's* are not always cumulative; each volume of *Shepard's* relates to a distinct period of time. As a rule of thumb, the older your case is, the more volumes of *Shepard's* you will need to examine.

Question: What if I never find any references in *Shepard's* for my case?

Answer: If your case is new, it is possible that no other cases have yet discussed your case; however, it is possible that you have transposed numbers in your citation. Thus, carefully check your citation for accuracy.

B. Using *Shepard's* in Print Form to Shepardize Other Authorities

1. Shepardizing Statutes, Constitutions, and Administrative Regulations

Just as you must Shepardize a case to determine whether it is still "good law," you must Shepardize the other primary authorities you rely on: statutes, constitutions, and administrative regulations (such as the regulations of the Federal Communications Commission). The process of Shepardizing these authorities is the same as that for cases.

- Locate the volume(s) of *Shepard's* you need, titled *Shepard's* [State] *Citations for Statutes*, *Shepard's Federal Statute Citations*, or *Shepard's Code of Federal Regulations Citations*.
- Examine the upper right and left corners of the pages in *Shepard's* to locate the title or article of the provision you are Shepardizing.
- Scan down the page, looking for a boldfaced entry for the particular section in which you are interested.
- Carefully examine the entries listed, paying particular attention to the history of your statute, constitutional provision, or regulation (for example, whether the statute has been amended or repealed by the legislature) and then to its treatment by later cases (for example, whether a case merely discussed your statute or decided your statute was unconstitutional). Each volume of *Shepard's* will contain a Table of Abbreviations for any abbreviations used. Examine other sources, such as law review articles and annotations, if desired.
- Carefully analyze all troublesome entries. For example, "A2004C37" means that your statute has been amended and that the amending language can be found in Chapter 37 of your state's session laws for 2004.

2. *Shepardizing Other Authorities*

There are several other authorities that you can Shepardize, including Restatements, court rules, and treaties. You will then be directed to authorities that have discussed your Restatement provision, court rule, or treaty.

Help Line: Shepard's *Daily Update Service*

The print volumes of *Shepard's* are updated approximately every six weeks. To make sure that nothing has happened in the past six weeks that negatively affects your case or statute, use *Shepard's* Daily Update Service. Call (800) 899-6000 to determine what has happened to your case since your last print supplement arrived. Information may be as current as 24 to 48 hours from the time of decision from the courts. The service is also available on the Internet. Send an email to helpcite@lexisnexis.com.

C. Electronic Updating of Legal Authorities

1. *Introduction to Electronic Updating*

For nearly 100 years, legal researchers updated their legal authorities through the conventional print versions of *Shepard's*. Electronic updating, however, provides more up-to-date validation of legal authorities and is easily accomplished. There is no need to learn quirky abbreviations. Negative history, such as reversal of a case, appears in plain English. Electronic updating eliminates the worry that you do not have all of the print volumes in a set of *Shepard's*. Updating and checking your adversary's citations are easily accomplished. Finally, references are available online far more quickly than the print versions of *Shepard's* are published, thus giving you the most recent treatment of your authorities. Consequently, updating electronically is the preferred method for nearly all legal professionals. In fact, most law firms and law libraries no longer subscribe to the print volumes of *Shepard's*, and all updating is accomplished electronically, through the use of *Shepard's* online (offered by LexisNexis) or through West's online product, KeyCite.

2. *Shepardizing Online*

a. How to Shepardize Cases Online Using LexisNexis

Assume the case you are updating is *United States v. Falstaff Brewing Corp.*, 332 F. Supp. 970 (D.R.I. 1971).

- If you are viewing this case on the LexisNexis screen, a *Shepard's* signal indicator will be displayed on the screen. If you click it, *Falstaff* will be immediately Shepardized.
- If you are not currently viewing *Falstaff* on your screen but are instead perhaps validating a written brief that mentions *Falstaff*, follow these steps:
  - Sign on to LexisNexis.
  - Click the *Shepard's* tab at the top of your screen.
  - Type in your citation (332 fs 970) in the open field.
  - By clicking the word "Check" on your screen, select one of the following options: "*Shepard's* for Research" (also called "FULL"), which will list every authority that mentions *Falstaff* or "*Shepard's* for Validation" (also called "KWIC"), which will provide you with negative history only, rather than all authorities that mention *Falstaff*. (See Figure 11-3.)

You are now ready to interpret your results. You will be informed, in plain English, whether *Falstaff* has been distinguished, criticized, followed, and so forth. If you are interested in one of these references, click on it and you will be immediately transported to that reference, thereby eliminating the need for you to run around the library collecting references that distinguish, criticize, or follow *Falstaff*.

Shepard's uses *Signal Indicators* to inform you at a glance of the status of your case. These signal indicators appear at the top of the authority you are viewing on the screen. The following signal indicator graphics are used:

- **Red Stop Sign:** This signal warns that your case has strong negative history or treatment (such as being reversed).
- **Red Exclamation Point in a Red Circle:** A statute has been treated negatively by a later case.
- **Letter "Q" in an Orange Square:** The validity of your case has been questioned by other cases.
- **Yellow Yield Sign/Triangle:** This signal indicates that your case may have some negative history or treatment (such as being criticized).
- **Green Plus Sign:** Your case has positive history (such as being affirmed).
- **Letter "A" in a Blue Circle:** Your case has been analyzed in a neutral manner (such as being explained by a later case).
- **Letter "I" in a Blue Circle:** Other citation information is available for your case (such as a law review article that mentions your case).

Figure 11-3
Reviewing *Shepard's* Results Online

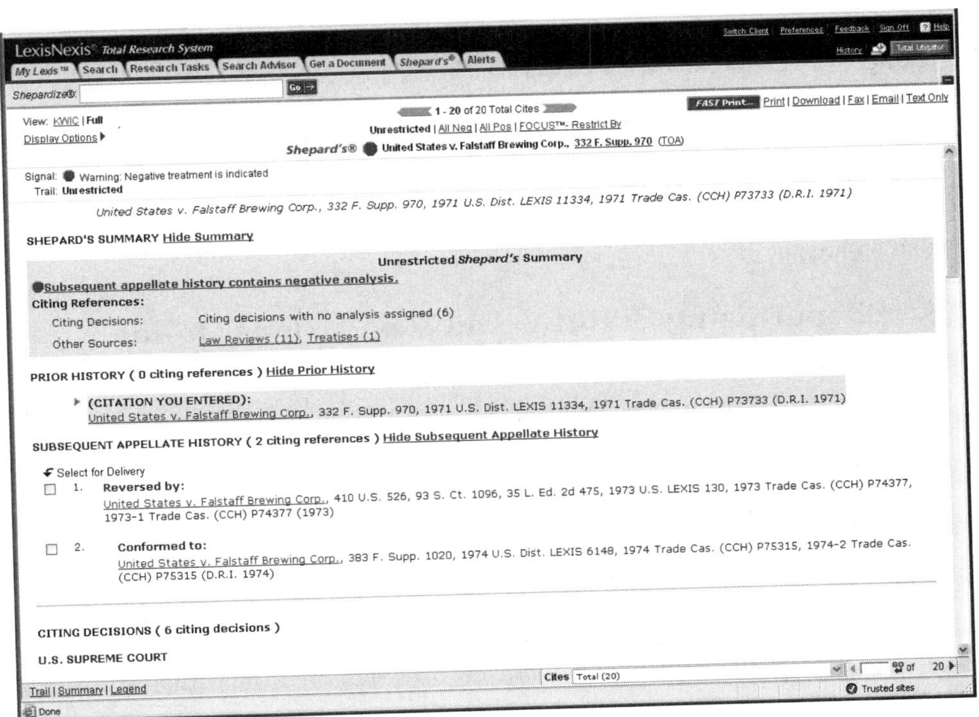

These signals make Shepardizing online extremely easy because they tell you at a glance whether your citation is in trouble or whether it is cleared for your use. Note, however, that a red stop sign does not necessarily mean that your case is no longer good law; it simply means that your case has received some negative treatment that you need to analyze.

b. Features of *Shepard's* Online

Shepard's provides a number of tools to maximize your research efforts:

- **FULL.** If you select "FULL" you will be given all prior and subsequent appellate history of your case and every reference from any case, law review, periodical, treatise, and A.L.R. annotation that mentions your case.
- **KWIC.** Selecting the KWIC option provides a quick answer to the question, "Is my case still good law?" You will not be sent to law review articles and other authorities that merely mention your case. Use KWIC when you are satisfied with your research efforts and only want to confirm that your case is still valid.
- **Summary.** Begin your analysis with *Shepard's* "Summary," which presents a readable summary showing why your case received a signal indicator. For example, you might be informed that your case was distinguished two times, followed once, and mentioned in six law reviews.
- **Custom Restrictions.** *Shepard's* allows you to narrow the results you desire by selecting groups of citations to review by date, jurisdiction, and so forth. For example, you can elect to see only those cases that explain *Falstaff* or only those cases that follow *Falstaff* after a certain date.
- **Alert.** Alert is a clipping service that automatically reports changes in the treatment of *Falstaff*. You can elect to be notified daily, weekly, and so forth, by email message.
- **Table of Authorities.** Assume that *Falstaff* relied on and cited four cases. *Shepard's* validation tool called *Table of Authorities* analyzes those four cases cited in *Falstaff*, allowing you to reevaluate the cases on which *Falstaff* relied (because if their authority is weakened, *Falstaff* may also be suspect).

c. Shepardizing Statutes and Regulations Online

Shepardizing statutes or regulations online is nearly identical to Shepardizing cases online. To Shepardize 18 U.S.C.S. § 212 (LexisNexis 2000), follow these steps:

- Sign on to http://www.lexisnexis.com.
- Click the *Shepard's* tab at the top of your screen.
- Type in your citation (18 uscs 212) in the open field.
- Select "FULL" (and you will be given every authority that mentions your statute) or "KWIC" (and you will be given negative history only rather than all authorities that mention your statute).

d. Other *Shepard's* Products

(1) *Automatic Validation Through BriefCheck*

One of the most significant advances in validating citations is the availability of software programs that automatically check whether your legal authorities are still good law. Assume your research project cites 20 cases. Keying in 20 separate entries and then reading the results for these 20 cases can be time consuming.

Shepard's offers a software program called *BriefCheck* (formerly known as CheckCite), which automatically checks all citations in your brief, without the necessity of your keying in a single citation. The program "reads" your brief, locates and extracts your citations, checks them, and then provides the results either on your screen or in a separate printed report. You can elect "FULL" Shepardizing or the "KWIC" option. BriefCheck also checks your quotations for accuracy and locates discrepancies in case names, dates, and page numbers. BriefCheck is also useful for checking your adversary's documents to determine whether authorities cited are still good law.

(2) *StyleCheck*

StyleCheck (formerly known as CiteRite) is Lexis's citation-checking software program that checks your citations for proper form using *Bluebook* rules (or the *California Style Manual*). You will be given parallel cites and informed of errors in punctuation (such as neglecting the period after "Cal"), incorrect abbreviations, and other errors. It is unclear, however, whether StyleCheck can thoroughly master the intricacies of citation form, such as when you may abbreviate "Western." Nevertheless, it is a valuable tool for preliminary checking of citation form errors in both primary and secondary authorities.

(3) *FullAuthority*

Many courts require that briefs submitted to them include a table listing each authority cited in the brief with a reference to the pages in the brief on which the authority is cited. *FullAuthority* reads your brief or document and automatically creates a *table of authorities* for you, separating federal cases from state cases, and so forth, eliminating the need for you to create this table manually. Always double-check the table generated by FullAuthority to ensure it is correct and to make sure case names are presented consistently.

(4) Shepard's *Link*

A new software application called *Shepard's Link* (formerly known as LEXLink) identifies citations in a word processing document (for example, a brief you are drafting) and creates hyperlinks to LexisNexis so readers of your document can instantly link to the cases you cite.

3. *KeyCite*

a. How to KeyCite Cases Using Westlaw

KeyCite is West's service that electronically updates and validates your legal authorities. KeyCite can be accessed on the Internet through http://www.westlaw.com. Although there are some differences between online Shepardizing and KeyCiting, the services are probably more alike than different.

Assume you want to KeyCite the *Falstaff* case.

- If you are viewing this case on the Westlaw screen, a KeyCite status flag will be displayed at the top of your case (red, yellow, or a blue "H") or the word "update" will be displayed. Click the flag or "update" to access KeyCite.
- If you are not currently viewing *Falstaff* on your screen but are instead perhaps validating a written brief that mentions *Falstaff*, follow these steps:
  - Sign onto Westlaw at http://www.westlaw.com.
  - Click the KeyCite tab on the toolbar at the top of your screen.
  - Type in your citation (332 fs 970) in the open field and click "Go."
  - Alternatively, you may type a citation in the "KeyCite this citation" text box that is displayed in the left frame of many screens.

You are now ready to interpret your results. The first thing that appears is any history of the case. Like *Shepard's* online, KeyCite uses signal indicators or graphics to instantly convey information to you about the status of your case:

• **Red Flag.** A red flag warns that your case is no longer good law for at least one of the issues it discusses (such as being reversed or overruled).

• **Yellow Flag.** A yellow flag warns that the case has some negative history, such as being criticized or limited.

• **Blue "H."** The case has some history, such as being explained or having certiorari granted.

• **Green "C."** This signal indicates that the case has been cited by some references but there is no direct history or negative citing references. (See Figure 11-5 for some KeyCite graphics.)

You can easily link to cases that discuss *Falstaff* by clicking on them.

b. Features of KeyCite

KeyCite offers several features (see Figures 11-4 and 11-5) to assist you with your citation updating and validating:

• **Citation History Options.** You can customize your KeyCite results to display different types of case history for your case. By clicking on "Full History," you will be given the complete history of your case; by clicking on "Citing References," you will be directed to other cases and sources that mention or discuss your case, including secondary sources and briefs that cite your case.

- **Graphical Display of Direct History.** A new Westlaw feature shows you the direct history of your case in an easy-to-understand flowchart format. For example, you would be shown in graphical format, using arrows, how your case progressed from trial, through its initial appeal, when certiorari was granted, and then what the United States Supreme Court held. You may easily link to the court briefs and motions filed at each level of the case's history.
- **Limit KeyCite History Display.** If the list of sources that mention your case is lengthy, you can restrict or narrow your list. Select the "Limit KeyCite Display" button at the bottom of the screen to narrow results by date, jurisdiction, headnote, and so forth. For example, you elect to view only cases that discuss headnote 2 of *Falstaff*.
- **Depth of Treatment Stars.** As KeyCite lists the cases that mention *Falstaff*, a number of green stars may be displayed next to each citation. These stars tell you the extent to which a citing case discusses *Falstaff*. Four green stars means that the case examines *Falstaff* in depth; three green stars indicates a substantial discussion of *Falstaff*; two stars means there is some brief discussion of *Falstaff*; and one star indicates that *Falstaff* was mentioned in passing, usually in a string citation. (See Figure 11-5.)

Figure 11-4
KeyCite Screen Showing History of Case

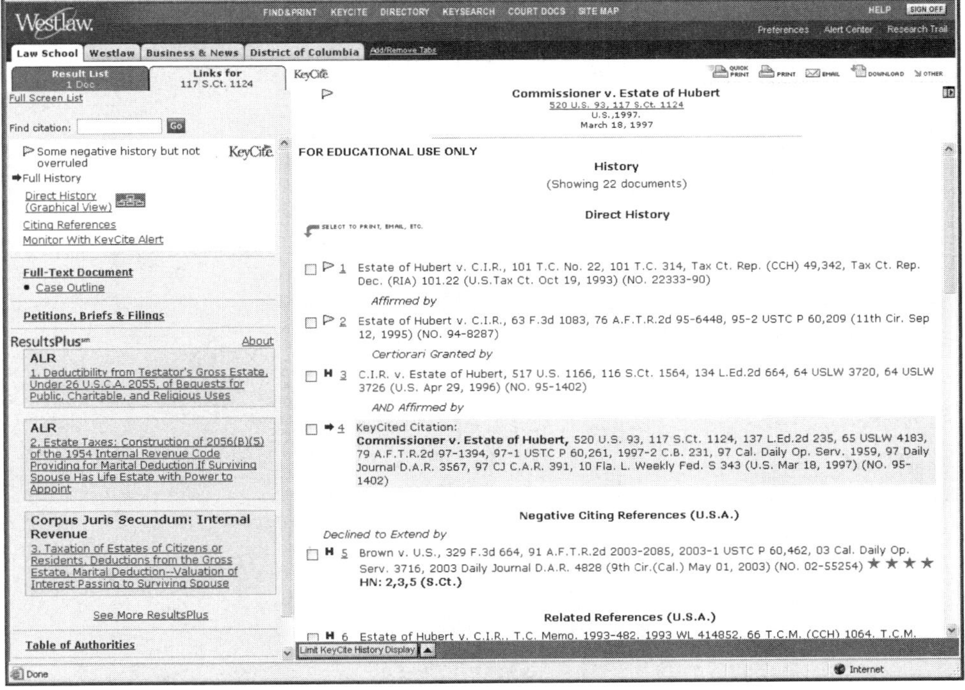

Figure 11-5
KeyCite Symbols

Red Flag - Your case is no longer good law for at least one of the points it contains.

Yellow Flag - Your case has some negative history, but hasn't been reversed or overruled.

H **Blue H** - Your case has some history.

C **Green C** - Your case has citing references but no direct or negative indirect history.

Depth of treatment stars help you determine how extensively your case has been discussed in a citing case:

★★★★ Examined
★★★ Discussed
★★ Cited
★ Mentioned

" **Quotation Marks** - Indicate that some language from your case is quoted word for word in the citing case.

HN (Headnote) - "HN#" indicates the legal issue(s) for which your case was cited.

• **Quotation Marks.** If KeyCite displays quotation marks (") after a case citation, it means that the case quotes from *Falstaff*. (See Figure 11-5.)

• **Headnote References.** *Falstaff's* headnote references are clearly displayed. Thus, a reference to **"HN:3"** means that the case discusses the point of law discussed in headnote 3 of *Falstaff*. (See Figure 11-5.)

• **KeyCite Alert.** KeyCite Alert is a clipping service that automatically notifies you of any changes in the treatment of *Falstaff*. You can restrict its coverage so that, for example, you are only notified of later negative treatment of *Falstaff*. You can elect to be notified daily, weekly, and so forth, by email message.

• **Table of Authorities.** Once again, assume that *Falstaff* relied on and cited four cases. West's validation tool called *Table of Authorities* analyzes those four cases cited in *Falstaff*, allowing you to reevaluate the cases on which *Falstaff* relied (because if their authority is weakened, *Falstaff* may also be suspect). This product is identical to LexisNexis's product (which shares the same name) and is useful for finding weaknesses in cases relied on by your adversary.

• **Petitions, Briefs & Filings.** By selecting this button, you will be linked to various court documents and briefs filed by the attorneys for the parties in the *Falstaff* case.

c. KeyCiting Statutes and Regulations

KeyCiting statutes or regulations online is nearly identical to KeyCiting cases online. To KeyCite 18 U.S.C.A. § 212 (West 2000), follow these steps:

- Sign on to http://www.westlaw.com.
- Click the KeyCite tab at the top of your screen.
- Type in your citation (18 usca 212) in the open field and click "Go." Alternatively, you may type a citation in the "KeyCite this Citation" text box that is displayed on the screen and click "Go." If you are viewing the statute on your screen, simply click on its flags or signals displayed at the top of your screen.
- After you enter your statute citation in KeyCite, you may either select "History" (to view the history of a statute, including links to recent session laws that amend or affect your statute and historical and statutory notes describing the legislative changes affecting your statute); "Citing References" (to view cases and other authorities that mention your statute); or "Graphical Statutes" (to view a timeline showing you the enactment history of the statute and allowing you to link to prior versions of the statute, conference reports, and other pertinent legislative materials).

You may also limit your results by selecting specific jurisdictions that have issued cases citing your statute, selecting documents mentioning your statute during specific time periods, and so forth. KeyCite provides status flags for statutes as well as cases, using a red flag to warn you that a statute has been amended, repealed, or held unconstitutional; a yellow flag to indicate that the statute has been limited or is subject to pending legislation; and a green "C" to show that various authorities cite your statute. The process for updating regulations is nearly identical to that of updating statutes.

d. Other West Products

(1) Automatic Citation Validation Through WestCheck

Similar to LexisNexis's BriefCheck, West offers a software program called *WestCheck*, which automatically extracts citations from your document, checks their validity, and produces a printed report with the results of the check. WestCheck can also create a table of authorities listing the cases and authorities you have cited in your document. The advantage of using WestCheck rather than KeyCiting each individual case is that WestCheck automatically "reads" your document and validates your citations, thus saving you the time of keying in each citation you wish to check.

The process is easily accomplished. Once the software is "loaded" onto your computer, you merely open your brief or other document that contains the citations you wish to check and then click the WestCheck button on your toolbar.

WestCheck is also now available to anyone with Internet access. This product (WestCheck.com) eliminates the need to load software onto your computer. You simply attach your Word or WordPerfect document and run it through WestCheck.com, which will automatically extract and check your citations to ensure they are still good law. Alternatively, you can "cut and paste" your brief into a text box. An easy-to-read online report (using KeyCite flags and symbols) is provided. Access http://westcheck.com to use the service or take a training tutorial. This Internet-based service allows legal professionals to use their BlackBerrys and perform a last-minute validation check on the way to the courthouse.

(2) WestCiteLink

A new product from West, *WestCiteLink* (similar to LexisNexis's *Shepard's* Link), can create hyperlinks to the cases you cite in a brief, allowing the reader of your document to have instant access to the full text of each case you have cited. WestCiteLink can also automatically create a table of authorities in your brief that lists the cases and other documents you have cited, including the page numbers on which they appear. WestCiteLink is a software program that is "loaded" onto your computer. If available at your school or law firm, a WestCiteLink will appear on your toolbar.

(3) BriefTools

West's new product *BriefTools* is a cutting edge tool that offers the following features (primarily for litigators):

- It KeyCites your authorities as you write your document and creates links from the citations in your document to the full-text document in Westlaw.
- It monitors the status of authorities you have cited in your brief or document.
- It retrieves all of your firm's internal documents that contain a particular citation.

4. *Comparing Shepardizing Online with KeyCiting*

Most schools and large law firms afford access to both LexisNexis and Westlaw, realizing their legal professionals develop distinct preferences. Although it is impossible to make absolute statements as to pricing and costs (because most firms have negotiated pricing schedules), nevertheless, fees for Shepardizing online or KeyCiting are usually assessed on a per-case basis. Generally, it costs about $7 to check any one citation. Additional fees will be charged by your law firm to the client for your time in performing the updating and reviewing results. Because fees are roughly equivalent, a decision whether to Shepardize online or KeyCite is not usually based on cost.

Beginning researchers often wonder, "Which service is better?" Both offer many of the same features: rapid and easy citation validating; the use of easy-to-understand, colorful graphics (signs and flags) to tell you at a glance that your citation is in trouble; the ability to limit or narrow your results; and the ability to immediately link to an authority that mentions your case or statute. Both services offer automatic citation updating so you need not key in individual citations.

In sum, the use of *Shepard's* online or KeyCite is usually a matter of habit, convenience, or preference. Additionally, because deciphering the reports generated by *Shepard's* online or KeyCite can be somewhat difficult (primarily because so much information is given on each screen), legal researchers tend to stick with one service after they have become familiar with its formatting and layout. Note, however, that at least one expert who has compared *Shepard's* online and KeyCite recommends that citations be checked in both databases because in his samples, between ten and thirty-seven percent of the references were missed if the citation was checked in only one system. William L. Taylor, *Comparing KeyCite and Shepard's for Completeness, Currency, and Accuracy*, 92 Law Libr. J. 127, 134 (2000), *available at* http://www.aallnet.org (select "Products & Publications").

Ethics Alert: *Duty to Update and Validate Cases*

A number of cases have reminded legal professionals of their ethical duty to update and validate the cases they cite. In *Gosnell v. Rentokil, Inc.*, 175 F.R.D. 508, 509 n.1 (N.D. Ill. 1997), the court sternly admonished the attorneys involved as follows:

> It is really inexcusable for any lawyer to fail, as a matter of routine, to Shepardize all cited cases (a process that has been made much simpler today than it was in the past, given the facility for doing so under Westlaw or LEXIS). Shepardization would of course have revealed that the "precedent" no longer qualified as such.

5. *Other Electronic Citator Services*

Although LexisNexis and Westlaw are the giants in computer-assisted legal research systems, remember from Chapter Eight that three other systems provide citation updating: Loislaw, JuriSearch, and VersusLaw. These companies generally aim their services at smaller firms or sole practitioners and charge reasonable fees, but they offer much smaller databases than LexisNexis or Westlaw. Loislaw's citator is called GlobalCite, and JuriSearch's citator is called CheckMate. Their use is similar to that of Shepardizing online or KeyCiting, but, in general, they offer fewer enhancements and features for customization. VersusLaw offers only rudimentary updating through its v.cite feature.

6. *Summary*

Updating and validating your primary authorities is the second component of cite-checking (the first being to place citations in proper *Bluebook*, *ALWD*, or local format). Although the primary function of updating is to check the status of your primary authorities, a related important function is to allow you to tap into additional legal research, because both *Shepard's* (in print form or online) and KeyCite will direct you to cases, periodicals, attorneys general opinions, annotations, and other sources that mention the authority you are updating.

The determination of when to perform your updating task is a matter of individual discretion, although updating early in the research process will not only alert you to an invalid or weakened case, statute, or regulation but also enhance your efforts by directing you to additional research sources.

Nearly all legal professionals update electronically rather than by using *Shepard's Citations* in print form. The print forms of *Shepard's Citations* will soon be relics. *Shepard's* online and KeyCite provide easy and very recent validation of legal authorities. Moreover, their new software programs (BriefCheck and WestCheck, respectively) offer automatic updating, eliminating the necessity of keying in any citations. Moreover, both LexisNexis and Westlaw are now available on handheld BlackBerry devices or iPhones, allowing legal professionals to Shepardize or KeyCite on-the-go.

Once you have Shepardized or KeyCited a few times, you will quickly get the hang of it and will find that it is an easily accomplished task. Do not assume that because Shepardizing and KeyCiting are easy and routine that they are unimportant. On the contrary, updating is one of the most critical aspects of legal research, and no project is complete until every reference to a case, statute, constitutional provision, or regulation has been updated and validated.

CyberSites

http://www.lexisnexis.com/infopro/training/reference/Shepards/Shepardscompgd.pdf	This "How to Shepardize" pamphlet offered by LexisNexis provides instructions on Shepardizing in print form and electronically.
http://web.lexis.com/help/multimedia/shepards.htm	Take a tour of various *Shepard's* services.
http://law.lexisnexis.com/shepards	*Shepard's* reference desk informs you of information relating to print *Shepard's*.
http://west.thomson.com/support/westlaw/training	West's website provides information about its products, including KeyCite and WestCheck, and offers free tutorials.
https://westcheck.com/Default.aspx	Information about WestCheck and a free tutorial are available at this site.
http://www.ll.georgetown.edu/tutorials/cases/index.cfm	Georgetown Law Center offers a tutorial on Shepardizing and KeyCiting.
https://www.lectlaw.com/files/lwr17.htm	The 'Lectric Law Library offers an excellent description on "How to Shepardize" using print volumes of *Shepard's* Citators.

Research Assignment Using Print Volumes of *Shepard's*

1. Locate the first time *Shepard's* mentions 674 P.2d 145.
   a. Give the parallel citation for this case.
   b. What negative subsequent history is given for headnote 16 of 674 P.2d 145 in this volume?
2. Use *Shepard's Federal Citations* and find the first time *Shepard's* mentions 33 F.3d 754.
   a. What Seventh Circuit case followed 33 F.3d 754?
   b. What Fifth Circuit case mentions this case in a dissent?
3. Use *Shepard's United States Citations* and find the first time 468 U.S. 491 is mentioned. What was the first case to explain this case?
4. Use the appropriate volume(s) for *Shepard's Federal Statute Citations* and Shepardize 36 U.S.C. § 5703. Give the negative history for this statute.

Research Assignment Using *Shepard's* on Lexis

1. Shepardize 222 F.3d 1298 and select the *Shepard's* icon.
   a. What is the subsequent appellate history of this case?
   b. What 2007 law review article discusses this case?
2. Shepardize 309 F. Supp. 2d 780.
   a. What is the subsequent appellate history for this case?
   b. Why does this case display the "green plus sign" *Shepard's* icon?
   c. Select "All Neg." What result are you given?
3. Shepardize 605 S.W.2d 73.
   a. What *Shepard's* icon is displayed? Why?
   b. What dissenting opinion cited your case?
4. Shepardize 490 U.S. 319.
   a. Select "TOA." How many decisions were cited by 490 U.S. 319?
   b. Why does this case have negative analysis?
5. Shepardize 524 U.S. 274.
   a. Which *Shepard's* icon is displayed? Why?
   b. How many references cite 524 U.S. 274?

6. Shepardize 45 Cal. 4th 116.
   a. What was the citation for this case at the lower California Court of Appeals?
   b. How was 45 Cal. 4th 116 later modified?
7. Shepardize 18 U.S.C.S. § 283. Select "Practitioner's Toolbox" for this statute. What is the status of this statute?
8. Shepardize 10 U.S.C.S. § 332. What is the treatment of this statute by later cases?
9. Shepardize 110 Yale Law Journal 549.
   a. Give the citation to the 2008 Alabama law review article that cites your law journal article.
   b. How many cases did 110 Yale Law Journal cite? Have any of these cases been questioned? If so, give the citation.

Research Assignment Using KeyCite on Westlaw

1. KeyCite 102 F. Supp. 2d 113 and select "Citing References."
   a. What case quotes from headnote 9 of your case?
   b. What appellate brief quotes from headnote 14 of your case?
2. KeyCite 301 F.3d 441.
   a. Select "Direct History (Graphical View)." Give the citation for your case at the trial level at the agency.
   b. Why does your case display a yellow flag?
   c. Select "Citing References." What 2004 trial court motion cited your case?
3. KeyCite 548 U.S. 212.
   a. What case declined to extend your case?
   b. Review the Petition for a Writ of Certiorari filed on July 13, 2005. What was the question posed?
4. KeyCite 545 U.S. 353. Select "Citing References" and then "Limit KeyCite History Display." Review only the law reviews that mention your case.
   a. Give the citation to the 2006 Fordham Law Review article that mentions your case.
   b. Select this law review article. Where in the article is your case mentioned?

5. KeyCite 15 U.S.C.A. § 1058.
   a. Select "Graphical Statutes." What is the public law number of the current statute text?
   b. Select this public law number. What number was assigned to this legislation in the House of Representatives?
6. KeyCite 104 Michigan Law Review 101. What Northern District of California case cites this article?
7. KeyCite 28 U.S.C.A. § 1255. What negative history are you given?

Research Assignment Comparing Shepardizing Online with KeyCiting

1. Shepardize and then KeyCite Restatement (Second) of Contracts § 51.
   a. What is the most recent federal case that cites this Restatement provision?
   b. How many citing references do Shepardizing and KeyCiting disclose for this Restatement provision?
2. Shepardize and then KeyCite 262 N.W.2d 660.
   a. What *Shepard's* and KeyCite icons are displayed?
   b. Why were these icons assigned to your case?
3. Shepardize and then KeyCite 405 So. 2d 116.
   a. How many later authorities does Lexis indicate that cited your case? Did any later cases follow your case?
   b. How many later authorities does Westlaw indicate that cited your case? Did any later cases follow your case?
4. Shepardize *People v. Horton*, 598 N.E.2d 452.
   a. How many later authorities does Lexis indicate that cited your case?
   b. Select Table of Authorities. How many cases does *People v. Horton* cite? Do any of them have any negative treatment?
5. KeyCite *People v. Horton*, 598 N.E.2d 452.
   a. How many later authorities does KeyCite indicate that cited your case?
   b. Select Table of Authorities. How many cases does *People v. Horton* cite?
   c. Do any of them have any negative treatment?

Internet Assignment

1. Access http://law.lexisnexis.com/shepards.
   a. How soon are *Shepard's* treatment and history analyses updated?
   b. Select "Brochures" and then "Shepard's Citations Service Overview." In what two ways may you use *Shepard's*?
   c. Select "Brochures" and then "Shepard's Differentiations." Why would one Shepardize a headnote?

2. Access http://law.lexisnexis.com and locate the brochure "How to Shepardize." Review the material on using *Shepard's* in print. What are the most common mistakes made when one Shepardizes using the print volumes?

3. Access West's site at http://west.thomson.com/westlaw/advantage/keycite.
   a. Select "Graphical KeyCite." What does Graphical KeyCite usually depict?
   b. Select "Get a User Guide" and review the user guide titled "KeyCite at a Glance." What does a yellow flag mean with reference to a statute?
   c. Select "Get a User Guide" and review the user guide titled "Using KeyCite on Westlaw." When direct history in the Graphical View format is displayed, what is the import of the size of the boxes?

Putting It Together

An Overview of the Research Process

Chapter 12

Overview of the Research Process

Chapter Overview

Among the most difficult tasks in performing legal research are beginning and ending the project. It is easy to become so overwhelmed at the task ahead of you that you become paralyzed at the thought of how and where to begin your legal research. Part of the difficulty lies with the tremendous mass of legal publications: millions of cases, volumes of codes, and so many secondary authorities that a researcher does not know where to turn first. LexisNexis, Westlaw, and the Internet add another layer of complexity to the research process.

Similarly, once you have begun delving into these authorities, it is difficult to know when and where to stop. This chapter offers some practical guidelines on beginning your research task and knowing when to end it.

A. How to Begin

1. Introduction

There are few inflexible rules in legal research. It is not nearly so precise as a field such as mathematics, which provides step-by-step logical guidelines to enable you to systematically reach a solution to a problem. In legal research you are asked to provide an answer to a legal question. To reach that answer, there are a number of strategies available to you. The sheer number of authorities to consult offers not only great flexibility, but also produces great uncertainty: Where do I begin? How do I begin?

Moreover, researching is rarely a straight line but often involves backtracking and revisiting sources, requiring patience and flexibility.

This chapter offers you some guidelines and strategies on getting started; however, the best approach is the one that works best for you. If everyone you know prefers to consult an annotated code first but you like to gain familiarity with a topic by reviewing an encyclopedia, then that is the best approach.

In fact, although the number of sources you can examine may be staggering, this in itself is one of the benefits of our system of legal publishing. If you cannot locate a case or statute using one research technique, there are many alternatives available to you to help you find those authorities.

2. *Thinking Things Through*

Although it is tempting to run to the library and start grabbing volumes of books as soon as you are given a research task, the time you spend thinking about a project before you begin is time well spent.

It may be helpful to write down the central question or issue. This will help you "frame" the issue and in and of itself may impose some structure on the project and suggest certain approaches to follow. After you write out the issue, develop a list of descriptive words and phrases. Because almost all legal authorities are accessed by alphabetically arranged indexes, and the descriptive word approach is usually the most efficient method of using an index, jot down the words that initially occur to you in examining the issue. These will be the words you will use in examining the indexes or online sources.

After you have considered the most obvious words, facts, and phrases, expand your list by thinking of related words, such as synonyms or antonyms. Consider the following questions, which will help you develop a list of descriptive words or phrases:

Ethics Alert: *The Two Inflexible Rules of Legal Research*

There are really only two inflexible "rules" that you must follow when you perform legal research to ensure you comply with your ethical duties of competent representation:

- If the source you review has a supplement or pocket part, you *must* check it; and
- You *must* Shepardize or KeyCite all primary authorities.

As long as you always perform these two tasks, you have tremendous freedom in solving your legal research problem.

Who is involved? Landlords? Employees?

What is the issue being considered? Termination of a lease? Wrongful discharge of an employee?

Where did the activity take place? On the leased premises? At the place of employment?

When did the activity take place? Within the last month? Year?

How did the problem arise? The tenant complained to authorities about defects at the premises? The employee alleged sexual harassment?

3. *Narrowing Down the Possibilities*

Once you have given some initial thought to your project and prepared your list of key descriptive words and phrases, narrow the universe of research sources by considering five core issues:

- **Criminal or Civil Law.** You must first determine if the action is a criminal action, brought by the federal government or your state for a wrong done to society, or a civil action, brought by a private party for a wrong done to him or her. The legal authorities, burdens of proof, punishments, and remedies are far different in criminal cases than in civil cases.
- **Jurisdiction.** You must consider which jurisdiction's authorities you will examine. If the issue is one of Texas law, then you should likely restrict your research strictly to Texas authorities. If the issue is one of federal law, narrow the focus again by considering which district court or circuit is involved. Thus, if a case for copyright infringement is filed in the U.S. District Court for the Southern District of Florida, examine cases from that district before others. Similarly, because Florida is in the Eleventh Circuit, look for other cases from the Eleventh Circuit (or U.S. Supreme Court cases).
- **Action.** Consider the legal issues involved in the case: Ask yourself what the plaintiff would allege in a lawsuit based on this issue. Would the plaintiff's action be for breach of contract? Medical malpractice? Trespass?
- **Defenses.** Once you have considered the plaintiff's "gripes," put yourself in the place of the defendant and ask what defenses the defendant would assert. Would the defendant allege that although there was a contract, he fully performed its terms? That the statute of limitations for medical malpractice has expired? That the plaintiff invited the defendant to enter his property?
- **Remedies.** After you look at the issue from the perspectives of both parties, consider what remedies the plaintiff is seeking. Is the plaintiff asking for money damages for breach of contract? For an injunction?

Figure 12-1 provides an approach that you may wish to follow to help develop your research strategy. This outline will also help you develop words to use in formulating a LexisNexis or Westlaw query.

Figure 12-1
Research Project Planner

Name: ____________________

Client Name: ____________ Case Name: __________ Assigning Attorney: ________

Client/Billing No.: _______ Date Given: ______________

Date Due: ____________

Issue/Question/Task:

____

____

____

Law Category	Jurisdiction	Descriptive Words	Synonyms	Antonyms	Plaintiff's Action	Defenses	Remedies
Civil ___ Criminal ___ Administrative ___ International ___ Municipal ___ Other ___	State ___ Federal ___ • District ___ • Circuit ___						Money Damages ___ Compensatory ___ Punitive ___ Equitable Relief ___ Injunction ___ Other ___

Practice Tip: Using West's Digest Topics

If you are unsure what words to look up in a descriptive word index, review West's list of more than 400 topics of the law (http://www.westgroup.com/documentation/cdrom/cddoc/cdsupp/digtopcd.pdf#search=%22west%20400%20digest%20topics%22). Use this list as a "menu," and pick and choose the words and topics that fit your research problem.

B. Tackling the Project

Once you have formulated the descriptive words and phrases that you will look up in an index, you need to decide with which sources to start. Remember that there are two categories of sources you can consider: primary authorities (cases, constitutions, statutes, and administrative regulations) and secondary authorities (everything else). You can also use digests to help you find cases.

Some research questions will immediately suggest the source to consult. For example, if the question relates to the statute of limitations for a medical malpractice action against a doctor, you should begin with your state's annotated statutes, looking up descriptive words in the index, reading the statute, and then reviewing the cases that interpret the statute.

If you do not know which source to consult initially, consider the following strategy:

- **Familiarize Yourself.** When you are unsure where or how to start a research project, invest an hour or two in becoming familiar with the area of law involved (contracts, property, wills). The best place to "get your feet wet" may be an encyclopedia, which will offer you introductory information on an area of law. Unless your state has its own local encyclopedia, start with C.J.S. (noting pertinent topic names and key numbers) or Am. Jur. 2d (noting pertinent A.L.R. annotations). Additionally, these sources often provide suggestions for search queries for LexisNexis and Westlaw. Consider reviewing a treatise on your general topic, because it will provide excellent analysis as well as references to supporting case law and other authorities.
- **Consult Primary Sources.** After you have begun to feel comfortable with the subject matter, consult the primary authorities: constitutions, statutes, and cases (and, if applicable, administrative regulations).

  - **Constitutions.** If your issue is a federal one, it may be governed by the U.S. Constitution, included in U.S.C.A. and U.S.C.S., which provide the text of the Constitution and then references to cases interpreting it.
  - **Statutes.** Always examine an annotated code because it will send you to cases interpreting your statutory provision. For federal questions, use U.S.C.A. or U.S.C.S. For state statutes, examine your state's annotated code. Always check the pocket parts or supplements.
  - **Cases.** If reviewing the annotations for a federal or state statutory provision does not produce any cases on point, use digests, which function as case finders. If you can find "one good case," you can use its topics and key numbers to locate other cases in West's Decennial Digest System, and then you can Shepardize or KeyCite those cases to find other authorities.

Figure 12-2 provides a chart showing the sets to review when conducting research using primary authorities.

Figure 12-2
Chart of Primary Authorities

	Federal	*State*
Constitutions	Consult U.S.C.A. or U.S.C.S.	Consult your state's annotated code.
Statutes	Consult U.S.C.A. or U.S.C.S.	Consult your state's annotated code.
Cases	Consult digests (American Digest System or Federal Practice digests)	Consult your state's digest or a regional digest.
Regulations	Consult C.F.R.	Consult your state's administrative code.

• **Consult Secondary Sources.** After reviewing the pertinent primary authorities, review the secondary authorities to fill in the gaps. Most secondary authorities will refer you to cases, thus ensuring you find the case law relating to your topic. The most commonly consulted secondary authorities are A.L.R. annotations, encyclopedias, periodicals, Restatements, and texts and treatises.

There are many secondary sources, and you should examine the list of secondary authorities shown in Figure 12-3, and ask yourself if your issue would be addressed by the particular authority in question. You need not examine every secondary authority for every issue you research. It is possible that a review of a treatise and an A.L.R. annotation may provide you with useful information as well as sufficient references to cases that you need not examine other secondary authorities.

Figure 12-3
Chart of Secondary Authorities

Secondary Authority	*Coverage*	*To Use*
Encyclopedias		For all sets, consult alphabetically arranged index.
• C.J.S. and Am. Jur. 2d	• All U.S. law	
• State-Specific Sets	• Law of one state	
A.L.R. Annotations		For all A.L.R. sets, consult *A.L.R. Index*.
• A.L.R. Fed. and A.L.R. Fed. 2d	• Federal issues	

Figure 12-3 *(Continued)*

Secondary Authority	*Coverage*	*To Use*
A.L.R. A.L.R., A.L.R.2d, A.L.R.3d, A.L.R.4th, A.L.R.5th, A.L.R.6th	• State and common law topics	
Texts and Treatises	Law related to one topic	Consult alphabetically arranged index or table of contents.
Periodicals	Various topics	Use *Index to Legal Periodicals & Books* or *Current Law Index* (or their online versions).
Restatements	Various topics	Consult alphabetically arranged index to each Restatement.
Attorneys General Opinions • U.S.A.G. Opinions • State A.G. Opinions	• Federal topics • State topics	For all sets, consult alphabetically arranged index.
Dictionaries	Legal words and phrases	Look up alphabetically arranged words or phrases.
Form Books	Various topics	Consult alphabetically arranged index.
Uniform Laws	Various topics	Consult *Uniform Laws Annotated* and *Uniform Laws Annotated Directory of Acts* (or access http://www.nccusl.org).
Looseleaf Services	Various topics	Consult alphabetically arranged index.
Jury Instructions	Various topics	Consult alphabetically arranged index.

• **Review Miscellaneous Research Guides.** In addition to the primary and secondary authorities, use *Shepard's Citations* or KeyCite not only to tell you whether your primary authorities are still valid, but also to lead you to other sources, such as law review articles and A.L.R. annotations. Don't forget to use common sense. If a question can be easily answered by an individual or organization, call or email. Also, browse the library shelves for useful materials. For example, once you locate the bankruptcy section, scan the shelves for helpful sources. When you come to a dead end, ask the law librarian for help.

Practice Tips: *Legal Research in Five Easy Steps*

To ensure your research is sufficiently thorough:

- Use encyclopedias to obtain some background on the topic you research.
- Always examine the statutes. Use an annotated code, because it will refer you to cases.
- Use a treatise (or looseleaf service) for more thorough analysis of a topic and to direct you to cases and other authorities.
- If you cannot locate any cases through annotated codes or treatises, use digests.
- Shepardize or KeyCite your cases and statutes to ensure they are still valid and to be directed to A.L.R. annotations, periodical articles, and other relevant sources.

• **Consider the Quality of the Sources.** Once you have collected your authorities, consider their quality, credibility, and reliability. Although primary sources are binding and secondary sources are persuasive only, a project composed solely of nearly ancient cases will not be as authoritative as one composed of those cases that are then supported by credible secondary sources. For cases, remember that, in general, you should read or sort out cases following these guidelines:

- Read newer cases before older ones;
- Read cases from higher courts before those from lower ones;
- Read cases from your forum jurisdiction before expanding your search to foreign jurisdictions.

Similarly, remember that some secondary authorities are considered more authoritative than others. The Restatements have a status nearly equal to that of court decisions; law review articles written by well-known experts, judges, and academics often carry great weight; and many treatises are so highly regarded that a citation to one of them is of significant value to a court. Remember the signals that show a treatise is well respected: It is published in multiple editions, cases routinely cite it, and the author has produced other writings on this topic. Avoid citing to an encyclopedia; a reference to an encyclopedia is nearly equivalent to screaming, "I couldn't find anything else to support my position!"

C. Working with the Authorities

1. Note-Taking Techniques

As you begin to read the primary and secondary authorities, you need to develop a focused plan for taking and organizing notes during your research efforts so you can effectively use them to write your project. There are several approaches to note-taking:

• **Looseleaf Notebooks.** Using a looseleaf notebook or binder that is divided into separate sections through the use of tabs or dividers is an effective organization technique. You can then devote each section to a particular issue. Additional dividers can be inserted as needed, and pages can be moved to different sections if you decide to discuss issues in a different order than originally planned. You can also use different-colored sticky flags for different issues so that your notes give you visual cues about their contents.

• **Index Cards.** Many individuals use index cards when taking notes. Use different-colored index cards for different issues, which will allow immediate recognition or retrieval of the sections you later need to review. Devote a separate card to each case, law review article, or other authority. Record only the critical portions of a case or authority; there is no need to write out the entire case in longhand.

• **Printed or Photocopied Cases.** If your research produces several cases, you may choose to photocopy or print them. Mark or highlight the significant portions of any case, so later you can readily locate relevant sections. Use different-colored pens or highlighters to reflect different issues. For example, highlight all portions relating to damages in yellow. Give a "grade" to the cases (from A to F); this will later jog your memory as to whether the case will be useful to you and allow you to weed out weaker authorities.

• **Electronic Note-Taking.** New software packages allow students to simulate highlighting, bookmarks, and sticky notes as they take notes on their laptops while in the law library. This form of electronic note-taking is easy and convenient, and hyperlinks to cases and authorities of interest can be inserted in the notes. Any kind of text can be stored in your "infobase," and you can insert notes wherever you like, just as you would attach sticky notes to a text you read. Finally, text searching is easily accomplished, allowing you later to locate immediately your notes and information on "venue" or "deeds."

2. *Contents of Notes*

Your notes need not be perfect. They should contain only the most important and relevant information. You can "fill in the gaps" when writing your project by referring to your photocopied materials themselves. Your notes are for reference purposes only. Although your notes need not be perfect to be useful, they must be sufficiently complete so that they allow you to write your project. If you need to return to the library or log on again during the writing phase to get a parallel cite or the name of a law review author, your note-taking was ineffective. Follow these tips to ensure your notes are complete:

• **Citations.** Citations to all authorities should be complete and in *Bluebook* or *ALWD* form. You may be tempted to jot down part of a citation and then start taking notes, figuring you will obtain the complete cite later. Resist this temptation, and always include all information you need for citation purposes. This will save time later.

• **Quotations and Paraphrases.** Clearly identify whether your notes reflect a direct quotation or merely paraphrase the judge's or author's statements. It is nearly impossible to remember days after your research whether a statement in your notes is a quotation or your own summary of a case unless your notes remind you. Any system is sufficient so long as it works for you. Use quotation marks only for direct quotes and then any material not in quotes is a paraphrase, or else label each statement in your notes with a "q" or a "p."

• **Include Pinpoints and Headnote References.** Record the pages for all quotations and paraphrases because you will need these pinpoints later when you give your citations. Similarly, if your quotation appeared in headnote 6 of a case or you are relying primarily on headnote 6 of a case, indicate this in your notes as **[6]**. When you later Shepardize or KeyCite, you will be able to focus on the treatment of this portion of the case by later authorities and not waste time reading later cases relating to headnote 3 when you were not relying on that portion of a case.

3. *Staying Focused*

One of the most difficult tasks in performing legal research is staying focused on a specific issue or question. Students commonly report that as they are in the process of researching an issue such as fraud and reading a pertinent case, they come across a reference to what appears to be a promising law review article. Without completing the reading of the case, they locate the law review article, which then refers to two other promising cases. These new cases are then retrieved. At the end of several hours of research, the student is surrounded by a pile of books, none of which has been thoroughly analyzed, and some of which, when later re-read, are a mystery as to their relevance because they discuss topics completely unrelated to the original topic of fraud.

This "hopscotch" approach occurs whether you are reviewing conventional print materials or whether you are online and routinely hyperlink from one authority to the next. The reason it occurs so frequently is that it is incredibly tempting to interrupt your analysis of an issue with the thought that the "perfect" authority is the next one, or that if you do not grab the authority now, you will forget about it later.

Train yourself to stay focused on each specific issue. For example, decide that the first three research hours will be devoted to fraud. If you come across cases or references that relate to other issues during this time, mark them with sticky flags or jot the citations in your notes so you can retrieve them later, but do not interrupt your research on the assigned issue. With any luck, when it is time to research later issues, you will already have a list of promising leads, eliminating the need to start at the beginning with encyclopedias or digests. Use electronic aids, such as Google's "Scratch pad," to take notes, maintain your "to do" list, and record websites of interest on a sidebar displayed on your screen at all times.

Be especially careful not to get sidetracked when you Shepardize or KeyCite. If you interrupt your Shepardizing or KeyCiting to read promising cases, you may forget where you are in the validation process. Thus, when you return to the task, you may assume you completed validating your original case when in reality you examined only some of the references.

D. When to Stop

One of the most difficult tasks in legal research is knowing when to stop. It seems that some issues can be researched endlessly. If you read a promising case, it may refer to six other cases, which you may also decide to read. When you Shepardize or KeyCite these cases, you discover each of them has been mentioned or discussed in ten other cases, as well as numerous law review articles and other resources. You now have 60 other cases that could be examined and then Shepardized or KeyCited. This process could continue indefinitely, and is a bit like a funnel that gets wider and wider. Eventually, you need to call a halt to your research.

1. *Practical Considerations*

There is often a practical reason for stopping your research. If the client's claim is for $40,000, you cannot possibly afford to expend $20,000 in legal research and then present the client with a bill after the trial that charges for that legal research and $10,000 for costs and other attorneys fees, leaving the client with a mere $10,000 recovery. Thus, in many cases economics will govern the scope of your research. When the client's budget dictates the amount of research that can be performed, you will have to be as efficient as possible. Keep track of your hours as you go along, and after a few hours report back to your assigning attorney on your progress. Estimate how much longer you think will be required. In many instances, when you are assigned a project, you may be instructed to allot a stated number of hours for research.

The balance between the duty to research adequately and the economic realities of a case is a delicate one. At the beginning of your legal career, it is the supervising attorney's task to resolve this issue and give you proper guidance. If you receive no instructions, take the initiative and state that for time-management purposes, you would like to inquire when the project is due (this in and of itself may give you a clue as to how thorough the project is to be) and a range of time the attorney estimates for the research. Alternatively, give your supervisor a brief status report after a few hours of research; a quick email will allow your supervisor to redirect you, if necessary.

Do not be embarrassed to ask for direction or acknowledge that you are having difficulty. Your supervising attorney would much prefer to discover this after six hours of your research than after 30 hours that cannot be billed to the client. If your project is more complex than originally anticipated, stop your research and explain your progress thus far to your supervisor and ask for direction. Send an email stating, "I've spent the six hours you suggested and because the circuit courts are in conflict on this issue, I think I need two to three more hours. Will the client approve this additional time?"

2. *Complex Projects*

If the project is complex, you may find yourself in the "funnel position" described previously, in which there is an ever-expanding list of authorities that could be reviewed. One clue that your research is complete is that you keep bumping into the same authorities. For example, assume that you locate the *Lynch* case, which itself refers to *Lyons*, an earlier landmark case. Later cases all refer to *Lynch* and *Lyons*, and when you Shepardize or KeyCite *Lynch* and *Lyons* you turn up no new lines of case law.

These references to the same authorities are a signal that your research is complete. You may want to "flesh out" your research by reviewing a current law review article or other secondary authority, but if these confirm the results of your earlier research, you will know you have been sufficiently thorough.

Beginning researchers often lack the confidence to stop researching; they are convinced that there is one perfect case to find, if they can only devote enough time to the effort. This is almost always a fallacy. Seldom, if ever, will you find a "perfect" case; no two cases are ever exactly alike. You will, however, find cases that are similar to yours, and you will be able to argue that because the cases are similar in reasoning and facts, the reported cases should apply to your research problem. It is only when you neglect to review the cases interpreting a statute or fail to update by checking pocket parts and Shepardizing or KeyCiting that your research is an unexploded minefield.

3. *Quick Questions*

Often, your research issue is specific and well defined. You may be asked to check how many days' notice a landlord must give a tenant before initiating eviction proceedings. Such specific questions are usually easily answered by starting with your state's annotated code. Review the statute and a few cases construing it. Check the pocket parts and Shepardize or KeyCite. This approach is sufficient to answer questions that are straightforward.

4. *Established Issues*

If your research relates to an established area of the law, such as a landlord's duty to provide habitable premises to a tenant or the damages available for fraud, you may find a multitude of authorities. Some of them may be decades old, and there may be numerous cases, periodical articles, and discussions in treatises. These authorities, however, may reflect remarkable unanimity. Researching an issue related to an established area of law usually produces numerous authorities in agreement.

Determining when to stop researching will be relatively easy because the authorities will begin referring to each other over and over again. Once you update and Shepardize or KeyCite to ensure that the primary authorities are still valid, your task is complete.

5. *Newly Emerging Issues*

Researching newly emerging areas of law can be frustrating because there may be substantial conflict among courts as judges grapple with a difficult issue and try to establish rules of law. Thus, research relating to the liability of an Internet service provider for defamatory statements posted on a website may produce a patchwork quilt of conflicting results. Often periodical articles or A.L.R. annotations will be most helpful because they will offer an overview of new topics and attempt to explain and reconcile conflicts. Computer-assisted legal research, with the ability to locate hundreds of documents and sort them by date, is ideal for newly emerging areas of the law.

6. *Issues of First Impression*

Often the most difficult research task is the one that yields no results whatsoever. Thus, after hours of research, you may not have found any authorities. There are two conclusions to draw from this occurrence: "There are no authorities relating to this issue" or "I must be doing something wrong, because I can't locate any authorities." Beginning researchers will always draw the second conclusion and refuse to stop researching, even though they are retracing their steps over and over again.

It is possible that an issue is one of *first impression*, that is, one not previously considered in your jurisdiction. Although there is no foolproof way to determine this, there are two techniques you can use to assure yourself that it is not your research strategy that has resulted in a lack of authorities.

First, select a populous and varied jurisdiction, such as California or New York, which has a rich body of law. Use the same research techniques and sets of books that you used in your home jurisdiction. If you obtain results, you will know that your strategies were sound and that the lack of authorities in your jurisdiction is the result of an issue of first impression, not misguided research efforts.

Second, computer-assisted legal research, with its ability to search for thousands of documents that contain specific terms, will help verify your research techniques. If your search query is sound and you selected the database for all Utah statutes and cases and yet no authorities are produced, you should feel more confident that Utah has simply not considered your issue. To achieve a final comfort level, contact the service representatives for LexisNexis or Westlaw and ask for help in formulating a search query.

If your jurisdiction has never before considered your issue, you may search in other states or jurisdictions. Remember, however, that these authorities are not binding in your jurisdiction, although they may be persuasive.

7. *How Many Authorities Are Enough?*

Beginning researchers usually want to know how many cases or authorities should be cited in a brief or project. There is no answer to this question. As a general rule, however, you will need fewer authorities to support a well-established principle and more authorities to discuss an emerging area of law or one in conflict.

Help Line: *Research Assistance from LexisNexis and Westlaw*

Both LexisNexis and Westlaw are extremely helpful in providing research assistance if you encounter difficulties when performing research.

- **LexisNexis:** Call (800) 543-6862 for 24/7 research help.
- **Westlaw:** Call (800) REF-ATTY for research assistance.

Additionally, both services offer "real-time" online assistance. When you are researching online, simply send an email with your question, and you will be given research assistance within minutes.

Is one citation enough? It is possible that one or two citations may suffice to answer a quick question. Thus, the question how many days one has to answer interrogatories served by mail may be answered as follows: "A party served with interrogatories has 30 days after the date of service to answer or object to the interrogatories. Fed. R. Civ. P. 33(b). The answering party has three extra days to respond if served by mail, and if the last day is a Saturday, Sunday, or holiday, the party has until the next business day. Fed. R. Civ. P. 6(a), (e)." More complex questions, such as the test for determining patent infringement, may require careful reading of several cases, statutes, and other authorities.

You should always aim to have at least one primary authority to support each of your arguments. Consider selecting the landmark case in the area and then one recent case from your highest court. This may be sufficient for areas of law that are fairly well established. See Figure 12-4 for a blueprint for conducting legal research.

Cite secondary authorities if they provide useful analysis or if the author is a renowned authority in that field. Consider combining primary authorities with a secondary authority to support your argument. Do not, however, believe that legal research is like a recipe, and that if you always cite two cases and a law review article, your argument will win. Different topics require different levels of analysis, and you will need to exercise your own discretion to determine how many authorities are enough. Although there is no perfect rule for when to stop conducting legal research, consider that it is likely time to stop when:

- You keep bumping into the same authorities and their commentary is much the same;
- You have read the same point in a number of different sources, with nothing new added;
- The same citations keep showing up; and
- Your Shepardizing or KeyCiting reveals no changes in the law.

Figure 12-4
A Blueprint for Legal Research

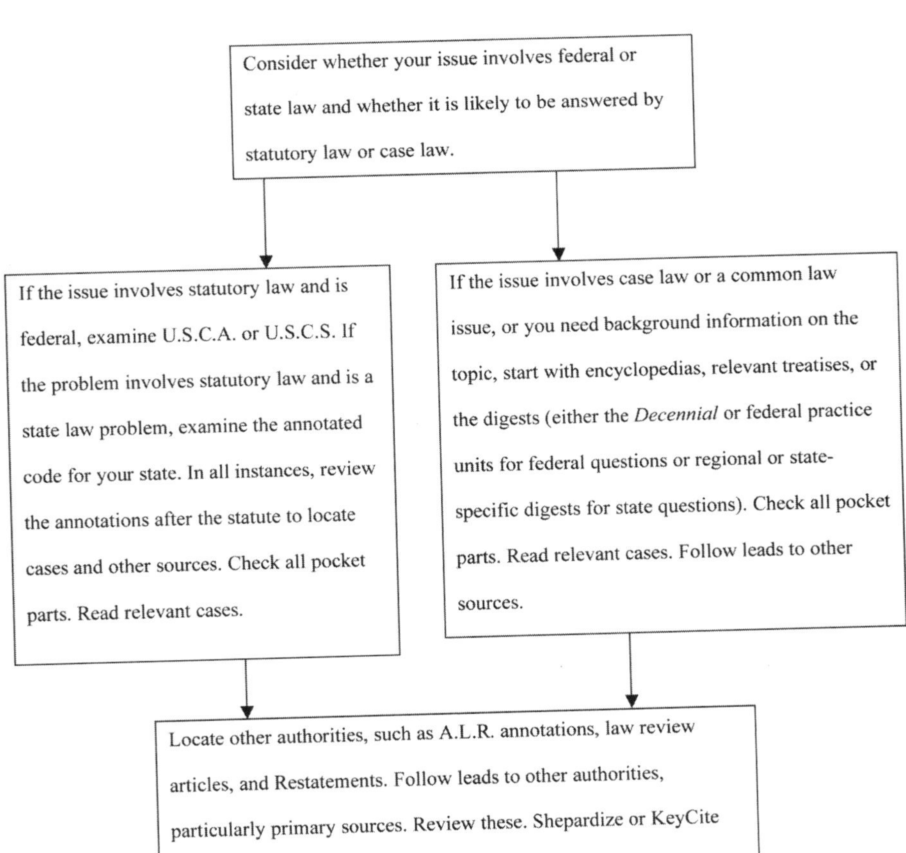

8. *Ten Tips for Effective Legal Research*

• **Be Prepared.** The time you spend thinking about a project before you begin is time well spent. Give yourself a few minutes to plan your research strategies.

• **Be Flexible.** If the books you need aren't on the shelf or if your efforts are not yielding results, switch to another set of books or source. Consider a variety of research methods (print, computer-assisted legal research, and the Internet) to achieve the best results.

• **Be Thorough.** Check all pocket parts and supplements. Shepardize or KeyCite all primary authorities to make sure they remain valid. Take complete notes.

• **Be Patient.** Research can be a difficult process. Expect some roadblocks.

• **Be Organized.** Tackle one topic at a time. Avoid getting sidetracked on a minor issue. Address each research issue with a laser, not a buckshot, approach.

• **Be Efficient.** Gather together all of the materials you need so you don't waste time wandering around the library.

• **Be Creative.** If all of your colleagues are beginning their research in one set of books, begin in another to avoid the crowd as well as the crowd mentality. Try contacting agencies and individuals and asking for assistance rather than depending exclusively on the books in the stacks.

• **Be Wary.** Approach your problem from all angles. Play devil's advocate. What will the adversary argue?

• **Be Resourceful.** Look for law review articles and A.L.R. annotations on your topic. If someone has already written a thorough analysis of an issue, why reinvent the wheel?

• **Be Calm.** If you get stuck, ask a librarian for help. That's what they're there for.

E. Presenting the Results of Your Research

Research is seldom conducted in a vacuum. You will almost always be required to present the results of your research. You may be providing your supervising attorney with a legal memorandum; you may be preparing a letter to a client explaining an issue; you may be drafting a brief for a court. Each of these specific writing projects has its own style, and books on writing fully address the most commonly prepared documents in law practice, discussing their purpose, audience, and structure. Nevertheless, because legal research and writing are invariably linked, and writing is the logical step after research, this section of the chapter presents some basic information on writing and an introduction to one of the most common writing projects: the legal memorandum.

1. *The IRAC Method of Analyzing Authorities*

One threshold question for legal writers is exactly *how* to discuss the legal authorities that have been located in the research process. In discussing and analyzing authorities, many writers follow what is referred to as the "IRAC" method. "IRAC" is an acronym for Issue, Rule, Analysis or Application, and Conclusion. First, the issue is presented (*Does the Uniform Partnership Act govern a partnership that has no written agreement?*). Next, the rule or legal authority that governs the issue is discussed. Then the writer analyzes and applies the rule to the writer's particular case situation. After a thorough analysis, in which authorities are compared and contrasted, a conclusion is presented.

Other writers use a variation of IRAC, usually called "CRAC" (for Conclusion, Rule, Application, and Conclusion). In this type of analysis, the conclusion is given first, followed by the rule of law that supports the conclusion. The rule is explained and illustrated through citation to legal authorities. The rule is then applied to the writer's particular case, and then the conclusion is restated. The CRAC method is often used by authors of court briefs, which are persuasive documents, because stating the conclusion first is a more powerful way to begin an argument than merely identifying the issue the document will examine.

Still another variation of IRAC is "CRuPAC" (for Conclusion, Rule, Proof, Application, and Conclusion). In this analysis, the conclusion is first stated, followed by the pertinent rules that govern the issue. The proof section then analyzes the relevant case precedents. The rules and proof are then applied to the specific facts in the case, and the second conclusion reiterates the introductory conclusion.

Although methods of analyzing cases vary, some techniques are common to all analysis:

- Analyze rather than merely summarize the legal authorities you rely on. Describe the cases you rely on, giving sufficient facts from those cases so the reader may readily see how and why those cases apply to your situation.
- Give the holding and the reasoning from the cases you rely on. Then, compare and contrast the cases you rely on with your particular issue or problem.
- Convince by applying the holding and reasoning from the cited authorities to your case. Complete the analysis by giving a conclusion for the reader. Don't force the reader to guess at a conclusion.

2. *The Legal Memorandum: Its Purpose and Format*

A *legal memorandum* or research memorandum is a document designed to provide information about a case or matter. It is one of the best-known documents in legal writing; it calls for you to research a question and then provide your answer in the form of a written memorandum or "memo." The memo is an internal document, meaning it is prepared for use within a law firm or company. It is generally protected by the work product privilege and thus is not discoverable by an adverse party. Because it is not discoverable, its primary characteristic is its objectivity. The most difficult part of writing a memo is remaining neutral and objective. You must point out any weaknesses and flaws in the client's case. Your goal is to explain the law, good and bad, not to argue it.

In addition to research memoranda, many firms use memoranda to report the results of client interviews or investigations. Some law firms use specific formats for their memos. Most memos, however, share the following common features:

- **Introductory Information.** This section identifies the document, the person for whom the memo is prepared, the author's name and position, the subject matter of the memo, and the date it is prepared.
- **Question(s) Presented.** This section sets forth the legal questions or issues the memo addresses. If the memo discusses more than one issue, number each one. Most writers use a true question form, such as *In Florida, are punitive damages recoverable in fraud actions?*
- **Brief Answer(s).** This section of the memo briefly answers the questions you set forth, in the order you presented them. Each answer should be no more than one or two sentences. Do not include formal citations.
- **Statement of Facts.** The statement of facts will be based upon what you know about the case, what the client has said, and your review of the file. Remember to be objective and include all facts, even if they are unfavorable to the client's position. The most common approach in stating the facts is to present them in the past tense and in chronological order. Some writers place the Statement of Facts before the Questions Presented section.
- **Analysis or Discussion.** The heart of the memorandum is the analysis or discussion section. This portion of the memo provides an in-depth analysis of the issues presented. Cases, statutes, and other legal authorities will be discussed. Citations usually appear in the body of the memo rather than as footnotes. Consider using the IRAC approach to analyze the issues. Use headings and subheadings throughout this section to alert the reader to new topics. Write in the third person in your discussion.
- **Conclusion.** The conclusion should be brief (probably no more than one paragraph) and should not include formal citations. The conclusion should summarize your analysis section.

See the Appendix for a sample form of a legal memorandum.

CyberSites

http://www.ll.georgetown.edu/tutorials/index.cfm	Georgetown Law Center offers several valuable tutorials relating to legal research.
http://www.bc.edu/schools/law/library/research/researchguides.html	Boston College Law Library offers legal research guides.
http://www.law.syr.edu/lawlibrary/electronic/researchguides.aspx	Syracuse University offers legal research guides.
http://ualr.edu/cmbarger/Memofrmt.htm	Professor Coleen Barger of the University of Arkansas at Little Rock provides information on memo formats and a sample memo.

Research Assignment

Answer the following questions, and give the citation to the legal authority that supports your answer.

1. Under federal law, when a statute prohibits a "person" from doing an act, does the statute apply to corporations and other associations as well as to individuals?
2. ABC Inc. is a corporation that owes money to three creditors, each of whom is owed $4,500. May these three creditors commence an involuntary bankruptcy action against ABC Inc.?
3. Andrew has written and illustrated a comic book featuring a unique character. Is the comic book copyrightable?
4. Smith is a prisoner confined to the federal prison Leavenworth in Kansas. Smith is serving a sentence of life imprisonment. While in prison, Smith murdered another prisoner. What punishment might Smith receive for this crime?
5. In Colorado, would the following be allowed as names for a business that wishes to form as a corporation?
   - ABC Inc.
   - ABC Co.
   - ABC Group
6. Ben and Sarah Bailey moved to Florida three months ago and would like to divorce. May they file their petition to dissolve their marriage in Florida?
7. Phil is a resident of and works in Phoenix, Arizona. Phil would like to sue his former employer for breach of his employment contract. The breach occurred ten months ago. When must Phil commence his action?
8. Al is a landlord in California who would like to evict his tenant, Tina, for failure to pay rent for the leased premises. How many days' notice must Al provide to Tina before filing his action to evict her?
9. Frank made his will in Massachusetts ten years ago, leaving all his property to his three children. Last year, Frank had another child (who is not included in the will prepared ten years ago). Will this child share in any portion of Frank's estate?
10. What is the definition of "farm animal" under Wisconsin law?
11. Susan is employed by ABC Inc., a small company with only 35 employees. Susan has worked at ABC for five years and wishes to take maternity leave to care for the birth of her newborn child. Must ABC provide Susan with unpaid leave under the Family and Medical Leave Act?

Internet Assignment

1. Access Georgetown Law Center's site at http://www.ll.georgetown.edu/research/browse_techniques.cfm and select "Online vs. Books Research Guide." Indicate whether you should start your research online or in books for the following situations:
   - The area of law is new or emerging.
   - You are researching a complex concept or legal theory.
   - Your search terms are ambiguous.
   - You are looking for unpublished opinions.
2. Access Georgetown Law Center's tutorials, select "Case Law Research Tutorial," and then select "How to Find Cases." How do you find a case when you have no citation?
3. Access Georgetown Law Center's guide to cost-effective legal research at http://www.ll.georgetown.edu/guides/cost.cfm.
   a. What are the first three tips given to keep research costs under control?
   b. What is "transactional pricing" charged by Lexis and Westlaw?
4. Access the University of Washington School of Law's legal research guides at http://lib.law.washington.edu/ref/basic.html. Select "What You Always Wanted to Know About Legal Research but Were Afraid to Ask."
   a. What are the three overarching themes of legal research?
   b. Review the Final General Tips. What are the computer-assisted legal research tips, and when is it okay to stop researching?
5. Access Cornell University's Law Library Research Guides at http://library.lawschool.cornell.edu/WhatWeDo/ResearchGuides. Select "Basics of Legal Research." Why do many researchers recommend beginning with secondary sources?

APPENDIX

MEMORANDUM

To: Joanne DeRoache, District Attorney
From: Lane Gammon, Paralegal
Re: *State v. Davis* Terroristic Threatening
Date: January 30, 2010

ISSUES

1. In Delaware, does the offense of terroristic threatening require that the threat be communicated to the person threatened?
2. Is a threat to kill protected under the First Amendment?

BRIEF ANSWERS

1. No. A threat need not be communicated directly to the person threatened for terroristic threatening to have occurred.
2. No. An unequivocal threat to kill another is not speech that is protectable under the First Amendment.

FACTS

Robert Davis ("Davis") was recently charged by the State of Delaware with "terroristic threatening," a violation of Del. Code Ann. tit. 11, § 621 (2002). The charge arose out of the following incident. After his girlfriend, Gina Gersten, broke up with him, Davis saw Ms. Gersten with another man. Davis angrily told his friend, Allen Franklin, "I'll kill Gina if I ever see her with another man again. You know I have a gun, and I'll do it." Concerned, Mr. Franklin told Ms. Gersten about Davis's threat. Ms. Gersten reported the threat to the police, who charged Davis with "terroristic threatening," a violation of Del. Code Ann. tit. 11, § 621 (2002).

Davis contends that because the threats were not uttered to the intended victim, Ms. Gersten, they cannot constitute terroristic threatening. Davis has also contended that his statement is protected free speech under the First Amendment.

DISCUSSION

Terroristic Threatening

Del. Code Ann. tit. 11, § 621 (2002) provides, in pertinent part, that "a person is guilty of terroristic threatening when he or she . . . threatens to commit any crime likely to result in death or in serious injury to person or property." The language of the statute does not specify that the threat must be made directly to the person to whom the threat is addressed. Moreover, there is no case law in Delaware addressing this issue. Case law from other jurisdictions, however, with statutes similar to those of Delaware supports the conclusion that a threat to a third party, rather than to the threatened person directly, can constitute the offense of terroristic threatening.

In *State v. Alston*, 865 P.2d 157, 162 (Haw. 1944), the defendant, Alston, was seated in a restaurant and threatened a waitress who was scheduled to be a witness against him in court. Two police offers were present and asked Alston to go outside with them. While outside, Alston pointed at the waitress through the window and angrily told the officers that he was "tired of that [expletive]" and that if he were arrested, he would "go home and get his pistol and tie up this end once and for all." Alston immediately told another woman present to go to his home and get his gun so he could "take care of that [expletive] once and for all." *Id.*

Alston was charged with terroristic threatening for the threats to the waitress made in front of the two police officers. He argued that the threats made in front of the officers could not constitute terroristic threatening because the threats were never communicated to the person against whom the threats were made. The Hawaii Supreme Court held that the threat did not need to be communicated to the victim. The court noted that for one to be subject to criminal prosecution for terroristic threatening, "the threat must be conveyed to either the person who is the object of the threat *or to a third party*." *Id.* at 168. Once the threat is communicated to anyone, terroristic threatening has occurred.

Similarly, in *State v. Chung*, 862 P.2d 1063 (Haw. 1993), a teacher (who was holding a clip of bullets) made a threat against the school principal in front of other teachers, but without the principal present. The court held that this threat constituted terroristic threatening. Moreover, the court noted that actual terrorization is not a material element of the offense of terroristic threatening. To be subject to criminal prosecution for terroristic threatening, one need only make a threat either to the person who is the object of the threat or to a third party. *Id.* at 1071.

In *Richards v. State*, 585 S.W.2d 375, 377 (Ark. Ct. App. 1979), the defendant, Richards, while holding a gun, stated that he intended to shoot a former coworker, Roberts. The threat was made to a third party, and Roberts did not hear it. The third party promptly communicated the threat to Roberts. On appeal, the defendant challenged his conviction on the ground that the threat had not been communicated to the intended victim. The Arkansas statute prohibiting terroristic threatening was nearly identical to the Delaware statute at issue in this case. The court held that because the statute did not include language specifying that the threat must be communicated directly to the person threatened for the offense to have taken place, terroristic threatening can occur even though the intended victim does not hear or know of the threat. Thus, Davis's threat to kill Ms. Gersten constitutes terroristic threatening under the Delaware statute even though the threat was made to a third party and not directly to Ms. Gersten.

First Amendment Defense

Davis has asserted that his statement that he would kill Ms. Gersten if he ever saw her with another man again is protected by the First Amendment right of free speech and expression. *See* U.S. Const. amend. I.

The U.S. Supreme Court has already addressed the issue whether an unequivocal threat is protected under the First Amendment and has firmly stated, "[A] statement that amounts to a threat to kill . . . would not be protected by the First Amendment." *Rankin v. McPherson*, 483 U.S. 378, 386-87 (1987). Although threats made in jest and that when taken in context are not true threats because they are conditional are protected under the First Amendment, *Watts v. United States*, 394 U.S. 705, 708 (1969), if language used in a threat conveys a gravity of purpose and likelihood of execution, it is not protected speech, *United States v. Kelner*, 534 F.2d 1020, 1026-27 (2d Cir. 1976). If a statement on its face and in the circumstances in which it is made is so unequivocal and unconditional as to convey a gravity of purpose and imminent prospect of being carried out, such is not protected speech under the First Amendment. *Id.*

In the present case, Davis's threat was made in anger, not in jest, and stated his clear and unequivocal intention to kill Ms. Gersten. Davis's statement included specific details as to how this killing would occur. Moreover, Franklin understood the threat to be sufficiently serious that he immediately conveyed the threat to Ms. Gersten. Such an unequivocal and unconditional threat is not protected free speech.

CONCLUSION

Because there is nothing in the Delaware statute requiring an applicable threat to be made directly to the threatened person, a threat made in front of a third party who later communicates it to the victim can constitute terroristic threatening. Thus, Davis has committed the threat of terroristic threatening. Moreover, because Davis's threat was unequivocal and unconditional and not made in jest, it is not protected free speech under the First Amendment.

Glossary

Adjudication: An administrative proceeding before an administrative law judge.

Administrative agency: A governmental body (federal or state) that enacts rules and regulations on a specific topic and settles disputes relating thereto, for example, the FCC or FDA.

Administrative law: The law relating to administrative agencies.

Administrative law judge: An individual who presides over an administrative adjudication.

Administrative rule: A regulation promulgated by an administrative agency such as the Securities and Exchange Commission; also called *administrative regulation.*

Advance sheets: Temporary softcover books that include cases prior to their publication in hardbound volumes.

Alert: Electronic clipping service offered by both LexisNexis and Westlaw that automatically updates research requests or reports changes in the law.

A.L.R.: *See American Law Reports.*

***ALWD* citation system:** A system introduced in 2000 by the Association of Legal Writing Directors (ALWD) to provide an easily understood citation format.

Am. Jur. 2d: A general or national encyclopedia published by West covering all United States law; formal name is *American Jurisprudence, Second Series.*

***American Digest System*:** West's comprehensive set of digests designed to help researchers find cases from all over the United States; also called "Key Number System."

***American Law Reports* (A.L.R.):** Sets of books publishing appellate court decisions together with comprehensive essays or articles, called "annotations," relating to the legal issues raised by those cases.

Annotated: Literally, "with notes"; manner of publishing statutes together with case summaries interpreting statutes.

Annotated code: Set of statutes organized by subject matter that contain material accompanying the statutes, chiefly references to cases.

Annotated law reports: *See American Law Reports.*

Annotation: One-sentence description of case, which follows statute; essay published in *American Law Reports.*

App: Database of material available on iPhones, BlackBerrys, and similar devices.

Article: Portion of a law review written by professors or other scholars, which analyzes a legal topic in depth.

Article III judge: A federal judge appointed pursuant to Article III of the U.S. Constitution.

Attorneys general opinions: Opinions by executive officials on various legal topics; opinions by the U.S. Attorney General or individual state attorneys general.

Auto-Cite: A computer service provided by *Shepard's* showing the appellate history of a case, used primarily to confirm that the authority in question is still good law.

Bicameral: A two-chamber legislature.

Bilateral treaty: A treaty between two parties.

Bill: A proposed law.

Bill of Rights: The first ten amendments to the United States Constitution.

Binding authority: Legal authority that must be followed by a court.

Blawg: An online journal related to legal topics.

Block quotation: A quotation from another source of 50 words or more, indented (typically ten spaces) left and right, that appears without opening and closing quotation marks.

Blog: An online journal or diary (short for "weblog").

Blue and White books: Books published by West for individual states that include conversion tables for locating parallel citations.

***Bluebook*:** The best-known and used guide for citation form; subtitled *A Uniform System of Citation*, now in its 18th edition.

Bluepages: Section of *The Bluebook* printed on light blue paper, providing rules and examples for practitioners (rather than the citation form used for law review articles).

Book briefing: *See* Technicolor briefing.

Boolean searching: A method of conducting research online using symbols, terms and connectors, and characters rather than plain English.

Brief: A summary of a case (also called "case brief") or a written argument presented to a court.

BriefCheck: A LexisNexis software program that automatically validates all cases cited in a document.

BriefTools: A West product for use by litigators that monitors citations, inserts KeyCite status flags, and retrieves a firm's internal documents that contain a particular citation.

Case brief: *See* Brief.

Case synopsis: *See* Synopsis.

CataLaw: A catalog of worldwide law on the Internet; a metaindex that arranges law by topic, region, or special subjects called "Extras."

Certification: The process by which a court of appeals refers a question to the United States Supreme Court and asks for instructions and direction.

***Certiorari*:** Writ of *certiorari*; the most widely used means to gain review of a case by the United States Supreme Court; issuance of the writ (meaning a decision to review a case) is discretionary with the Court.

Charter: Governing document for a municipality.

Circuit: A geographical area in which courts are located; the

Untied States is divided into 13 circuits, each with its own court of appeals.

Citation: A reference to a legal authority.

Citation signal: Words and abbreviations that indicate the degree of support (or contradiction) of an authority cited.

Citators: Sets of books published by *Shepard's* or online services, such as Westlaw's KeyCite service that direct one to other materials discussing or treating legal authorities.

CiteAdvisor: West's product that creates a table of authorities and suggests correct citation form.

Cite-checking: The process of verifying that citations in a document are accurate and in compliance with rules for citation form and then verifying that the authorities are still "good law."

Civil law: A body of law depending more on legislative enactments than case law; often seen in non-English-speaking countries.

C.J.S.: A general or national encyclopedia published by West covering all United States law; formal name is *Corpus Juris Secundum*.

Code: A compilation of statutes or regulations arranged by subject or topic.

Code of Federal Regulations: The codification of administrative rules and regulations, by subject, into 50 titles.

Codification: Process of organizing statutes, bringing together all valid laws on the same subject with their amendments.

Comment: Shorter piece in a law review authored by a student; also called "Note."

Committee report: Document reflecting decisions reached by legislative committees considering proposed legislation.

Committee transcript: Report of proceedings before committee considering proposed legislation.

Common law: The body of law that develops and derives through judicial decisions rather than from legislative enactments, usually seen in English-speaking countries.

Competitive sets: Sets of books or resources that are substantially equivalent to each other.

Compiled legislative history: "Prepackaged" legislative history, usually compiled for significant legislation.

Computer-assisted legal research: The process of conducting legal research through computer rather than conventional print sources.

Concurrent jurisdiction: The sharing of jurisdiction over a case by federal and state court so that a litigant may select which forum in which to bring the action.

Concurring opinion: Persuasive but not binding pinion written by a member of the majority who agrees with the result reached in a case but disagrees with the reasoning of the majority.

Conference committee: Congressional committee charged with reconciling differing versions of a bill.

Congress: The lawmaking body of the federal government, composed of the Senate and the House of Representatives.

"Congressional"**:** Source provided by LexisNexis offering rich and varied congressional information, including bills, hearing transcripts, committee reports, and the *Congressional Record*.

Congressional Information Service**:** Sets of books used to compile legislative history.

Congressional Record**:** A publication that publishes the remarks of the speakers debating a bill; prepared for each day Congress is in session.

Connectors: Symbols used by LexisNexis and Westlaw to construct a research query.

Constitution: The document that sets forth the fundamental law for a nation or state.

Constitutional court: A court that exists pursuant to the U.S. Constitution, namely, the U.S. District Courts, the U.S. Courts of Appeal, and the U.S. Supreme Court

Convention: A type of treaty, usually relating to a single topic.

Court reports: Sets of books that publish cases.

Court rules: *See* Rules of Court.

Courts of appeal: Intermediate appellate courts; in the federal system, these are sometimes called "circuit courts."

Courts of first resort: Trial courts.

Courts of last resort: The highest court in a judicial hierarchy.

CRAC: Acronym for Conclusion, Rule, Analysis, Conclusion; method of analyzing cases by setting forth conclusion, rule, analysis, and conclusion.

Critical: Treatment of a topic in an analytical or critical rather than explanatory manner.

CRuPAC: Acronym for Conclusion, Rule, Proof, Application, Conclusion; method of analyzing cases by setting forth conclusion, rules, proof, application, and conclusion.

***Current Law Index*:** Separately published index designed to direct researchers to periodicals, such as articles in law reviews.

Cyberspace: The electronic or computer world in which vast amounts of information are available; sometimes used as a synonym for the Internet.

***Daily Compilation of Presidential Documents*:** Publication including materials relating to the executive branch (formerly called the *Weekly Compilation of Presidential Documents*).

Database: Westlaw's groupings of materials offered in its computer-assisted legal research system.

Database Wizard: A service offered by Westlaw designed to help researchers select the right computer database; Database Wizard assists in selecting a database and narrowing research options.

Decennials: Digest books published by West that arrange cases by subject in ten-year groupings; *see American Digest System*.

Decision: Technically, the final action taken by a court in a court case; generally, the term "decision" is used synonymously with "opinion," "judgment," or "case."

Depository library: A library designated by the United States government to receive selected government materials and publications.

Descriptive word approach: A method of locating legal materials by inserting words describing a problem or issue into an index that then directs the reader to relevant information; also called "index method."

Dictionary (legal): An alphabetical arrangement of law-related words and phrases providing the meaning or definition of those words and phrases.

Dictum: Technically, "obiter dictum"; a remark in a case used for purposes of illustration or analogy; dictum is persuasive only.

Digests: Books or indexes that arrange one-sentence summaries or "digests" of cases by subject.

Directory: A list of lawyers.

Dissenting opinion: An opinion written by a judge in the minority who disagrees with the result reached by the majority of a court; persuasive only.

District courts: The 94 trial courts in our federal system.

Diversity jurisdiction: A basis on which federal courts take cases, due to the different or diverse citizenship of the parties in the case.

Docket number: A number assigned to a case by a court to track its progress through the court system.

Easy Search: Electronic search method offered by LexisNexis, similar to using an Internet search engine such as Google, providing easy searching and ranked results.

Ellipsis: Three periods separated by spaces and set off by a space before the first and after the last period, used to indicate omission of a word or words in a quotation.

Enabling statute: A statute that creates an administrative agency such as the FDA or FCC.

En banc opinion: Literally, "in the bench"; an opinion in which all judges in an appellate court participate.

Encyclopedias: Sets of books that alphabetically arrange topics related to legal issues; treatment of legal issues is somewhat elementary; the best-known general or national sets are C.J.S. and Am. Jur. 2d; some state-specific sets exist.

Exclusive jurisdiction: The basis on which a court's ability to hear a case is exclusive to the federal court, such as a bankruptcy case, and which cannot be heard by another court.

Executive agreement: An agreement entered into with a foreign nation by a president without Senate approval.

Executive branch: The branch of a government that enforces laws.

Executive order: Binding regulations issued by a president or governor to direct government agencies.

***Ex rel.*:** Latin for "upon relation of"; a designation in a title of a case filed on behalf of the government but at the instigation of a private party.

***Federal Appendix*:** West's set of books that prints unpublished federal courts of appeal cases.

Federal Depository Library: A library designated by the federal government to receive certain government publications.

Federalism: Sharing of powers by the federal and state governments.

Federal question jurisdiction: The power of a federal court to hear a case based on the fact the case arises under the U.S. Constitution or a U.S. law or treaty; also called "subject matter jurisdiction."

***Federal Register*:** A pamphlet published every weekday relating to administrative law and publishing agency rules and regulations.

***Federal Reporter*:** West's unofficial publication containing cases from the federal courts of appeal.

Federal Rules of Civil Procedure: Rules governing practice in federal district courts.

***Federal Supplement*:** West's unofficial publication containing cases from the federal district courts.

File: Westlaw's subdivisions within its databases of computer materials.

FindLaw: Internet site providing free access to many legal authorities.

First impression: A case presenting a novel issue not previously considered in a jurisdiction.
Form books: Sets of books including forms for use in the legal profession; may be general or related solely to one area of law.
FULL: A feature of "*Shepard's* for Research," a software program provided by LexisNexis that lists every authority that mentions a case or other source being Shepardized.
FullAuthority: A LexisNexis software program that automatically generates a table of authorities cited in a brief or other document.

General encyclopedia: *See* Encyclopedia.
GlobalCite: Loislaw's citation validation tool, used to ensure cases are still good law.
Global Legal Information Network: A database of the official text of laws, regulations, cases, and other sources from more than 50 countries; available at http://www.glin.gov.
Google Scholar: A free search service offered by Google allowing one to access federal and state court cases by case name or topic.
GPO Access: Internet source provided by the federal government, which offers free direct links to information about government agencies, and links to the *Federal Register*, C.F.R., Congressional, and executive materials.
***Guide to Microforms in Print*:** Alphabetical list of more than 200,000 books, journals, and other materials currently available in microform.

Headnotes: Short paragraphs prepared by editors, given before a case begins to serve as an index to the points of law discussed in a case.
History references: References provided by *Shepard's* relating to the subsequent history of a primary authority.
Holding: *See* Decision.
Hyperlink: A method of instantaneous electronic transport to another destination; hyperlinks are often underscored or appear in different color on the computer screen; by clicking the colored links you will be immediately transferred to that particular site or page.

***Id.*:** A citation short form used in citation form to direct a reader to an immediately preceding citation.
Index: An alphabetical arrangement of words and terms designed to direct researchers to relevant cases, statutes, or legal information; usually found in the last volume of a set of books or in separate volumes after the last volume.
Index method: *See* Descriptive word approach.
***Index to Legal Periodicals & Books*:** Separately published index designed to direct researchers to periodicals such as articles in law reviews.
***Infra*:** A citation short form used in books or citation form meaning "below" directing a reader to a later citation.
International Court of Justice: A court under the responsibility of the United Nations, created to hear and decide disputers between and among nations; also called the "World Court."
International law: The law relating to relations among nations.
Internet: A collection of worldwide interconnected computer networks, which are linked together to exchange information.
IRAC: Acronym for Issue, Rule, Analysis, and Conclusion; method

of analyzing cases by setting forth case issue, rule, analysis and conclusion.

Judge: Individual who sits on a lower court.
Judiciary: The branch of the government that interprets laws.
Jump cite: *See* Pinpoint citation.
Jurisdiction: The power of a court to act.
Jury instructions: Sets of books containing proposed instructions to be used to charge a jury in a civil or criminal case.
Justice: Individual who sits on a state's highest court or on the U.S. Supreme Court.

KeyCite: Citation service offered through Westlaw providing valuable and automatic information relating to the validity of primary authorities cited in a document.
KeyCite Alert: A software clipping service that automatically notifies a researcher of changes in treatment of a case or other authority being validated.
Key Number: West's assignment of a number to a particular topic of law, allowing researchers to retrieve numerous cases dealing with the same point of law.
Key Number System: West's arrangement of cases by topic name and specific number, allowing researchers to find cases on similar points of law; also called "American Digest System."
KWIC: A computer program offered by LexisNexis that provides subsequent appellate history of a case; used primarily to confirm that authority in question is still good law by showing negative history only; also a method of displaying a band or window of words around a requested search term or phrase.

Law: *See* Statute.
Law review: The periodical publication by a law school providing scholarly treatment of a legal topic; sometimes called "law journal."
Legal dictionary: *See* Dictionary.
Legal directory: *See* Directory.
Legal encyclopedia: *See* Encyclopedia.
Legal memorandum: *See* Memorandum.
Legal periodical: *See* Periodical.
Legal Periodicals & Books: The online version of *Index to Legal Periodicals & Books*.
Legal thesaurus: *See* Thesaurus.
LegalTrac: An online index to articles published in *Current Law Index*.
Legislation & Politics: A LexisNexis database library for legislative information.
Legislative courts: Specialized courts, such as the United States Tax Court, which do not exist under the Constitution and whose judges are appointed for specific terms.
Legislative history: The documents reflecting the intent and activity of a legislature at the time it enacts a law.
Legislature: The branch of the government that makes law.
LexisNexis: A publisher of legal books; the computerized legal research system offered by Reed Elsevier; often referred to as "Lexis."
Libraries: *See* Sources.
Library references: A feature of U.S.C.S. comparable to that of U.S.C.A. in that it provides cross-references as well as directing researchers to books, encyclopedias, annotations, and a wide variety of law review articles.
Listserv: A system that allows groups of people to email each other and participate in group

discussions, usually about a topic of common concern; for example, there may be a listserv for law students, and when one message is sent by a user, it is automatically sent to all others in the group; sometimes called "newsgroup."

Local encyclopedia: A legal encyclopedia devoted to the law of one state; also called "state-specific encyclopedia."

Loislaw: The computerized legal research system offered by publisher Wolters Kluwer, often used by sole practitioners or smaller law firms.

Looseleaf (or looseleaf services): A set of materials collected in ringed binders due to the need for frequent updating and related to a specific area of law such as labor law or tax; includes both primary and secondary authorities.

Majority opinion: Any judicial opinion written by a member of the majority after a court reaches a decision; has binding effect.

***Maroon Book*:** A citation manual published by the University of Chicago Law School and used in the Chicago area.

***Martindale-Hubbell Law Directory*:** A comprehensive directory of lawyers in the United States and in foreign countries, which also includes summaries of law for various foreign countries.

Material fact: *See* Relevant fact.

MegaLaw: Internet site providing free access to many legal authorities.

Memorandum: A document explaining legal issues involved in problem or case in a neutral and objective manner; also called *legal memorandum* or *research memorandum*.

Memorandum opinion: An opinion that provides a result but offers little or no reasoning to support that result.

Metadata: Information relating to the history, management, and tracking of electronically created documents.

Microfiche: Celluloid strips of film used in cataloging or archiving documents.

Microfilm: 16-mm or 35-mm film containing images displayed on screens and often used for efficient storage of voluminous records.

Microform: A type of technology embracing microfilm, microfiche, and ultrafiche, based on photography and that stores materials more efficiently than print sources.

Model act: Proposed law intended to be used as a guideline for actual legislation.

Moot: Resolved; cases that have been resolved or settled in some manner are said to be moot.

Multilateral treaty: Treaty between more than two parties.

National encyclopedia: *See* Encyclopedia.

National Reporter System: A set of unofficial court reporters published by West and including federal and state cases.

Natural Language: A "plain English" computer method of conducting legal research in contrast to using Boolean terms and connectors.

Neutral citation: A citation that does not refer to a particular vendor or to a particular type of source; also called *public domain citation* or *universal citation*.

Newsgroup: Electronic communications method allowing its participants to view, post, and reply to messages on the Internet.

Noncritical: Treatment of a legal topic in explanatory rather than analytical or critical manner.
Notes: *See* Comment.

Obiter dictum: *See* Dictum.
Official: Government-approved publication of cases, statutes, or other legal materials as directed by a statute.
On all fours: *See* On point.
Online: The process of being connected to the Internet through electronic communication.
Online catalog: An electronic database used by libraries in place of a conventional card catalog to catalog materials owned by the library.
Online journal: A journal that is published exclusively online, not in print form.
On point: A case that is factually similar and legally relevant and that controls another case; sometimes called a case "on all fours."
Opinion: A court's explanation of the law in a particular case; also called "case" or "decision."
Ordinance: A local law.
Original jurisdiction: The ability of a court to act as a trial court.
Overrule: The overturning of a case by a higher court considering a different case on appeal.

PACER: Service of U.S. Judiciary allowing access to documents filed in federal courts.
Parallel citation: Two or more citations to the same case allowing researchers to read a case in two or more sets of reports.
Per curiam: An opinion by the whole court in which a specific author is not identified.
Periodical: A publication issued on a periodic (such as a monthly or quarterly) basis; for example, the *Computer Law Journal*.
Permanent law: A law that remains in effect until it is expressly repealed.
Persuasive authority: Legal authorities that a court is not required to follow but might be persuaded to do so; secondary authorities are persuasive.
Pincite: *See* Pinpoint citation
Pinpoint citation: A reference to the exact page in a source to which a reader is directed; also called a "pincite" or "jump cite."
Plain English searching: See Natural Language.
Plurality opinion: The result reached when separate opinions are written by members of a majority.
Pocket part: A booklet or pamphlet inserted into the back of a hardbound volume to provide more current information than that found in the volume.
Popular name: The practice of calling certain statutes or vases by a popular name.
Popular name approach: A method of locating cases or statutes by looking up their "popular names"; generally, the names of the sponsoring legislators, the parties to the case, or a name assigned by the media.
Posting: The entering of information or messages into a network, for example, cases are "posted" to the website of the United States Supreme Court, and legal professionals "post" messages on a listserv.
Primary authority: Official pronouncements of the law, chiefly cases, constitutions, statutes, administrative regulations, and treaties, all of which are binding authorities.
Private international law: The law relating to which country's law will govern a private contractual transaction or arrangement.
Private law: A law affecting only one person or a small group of persons, giving them some special benefit not afforded to the public at large.

Procedural history: The path a case takes, for example, from trial court to appellate court.
Proclamation: A statement issued by a president that may or may not have legal effect.
Public domain system: With regard to format- or vendor-neutral citation systems, the citation appears the same whether the reader has accessed the case by conventional print format or by electronic methods, such as Lexis-Nexis, Westlaw, or the Internet.
Public international law: The law relating to the conduct of foreign nations.
Public law: A law affecting the public generally.

Query: A search request used to access a computer-assisted legal research system.
Quick Index: An easy-to-use one-volume index published by West that directs the researcher to A.L.R. annotations. Note that there is also an A.L.R. Federal Quick Index.

Ratio decidendi: The "reason for deciding"; the holding of a case.
Regulation: A pronouncement by an administrative agency; synonymous with "rule."
Regulatory body: An administrative agency, whose function is to regulate a body of law
Relevant fact: A fact that might affect the outcome of a case; also called material fact.
Remand: An order by a higher court that returns a case to a lower court, with directions.
Removal: Sending of a case from one court to another.
Report: Set of books publishing cases (often an official set).
Reporter: Set of books publishing cases (often an unofficial set).
Research memorandum: *See* Memorandum.
Restatements: Publications of the American Law Institute designed to restate in a clear and simple manner legal doctrine in specific areas, such as contracts, torts, or trusts.
Reverse: The overturning of a lower court decision by a higher court considering that same case on appeal.
Rule: *See* Regulation.
Rules of court: Procedural requirements issued by courts and that must be followed by litigants.
Rules of procedure: Rules governing practice before a court, such as the FRCP, which govern significant matters.
Running head: The printed line across the top of published cases that identifies the parties' names and case citation.

Scope note: A brief paragraph outlining the matters treated in a legal discussion and those to be treated elsewhere.
Search box: A blank box on a computer screen, in which you type or key in the word or terms you are interested in researching.
Search engine: A particular service that helps one locate useful information on the Internet, usually through the use of keywords; common search engines are "Yahoo!" and "Google." A search engine is a website that looks for and retrieves other websites. Search engines look for words in the millions of web pages on the Internet and direct you to pages that include the search words or keywords you enter in a search box.
Secondary authorities: Any legal authority that is not a primary authority; secondary authorities explain, discuss, and help locate primary authorities; include encyclopedias, A.L.R. annotations, law reviews, texts, and treatises.

Selective publication: The process whereby not all cases are published but rather only those that advance legal theory are published.
Series: Newer or more recent editions of cases or other legal materials.
Session laws: The chronological arrangement of laws before their arrangement in a code.
Shepardizing: The process of ensuring that authorities are still "good law."
***Shepard's*:** Sets of books that allow researchers to verify that primary authorities are still "good law."
Shepard's Link: A LexisNexis software tool that identifies cites in a document and creates hyperlinks to them.
Short form citation: An abbreviated form of a citation used after a citation has been given in full.
Signal indicator: A symbol or graphic displayed on a computer screen that informs the user of the precedential status of an authority by indicating through colors, letters, or symbols the history and treatment of an authority.
Signals: In citation form, words indicating how a citation supports or contradicts an assertion; references to preceding or later-given citations in a legal writing.
Slip law: Law initially published on looseleaf sheet(s) of paper.
Slip opinion: A court decision available on looseleaf sheets of paper; one not yet available in a published reporter.
Sources: LexisNexis's databases of materials; also called "Libraries."
Special subject encyclopedia: An encyclopedia devoted to one legal topic.
Stack: Shelf in a library.
Standing: Personal injury or damage sustained by a plaintiff enabling the plaintiff to bring suit.
***Stare decisis*:** The concept whereby courts follow and adhere to previously decided cases.
Star paging: A technique to convert page numbers in cases published in unofficial sets to page numbers in cases published in official sets.
Start page: Internet page routinely accessed by researchers.
State-specific encyclopedia: *See* Local encyclopedia.
Statute: An act of a legislature declaring, commanding, or prohibiting something; also called law.
String citing: The practice of citing more than one authority in support of a proposition.
StyleCheck: A LexisNexis citation checking software program that checks citations for proper form using *Bluebook* rules or the *California Style Manual*.
Subject matter jurisdiction: *See* Federal question jurisdiction.
Supplement: A softcover book that updates a hardcover volume.
***Supra*:** A citation short form used in books or citation form meaning "above," directing a reader to a preceding (though not immediately preceding) secondary authority.
Syllabus: A comprehensive but unofficial summary preceding an opinion of a court, prepared by the court's reporter of decisions or the publisher.
Synopsis: A brief summary of a case prepared by editors to provide a quick overview of the case and given before the case begins.

Table of Authorities: LexisNexis and Westlaw feature that analyzes cases cited by another case; also, a list of authorities cited in a brief or document and that must be arranged in a certain order.

Technicolor briefing: The technique of using colored markers and pens to highlight sections of cases as they are read; also called "book briefing."

Temporary law: A law that has specific language limiting its duration.

Terms and Connectors: A method of searching on a computer, using words, symbols, and characters rather than plain English; often called "Boolean searching."

Thesaurus: In law, a book providing synonyms and antonyms for legal words and terms.

THOMAS: Website for legislative information provided by the federal government that offers text of proposed and enacted legislation, committee information, calendars for hearings scheduled, and House and Senate directories.

Title approach: *See* Topic approach.

Titles: Categories of statutes.

Topic approach: A method of locating legal materials by bypassing the general index and going directly to the appropriate title or topic in a source; also called "Title approach."

Total Client-Service Library: Collectively, the set of books published by LexisNexis (formerly published by Lawyers Cooperative Publishing Company) and including U.S.C.S., Am. Jur. 2d, A.L.R., *Proof of Facts*, *Am. Jur. Trials*, and various form books.

Treatise: A scholarly book (or set of books) devoted to the treatment of a particular topic, such as *Treatise on the Law of Contracts*.

Treatment references: References provided by *Shepard's* relating to the later treatment and discussion of primary authorities by other cases, attorneys general opinions, law review articles, and so forth.

Treaty: An agreement between two or more nations.

Ultrafiche: An enhanced microfiche holding a great many images.

Unicameral: A one-house legislature.

Uniform law: Model legislation prepared by the National Conference of Commissioners on Uniform State Laws on various legal topics, such as the Uniform Commercial Code, and designed to be adopted by the 50 states.

***United States Code (U.S.C)*:** The official publication of all federal laws, arranged by subject.

***United States Code Annotated (U.S.C.A.)*:** West's annotated version of the *United States Code*, including all federal statutes arranged by subject.

***United States Code Congressional and Administrative News*:** A publication including public laws, legislative history of selected bills, summaries of pending legislation, presidential proclamations and executive orders, various federal regulations, and court rules.

United States Code Service: Annotated set of federal statutes arranged by subject and published by LexisNexis.

United States Courts of Appeal: Intermediate courts in the federal system.

United States District Courts: Trial courts in the federal system.

***United States Government Manual*:** A manual or handbook providing information about the United States government, particularly the administrative agencies.

***United States Law Week*:** A weekly publication that prints the text of significant public laws and recent U.S. Supreme Court cases.

***United States Reports*:** The official publication containing cases from the United States Supreme Court.

***United States Statutes at Large*:** The set of books containing all federal laws, arranged in chronological order.

United States Supreme Court: The highest court in the federal system.

Universal citation: *See* Public domain system.

Universal symbols: Symbols and characters used in constructing a search on LexisNexis or Westlaw; sometimes called "root expanders."

Unofficial: Private publication of law or case; publication not mandated by statute.

Unpublished case: Generally, a case that a court has not designated for publication, although it may be available from LexisNexis, Westlaw, or on the Internet; its precedential value varies from jurisdiction to jurisdiction; *see* Unreported case.

Unreported case: A case marked "not for publication" by a court; persuasive authority.

VersusLaw: A commercial legal research system offering cases through the Internet for a moderate fee.

Website: A collection of web pages. For example, IBM's website (http://www.ibm.com) consists of numerous "pages" or screens, each of which is devoted to a specific topic. A website always begins with a "home page," which is the first screen viewed when the website is accessed.

***Weekly Compilation of Presidential Documents*:** *See Daily Compilation of Presidential Documents*.

West: The common name of the largest law book publisher in the United States; formerly West Publishing Co. and now owned by Thomson Reuters

Westlaw: The computerized legal research system offered by West.

WestlawNext: A new, user-friendly research platform that allows easy "Google" type searching of Westlaw, with results ranked in order of importance.

WestCheck: A West software program providing automatic validation of all cases cited in a document.

WestCiteLink: Westlaw's software product that automatically creates hyperlinks to cases cited in a document.

***Words and Phrases*:** A multivolume set of books directing researchers to cases that have construed certain terms.

World Court: *See* International Court of Justice.

Writ of certiorari: *See* Certiorari.

Index